The Official Guide to
Authorware 4

Nick Roberts

macromedia®
PRESS

The Official Guide to Authorware 4
Nick Roberts

Peachpit Press
2414 Sixth Street
Berkeley, CA 94710
510/548-4393
510/548-5991 (fax)

Find us on the World Wide Web at: **http://www.peachpit.com**

Published by Macromedia Press, in association with Peachpit Press,
a division of Addison Wesley Longman Company.

Copyright © 1997 by Nick Roberts

Peachpit Editor	Jeremy Judson
Project Editor	Karen Whitehouse
Tech Reviewers	Authorware QA Team
Book Designer	Michael J. Nolan
Cover Designer	TMA Ted Mader Associates
Book Production	Michael J. Nolan
Proofreader	Marta Partington
Indexer	Sharon Hilgenberg

ISBN 0-201-68899-9

9 8 7 6 5 4 3 2

Printed on recycled paper

Printed and bound in the United States of America

Acknowledgments

This book was written with the generous help of a great many people, who contributed time, energy, ideas, suggestions, reviews, and a great deal of encouragement while it was being completed. A very big thanks to the following people:

Karen Whitehouse for the editorial focus and words of guidance; Michael Nolan for the wonderful book design and layout; Mick Khavari for designing the example files included on the CD; David Rogelberg at Studio B Productions for invaluable feedback and management behind the scenes; Tim Bigoness at Macromedia Press for giving me the opportunity; Jeremy Judson, Nancy Runzel, and all at Peachpit Press for keeping all of us on track; Jeff Schwamberger at Macromedia, who kept us in the loop and provided the original content direction for this book along with Joe Schmitz; Sharon Hilgenberg for indexing; Marta Partington for proofing of the final manuscript; Ronni Asrouch, Andrew Chemey, Peter Li'ir Key, Patrick O'Connor, Fran Taylor, and Stan Wong for providing invaluable technical reviews of the manuscript; Patricia Barkman, Randy Cox, Tom Dinger, Brian Dister, Aram Gerstein, Brian Herring, Bob Reine, Mark Schneckloth, Mike Schroeder, Dietrich Schultz, Ed Skwarecki, Michael Thompson, Kevin Wallace, Jamil Zainasheff and the rest of the Authorware development team for generously answering questions and providing technical feedback; and Karen Silvey and Carrie Myers for the great beta site support…

Many thanks to those whom I've worked with at Macromedia and elsewhere while learning the ropes:

Lee Allis, Ed Baldwin, Peter Caban, John Dowdell, Stefanie Dworkin, Brian Ellertson, Craig Goodman, Josh King, Ed Krimen, John Lorance, Jack Moreno, Tyson Norris, Dan Read, Jeff Schick, Bob Tartar, Henry Warwick, Joanne Watkins, Eric Wittman and other present (and past) members of the Macromedia technical support group; Eastman Webber, Dennis Ferrell, John Szymanski, Sherry Flanders-Page, Karen Tucker, Victoria Avdienko, Monica Dahlen, Steve Shannon, David Edwards and David Lasner for extreme faith; Larry Doyle and John "J.T." Thompson for the Lingo tips; Dennis Kerr and Erin Rosenthal at RKG Interactive for necessary comic relief; Joan Mackrell, Olivia Rodriguez, E. Lisette Gerald-Yamasaki, Stan Young, Sharon Martin, Mike Smith and all at Apple; Karen Nelson and Bob Dennis at Pacific Media; Marvin Avilez and Paul Hamilton, the mBed crew; Robert Milton at Terrapin Design; Terry Schussler at gMatter; Lee Swearingen at DXM; Danny Engelman, Wade Wells, and all other AWARE members worldwide; Dr. Robert Winter for getting me on the road; and Jim Schwartz, for keeping me headed in the right direction…

Finally, to my family (Glenna, Greg, and Leroy), and to the many friends who have shared in this experience with me from the start: thank you for being there unconditionally, always with a smile and a good story to share…

Contents at a Glance

Contents

Part V: The Final Stages   *511*

Introduction

Welcome to *The Official Guide To Authorware 4*. This book is for beginners and advanced users alike to showcase the latest features of Macromedia Authorware—a tool that has become a leading standard in interactive design and digital publishing.

The primary focus of this book is how Authorware's ease of use, wide range of multimedia features, and unparalleled support for cross-platform and Internet/intranet development set it apart from other authoring tools. Many multimedia developers all over the world have come to rely on Authorware for prototyping and designing sophisticated applications quickly without relying on a specialized programming language.

This book discusses the ways you can use Authorware to create applications in every area imaginable—from corporate-wide tracking and training applications to children's CD-ROM game titles; and more recently, as an advantageous way to deliver interactive content over the Internet using Macromedia's Shockwave technology.

Authorware enables the creative process, allowing developers to reach beyond their technical limitations and instead focus on the process of designing sophisticated interactive content for their audiences. While this book covers the many technical issues involved with developing a piece in Authorware, you'll find that Authorware is first and foremost a creative tool—one that allows you to design, implement, and refine the ways you communicate your ideas. By learning about the ways you can use Authorware, you will be well on your way to developing your own applications in Authorware.

The Official Guide to Authorware 4 includes step-by-step examples, comments, and suggestions that are designed to get you started creating your own pieces in Authorware. This book also addresses the issues that all Authorware developers face when working on all phases of creating your piece. By learning both sides of the development process, you will be well on your way to creating sophisticated multimedia applications that you can deliver on the Macintosh and Windows platforms, as well as the Internet.

As you go through the book, you will learn all aspects of how to develop a piece in Authorware. Some of what you'll learn includes working with the interface elements, designing, managing and delivering your content, optimizing your design and implementation strategies, and extending the range of Authorware's functionality by utilizing Shockwave and Xtras—the latest enhancements to Authorware's already powerful set of built-in tools.

How you use this book depends on how much experience you already have working with Authorware. Most likely, you are approaching this book from one of three perspectives:

- If you are a beginner, this book provides in-depth guidance on all aspects of creating multimedia applications with Authorware.

- If you have already know how to work with Authorware, you nonetheless can use this book to improve your authoring skills, and learn a great deal more about using the new features included in Authorware 4.

- If you are a serious Authorware developer, you can use this book to gain additional insight into how to develop and refine your own interactive applications. This is especially true if you are interested in developing content for the Internet and intranets using Shockwave.

Although it's not required, it's assumed that you have spent some time looking at the documentation that is included with Authorware, and that you have the application installed on a system already so that you can follow along with the examples included in each chapter.

Each chapter in this book explains techniques essential to the process of creating a piece from start to finish in Authorware. There are five main parts of the book with each part focusing on a specific aspect of developing a piece:

Part I, "Creating and Managing Content," starts you off by showing you how to work with Authorware's two basic design elements: the icons and the flowline. You also learn about the main issues that you need to know when beginning a piece, including working with files and fonts and setting up your piece for different platforms. After you learn how to add text, graphics, animation, sound, and video to your piece, you are shown ways to manage your content and organize your flowline logic more efficiently in preparation for larger projects.

Part II, "Developing Interactivity," explores the various techniques you can use in Authorware to add user interactivity to a piece. First you learn how to create interactions in Authorware by creating simple buttons, hot spots, and hot objects on which the user can click. You then explore the ways other types of interactivity—including movable objects, custom menus, and text entry fields—are added to a piece. This part of the book concludes by looking at ways to respond automatically to events happening in the background of a piece while the user performs other tasks.

Part III, "Controlling Navigation," focuses on how to structure the content of your piece using Authorware's set of navigation tools. You first learn how to add simple paging structures to your piece; then you explore how to create more complex types of navigation in a piece using jumps, hypertext links, and search functionality. You also learn some useful techniques for optimizing the flowline structure of a piece by looking at decision paths and branching.

Part IV, "Using Scripting and Data Tracking," provides an in-depth focus on the various scripting and data-handling tools available to you in Authorware. After getting a feel for how to build your own custom scripts, you look at ways to work around difficult development issues using scripting to control the flowline. You also learn how to take advantage of automatic tracking of user data inside a piece, as well as the primary ways to manage this information.

Part V, "The Final Stages," completes your look at developing a piece in Authorware by focusing on the process of preparing your piece for delivery. Part of this process is learning how to troubleshoot problems that you encounter when testing your piece. You also learn about ways to expland the functionality of Authorware by using Director movies, Xtras, and external function libraries.

In addition, the appendices at the end of the book and the accompanying CD-ROM provide late-breaking news on using Authorware 4 and resources that you can use to learn more about Authorware on your own.

Conventions used in this book...

Each chapter includes step-by-step procedures that allow you to develop your skills while learning more about the types of applications that you can create in Authorware. While you follow along in each chapter, you will see certain elements on the page that help explain procedures, point out a useful tip, or offer additional guidance. These types of hints are explained in more detail below.

Words **in bold** indicate something that you need to type in while working through an example.

```
Words shown in this font indicate an
Authorware scripting element or example.
```

Shortcut: This indicates a keyboard or mouse shortcut. Key combinations are indicated with a + placed between each key (e.g., Ctrl+A). Both the Windows and the Macintosh shortcuts are included whenever possible.

TIP Tips provide helpful suggestions along the way. In most cases, they provide additional information that may help you understand the examples described in the text. They also occasionally refer you to places to go outside of the book for additional information.

NOTE Notes are used to point out ways to get around a particular issue or explain a step of a procedure in more detail. They also provide help on what to do if you run into problems while working through an example.

 The CD icon is used to point you to the various types of example files included on the CD accompanying this book. They include sample Authorware pieces, information resources, and additional software tools that you can try out on your own.

Sidebars like this provide additional insight about the topic discussed in the current chapter. Many of the sidebars include useful tips on how to optimize your piece for delivery over the Internet using Shockwave.

Where To Go From Here...

The Official Guide to Authorware 4 is the result of many thousands of hours of collective experience—not only from the projects I've developed on my own, but also from discussions with other developers working with the product, and the people at Macromedia who design, develop, test, and provide support for Authorware. It is our hope that by reading and understanding this book, you too will soon be well on your way to becoming a successful Authorware developer.

When it comes time to develop your own applications and you run into problems, spend some time outlining all the ways in which you might be able to approach a specific design or development issue. The most difficult issues are often resolved by asking yourself, "How can I do this differently?" Quite often, the answer presents itself after you've made a mental list of all the options that Authorware provides.

In addition to the text, you can use the supplementary CD with this book to point you in the right direction once you begin developing your own applications. However, it's important to learn the basic steps in Authorware first before you try your own moves.

Creating multimedia content is a great deal of fun, and it can be approached in many different ways. There are very few people that can claim to know everything about using Authorware, and every author develops his or her own special techniques. However, the examples, tips, and suggestions included in this book will give you a firm foundation that you can use to begin improvising freely on your own with the program and improving your skills through practice.

Good luck, and have fun!

Nick Roberts
nroberts@ctrl-z.com

Creating and Managing Content

A multimedia piece can fit many profiles. It can be a training piece that teaches system technicians how to use a complex piece of software, or an interactive sales kiosk that lets the user to browse through a company's latest catalog of fashions to customize an order. It can be a CD-ROM magazine that features artist interviews and music videos, or an Internet site that explores DNA sequencing by including 3D models and commentary from the worldwide scientific community.

These examples are as varied as the types of projects you may create. What they have in common, however, is their unique capability to integrate all the basic media formats: text, graphics, sound, and video into a single, seamless presentation format that can be delivered on a personal computer. Part I, "Creating and Managing Content," focuses on how to integrate these types of elements into the piece you're creating, using Authorware's set of content design and management tools.

Getting Started

Chapter 1

Creating sophisticated multimedia content is not
an easy process, especially for those who are coming
to it for the first time. Because you must address so
many issues, it's not unusual for even experienced
multimedia authors to feel a bit overwhelmed when
starting a new project.

Fortunately, Authorware helps you where you
need it most—at the design level, where most mistakes
happen early and often. Authorware's visual user
interface enables you to focus on designing your
content, which you can test along the way. Once
you understand the basic tools used in Authorware,
you can focus on the end result—delivering sophisticated multimedia pieces to your audience.

This chapter gives you a first look at Authorware's
feature set by introducing you to the icons, the
flowline, and the other basic components that make
up the Authorware environment. As you become
comfortable working in the Authorware development
environment, you'll find that the process of creating
Authorware pieces will flow more naturally.

What you'll learn...

Getting into the flow

**The main interface
components**

**Working in the
Design window**

**Working in the
Presentation window**

If you have experience with instructional media design or multimedia authoring, you probably have spent some time working with flow-charts. However, if you're new to the process of creating a multimedia piece, you may be unfamiliar with them. It's essential to know a bit about flowcharts before looking at the Authorware programming environment, because it's the metaphor that you work with when creating a piece in Authorware.

When you need a step-by-step overview of how your software will function before you start, turn to a flowchart. A flowchart is a tool used to map out the structure (or logic) of a program by showing connections between main components of a program or process. Traditionally, these components are represented visually, using rectangles and lines or arrows to connect them. The rectangles represent the main steps that divide the program. These rectangles (or steps) are connected by lines in the flowchart to indicate the order in which you will perform the steps.

Figure 1.1 is a sample flowchart diagram of an instructional piece that teaches people about setting up an Internet site. As you can see, the flowchart is divided into four content segments, which are connected by a main overview segment. For instance, you might have a menu screen with four buttons that you can select from to take you to the different areas of focus. The following example is as simple as possible to demonstrate how a flowchart works. However, all pieces tend to look something like this when you first start designing them.

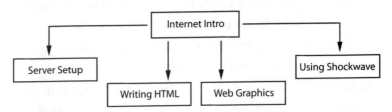

Figure 1.1
A flowchart for a piece about creating an Internet site.

It is helpful to begin a project by mapping out the structure of your piece in this way. It helps you organize your ideas and allows you to think about how to assemble your content into separate elements. After defining the elements your piece needs, you can assemble them inside Authorware using its flowchart metaphor.

Building a piece in Authorware is very similar to the process used to diagram a flowchart on paper, except that you have a wider range of options. Rather than creating a content structure using rectangles and lines, you use icons and the Authorware flowline. In **Figure 1.2**, you can see what the Internet site instructional piece might look like once you start building it inside Authorware.

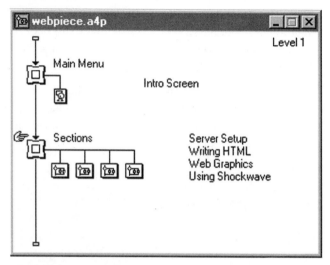

Figure 1.2
Using Authorware's flowline and icons, the sample piece now resembles the structure of a flowchart.

As you can see from this example, Authorware takes care of filling in the necessary connection between the icons—creating a logical structure for your piece that you can edit and rearrange while building it. After you create your flowline structure in Authorware and assign the icons different properties and options, what you end up with isn't just a representation of the piece but the source code itself, which you package and deliver to the end user.

Understanding the visual process of joining icons on the flowline is the first step in learning to use Authorware. After spending some time working with the interface, you quickly learn to recognize the various relationships among the icons on the flowline and how these relationships affect what the user sees and hears.

The next section explores this new way of working by discussing the main components of the Authorware interface.

Authorware's main interface components are visible when you launch the application for the first time. Since this chapter refers to many of the interface elements in Authorware, now may be a good time for you to open the application (if you've installed it) and follow along.

NOTE You'll need to install Authorware on your machine in order to follow along with some of the examples in the chapters. You also may want to check out the CD-ROM bundled with this book. Occasionally, in order to explain a complicated procedure, sample files included on the CD are referenced in the text.

The Authorware interface has five basic components: the icon palette, the menu bar, the toolbar, the Design window, and the Presentation window. However, if you've just opened the application, you will see only four of them, as shown in **Figure 1.3**.

The menu bar ——

The toolbar ┘

The icon palette ——

The Design window ——

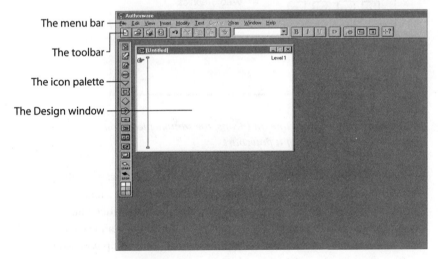

Figure 1.3
The basic interface components that make up Authorware.

NOTE The fifth element, the Presentation window, isn't visible until you run a piece.

As you can see in the icon palette, there are 13 different icons in Authorware. Each icon represents a different type of media or action that you can add to the flowline. The positioning of these icons on the flowline determines the sequence or order in which Authorware presents the various components of your piece to the user.

The icons and the flowline give you control over the order of events that occur in a piece. Events can be as simple as displaying a graphic on screen, or as complex as reading in a text file line by line. At any time, you can change the order of the events in a piece by changing the order of the icons on the flowline.

The icon palette

When you first open Authorware, the Design window appears along with a palette of icons, as shown in **Figure 1.4**. On the Macintosh, this palette is movable so that you can reposition it on screen. The icon palette contains most of the tools available in Authorware to build your multimedia piece.

To build the structure of your piece, you simply drag the icon that you need from the icon palette onto the flowline; then select the appropriate options you want applied to the icon. Each type of icon controls different aspects of how Authorware presents the content to the user inside the Presentation window.

Now that you have located the icons, the following information explains how they are used.

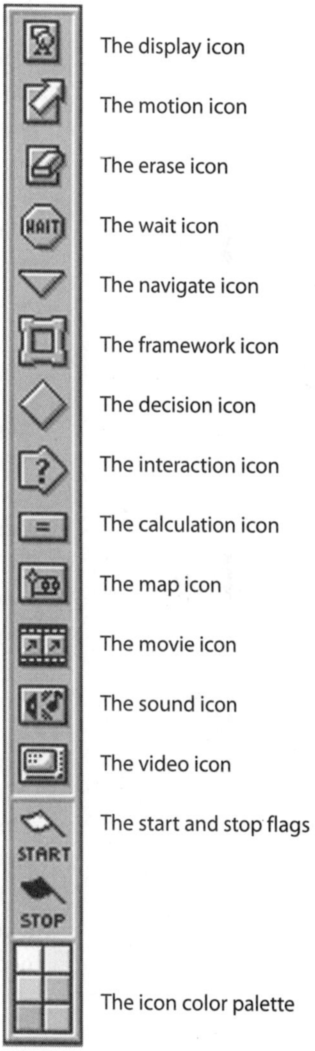

The display icon
The motion icon
The erase icon
The wait icon
The navigate icon
The framework icon
The decision icon
The interaction icon
The calculation icon
The map icon
The movie icon
The sound icon
The video icon
The start and stop flags
START
STOP
The icon color palette

Figure 1.4
The icon palette appears in the Design window.

The display icon

Use the display icon in a piece to present graphics and text to the user. You can create your own graphics and text using Authorware's built-in tools, or you can import graphics or text created in other programs such as Macromedia xRes and Macromedia FreeHand, or Microsoft Word. You also can link a display icon to an external graphic stored on your hard disk.

For information on how to use display icons, see Chapter 3, "Working with Text and Graphics."

The motion icon

You use motion icons to animate objects across the screen to a single destination point or along a designated path. You only use motion icons with those icons that display content on screen—namely, the display and movie icons. The motion icon gives you a great deal of customizable options for moving objects on screen. With the motion icon, you can update an object's position on screen through user interactivity or a condition that changes continually in the piece.

For information on how to use motion icons, see Chapter 4, "Adding Motion."

The erase icon

Use the erase icon in a piece to remove any or all objects from the screen, including graphics and movies. You also can specify that a transition effect display when an object erases from the screen. Like the motion icon, the erase icon affects only those icons that display content on the screen.

For information on using erase icons, see Chapter 3, "Working with Text and Graphics."

The wait icon

The wait icon pauses presentation of icons, or waits for a specified amount of time to pass before continuing forward in the flowline. In addition, you can specify the icon to wait until the user presses a key or mouse button, making it a convenient icon to use if you need only minimal user interactivity in a piece.

The navigate icon

The navigate icon defines links between sections of content attached to a framework icon. It also has several options that allow you to limit or expand its navigational properties, which include useful functions such as making callouts to related content or searching a piece for a specific text item or keyword.

For information on how to use the navigate icon, see Chapter 11, "Working with Pages."

The framework icon

The framework icon creates the main navigation structure of your piece. Its built-in controls for paging, navigation, and resource management make developing larger pieces much easier to handle.

For information on using the framework icon, see Chapter 11, "Working with Pages."

The decision icon

The decision icon sets up a path of options that Authorware evaluates and executes automatically on the flowline. You can set up these paths to make choices for the user automatically, add an element of randomness to your piece, or create logic that repeats until a condition is met.

For information on how to use decision icons, see Chapter 13, "Creating Decision Paths."

The interaction icon

The interaction icon creates the majority of interactivity in your piece. You can use it to check for user responses from a mouse, menu, or keyboard. You also can program interactions to give automatic feedback to the user based on a condition that you set, or use custom controls like the ActiveX Xtra.

For information on how to use interaction icons, see Chapter 7, "Creating Basic Interactivity."

Custom controls like the ActiveX Xtra are explained in more detail in Chapter 20, "Developing with External Code."

The calculation icon

You can use the calculation icon to build custom scripting into your piece. This enables you to evaluate expressions, run functions, and keep track of internal variables and custom variables that you create. You also can place comments into calculation icons to describe in detail what is happening on the flowline.

For information on using calculation icons, see Chapter 14, "Using Functions and Variables."

The map icon

The map icon simplifies and organizes the flowline by breaking it into smaller segments. You can place groups of icons into a map icon to keep your code organized when creating more complex logic structures. You can open a map icon to display its segment of the flowline in a separate Design window.

You'll learn more about working with the map icon later in this chapter.

The movie icon

The movie icon controls the playback of the most common digital movie and animation formats, including Macromedia Director, QuickTime, Video for Windows, and MPEG. When using Director movies, you can take advantage of any interactivity built into the Director movie.

For information on using movie icons, see Chapter 5, "Adding Sound and Video."

The sound icon

The sound icon controls the playback of digitized sound (i.e., music, speech, or sound effects) recorded and saved using a digital sound editing tool such as Macromedia SoundEdit 16 plus Deck II (Macintosh), or SoundForge (Windows).

For information on using sound icons, see Chapter 5, "Adding Sound and Video."

The video icon

The video icon controls the playback of frames and sequences of video from external videodisc or videotape sources. When using the video icon, you can play these sequences on an external monitor or inside Authorware.

For more information on using video icons, see Chapter 5, "Adding Sound and Video."

The start and stop flags

The start and stop flags enable you to "zoom in" on a specific portion of the flowline and run it without starting at the beginning of a piece. The start flag marks the start point of a flowline segment that you want to run; the stop flag marks the stop point of a flowline segment.

You use the start and stop flags primarily to speed up development by testing segments of the flowline as you create them. You will find yourself frequently using flags while troubleshooting or debugging a piece.

For information on how to use the start and stop flags to trouble-shoot problems, see Chapter 18, "Debugging Your Piece."

The icon color palette

Use the icon color palette to apply colors to selected icons. This helps you organize your flowline by color coding icons that share similar properties or functions. It is also a helpful way to keep track of revisions made on a particular file.

For information on using the icon color palette to organize your work, see Chapter 6, "Managing Your Content."

What is an Xtra?

In Authorware 4, you now can include other types of elements in your piece by using Xtras created for Authorware. These might include Xtras designed to import a specific type of image, sound, or video file; or an Xtra designed to give you additional control over elements in your piece that use custom scripts.

You also can use Xtras that support different types of networking functions with Authorware's Shockwave plug-in to create pieces that run over an internal network (intranet) or the Internet. Throughout this book you will find information about how to work with Shockwave, as preparation for delivering your pieces on a variety of platforms.

For more information on using Xtras to expand your piece, see Chapter 20, "Developing with External Code."

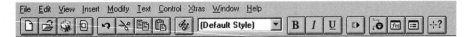

Figure 1.5
The Authorware toolbar appears below the menu bar.

The menu bar and toolbar

Many of the tasks you do to build a piece are accessed and controlled through the menu bar located at the top of the Authorware window. These menu commands allow you to do everything from opening and creating new files to copying and pasting icons, opening tool windows, and formatting text. You also can access menu commands quite easily using the toolbar, which appears just below the menu bar, as shown in **Figure 1.5**.

If you don't see the toolbar on your monitor, you can activate it by choosing the Toolbar command from the View menu. You can toggle between showing and hiding the toolbar using this menu command. This comes in handy if you are developing your piece on a 14-inch monitor and need extra room in the Design window.

Shortcut: To toggle the toolbar on and off, use Control+Shift+T (Windows), or Command+Shift+T (Macintosh).

The toolbar provides a set of buttons that performs many of the same functions as those accessed through the menu bar. These functions include opening, saving, and closing files; copying and pasting icons or content; and opening or closing the various Authorware windows used to create a piece. Most of these menu or toolbar commands are also available using defined keyboard shortcuts, which you will find highlighted throughout the book.

NOTE For a complete list of the keyboard shortcuts available in Authorware 4, see *Using Authorware* or Authorware Help.

The chart below identifies the buttons on the Authorware toolbar and how you use them.

This button...		*Does this...*
	New	Creates a new file or library.
	Open	Opens a file or library.
	Save All	Saves all currently open files, including libraries.
	Import	Opens the file import dialog box.
	Undo	Cancels the previous user action.
	Cut	Cuts the selected item.
	Copy	Copies the selected item to the Clipboard.
	Paste	Pastes the selected item.
	Find	Opens the Find/Change dialog box.
	Text Styles	Allows you to apply a text style to a selected text field.
	Bold	Makes selected text bold.
	Italic	Makes selected text italic.
	Underline	Makes selected text underlined.
	Restart	Runs the piece from the beginning, or from the start flag if it is in the flowline.
	Control Panel	Opens the Control Panel window.
	Functions window	Opens the Functions window.
	Variables window	Opens the Variables window.
	Help	Activates the help system pointer.

You use both the Design window and the Presentation window to create a piece in Authorware. When working in the Design window, you have access to all icons and menu commands. These features enable you to add or edit content and to define the relationships between icons. You can switch to the Presentation window at any time, where you can preview how the piece will run in its final form. Because Authorware is extremely flexible, you also can edit objects while they appear in the Presentation window—testing the interactivity of your piece while it runs.

Figure 1.6 shows an example of the Design window when using the flowline to create a piece. The Design window in this example illustrates how you might start building a simple kiosk piece that displays a company's animated logo, erases it, and then displays a background screen that contains text describing the company and its products.

The movie icon plays the animation.

The erase icon erases the animation.

The display icon displays the background and text.

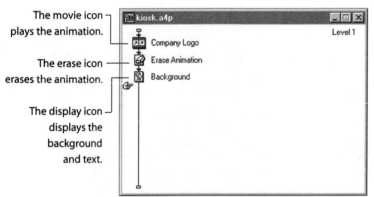

Figure 1.6
Creating the flowline structure in the Design window.

In this example, I used three different types of icons: the movie icon, which plays the animation; the erase icon, which erases the animation; and the display icon, which displays the graphics and text. As you can see, the icons are placed one after another on the flowline in the order that the piece should run.

 If you want to take a closer look at the kiosk piece, you can look at the file named KIOSK.A4P, included in the Chapter 1 examples folder on the CD-ROM accompanying this book.

To get a better idea of how the piece runs, switch to the Presentation window using the Control menu commands and play the piece, as shown in **Figure 1.7**. When playing a piece, Authorware moves from the top of the flowline to the bottom, performing the actions defined by the placement of the icons on the flowline. Authorware displays the piece for you in the Presentation window.

Control	Xtras	Window	Help
Restart		Ctrl+Alt+R	
Stop		Ctrl+Alt+.	
Play		Ctrl+Alt+P	
Reset			
Step Into		Ctrl+Alt+Shift+RtArrow	
Step Over		Ctrl+Alt+Shift+DnArrow	
Restart from Flag		Ctrl+Alt+Shift+R	
Reset to Flag			

Figure 1.7
The Control menu allows you to play back your piece in the Presentation window.

The Presentation window is similar to the stage feature in Director (for those of you who have worked with this tool in the past), in that you can work with graphics, sounds, videos, and any interactions there, as well as preview your work. As mentioned before, the progression of screens or "scenes" that you see is defined by the order of the icons on the flowline. In the example, the animation plays first and is erased, and then the background screen appears with text. This is shown for you in **Figure 1.8**.

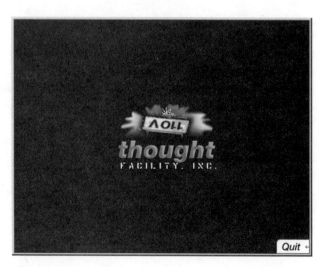

Figure 1.8
The kiosk piece, as it appears in the Presentation window.

After you run a piece several times, you may decide that the animation should come after the background screen displays. By rearranging the icons on the flowline—in this example, moving the display icon above the movie icon—you can rework the piece and change the order of the events or actions. **Figure 1.9** shows you what the flowline looks like now, after the icons are repositioned.

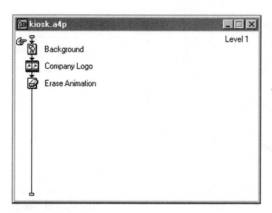

Figure 1.9
The background screen now appears before the movie plays.

Working in the Design Window

The Design window is the canvas that holds your design structure. By placing icons onto the flowline, you create the structure that holds your content together. The next few sections describe some of the common ways to work with icons in the Design window.

Naming icons

In order to better organize your piece, you'll want to keep on top of naming all icons that you drag onto the flowline. All icons, except the navigate and wait icons, Authorware names "Untitled" when initially added to the flowline. (Navigate icons receive the title "Unlinked." Wait icons appear without a title.)

On a hypothetical scale of one to ten (with ten being nirvana), naming icons rates about a 9.5 in terms of keeping you and your Authorware piece in a state of harmonious bliss. If you start scattering unnamed icons around, you'll find it far more difficult to organize content, make edits, and hand off the file to someone helping you with the project.

The basic method for naming icons is very simple:

1. Click on the name of the icon that appears in the flowline.

2. Type a new name into the text field to the right of the icon while you have the icon selected.

Authorware stores the new title in the file when you save your changes.

TIP You can title a sequence of icons by typing the first title and then pressing the Return key; Authorware then automatically selects the next icon on the flowline.

From the moment you start working on a piece, it's very important that you use icon titles that are descriptive. This way, you quickly can refer to them later and have a general idea of what they contain. As files get larger and the icon count grows, problems can arise when you lose track of what you've added to the flowline.

Although you can give an icon any title you want, you should try as often as possible to provide unique titles for them. This is particularly important for display, sound, video, and interaction icons because when you use one of them with a function in a calculation icon, you need to refer to it with an unique name.

It's also a good idea to use a set naming convention for your icons. One common approach is to include a reference in the icon title to the name of the original file used to create the icon. In such a case, you might name a movie icon "mymovie.mov," referring to the original file that you imported into the icon.

You also can integrate naming conventions into your design. By including a numbering scheme in the title, you can distinguish your icons from one another if they contain similar content. For example, you could name a sequence of text icons that appear next to each other "introtext 01," "introtext 02," and so on. Because you labeled the icons clearly, it is easier to move them to another part of the flowline if you need to reorganize your logic.

Rearranging icons on the flowline

Shifting icons in a file is a common practice. You begin a piece thinking you need to display images in a certain order, and then realize you want to reverse that order. Or you place a movie in one part of the flowline, but find out later you need to move it into another section.

Rearranging icons in a piece is pretty much a drag-and-drop exercise—although you can use the Clipboard to copy and paste them in new locations. Usually when changing the placement of a specific icon on the flowline, it's faster to select the icon and move it to the new location using your cursor.

To move an icon:

1. Click on the icon you want to move.

2. Drag and drop it to a new location.

Authorware inserts the icon at the spot in the flowline where you released it. When moving an icon to a position close to an interaction, framework, or decision icon, you need to remember to position the cursor to the right of the icon before releasing the mouse button, as shown in **Figure 1.10**. If you don't, it is placed below the interaction, framework, or decision icon.

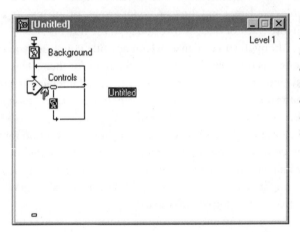

Figure 1.10
Release the icon to the right of a framework, interaction, or decision icon to move it into place.

Moving multiple icons is a bit more complex. You can use the Copy and Paste commands to insert the icons into their new locations.

To copy and paste an icon or group of icons:

1. Select the icons you want to move by highlighting them. You can hold down the Shift key and click on each icon separately, or you can use the mouse to create a rectangular selection, which highlights all the icons within the selection.

2. Choose Copy from the Edit menu. This copies the icons to the Clipboard.

Shortcut: To copy, use Control+C (Windows), or Command+C (Macintosh).

---

3. Click in the flowline where you want to paste the icons.

The paste hand appears where you clicked.

4. Choose Paste from the Edit menu.

Shortcut: To paste, use Control+V (Windows), or Command+V (Macintosh).

Authorware pastes the icons where you positioned the paste hand, as shown in **Figure 1.11**.

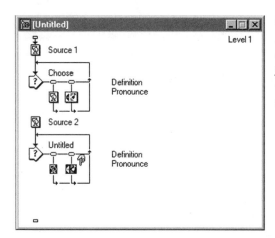

Figure 1.11
The paste hand acts as a guide, showing you where Authorware will paste the icon into the flowline.

Copy and Paste is useful when you need to add content to your piece and don't want to create it from scratch. You can copy a group of icons that you've already created and paste this group in another location on the flowline. When you copy and paste an icon, Authorware retains the icon's properties, including any transition effects that you applied to it.

NOTE Because framework, decision, and interaction icons have other icons attached to them, you can't cut a framework, decision, or interaction icon without also cutting the icons attached to it.

Grouping icons

As you've probably noticed, there are no scroll bars in the Design window. While this may seem limiting at first, there are several techniques in Authorware available to build larger files, one of which is using the map icon. Having no scroll bars is beneficial in many ways because it encourages you to keep your file tightly structured in compact groups of icons.

When you start working on larger pieces with many icons, you can use the map icon to organize your logic into separate "containers." The map icon creates separate windows of icons that you can edit later by opening the map icon, as shown in **Figure 1.12**. This gives you greater flexibility in designing your piece because you are no longer limited to the size of the Design window.

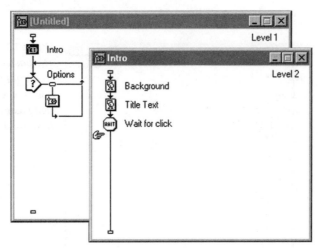

Figure 1.12
The map icon contains nested logic that you can view and edit at any time.

Instead of using Copy and Paste to move multiple icons, you can group them in a map icon and then drag-and-drop the map icon to a new location.

To group icons into a single map icon:

1. Select the icons you want to group.

2. Choose Group from the Modify menu.

Shortcut: To group icons, use Control+G (Windows), or Command+G (Macintosh).

Authorware replaces the group of icons with an untitled map icon that contains the group. You can name the map icon either before or after you move it. After you move it to a new location, you can ungroup the icons using a similar command.

To ungroup a set of icons:

1. Select the map icon that contains the group of icons.

2. Choose Ungroup from the Modify menu.

Shortcut: To ungroup icons, use Control+Shift+G (Windows), or Command+Shift+G (Macintosh).

When you ungroup icons in a map icon, Authorware places them in the part of the Design window that is currently active, as shown in **Figure 1.13**.

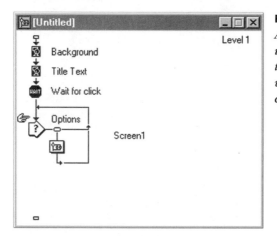

Figure 1.13
Authorware places ungrouped icons into the part of the Design window that is currently active.

Editing an icon

Moving and grouping icons are not the only types of icon editing available to you. After you add an icon to a piece, you usually find yourself going in and editing it to update a graphic, import additional text, or reposition text in the Presentation window. To edit an icon, you simply open the icon by double-clicking it. Authorware then presents the tools or options available for that icon.

Icons dedicated to displaying content on screen—namely, the display, interaction, movie, and video icons—open the Presentation window when you edit them and display their contents. An interaction icon also displays its associated responses on the screen. These may include buttons, hot spots, or a text entry field attached to the interaction icon, as shown in **Figure 1.14**.

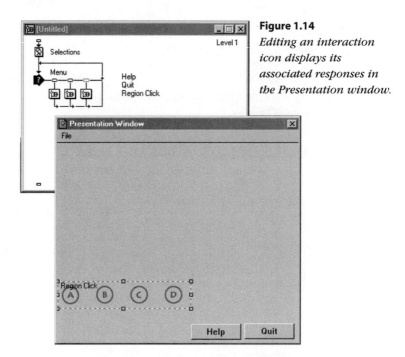

Figure 1.14
*Editing an interaction
icon displays its
associated responses in
the Presentation window.*

When you edit a display or interaction icon, the Authorware
toolbox appears in the Presentation window, allowing you to change
the contents of the display icon. See Chapter 3, "Working with Text
and Graphics," for more information on how to use the toolbox.

NOTE The Presentation window doesn't appear when icons that
don't utilize it (such as navigate, wait, and calculation icons) are open
for editing. Instead, Authorware opens the icon's corresponding
Options dialog box or window.

If you want to display the contents of more than one icon
at a time, you can do so by using the following steps:

1. Double-click the first icon to open it. It displays in the
Presentation window.

2. Return to the Design window by clicking the close box on
the toolbox.

3. Hold down the Shift key and double-click on subsequent icons.

As long as you continue to hold down the Shift key, Authorware
displays each subsequent icon you double-click in the Presentation
window, in addition to the first object you edited.

Most of your work in editing icons probably will take place in the Design window. In several cases, however, you may want to take advantage of Authorware's running, pausing, and editing features to edit content on-the-fly in the Presentation window.

Working in the Presentation Window

The Presentation window gives you the chance to preview and edit your piece while it runs. As you author a piece, you'll find yourself frequently running it in the Presentation window to see how images appear and whether the interactivity works correctly.

At any time, you can preview a piece from the beginning by choosing Restart from the Control menu. This action displays your flowline events inside the Presentation window.

Shortcut: To restart a piece, use Control+Alt+R (Windows), or Command+Option+R (Macintosh).

Running a piece from the beginning, however, forces you to sit through everything that happens up to the point that you want to preview. In most cases, you only want to get a quick preview of a particular section of the flowline to see if a graphic appears correctly or a sound plays. If you need to preview a small portion of the flowline, use the start and stop flags, as shown in **Figure 1.15**.

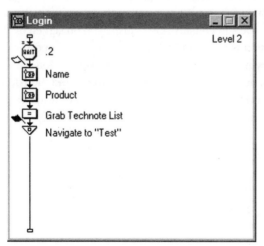

Figure 1.15
The start and stop flags control which segment of the file runs.

To run a segment of a piece:

1. Drag a start flag to the segment's starting point on the flowline.

2. If needed, drag a stop flag to the segment's stopping point on the flowline.

3. Choose Restart from Flag from the Control menu.

Shortcut: To restart from a flag, use Control+Alt+R (Windows), or Command+Option+R (Macintosh).

Authorware starts the piece where you placed the start flag and stops presentation when it reaches the stop flag. It isn't necessary to use the stop flag each time you use the start flag. It simply gives you more control over which icons you view in the Presentation window.

NOTE Many of the commands you use when running a piece are accessible from the Control Panel window. The Control Panel window gives you greater control over running a piece, allowing you to trace the steps that happen in a particular area of the flowline. Chapter 18, "Debugging Your Piece," takes a closer look at how you can use the Presentation window for troubleshooting.

Editing while running a piece

Authorware's interface is unique because it allows you to edit an icon while testing a piece. While running the piece in the Presentation window, you can edit any object displayed on screen by pausing the Presentation window and clicking the object. You can work through the following examples to see this process in action.

First, drag a display icon to the flowline, and then double-click the display icon to open it. The Presentation window appears with the display icon's toolbox, as shown in **Figure 1.16**.

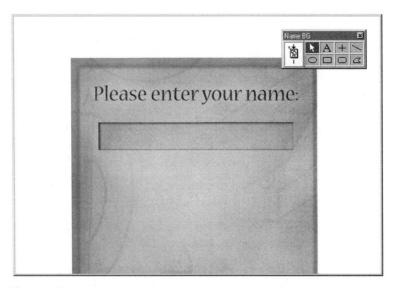

Figure 1.16
The toolbox appears when you open a display icon.

For now, create a simple graphic in the Presentation window so that you can see how the editing process works.

1. Select the oval tool from the toolbox (the button underneath the arrow pointer).

2. Draw a circle in the Presentation window. Close the window when you have finished.

3. Start the piece by choosing Run from the Control menu.

You should see the circle you created inside the Presentation window. You can reposition the circle displayed on screen by clicking it once and dragging it to a new spot.

NOTE Editing the position of a display object this way moves everything in the display icon. If you need to reposition only one element in the display icon, you should pause Presentation and open the display icon as described above.

However, you can't edit graphic properties such as size, color, or shape while the piece runs. First, you need to pause the Presentation window by choosing Pause from the Control menu.

Shortcut: To pause, use Control+P (Windows), or Command+P (Macintosh).

Because the object is still visible in the Presentation window, you can edit it now by double-clicking it.

1. Double-click the circle.

Once again, the toolbox appears allowing you to make corrections to the graphic.

2. Click the object and resize it using the drag handles.

After you edit the icon, you can continue to play the piece, resuming where you left off.

To resume the piece, select Play from the Control menu. You do not need to close the Toolbox window.

NOTE Choosing Stop from the Control menu halts playback and closes the Presentation window.

You can use on-screen editing to speed up your development process. While running a piece in the Presentation window, you can quickly switch to the Design window to view the current icon's position on the flowline. This is a simple way to find an icon buried in a map icon somewhere on the flowline.

To view the current icon, choose Current Icon from the View menu.

Shortcut: To view the current icon, use Control+B (Windows), or Command+B (Macintosh).

Selecting Current Icon displays the Design window and highlights the current icon, as shown in **Figure 1.17**. If you no longer want the Presentation window active, close it using the close box.

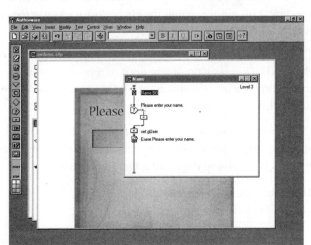

Figure 1.17
The Current Icon command highlights the icon displayed in the Presentation window.

TIP Additionally, you can build a skeleton structure for your piece by adding empty icons to the flowline and then running the piece. When Authorware encounters an empty icon, the piece stops automatically and the icon opens for editing.

Running, pausing, and editing is a regular ritual for most authors. Often you can take care of most of your positioning and screen layout issues by editing in the Presentation window. For instance, if you have a column of text that needs repositioning on screen to fit over a particular part of a bitmapped background, you can quickly adjust the position of the text by running the piece, pausing it, and then using the mouse to reposition the text.

TIP A more accurate way to reposition graphics or movies in the Presentation window is to use the arrow keys on the keyboard. Clicking the appropriate arrow key nudges the currently selected graphic or movie by one pixel in the direction you select on the keyboard.

Looking Ahead...

This chapter introduced you to the main components of the Authorware interface—the icon palette, menu bar, and toolbar, which help you work with content in the Design and Presentation windows. You should feel a bit more comfortable now working in Authorware's programming environment. As you can see, Authorware has many different features designed to make viewing and editing your content easier.

Before continuing, take some time to play around with the icons and the flowline, and familiarize yourself with the Design and Presentation windows—since you'll spend most of your time switching between the two while authoring. The best way to learn how to work with these features is to experiment on your own. Familiarizing yourself with the interface is the first step in learning to develop multimedia applications using Authorware.

The next chapter introduces you to the preliminary steps you need to follow when beginning a piece, and early design decisions you face before starting a new project.

Beginning a Piece

Multimedia developers often hear horror stories about how projects fall apart at the seams when going into final testing. While you can't anticipate all of the problems you may encounter when testing a piece, you certainly can learn to design it with cross-platform and delivery issues in mind.

This chapter discusses some of the common technical issues that you will face when starting a piece. These include setting up your piece for different monitor sizes, working with fonts, and setting paths to your external content. Knowing how to handle these types of issues will help you later when it's time to deliver your final piece. If you plan ahead when authoring, you will see more consistent results with your work, and spend less time on costly redesigns and code fixes during last minute crunches.

There are a few basics to working with files in Authorware. While you may not always begin a project by creating a new file, you definitely need to know how to save your work and open existing files (especially if another design team working on the project creates the files for you).

Creating a new file

The File menu gives you access to creating, saving, and closing both Authorware files and libraries. (You'll learn more about working with Authorware libraries later in Chapter 6, "Managing Your Content.")

When you launch Authorware, it automatically creates a new file for you in the Design window. However, at times you may need to create a new file while working on a project that you have loaded already. In that case, you simply choose New > File from the File menu.

Shortcut: To create a new file, use Ctrl+N (Windows), or Command+N (Macintosh).

When you create a new file, Authorware asks you if you want to save changes to the piece that is already open. After you make your decision, an untitled Design window and the icon palette appear, as shown in **Figure 2.1**. You then can start building your piece using the icons in the icon palette and the commands from the menu bar.

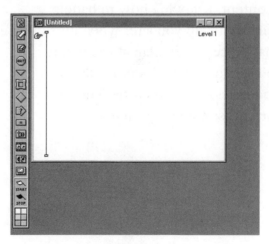

Figure 2.1
An untitled Design window appears when creating a new file.

Opening an existing file

Like other programs you use, there are different ways to open existing files. You can open a file from the desktop by double-clicking it; you can drag–and–drop the Authorware file from the desktop into the open Authorware application window; or, if you need to browse your hard disk, you can use the Open command to locate and open the file.

To open the file from the menu bar:

1. Choose Open from the File menu.

Shortcut: To open a file, use Ctrl+O (Windows), or Command+O (Macintosh).

The Open File dialog box appears, as shown in **Figure 2.2**.

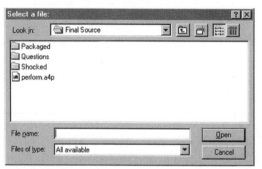

Figure 2.2
The Open File dialog box.

2. Go to the folder that contains your file.

3. Select the file by clicking its name in the list of available files.

4. Click Open.

After you select Open, the file's flowline content appears in the Design window and the icon palette and toolbar icons become active, allowing you to add additional icons to the flowline.

NOTE If you move a file from the Windows platform to the Macintosh platform and the file is not listed as available when trying to open it on the Mac side, select the Show All Files option in the Open dialog box. This option makes DOS-format files (files without a Mac resource fork) visible to you from the Macintosh desktop.

Saving a file

Saving files frequently is the most important step you can take when working on a project in Authorware. The hours needed to redo work that wasn't saved properly are not only time-consuming, but costly for you and your development team in the long run. When working with a file in Authorware, you have the following save options:

- Save the revised file with the same name, replacing the older version.

- Save the revised file with a different name, leaving the older version intact.

- Save the revised file using the Save and Compact feature, which streamlines the file by removing unused links and icon data.

When working on a piece, you should save the file constantly. (In Authorware, unlike other programs, there is no Auto-Save option available.)

To save a revised file with the same name, choose Save from the File menu.

Shortcut: To save a file, use Ctrl+S (Windows), or Command+S (Macintosh).

NOTE Authorware 4 now saves files on both platforms with an .A4P extension, and libraries with an .A4L extension. Chapter 6, "Managing Your Content," covers working with libraries in greater detail.

The Save As option is similar to the Save option, except that it allows you to save the revised version of your file with a different name.

1. Choose Save As from the File menu.

The Save As window appears, as shown in **Figure 2.3**.

Figure 2.3
The Save As window.

2. Select the folder where you want to save the file.

3. Enter a file name in the File Name field.

4. Click OK.

The third option, Save and Compact, rewrites the file to the hard disk after removing unused icon references and their associated data (stored in byte "records"). These records include any data that you imported into a specific icon, such as bitmap or sound data. When you delete an icon from the flowline, Authorware does not automatically remove the raw data stored in the file until you save and compact it.

To save and compact a file:

1. Choose Save and Compact from the File menu.

The Save and Compact window appears, as shown in **Figure 2.4**.

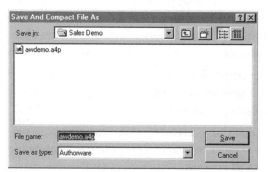

Figure 2.4
The Save and Compact window.

2. Choose a directory or folder from the scrolling list.

3. Enter a file name in the Save File As field.

4. Click Save.

Depending on the size of your file and the total number of icons, saving and compacting may take several minutes. During this time, a status bar displays to give you an update on Authorware's progress. After Authorware compacts the file, the new file opens in the display window.

TIP It is generally a good idea to use Save and Compact before you package a piece for testing or delivery because it streamlines the structure of the file and can shrink file size by 10–20 percent.

In general, here are some tips that can help you avoid problems while working on a piece:

- Use Save intermittently (every ten minutes or so) to back up your work.

- If you're working from a file server, it's always better to copy a piece to your local hard disk and work from the local copy. This helps improve performance—especially if the network is running slowly—and can prevent lost or damaged work if the file server unexpectedly goes down while making changes.

- Have a well-organized and well-documented system of creating and storing revisions to your files. This usually means creating a new version of the current file you're working on each day using Save As and, perhaps, giving it a name based on the current date or time and version number. If you run into a snag during development, you quickly can return to your archived files and back-track through different versions. This also helps you create a change/history document for your clients (a list of all changes made to the code from version to version).

- After every major production milestone, use Save and Compact to streamline the file for packaging and testing. Chapter 17, "Distributing Your Piece," covers this in more detail.

- If you don't have a reliable system to back up data in your studio or office, it's time to invest in one. You should diligently back up all your data once a week (at the very least), using an external data backup format such as Zip disk, recordable CD-ROM, removable optical, or DAT tape.

Following these pointers can help you prepare for the unavoidable things in life—like freak power outages or machine hardware lock-ups, things that can ruin half a day's work and possibly your entire weekend.

Moving files across platforms

With the release of Authorware 4, you now can take advantage of true cross-platform authoring by creating files that are binary compatible. Authorware's binary-compatible file format enables you to save a piece on Windows, copy it to a Macintosh, and open it without any type of file conversion process. The same applies to files created on the Macintosh and copied to a Windows machine.

If you're accustomed to finding clever ways to bridge the gap between the Macintosh and Windows platforms with previous versions of Authorware, then the new binary compatibility of Authorware 4 should strike you as a major revelation.

NOTE Only files saved in Authorware 3 or 3.5 can be converted to the new format when you open them in Authorware 4. Files created with earlier versions of Authorware cannot be converted to the new format.

Traditionally, developers have waited until the end of the authoring process to convert a piece to the other platform and test it so that they go through the conversion process only one time. However, now that you can transfer files easily from one platform to the other without converting the file format, you can spend more time developing your piece and testing it to see how it runs on both platforms.

Perhaps an even greater revelation—and one that certainly will change the way you create hybrid-format CD-ROM content with Authorware—is that you no longer need to worry about having two sets of library files for a piece that you are delivering on both platforms. With Authorware 4, library files you create for your piece are also binary compatible and can be shared across platforms.

NOTE By "hybrid" CD-ROM, I mean a CD-ROM that you can play on both the Windows and Macintosh platforms. This is different from a hybrid Shockwave piece that can incorporate both network and CD-ROM content into one application.

Binary compatibility can extend to the web, allowing you to create a single shocked version of your piece for the web. You still need to flatten external files on the Macintosh in preparation for delivery over the Internet, but you only need to worry about managing a single set of Authorware files. This material is covered in greater detail in Chapter 17, "Distributing Your Piece."

Regardless of which platform you develop on, you still need to keep many issues in mind when first beginning a piece. The two platforms can display your piece differently depending on how you design it. The next section looks at the options available to you for handling how your file plays back on different platforms.

A development platform's system-specific characteristics are referred to as the platform "environment." Every piece that you create in Authorware needs to be created with the platform environment in mind to maintain consistency when moving the piece from the development platform to another platform. However, some file properties settings, as you'll see in a moment, only apply to one particular platform.

Every file has a set of properties that you can adjust right away, before you begin working with your content. In Authorware 4, these settings are in the File Properties dialog box. You can acquaint yourself with these properties by creating a new file and playing around with the different properties.

To open the File Properties dialog box:

1. Create a new file.

2. Select File > Properties from the Modify menu.

Shortcut: To open the File Properties dialog box, use Ctrl+Shift+D (Windows), or Command+Shift+D (Macintosh).

The File Properties dialog box appears, as shown in **Figure 2.5**.

Figure 2.5
The File Properties dialog box.

There are a number of settings available to you in this dialog box. When switching between the Playback and Interaction tabs at the bottom of the dialog box, you will see two sets of options that control many of the overall conditions for the piece. These options include:

- The name of the Presentation window.

- The size of the Presentation window.

- The background color of the Presentation window.

- The default button used in a wait icon to pause presentation.

- The folders or directories Authorware searches first when trying to locate external files.

It's a good practice to set up these properties when you first start working on a piece. Although you can always return to the File Properties dialog box to change a setting later, you'll find that planning ahead can save you precious time when designing and testing your piece on different platforms.

For example, most developers create pieces for a standard VGA resolution (640 x 480 pixels, or the Macintosh standard 13-inch monitor) to make sure their pieces can run on the majority of machines available. Initially, setting the Presentation window to this size in the File Properties window assures that you won't have to go back and redesign your screens or reposition graphics and text halfway through development.

The File Properties dialog box contains several fields that give you valuable information about the current file, as labeled in **Figure 2.6**. This information is useful to reference when trying to find out the exact size of your file or how many icons your file contains.

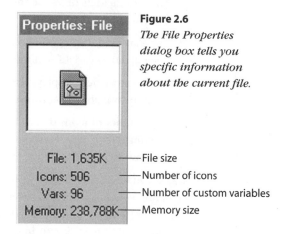

Figure 2.6
The File Properties dialog box tells you specific information about the current file.

These fields are always visible to you when the File Properties dialog box is open. You can utilize these fields as follows:

■ With the Title field, you can give your piece a title other than the name of the file. When you customize this field, Authorware displays the title you gave the file in the Windows or Macintosh title bar at the top of the Presentation window, as shown in **Figure 2.7**.

Figure 2.7

The file title displayed in the title bar at the top of the Presentation window.

■ The File Information field displays the size (in Kilobytes) of the current file.

■ The Icon field displays the total number of icons in the current file.

■ The Vars field displays the total number of custom (user-created) variables in the current file.

■ The Memory field displays the size (in Kilobytes) of system memory available to Authorware.

The number of icons that a single Authorware file can contain is approximately 32,000. However, you should try to keep your icon count below 10,000 to improve the file's overall performance.

TIP If you find yourself getting above this range, you should consider separating your large file into several smaller files using Authorware's JumpFileReturn system function to link them together. You'll see an example of how to do this in Chapter 16, "Tracking the User."

Modifying file playback options

Switch back to the Playback options and take a look at what you can do with them. Using these options, shown in **Figure 2.8**, you control the way your file appears when it plays back inside the Presentation window.

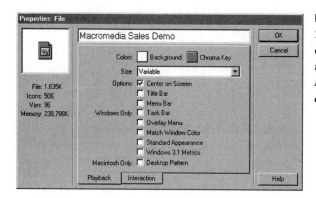

Figure 2.8

The Playback options appear in the File Properties dialog box.

When you adjust some of these options, you see the results immediately in the Presentation window. Other options, however, require that you first close the File Properties dialog box to see the result. You can set up your file using several of the available options:

1. Close the File Properties dialog box if it is open, and make the Presentation window active by selecting Presentation Window from the Window menu.

Shortcut: To switch to the Presentation window, use Ctrl+1 (Windows), or Command+1 (Macintosh).

The Presentation window appears on top of the Design window.

2. Open the File Properties dialog box and click on the Background color chip to display the Color Palette dialog box.

The Color Palette dialog box appears on top of the File Properties dialog box.

3. Change the background of the Presentation window to a different color by clicking on any one of the colors in the palette; click OK to close the Color Palette dialog box.

The Presentation window background changes to the color you selected. This is the color Authorware displays when you launch the piece. You won't see it, however, when you start layering graphics and movies on top of the Presentation window (unless you erase them from the screen using an erase icon).

Before taking a closer look at all the options available, make a couple other modifications to the Presentation window to give you a feel for how you can change the appearance of your piece.

For example, say that you have a really cool custom interface built with background graphics and buttons. In fact, the interface is so cool you want to hide the title bar and menu bar of your piece. You can do this using the following steps:

1. With the File Properties dialog box open, deselect the Title Bar and Menu Bar options, which are the default selections.

   Even though you've deselected them, these options have no effect on what you see until after you accept the changes by closing the dialog box.

2. Click OK to close the dialog box.

After closing the dialog box, the Presentation window changes appearance. The title bar and menu bar are no longer displayed in the Presentation window.

TIP When the title bar and menu bar are deselected, you should provide the user with a way to quit the piece, either through a custom button or other such device. Chapter 7, "Creating Basic Interactivity," discusses working with custom buttons.

You should now have a better feel for how you can use these options. There are many other options available for modifying playback of your piece, which are explained in more detail below.

Chroma Key

The Chroma Key option allows you to select the color that the video displays through when using a video overlay card with an external videodisc or videotape source. To learn more about how this works, see Chapter 5, "Adding Sound and Video."

Size

The Size option enables you to set the size of the Presentation window for your piece. It also affects how the Presentation window appears during authoring as well as playback. The most common setting used is 640 x 480 pixels (VGA, Mac 13-inch display). This creates a standard-sized Presentation window that can fit within the majority of monitor setups. Using the Variable setting allows you to resize the window anytime during playback. This is helpful when you need to accommodate a non-standard size display.

TIP If you want to dynamically change the size of the Presentation window in a piece, you can resize it using the `ResizeWindow` system function, which Chapter 14, "Using Functions and Variables," explains in more detail.

The Use Full Screen setting expands the Presentation window to fill the entire monitor. If the current monitor size is larger than the content displayed in the Presentation window, Authorware fills the rest of the screen with the background color you've selected, as shown in **Figure 2.9**.

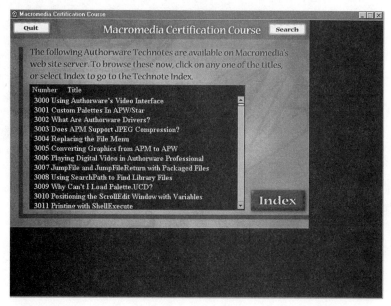

Figure 2.9
A piece 640 x 480 pixels, shown running in Use Full Screen mode.

NOTE None of these settings affects the actual size of the content in your piece. In other words, Authorware does not scale your graphics and other display objects to fit the current monitor setting. These settings only affect the dimensions of the Presentation window, so create your background screens at the size you want them displayed.

Center on Screen

Selecting the Center on Screen option centers the Presentation window on the monitor during authoring and playback, as shown in **Figure 2.10**.

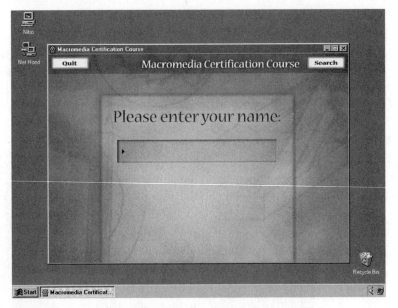

Figure 2.10
The Presentation window, centered on a monitor 1024 x 768 pixels.

NOTE If you have the Use Full Screen option for the Presentation window size selected, your piece does not automatically center on screen even if you have selected Center on Screen.

Title Bar and Menu Bar

As you saw earlier, selecting the Title Bar option displays the title bar in the Presentation window when you run your piece during authoring and final delivery, as shown in **Figure 2.11**. The title bar contains the title of the file as you've named it in the Title field.

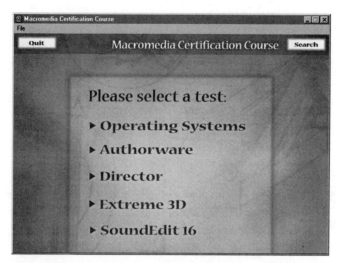

Figure 2.11
In this piece, both the title bar and menu bar display.

If you're developing a piece with a custom interface, you probably should turn this option off. Otherwise, the user has access to the minimize and close boxes on the title bar. This can cause problems if you want to control how the user exits the piece.

Notice that the Title Bar option has no effect on the Menu Bar option, as these are two separate settings. You also may have noticed that Authorware creates a default File menu for your file that allows you to quit the piece. If you're developing a custom piece and don't want to use the menu, simply deselect it, as you did earlier. You will learn more about creating and using menus in Chapter 8, "Keyboard and Menu Responses."

At times using a title bar and menu bar can lessen the overall effect you're trying to achieve if you have created a sophisticated graphical user interface. Sometimes it's best to create interface controls (such as buttons or hot spots) for the functions you need rather than inserting a menu bar into your piece. You should keep these issues in mind when you first start designing your piece.

NOTE The title bar of your piece does not display if you deliver your piece as a Shockwave file. Menus, however, normally appear at the top of the Presentation window, inside the browser running the piece. Chapter 17, "Distributing a Piece," talks about the Shockwave options available to you in more detail.

Platform-specific file options

Most of the File Properties settings are common to both platforms to ensure that a piece created on one platform plays back the same way on another platform. There are, however, several options available that are unique to each platform. These options are ignored on the other platform during authoring and final delivery—meaning, Macs ignore Window-specific options that you select, and vice versa.

Task Bar

If you select the Task Bar option, Authorware creates a Windows 95-style task bar for your Authorware piece, as shown in **Figure 2.12**. The Macintosh ignores this option because its operating system doesn't use a task bar.

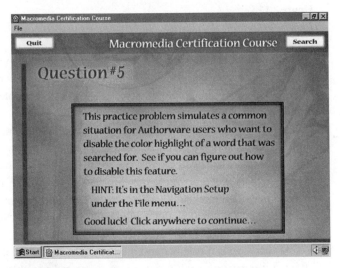

Figure 2.12
A piece with the Task Bar option enabled.

Having this option selected enables the user to switch between the Authorware piece and other open applications via the task bar. However, you should consider the following information before selecting this option:

- If you must have the task bar available in your piece, you need to be sure that your piece is delivered only to users running Windows 95 or Windows NT 4.

- You cannot make the task bar visible without also making the Authorware title bar visible. Authorware displays a title bar, even if the option is not currently selected.

- When a piece runs, the task bar may not display properly if the user has turned on Auto Hide in the Windows Task Bar properties or turned off the Always on Top option. This means that the user must have the correct Windows desktop settings preconfigured before running your piece.

Overlay Menu

In Windows 3.1, Authorware usually places the menu bar above the Presentation window so that the full-size window displays. However, if you select the Overlay Menu option, Authorware overlays the menu bar on top of the Presentation window, covering the top 20 pixels of the Presentation window.

The Overlay Menu option is useful when delivering a piece to users who are running a standard-size VGA (640 x 480 pixels) display. If you haven't selected this option, Authorware displays the menu bar above the Presentation window, forcing the remainder of the Presentation window to shift down by 20 pixels. This can cut off graphics or buttons that you've placed at the bottom of your piece.

TIP The best insurance against truncated graphics or buttons is to develop your design with screen layout issues and pixel trimming in mind. Avoid placing important objects at the very top or bottom edges of the screen.

Match Window Color

Unlike the Overlay Menu option, the Match Window Color option is Windows 95- and Windows NT-specific. If you select the Match Window Color option, the background of your Authorware piece automatically adopts the user's window color settings (which are set in the Appearance properties of the Display control panel). The default Windows setting is white, but the user can change the default.

NOTE If you select the Overlay Menu option, Windows 95 or Windows NT 4 ignores any background color that you assigned to the piece.

Standard Appearance

The Standard Appearance option applies to all versions of Windows. By default, Authorware displays Windows-style 3D controls such as buttons in grey. If you select the Standard Appearance option, Authorware relies on the user's Appearance settings when displaying buttons and other 3D objects in your piece. This procedure has no effect on custom buttons you import into Authorware, only on the default Windows-style buttons.

NOTE If you have selected the Standard Appearance option, you can preview your default controls by switching to the Interaction tab in the File Properties dialog box and looking at the default Wait Button.

Windows 3.1 Metrics

The Windows 3.1 Metrics option is another Windows-specific option available to you. Windows 95 and Windows 3.1 draw graphics to the screen using different sets of measurement rules. If you select this option, Authorware automatically adjusts the dimensions of your Presentation window, menu bar, and title bar to conform more closely to the system of screen metrics used in Windows 3.1. However, this may in result in graphics that are cut off by one pixel at either the top or bottom of your piece.

Desktop Pattern

The only Macintosh-specific option available is the Desktop Pattern option. When you select the Desktop Pattern option, the Presentation window automatically matches the Desktop Pattern setting on the user's Macintosh, which is set in the Desktop Patterns control panel. Like the Match Window Color option for Windows, this option ignores any background color you have assigned to the piece.

Modifying file interaction options

Like the Playback options, the Interaction options give you more control over how a piece looks and performs during playback and authoring. You access the Interaction options through the File Properties dialog box, as shown in **Figure 2.13**. The interaction options are described below.

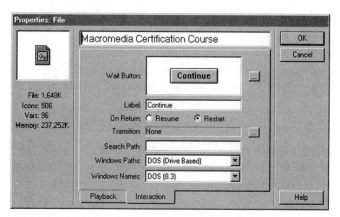

Figure 2.13
The Interaction options available to you in the File Properties dialog box.

Wait Button

The Wait Button option allows you to modify the default button that Authorware displays when it encounters a pause in the flowline. You can set up a pause using a wait icon, or by selecting the Pause Before Exiting option with interaction or decision icons (discussed in more detail in Chapter 7, "Creating Basic Interactivity").

To change the default wait button:

1. Click on the [...] button to the right of the default button, or simply click the button itself.

This opens the Button Library dialog box, as shown in **Figure 2.14**.

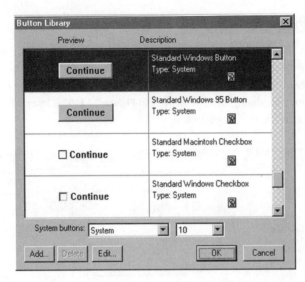

Figure 2.14
The Button Library dialog box allows you to select a different default wait button.

2. Select the button you want to use by scrolling through the available buttons and clicking one of them.

3. Click OK to close the Button Library window.

The new button now appears in the Wait Button preview window.

TIP If a wait button doesn't appear for a particular wait icon when you run your piece, make sure that you have selected the Show Button option in the wait icon's Options dialog box. (You'll see an example of this in Chapter 7, "Creating Basic Interactivity.")

Label

The Label field contains the name of the default wait button. The default wait button label is Continue. If you want to change the default label, simply type in a new label in the field. When the wait button next displays it has a new label. The button automatically resizes to fit the label you've entered here.

TIP You can change the default font used by the wait button and all other system buttons used in Authorware by modifying the default button text style inside the Button Editor. For more information about editing default buttons using the Button Editor, see Chapter 7, "Creating Basic Interactivity."

On Return

The On Return options allow you to control where the user begins
a piece after exiting the piece for the first time or jumping to another
Authorware file. Here's how the two options work:

- Selecting Restart for this option returns the user to the beginning of the piece and resets all system and custom variables
  to their initial values each time the file launches.

- Selecting Resume restarts in the place in the file where the user
  last exited, and maintains the values of all system variables from
  session to session.

Many Authorware training pieces consist of an initial "router"
or logon file that jumps the user to separate lesson files. Having the
Resume option selected provides one way to maintain user-specific
data created during sessions by keeping track of the user's location
and the value of all variables in a records file. For more information on
the records file and using routers, see Chapter 16, "Tracking the User."

Transition

The Transition option allows you to select a transition effect to
use when returning to the piece after having jumped out to another
Authorware file.

To select a return transition:

1. Click the [...] button to the right of the Transitions field.

This opens the Return Transitions dialog box, as shown in
Figure 2.15.

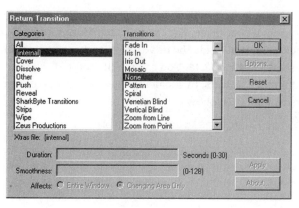

Figure 2.15
*The Return
Transitions
dialog box.*

2. Select the transition you want to use and click OK to close the dialog box.

NOTE The return transition effect doesn't affect the Presentation window when you first launch the file. If you want to use a transition effect at the start of your piece, you need to apply it to the first icon in the flowline that displays graphics. For information on how to apply transitions to icons, see Chapter 4, "Adding Motion."

see Chapter 4, "Adding Motion."

Search Path

The Search Path field enables you to designate the folders where you want to store the external content for your piece. When a piece first launches, Authorware uses the folder names specified in this field to locate any types of external files, including libraries and linked files.

The method for setting the Search Path is the same for both platforms, so you don't need to worry about changing this field when moving from one platform to the other. Authorware resolves any platform-specific naming issues automatically during playback of your piece.

To set up a new folder location in the Search Path, type in the name of the folder where the external content is located. Be sure to include either a colon [:] or a back-slash [\] after the name of the folder. If you use multiple folders, insert a semi-colon between the folder names.

After setting up your Search Path, it should look something like this:

```
Movies\;Sounds\;Resources\;
```

All folder names that you specify should be "relative" to the location of your piece. For example, the Movies folder is actually a folder located inside the drive or folder that contains your piece, as shown in **Figure 2.16**. You can specify "nested" folders, or folders within these folders, by including the full relative pathname to the nested folder, as follows:

```
Movies\Oldclips\;Sounds\Voices\;
```

Figure 2.16
The Search Path looks for folders relative to the location of your piece.

When you launch your piece, the information you entered in the Search Path appends to the `SearchPath` system variable. You also can modify the Search Path by specifying folders that a calculation icon will look for at the start of your piece. Chapter 14, "Using Functions and Variables," covers this in more detail.

In addition to these options, Authorware for Windows allows you to select the type of path and file system the piece should use when you deliver it on the Windows platform. These options not only affect the setup of the current piece, but any other files that you may need to access during playback.

Windows Path

This Windows Path option allows you to select the type of pathname that you want system functions and variables to use. Selecting DOS (Drive Based) requires that you refer to a directory or file using a specific drive letter. Selecting UNC (Universal Naming Convention) enables you to refer to a directory or a file that uses the name of the server where you have the file stored.

Using DOS (Drive Based) pathnames, you reference a file located on a server using the full path:

```
h:\images\graphic01.bmp
```

If you know the name of the server volume where the file is stored, you can reference the same file through UNC using the following pathname:

```
\\main server\images\graphic01.bmp
```

Because drive letters can change from machine to machine, the UNC option is helpful when you know ahead of time that your piece will need to access content from a file server running Windows NT or Novell Netware software.

NOTE The Search Path settings don't apply to externally linked content that uses an exact pathname or variable pathname. You'll see an example of how this works with externally linked files in Chapter 6, "Managing Your Content."

Windows Names

Using the Windows Names option allows you to select the file name format that you want system functions and variables to use, such as DOS (8.3), which allows eight characters plus a three-character extension; or Long Filenames, which allows 255-character file names. Although Windows 95 and Windows NT automatically create an alternative 8.3 file name when you view a file in Windows 3.1, you still need to refer to files in your application using the format you've selected in this option.

If you are creating your piece to run in only Windows 95 or Windows NT, you might want to select Long Filenames to give your application access to all files on the system. However, if your piece is to run in Windows 3.1, or if you are delivering it as a Shockwave application from a server configured for the Unix operating system; then, it's a good idea to stick with the standard DOS-naming convention so Authorware can locate specific files or folder names referred to in your piece during playback.

The Windows Names option has no effect on how the Macintosh treats names, if you plan to deliver the file as a cross-platform application. Names on the Macintosh use the Macintosh file-naming convention, which supports file names up to 32 characters long.

Handling Fonts

Fonts are the trickiest aspect of cross-platform authoring. The operating system uses fonts to display text on screen. Because the font formats are different on the Macintosh and Windows platforms, text that you create in a piece on one platform can look very different when you move your piece to the other platform to test it.

While there are several ways to minimize font-handling issues in your piece, you always should anticipate them—especially when designing your piece to run over the web or a local area network where it's accessible by both platforms simultaneously. In these situations, you can experiment with using font mapping to control how text will appear on the different delivery platforms.

Using font and character mapping

Whenever you move a piece from one platform to another, Authorware uses font and character mapping information to keep the formatting characteristics and screen size of the text consistent. You can adjust the font and character mapping options while authoring to get the best possible font handling between platforms.

Since you may be using fonts on one platform that don't exist for another platform, you can use the information contained in the Authorware font mapping table to help adjust the onscreen appearance of your text. When working on a file, you should regularly copy it from one platform to the other to see how Authorware remaps the text. Note the changes you see in text size and appearance so that you can later go to the font mapping table and adjust the mapping settings as needed.

For example, you might see some text in your piece on the authoring platform resized when displayed on the other platform, forcing some of the text off screen. As frustrating as this may sound, it's a pretty common event—especially when using a custom font that the other platform cannot remap easily. (See "Avoiding font problems" later in this chapter for some workaround solutions to this issue.)

NOTE When packaging a piece for distribution, Authorware adds font mapping information to the executable file so it doesn't need to be distributed separately. For more information on packaging, see Chapter 17, "Distributing Your Piece."

Specifying font mapping

Authorware stores all default font and character mapping information in a plain text file named Fontmap.txt (located in the same folder where you installed Authorware 4). This text file contains information that tells Authorware how to handle platform and size conversions for specific fonts used in the piece. It also contains a character mapping table that tells Authorware how to remap specific machine-code (or ASCII) characters used in the piece.

Whenever you move your file to another platform, Authorware uses the information in the font and character mapping tables to adjust the text inside the piece. At any time, you can replace the Fontmap.txt file with another text file that contains customized settings that you can create.

NOTE Authorware remaps all text objects using the Fontmap.txt file. This includes text fields, text entry fields, button labels, text in calculation icons, and text in attached libraries.

The font mapping information contained in Fontmap.txt specifies which font and size substitutions to make when moving a piece from one platform to another. If you open the Fontmap.txt file, you will see that Authorware uses the following format to specify font mapping definitions:

```
Originating Platform:Font Name => New Platform:
Font Name [MAP NONE] [old Size => new Size]
```

The MAP NONE and size tags are optional settings you can use. The size option only affects the font specified in this line. Specifying MAP NONE in this line turns off character mapping for the specified font. You should use this if you know that the Windows and Macintosh fonts you're using share the same ASCII values for special characters.

Because font mapping information is separate for each platform, each font that you use will appear in two separate lines. Some typical entries found in the Fontmap.txt file are shown below:

```
Win:"Courier"    => Mac:"Courier"

Mac:"Courier"    => Win:"Courier"


Mac:"Geneva"     => Win:"System" 12=>10 14=>12
18=>14 24=>18 30=>24

Win:"System"     => Mac:"Geneva" 10=>12 12=>14
14=>18 18=>24 24=>30


Mac:"Helvetica"  => Win:"Arial"

Win:"Arial"      => Mac:"Helvetica"


Mac:"Symbol"     => Win:"Symbol" Map None

Win:"Symbol"     => Mac:"Symbol" Map None
```

If you take a look at the default Fontmap.txt file, you'll see that all Windows entries are separate from all Mac entries. However, you should think about placing your fonts in pairs (as shown in the example above) to make it easier to edit. This becomes especially important when modifying the Fontmap.txt file by adding new font and size mapping information.

TIP To edit the settings in Fontmap.txt, use a text editing utility like Wordpad, Notepad, or SimpleText.

Specifying character mapping

Character mapping ensures that characters such as bullets, quotation marks, and accented characters appear correctly when moved from one platform to another. A character is mapped when a different ASCII value is substituted to preserve the appearance of the character. Use character mappings for all fonts except those you've specified not to map using the MAP NONE setting.

The following is the format for character mappings:

```
Platform: => Platform: oldChar => newChar
```

The default Authorware character mapping table provides a full set of bidirectional mappings for all ASCII values between 128 and 255. This applies to most characters that you will use in your pieces. Below is an example of what a character mapping line looks like:

```
Mac: => Win: 128=>196 129=>197 130=>199
131=>201 132=>209 133=>214 134=>220
```

NOTE Some characters are not available in both character sets; however, the mapping table preserves these characters even when you move a file to the other platform.

You probably won't need to modify the character mapping table as most fonts map correctly using the default settings. However, you always can change these settings if you're using a custom font and want to match the special characters as closely as possible on the other platform.

When working with a piece, you can save the current font mapping information from your file in a new text file so that it is easier for you to add new font and size information to the piece. You also can load new font mapping into your file to update or replace pre-existing font mapping information.

When importing and exporting font mapping information, you need to use the Font Mapping dialog box. To access the Font Mapping dialog box, choose File > Font Mapping from the Modify menu.

The Font Options dialog box appears, as shown in **Figure 2.17**.

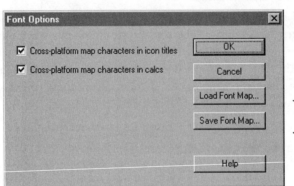

Figure 2.17
Use the Font Options dialog box to export and import font mapping information for your piece.

The Font Mapping dialog box presents several options:

- The Load Font Map button allows you to load in a text file with new or additional font mapping information. You can choose to either replace the existing font mapping information used in your file, or merge the new mapping information into your current font mapping.

- The Save Font Map button allows you to save the font mapping information so that you can edit it or use it later when moving your file to the other platform.

- The Map Characters in Icon Titles and Map Characters in Calcs checkbox options on the left of the dialog box control character mapping in icon titles and calculation icons, respectively.

If you deselect these options, you may run into problems later if you move your file to the other platform because the name of a referenced icon either on the flowline or in a calculation expression can change. Because of this, it is recommended that you leave them selected.

Saving and editing font mapping information

If you get into the habit of saving your font mapping information from a piece into a new text file, you'll have a clearer picture of the fonts you currently are using in your piece. You can use this information to help prepare the file for moving cross-platform.

To save your font mapping information:

1. Open the Font Mapping dialog box.

2. Select the Save Font Map button.

   The Save dialog box appears.

3. Select the location where you want to save the file using the list of available folders.

4. Type the name you want to save the file as in the Filename field and click Save.

This creates a new file that contains all the current font and character mapping information for your piece. Authorware lists all fonts used in your piece here.

If you want to make sure that all fonts used in your piece are remapped correctly on the opposite platform, you'll need to first edit this file, and then load it into the piece before you move it to the other platform.

If you've added a font to your piece that isn't included in the original Fontmap.txt file, you will see it listed on a single line in the new font mapping file you've saved, as shown below:

```
; These fonts are used but have no mapping.
;Win:"Wide Latin" => Mac:"" 10=> 24=>
```

The semicolon before the line indicates that you haven't yet provided Authorware with the cross-platform font mapping information it needs to correctly remap the font when you open it on the other platform. In the example above, a new font ("Wide Latin") was added to the piece on the Windows side, and then the font mapping information was saved. As you can see, a corresponding Macintosh font and font sizes have not yet been specified.

Before you move your piece to the other platform, it's important that you open your new font mapping text file to remove these semicolons and add the appropriate remapping information for the other platform. This way, your text will format correctly inside the Presentation window when you open the piece on the other platform.

To modify this information:

1. Remove the semicolon from the line.

2. Type in the name of the font and the size you want to use when opening the file on the other platform.

In the example above, the edited font mapping entry line would appear something like this:

```
Win:"Wide Latin" => Mac:"Lumina Bold" 10=>12
24=>26
```

NOTE The name that you specify in a mapped font entry must match the name of the font as it appears in Authorware when creating a new text object. This includes using the correct spacing and capitalization. Otherwise, your fonts do not map correctly.

After you've finished modifying the font mapping text file, you should use the Font Options dialog box to load the file back into the piece so that when you move the piece to the other platform, your fonts remap correctly. You will find that you may need to experiment with several different font combinations during this process to get the best font matching on both platforms.

Loading font mapping information

Say that you've modified your new font mapping information and want to replace the existing font mapping information in your file. To do this, use the Load Font Mapping option in the Font Mapping dialog box. This option enables you to either replace or append existing font mapping information in the current file.

To replace the default font mapping table with a new table that you've created:

1. Open the Font Mapping dialog box.

2. Select the Load Font Map button.

The Load Font Mapping dialog box appears, as shown in **Figure 2.18**.

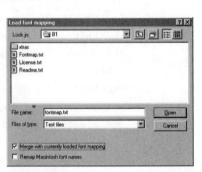

Figure 2.18
The Load Font Mapping dialog box enables you to replace or append existing font mapping information.

3. Select the file where you want your new font mapping information stored and click Open.

The new font mapping file loads, replacing the existing information.

Notice the two options you have when loading a font map into your piece. These are checkbox options that appear below the folder window, as shown in **Figure 2.18** above:

- Selecting the "Merge with currently loaded font mapping" option doesn't replace the existing font mapping information. It simply appends it using new settings stored in the file you modified. If you want to merge another file into your piece, Authorware ignores any duplicate font and character information.

NOTE If the Fontmap.txt file is missing when you move your piece over to the other platform, your text will appear, but it will be missing the styles and size information you'd applied to it. However, because Authorware retains all text style information, you can manually reload the font mapping information and see your styles reappear as normal using the merge technique.

- Selecting the "Remap [platform] font names" option ensures that Authorware replaces all font names used in the piece with the new ones you've saved in the new font mapping file. You need to deselect this option if you only want to replace the names of fonts on the current platform.

NOTE If the font mapping text file you select to load is empty (contains no characters), it clears all existing font mapping information from your piece and resets all text to the platform's default system font.

Avoiding font problems

Indeed, fonts are one of the most problematic issues you'll come across when authoring. The only comforting comment I can think to say at this moment is, "It happens to everyone." So, don't get too flustered and start throwing expensive equipment out the window (at least not the equipment that you own personally). Having said that, here are some basic guidelines you can follow to help minimize font problems you may encounter.

If you already know you will deliver on both the Windows and Macintosh platforms, your best bet is to stick with system fonts during development. These fonts (Arial, Courier, System, and Times New Roman on the Windows side; Chicago, Courier, Geneva, and Times on the Macintosh side) are installed with the operating system, so you don't have to worry about installing them when distributing a piece.

NOTE Keep in mind that any fonts you distribute with your piece (except for fonts that you've created yourself) must be licensed from the company you got them from before you can legally distribute them.

You also need to follow a simple golden rule that may save you in the end: "Test early, test often, test on all target platforms." For projects that are largely text-based, this rule helps you avoid finding yourself in a jam at the end. In any case, it's usually safest to stick with the standard system fonts and integrate them into your design.

TIP If you're developing strictly for the Macintosh platform, you have the option of packaging your Macintosh piece with the fonts included. However, this option applies only to fonts that are a TrueType (non-PostScript) format. See Chapter 17, "Distributing a Piece" for more information on other packaging options available to you.

If you need to use custom fonts in a piece, there are three recommended techniques you can use:

- Use a custom installer to install fonts on the user's system.
- Create a custom cross-platform font that can be used on both platforms.
- Bitmap your text.

Most of the time when you install an application to your hard drive, an installer copies the necessary files to a location you specify. You can do the same thing with an Authorware piece that you've created by placing the custom fonts on the user's system during installation.

Many third-party installers are available, including InstallShield for Windows and StuffIt InstallerMaker for the Macintosh. These utilities enable you to create a custom installation program that can copy resources (such as fonts to the user's hard disk) and then make the necessary modifications so the system recognizes the fonts. You will need to create two separate installers if you plan to deliver the piece on both Macintosh and Windows systems.

TIP The companies listed above have demo versions of their installer software that you can download and try on your own. See Appendix C, "Authorware Resources on the Internet," for the World Wide Web addresses of these companies.

Sometimes you can minimize the impact fonts have on your piece by using a font that maps for both platforms. Using a font editing package like Macromedia Fontographer, you can create custom fonts that you can use on both platforms. Like any other font, however, you still have to install it on the user's system.

There is one major caveat when creating custom fonts: If you have no experience creating type faces, you probably should hire someone who does. A badly designed font makes reading text virtually impossible, especially on the computer screen.

TIP More information about creating custom fonts can be found in the documentation for Fontographer or in the Fontographer area of the Macromedia web site (**http://www.macromedia.com/software/ fontographer**).

Bitmapping your text is a common production trick that you can use effectively in cases where you have a single screen or a line of text that doesn't require scrolling, as shown in **Figure 2.19**.

This text was created as part of the background image.

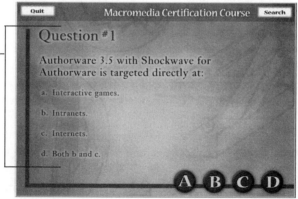

Figure 2.19
Using bitmapped text can improve the overall look of your piece, and doesn't require special font handling.

There are several ways of doing this. You can use a screen capture utility to capture the entire Authorware screen (once you have placed your text in Authorware) and save it as a bitmap image; or you can create the text as part of the image using a graphics production tool such as Macromedia xRes or FreeHand. When you import the graphic back into Authorware, your text is part of the graphic and doesn't require special font considerations when distributing your piece.

TIP To capture a screen in Windows 95 or NT, simply press the Print Screen button on your keyboard. This copies the contents of the entire display window to the Clipboard. Then you can paste the screen capture into your graphics editing tool, crop it, and save it as an image.

The only problem with using bitmapped text is that it consumes much more memory than plain text in a piece. Each full-screen graphic must be stored internally and usually takes up to 300K per screen, if you're developing with 8-bit graphics. If you're developing a piece with 24-bit graphics, keep in mind that these graphics are three times larger than 8-bit images, unless you're using a compressed image format such as JPEG or QuickTime.

In comparison, text on average takes up only a couple hundred kilobytes of storage space for the entire file. Those extra bytes saved can really improve the performance of your piece, especially if you're delivering it over the network as a Shockwave application. (You'll find more about the guidelines for using graphics with Shockwave in the next chapter, Chapter 3, "Working with Text and Graphics.")

Looking Ahead...

While you may want to jump right into production, be aware that many of the mistakes made on a project are made during the first few weeks. Mistakes made early and not caught until testing can result in a project that is late and over budget.

Each new project should begin by taking a look at the issues explained in this chapter: how your piece looks and functions on different platforms, the path and filename characteristics of your piece, and how you plan to handle such tricky areas as fonts and font mapping.

Once you are past this initial stage, you can begin building content by either creating your own text and images, or importing them into your piece. You'll learn more about how to do this in Chapter 3, "Working with Text and Graphics." Chapter 3 explains how you work with text by defining, modifying, and applying styles; and how you work with graphics by choosing and assigning colors, arranging graphics, assigning line width and fills, and much more.

Working with Text and Graphics

When developing your first Authorware piece, it may help to imagine the piece as a kind of book that encompasses all types of media—one that provides consistent visual clues to the user (your audience) on how to "read" it. Text and graphics make up the basic visual elements to help the user along the way, conveying information directly, providing visual reinforcement, explaining difficult concepts, and providing onscreen help with navigation.

Using the flowline, you can orchestrate when and how text and graphics appear in a piece to explain or illustrate the key concepts that you want to get across to the user. This chapter explores the basic techniques for adding text and graphics to your Authorware pieces.

Text is a key element of most Authorware pieces. You can use it for prompts, labels, titles, and simple directions; or, it can be the main feature of a piece, if you are creating a reference-based title or an online glossary or encyclopedia. As mentioned in the last chapter, handling fonts is a tricky aspect of development and because of this you probably will use tools such as Macromedia xRes or FreeHand to create some of your text elements. In most cases, however, text created in or imported into Authorware saves file space, easing the process of making your files deliverable over a network as a Shockwave piece.

With Authorware's text tools, you can create short text segments such as questions, comments, and headings. If your piece requires sizable portions of text from another source, you can write and format large blocks of text in a word-processing application, and then import it into Authorware with its formatting intact. After the text is in Authorware, you can edit its font, size, and style using the text tool and the Text menu, or by assigning a predefined style.

Creating text within a piece

When you open a display icon or an interaction icon to edit its contents in the Presentation window, the graphics toolbox appears in the upper right-hand corner, as shown in **Figure 3.1**. You use most of the items in the toolbox to create different kinds of onscreen display objects (as explained later in this chapter).

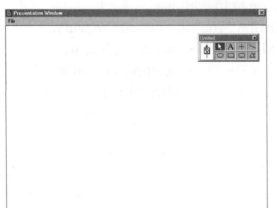

Figure 3.01
When you open a display or interaction icon, the toolbox appears.

You can create text fields inside the Presentation window using the text tool, labeled in **Figure 3.2**.

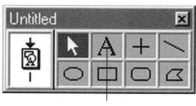

Figure 3.02
The text tool can be found on the toolbox.

The text tool

The Text menu, shown in **Figure 3.3**, gives you additional control over such properties as the font, size, and style of the object.

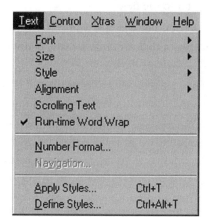

Figure 3.3
The Text menu enables you to set different properties for your text.

When adding text to a display icon or interaction icon, you open the icon first and then use the text tool to add the text.

Go ahead and create some text:

1. Create a new file, and add a new display icon to the flowline.

2. Double-click the display icon to open it.

The Presentation window opens and the toolbox appears.

3. Select the text tool by clicking it.

4. Click anywhere in the Presentation window.

Authorware creates a new text field where you click, as shown in **Figure 3.4**. The cursor indicates where you can enter text, and the paragraph ruler across the top of the text field lets you adjust the width of the field, as well as tabs and margins.

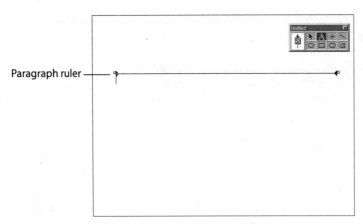

Figure 3.4
The new text field appears in the Presentation window.

Paragraph ruler

5. Type some new text into the field.

If you need to jump back a few letters, you can use the arrow keys on the keyboard, or click with the mouse. If you need to delete text, use the Delete or Backspace keys.

6. When you finish entering text, click the arrow tool in the toolbar.

When you click in the Presentation window with the text tool selected, you automatically create a new text field. If you create a text field and do not enter any text, Authorware automatically deletes the text field from the screen when you select the arrow tool or close the Presentation window.

One of the most time-consuming aspects of working with text is making sure that it looks good on screen. To ensure that your text looks good, you need to learn how to work with the text field in the Presentation window, as all text formatting takes place here. The next few sections take a look at the various ways you can format your text in Authorware.

Modifying text widths

You will find yourself frequently resizing text fields to accommodate more text, placement of the text field, or display size of the text.

To adjust the width of a text field:

1. Select the pointer or text tool and click in the text field you want to resize.

Adjustment handles appear on both sides of the text field, as shown in **Figure 3.5**.

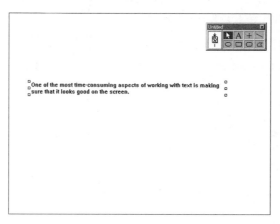

Figure 3.5
*When selecting
a text field,
adjustment
handles appear
on both sides
of the field.*

2. Drag the handles to adjust the size.

Authorware resizes the text field and adjusts the text to fit the new width.

NOTE If you have created a full screen of text, resizing the field may push some of the text off screen. If this happens, you need to either resize the object or change it into a scrolling field by selecting the Scrolling Text option in the Text menu.

After you create a text field, repositioning it on screen is easy. You simply move the field to its new position using the mouse.

TIP To move a group of text fields so they maintain the same position relative to each other, Shift-click the selected text fields before dragging them to a new location.

Modifying text color

Perhaps you have created your text and now want it to appear in a different color. You can change the color using the Colors Inspector, selecting any color from the current palette.

To change the color of your text:

1. Choose Inspectors > Colors from the Window menu.

The Colors Inspector window appears, as shown in **Figure 3.6**. This window displays the colors in the default Authorware palette. At the bottom of the window are three different color options: the text/line color fill, the object color fill, and the background color fill.

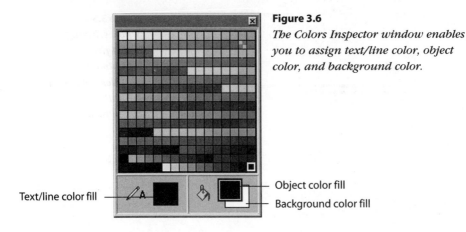

Figure 3.6
The Colors Inspector window enables you to assign text/line color, object color, and background color.

Text/line color fill

Object color fill
Background color fill

2. Select the text/line foreground color option by clicking on its color chip, located on the left side of the Color Inspector window.

NOTE A white highlight appears around the edge of any color chip when selected.

3. Select the color you want to use for the text by clicking anywhere in the color palette. You have 256 colors from which to choose.

4. Click on the Color Inspector window close box to close it.

You may want to experiment with different colors to see how they appear to you on screen. You also can try different combinations of foreground and background colors to determine the readability of the text. This usually depends entirely on the background color that you select for the Presentation window.

In most cases, you'll want to use the default Authorware palette when deciding colors for your text. If you need to use a custom color scheme, you may want to consider using bitmapped text created with a graphics tool like Macromedia xRes.

Keep in mind that light text on a dark background is the easiest to read on a computer screen. White or off-white text works particularly well in most cases, as shown in **Figure 3.7**.

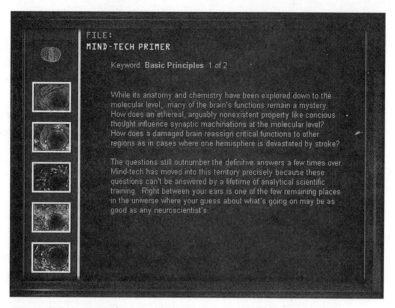

Figure 3.7
Try to design your screens using light text on a dark background.

Reading Text On Screen

Our eyes are accustomed to reading text from a printed page, which reflects light off its surface and into our eyes from an overhead light source. When reading text on a computer screen, the letters are created from a back-lit light source (the monitor), which forces the muscles in our eyes to work harder in order to focus on the images being created.

In any piece you design, keep in mind that onscreen readability is always a major issue. You need to spend time designing the text layout and styles used in your piece, as well as the background graphics on which they will appear.

Graphics and colored text usually appear a bit darker on the Windows platform because of hardware display differences. When creating content for both platforms, test your piece on the Windows side as you may need to lighten your graphics a bit inside the program that you used to create them.

If you plan to create a piece that is mostly text-based, make sure that you design your text and background graphics so they can be read easily on different screen sizes and monitors. You also will want to test your design on a number of test users.

In Authorware, you can modify text style by applying styles using the Text menu, or by defining styles using the Define Styles dialog box and applying the styles to text. For more information on creating styles, see "Using Text Styles" later in this chapter.

The text menu gives you full control over how your text appears on screen. Like any word-processing program, you can select different fonts to use, resize your text, or realign it.

To change the font, size, style, or alignment of text:

1. Select the text.

2. Choose the new font, size, style, or alignment from the Text menu.

Install any font you intend to use in a piece on the authoring system before you begin. In addition, you need to determine some method to get this font to the end user's machine.

However, if you're developing a Shockwave piece, you cannot install anything on the user's system, so you must rely on the user having the fonts installed. For this reason, many Authorware developers choose to use the standard system fonts, or bitmap their fonts after laying the text out in Authorware. For more information on bitmapping fonts, see Chapter 2, "Beginning a Piece."

In addition to font, size, style, and alignment, you have two other options, located on the Text menu, that you can apply to text fields:

- The Scrolling Text option adds a standard scroll bar to the text field, as shown in **Figure 3.8**. This option is useful for working with large fields that can't fit entirely on screen. Scrolling text fields also simulate real-world software more realistically.

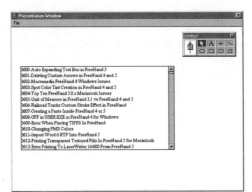

Figure 3.08

Scrolling text fields are useful for displaying large amounts of text on one screen.

■ The Run-Time Word Wrap option automatically reformats the line wrapping of your text when running the piece on another computer. This is a new feature to Authorware 4. It helps prevent text from cutting off at the end of the line when you move your piece between platforms.

Setting paragraph attributes

Paragraph attributes—like tabs, margins, indentation, and alignment settings—can be made at the same time as other formatting options. This feature enables you to preview and adjust your text layout inside the Presentation window.

You can set paragraph margins, indentations, and tabs in one of two ways:

■ You can use the paragraph ruler at the top of the text field. The paragraph ruler controls the attributes for selected paragraphs in much the same way as the ruler in a word-processing application.

■ You can import or paste text that already has these attributes set. This is discussed in greater detail later in this chapter in "Importing Text," which introduces you to working with RTF (Rich Text Format) files.

Setting paragraph attributes involves setting margins, tabs, and indentation. You also can align a paragraph's text with the left or right margins or center the text between the margins.

TIP You can use multiple paragraph attributes in a single text field by highlighting different lines and applying different attributes.

To set margins:

1. Use the text tool to select the text field.

The paragraph ruler appears above the block of text.

2. Drag the handles at the ends of the paragraph ruler to resize it.

To set a tab:

1. Click in the text field.

2. Click just above the paragraph ruler at the spot where you want to set the tab.

At the spot where you clicked, you should see a black arrow pointing downward, as shown in **Figure 3.9**. This is the tab marker. Slide the tab marker along the paragraph ruler to change the tab position.

The tab marker appears on the paragraph ruler.

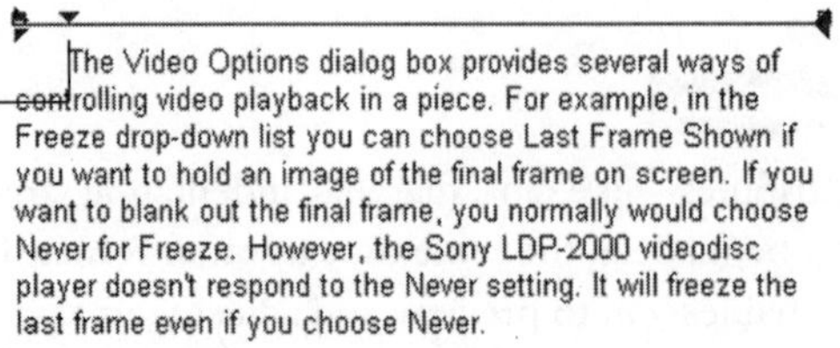
The Video Options dialog box provides several ways of controlling video playback in a piece. For example, in the Freeze drop-down list you can choose Last Frame Shown if you want to hold an image of the final frame on screen. If you want to blank out the final frame, you normally would choose Never for Freeze. However, the Sony LDP-2000 videodisc player doesn't respond to the Never setting. It will freeze the last frame even if you choose Never.

Figure 3.9
The tab marker, which appears on the paragraph ruler, indicates a tab setting.

TIP To delete a tab setting, drag the tab marker all the way to the left or right of the paragraph ruler.

Use the pair of triangle-shaped controls found to the left of the paragraph ruler to set indentations.

To change indentation settings for a paragraph:

1. Highlight the paragraph you want to indent using the text tool.
2. You now have the following options:
   - You can indent the left edge of the paragraph by dragging the top half of the triangle control to a new position on the paragraph ruler.
   - You can indent the first line of the paragraph by dragging the bottom half of the triangle to a new position on the paragraph ruler.
   - You can indent the right edge of a paragraph by dragging the triangle on the right end of the paragraph ruler.

Notice that when you drag the top half of the triangle, both halves move; when you drag the bottom half, only the bottom half moves.

To modify the alignment of a text field:

1. Click on the text field using the text or arrow tool.
2. Choose Alignment > Left from the Text menu to align the text with the left margin. You also have the option of choosing Center, Right, or Justify.

Your text justifies accordingly on screen.

TIP You can apply different text alignment styles to separate paragraphs in a text field by highlighting each paragraph and applying the desired style.

NOTE The Undo command cancels edits made to text, except for changes to tabs. Changes to paragraph styles cannot be undone.

Importing Text

If you're working on a piece that uses a great deal of text, simply import or paste text from other pieces or other applications into the flowline rather than creating it inside Authorware.

Why would you want to import and paste text?

- Importing text lets you bring entire documents into Authorware that you have created in a word-processing program like Microsoft Word.

- Pasting allows you to include sections of other documents that you have copied to the Clipboard into your piece.

Save the document you want to import into Authorware as either a plain text file or a RTF file. The advantage to using RTF files is that Authorware retains all text formatting characteristics saved with the file—except for headers, footers, footnotes, tables, and columns.

NOTE If you import headers, footers, footnotes, tables, or columns into Authorware as part of an RTF file, they appear in the Presentation window as regular paragraph text.

Save any multiple-page document in RTF-format with hard page breaks. When you import the file into Authorware, you can either ignore the page breaks and create one page, or import the file with page breaks and create separate pages (which Authorware imports into separate display icons). As with all other supported file formats, you can import text into Authorware using either the Import command or dragging and dropping a file from the desktop directly into the flowline.

If you have saved the text you want as a single-page document, you can use the following technique to import text:

1. Position the paste hand where you would like to add the page of text.

2. Choose Import from the File menu.

Shortcut: To import a text file (or any other supported file type) into Authorware, use Ctrl+Shift+R (Windows), or Command+Shift+R (Macintosh).

The Import dialog box appears.

3. Select the file and click Import.

The RTF Import dialog box appears and asks you how to distribute page breaks within icons, as shown in **Figure 3.10**. (Since you're importing a single-page document, you can ignore this dialog box.)

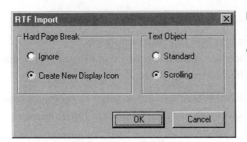

Figure 3.10
The RTF Import dialog box.

4. Click OK to import the text.

After importing the text, Authorware creates a new display icon in the flowline with the name of the text file you imported. To edit the text, apply a style, or change its formatting, simply open the display icon.

If you are importing a multiple-page RTF document into Authorware, you can create multiple pages instantly by importing the document into a display icon attached to a framework. For more information on creating pages automatically, see Chapter 11, "Working with Pages."

Pasting text

Sometimes it's easier to use the Clipboard to copy and paste text into an icon—especially if you're working with both Authorware and your word processor open. You also can paste text from one icon to another within Authorware.

You can use the text tool to choose the position on screen where you want to paste the text. When you select a text field, Authorware pastes the text at the text cursor. When no text field is selected, Authorware pastes the copied text into a new text field.

To paste text:

1. Copy the text to the Clipboard from the application that contains the text.

2. Switch to Authorware.

3. Open a display icon.

4. Select the text tool and position the cursor where you want to paste the text.

5. Choose Paste from the Edit menu.

Shortcut: To paste text into a display icon, use Ctrl+V (Windows), or Command+V (Macintosh).

Authorware pastes the text into the display icon.

Using Text Styles

When working with text in Authorware, you can assign specific text attributes (font, size, style, and color) to make the text easy to read, indicate its purpose, and look attractive in the piece.

It is possible that you're working with a designer who already has designed text styles with this specific purpose in mind. These are the rules that you will follow when laying out your text. You often assign different styles in a piece wherever text appears, sometimes within the same paragraph. You can apply attributes individually by selecting a portion of text and choosing characteristics such as Font and Size from the Text menu, but that isn't practical for applying sets of attributes to more than a few portions of text.

In Authorware you can use custom styles to make working with text easier. Using the Define Styles window and the Apply Styles palette, you can quickly select a text field and apply a style to it. Later, when you need to change the color, size, or font, you can simply update the style and Authorware takes care of adjusting each piece of text that is assigned the style.

One additional benefit to importing RTF files into your piece is that you can save styles directly in a document using a program like Microsoft Word. Any style that you've created for the document imports into Authorware. The name of the style appears in the list of available styles in your piece, and Authorware saves all text formatting characteristics of the style.

As you can see, learning to integrate styles into your work will save you a lot of time when authoring, especially when developing a piece with lots of text. Who wants to dig through the flowline each time a text item needs to be changed? Styles help you avoid this issue altogether.

NOTE You can add interactivity to a text style in Authorware by making it a hot text style. You can see an example of this in Chapter 12, "Creating Links and Hyperlinks."

Defining text styles

Create a text style in Authorware using the Define Styles dialog box. To use the style once you have defined it, simply apply it to a text field using the Apply Styles palette.

To define a text style:

1. Choose Define Styles from the Text menu.

Shortcut: To open the Define Styles dialog box, use Ctrl+Shift+Y (Windows), or Command+Shift+Y (Macintosh).

The Define Styles dialog box appears, as shown in **Figure 3.11**.

Select styles from this list.

Rename styles in this field.

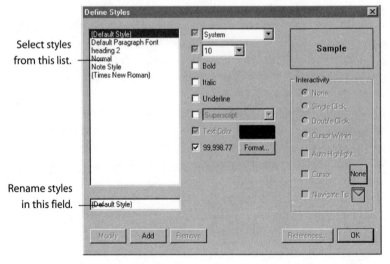

Figure 3.11
The Define Styles dialog box.

2. Click Add.

A style named New Style appears in the list of available styles. You can now change specific formatting characteristics of the style, including font, size, color, and interactivity. (See Chapter 12, "Creating Links and Hyperlinks," for an example of creating a hot text style.)

When you have finished defining the style's characteristics, give the style an unique name so that it doesn't conflict with any other styles you're using.

To rename the style:

1. Make sure that you have selected a style from the list of available styles. Its name should appear in the field in the lower left-hand corner.

2. Click Modify to apply the changes.

The new name appears in the list of styles. It also now appears in the Applied Styles palette when working with text in the Presentation window.

NOTE Use the Modify button when you want to change the formatting characteristics of a style.

Using the Define Styles dialog box

The Define Styles dialog box initially displays only the default text style used in your piece. As you continue to work with text and make changes, more styles are added to the styles list in the Define Styles dialog box.

If you modify text directly in the Presentation window, Authorware automatically creates a new unnamed style using the formatting characteristics you've selected. Working with unnamed styles can be a problem because they don't show up in the Apply Styles palette the way named styles do. Because of this, you should consider setting up several types of styles before you add any text to your piece so you can quickly adjust the text style using the Apply Styles palette without creating an unnamed style (see "Applying a text style" later in this chapter).

Unnamed styles appear in parentheses in the Define Styles list. For example, if you select a text field and set the font to 18-point Arial, Authorware automatically generates a style named (Arial 18). Rename these styles using the techniques described above.

You modify style characteristics inside the Define Styles dialog box the same way you rename a style. All the Text menu options for formatting a text field are available to you as checkbox items or drop-down lists in the Define Styles dialog box:

- Font

- Size

- Bold, Italic, or Underline

- Superscript or Subscript

- Color

- Number format

- Interactivity

To modify the style's formatting characteristics:

1. Open the Define Styles dialog box.

2. Select the style you want to change by clicking on its name in the list of available styles.

3. Select or deselect the style checkbox options depending on how you want the text to appear.

4. Click Modify to modify the style.

5. When you have finished, click OK to close the dialog box.

As mentioned earlier, you may find it easier to create a set of styles first and then import your text. You can quickly change the appearance of the text by applying a style to it, rather than using the Text menu (remember this creates an unnamed style, which you eventually rename anyway).

NOTE Changing the Default Style changes all text whose attributes aren't otherwise specified by another applied style. However, Authorware does not allow you to rename the Default Style.

Applying text styles

After you define a text style, you can apply it to a piece of text using the Apply Styles palette, shown in **Figure 3.12**. Any style given a name in the Define Styles window appears in Apply Styles palette. Any time you edit a text field, you also see the styles in your piece listed in the Text Styles drop-down list on the toolbar, as shown in **Figure 3.13**.

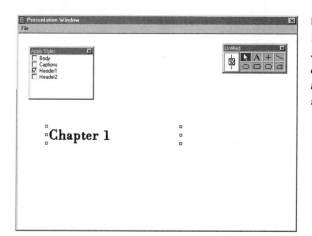

Figure 3.12
The Apply Styles palette displayed in the Presentation window.

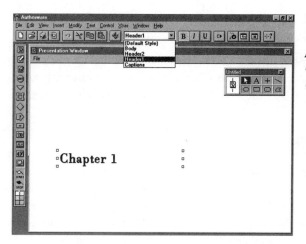

Figure 3.13
The Text Styles pull-down list displayed in the toolbar.

The Apply Styles palette remains available until you close it, except when the Define Styles dialog box is open. You can use the palette to apply text styles to other portions of text or to apply additional text styles to the same text.

To apply a text style:

1. Open a display or interaction icon that contains a text field.

2. Use the text tool to select a portion of text.

3. Choose Apply Styles from the Text menu.

Shortcut: To open the Apply Styles palette, use Ctrl+Alt+Y (Windows), or Command+Option+Y (Macintosh).

The Apply Styles palette appears.

4. Click on the style you want to apply to the text.

Authorware assigns the style to the selected text and a check-mark appears next to the name of the style in the Apply Styles palette.

If you apply more than one text style to the same portion of text, Authorware combines the styles and checks more than one item in the Apply Styles palette. For example, you may have a normal Body Text style that is set to 12-point Times; you also may have a Body Text Header style that is set to 12-point Times, boldface, and red. You can apply both of these styles to the same piece of text.

However, if you apply the Body Text style first and then the Body Text Header, your text will appear red. When the styles have different settings for the same attribute, the text style that you apply first becomes the default text style. Any occurrences of the other text style within a piece of text overrides the default text style.

TIP A display icon keeps its text styles when you paste it into another piece. Authorware adds the text style as long as the name of the text style isn't the same as any other text style in the piece.

Creating Graphics

Using graphics in a piece can provide the user with visual reinforce-ment of the key issues that you want to introduce. Graphics also can help improve the overall "value" of your piece by giving it a profes-sionally designed appearance, which helps keep the user interested and focused on what's on screen at any given time.

When designing photorealistic images and the main interface components, you probably will stick to a high-end graphics editing package, which can provide better control over paint options. With high-end graphics packages you can create photorealistic images from source material that you either photographed yourself or scanned from an outside source.

However, you also can create many of the visual elements for your piece directly inside Authorware's Presentation window using the toolbox. These elements could include bordered boxes that highlight definitions for you, a colored shape used for an animation effect, or drop shadows placed underneath a dialog box when the user tries to quit a piece.

Authorware stores graphics created with the toolbox as one-bit or "vector-based" graphics. If you're unfamiliar with this term, think of it as a way of storing graphics using only a basic description of the image—rather like a short text annotation. Because Authorware doesn't store all the bits of detail about the image, it can save file space and draw the image very quickly when you play it back. You should take advantage of this capability early, because it can drastically improve the performance of your piece when you distribute it as a Shockwave piece over a network.

 To see a piece created with one-bit graphics, look at the file named ONEBIT.A4P. It's included in the Chapter 3 examples folder on the CD accompanying this book.

Using the toolbox

Using the toolbox, you can quickly create simple visual elements in a piece. These might include one or two-color boxes, frames, and dividing lines. You can create toolbox objects directly inside the Presentation window when editing a display or an interaction icon. Each icon can hold more than one graphic object. You can group together multiple objects and then treat them as an individual object when you cut, paste, or move objects on screen. Objects can be both graphics that you create and graphics that you import into the piece.

The toolbox appears when the Presentation window is open for editing. With the toolbox, you can draw, resize, and rearrange graphics in the Presentation window. The line, oval, rectangle, rounded rectangle, and polygon tools draw simple two-dimensional graphics much like other paint programs do.

Take a closer look at what you can do with each of the items in the toolbox.

Arrow

The arrow tool allows you to select and move objects in the Presentation window. You click a single object to select and reposition it; or Shift-click to select multiple objects. You also can use the arrow tool to drag a handle on a selected object to resize it in the Presentation window. Selected objects could include text, graphics created in Authorware, imported graphics, and digital video files.

Text tool

The text tool allows you to create and edit text. Clicking in the Presentation window using the text tool creates a new text field; clicking in an existing text field opens it for editing.

Straight line tool

With the straight line tool, you can draw horizontal, vertical, or 45-degree lines. Click in the Presentation window to create the starting point of the line and then drag the cursor to draw the line. Lines created with this tool automatically snap to horizontal, vertical, or 45-degree positions.

Diagonal line tool

The diagonal line tool enables you to draw a line between any two points. Like the straight line tool, you click in the Presentation window to create the starting point of the line and then drag the cursor to draw the line.

TIP Holding down the Shift key while creating a line automatically locks the line to the Presentation window grid.

Ellipse tool

This tool is used to draw an ellipse or circle. To draw an ellipse, you click in the Presentation window to set the center point and then drag the cursor to create the dimensions of the shape.

TIP Holding down the Shift key while dragging the cursor creates a circle.

Rectangle tool

The rectangle tool allows you to draw a rectangular object. To create a rectangle, you click in the Presentation window to set the center point and then drag the cursor to create the rectangle.

TIP Holding down the Shift key while dragging the cursor creates a square.

Rounded rectangle tool

This tool enables you to draw a rectangle with rounded corners. You can use the control point that is inside the object to adjust the bevel of the corners by clicking and dragging it inside the object.

Polygon tool

The polygon tool enables you to draw irregular polygons or multiline objects. To create a polygon, you click in the Presentation window to set the first point, and then move the cursor around while clicking to create additional lines. To close the polygon, you double-click the last point.

TIP The polygon tool is particularly useful for creating irregularly shaped hot spots in your piece. Chapter 7, "Creating Basic Interactivity," takes a closer look at hot spots.

Using the Inspector windows

Using the Inspector windows you can apply different attributes (such as line, fill, transparency, and color), to any one-bit objects that you create in the Presentation window. All of the Inspectors are located in the Window menu, and are available to you each time you open a display or interaction icon to edit its content.

TIP To set the default color, fill pattern, and line width when you create a new object, open the Inspectors without editing a display icon and make the appropriate default selection. Authorware saves these settings until you quit the application.

The Inspector windows are floating windows that remain open until you close them, or until you close the display icon or the interaction icon that is currently open for editing. The next few sections describe how you use the Inspector windows when working with one-bit images.

Shortcut: To hide the open Inspector windows, use Ctrl+Shift+P (Windows), or Command+Shift+P (Macintosh).

Modifying line properties

The Lines Inspector allows you to set the width of a line created in Authorware using the line tools. You also can apply this attribute to a rectangle, oval, or polygon object to change the width of the stroke line around the object.

To change line width:

1. Select an object in the Presentation window.

2. Choose Inspectors > Lines from the Window menu.

Shortcut: To display the Lines Inspector window, use Ctrl+L (Windows), or Command+L (Macintosh).

The Lines Inspector appears, as shown in **Figure 3.14**.

3. Click a line sample to select that line width.

Figure 3.14
The Lines Inspector.

Authorware applies the line width to all selected objects.

TIP Use the dotted line sample at the top of the Lines Inspector to set an empty line or stroke.

Modifying fill properties

The Fills Inspector allows you to set the pattern or solid color fill for a rectangle, ellipse, or polygon object. Using the Fills Inspector, you can add a fill pattern or solid color to the center of the object. However, if you want to change the border color (the "stroke") of the object, use the Colors Inspector (see "Modifying color properties" below).

Fills are a convenient way to create an object that you can overlay on top of another object to partially mask it. You can use a pattern fill when you need to create a partially transparent drop shadow for a dialog box, as shown in **Figure 3.15**.

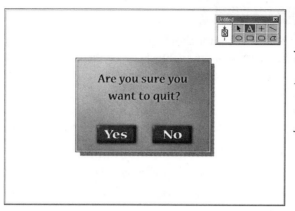

Figure 3.15
Here, a pattern fill was used to create a partially transparent drop shadow for a box.

To assign a fill to an object:

1. Select the object in the Presentation window.

2. Choose Inspectors > Fills from the Window menu.

Shortcut: To display the Fills Inspector, use Ctrl+D (Windows), or Command+D (Macintosh).

The Fills Inspector appears, as shown in **Figure 3.16**.

Figure 3.16
The Fills Inspector.

3. Click a pattern to select it.

Authorware applies the pattern to all objects that you have selected in the Presentation window.

Here are a couple of notes about the Fills Inspector:

■ The foreground and background colors of the fill pattern you apply to an object are the same foreground and background colors currently selected in the Color palette. To change the color of a fill, open the Colors Inspector and modify the currently selected foreground or background color. (See "Modifying color properties" below.)

■ Clicking the upper left-hand chip marked None gives the object an empty fill, creating a frame that you can place around other objects. You also can achieve this effect by filling the object with white and then changing the mode of the object from Opaque to Transparent using the Modes inspector. (See "Modifying mode properties.")

The Modes Inspector allows you to change the way the graphic overlays on top of other objects inside the Presentation window. The term "mode" is a bit confusing because it doesn't really change the way the graphic functions, only the way it looks on screen; however, it's a commonly used tool to create images that are transparent, matted, or blended with the other onscreen objects.

To change the mode of a graphic:

1. Select the graphic in the Presentation window by clicking on it.

2. Choose Inspectors > Modes from the Window menu.

Shortcut: To display the Modes Inspector, use Ctrl+M (Windows), or Command+M (Macintosh).

Figure 3.17
The Modes Inspector.

The Modes Inspector window appears, as shown in **Figure 3.17**.

3. Click one of the five settings (opaque, matted, transparent, inverse, or erase) in the Modes Inspector window.

How the image displays on screen depends on the mode setting you selected.

By default, any graphic object you import into Authorware is set to an Opaque mode—that is, it doesn't let anything else on screen show through it. New text that you import into the piece is set to Opaque mode.

However, if the object has any white pixels in it (this includes a text field's background color), you can use the white as a "masking" channel—that is, any white pixels in the graphic can be removed from the graphic to give it a transparent or matted appearance.

To create a transparent or matted object, change the mode setting from Opaque to Transparent or Matted inside the Modes Inspector window. If you select Transparent, Authorware removes any white pixels in the graphic, allowing other objects beneath it to appear, as you can see in **Figure 3.18**.

Figure 3.18
Other display objects appear behind an object set to Transparent mode.

If you select Matted, Authorware masks any white pixels outside the border of the object, as shown in **Figure 3.19**.

Figure 3.19
Authorware removes only the white border of a graphic when you use Matted mode.

The differences between Inverse and Erase modes are very subtle, and sometimes unnoticeable on many images. However, **Figure 3.20** shows the difference between the two using a color image placed on top of another color background image. The best way to think of these modes is that they are similar to the "subtractive" and "additive" blends used when compositing two images together in a graphics program such as xRes or Adobe Photoshop.

Figure 3.20
These images show the difference between Inverse mode (top) and Erase mode (bottom).

Since there may be many similar hues of "white" in a 24-bit image, you may be wondering exactly which "white" Authorware prefers when creating transparent and matted objects. There are two answers:

■ If you're working in Authorware, use the white color chip in the upper left-hand corner of the Colors Inspector window.

■ If you're working in a graphics program, set your fill color to a pure RGB white. If you're doing a single-color fill, look for a fill option named "white," or use the color picker tool to set your fill color to the RGB value 255, 255, 255.

TIP If Authorware masks out all white pixels, how can you create a graphic that has white in it? The answer is to fill areas of the graphic that you don't want to mask out with an off-white fill, something like RGB 253, 253, 253. It still appears "white" to the user, but its pixels are not masked out when you set the object's mode to transparent.

When setting an imported graphic to transparent mode, you may notice a "halo" of pixels around the outline of the image. This is because of the way programs like xRes and Photoshop handle "anti-aliasing." Anti-aliasing is used to smooth out "jaggies" (the jagged outlines you get when you paste a section of a graphic onto a solid background). In the process, however, the color values of pixels smooth out as well, so some of the white pixels around the edges darken, which creates the halo effect you see on screen.

TIP An essential trick to getting rid of the "jaggies" on a matted image is to turn off anti-aliasing when creating a selection inside xRes or Photoshop. If you are working with a graphic with anti-aliasing turned on, you may need to zoom in to the image and use the pencil tool to replace gray pixels around the edges of the object with RGB white.

Earlier in this chapter, you saw how to assign colors to text using the Colors Inspector window. You also can use the Colors Inspector window when adding color to one-bit graphics that you create in the Presentation window. This gives you a way to create color images without importing a bitmapped image into Authorware. Use the Colors Inspector to add colored borders and lines to your Shockwave pieces.

TIP Take advantage of using one-bit colored graphics in your Shockwave pieces because they take much less time to download.

To assign a color to a one-bit graphic:

1. Select the graphic in the Presentation window.

2. Choose Inspectors > Colors from the Window menu.

Shortcut: To display the Colors Inspector, use Ctrl+K (Windows), or Command+K (Macintosh).

The Colors Inspector window appears, as shown in **Figure 3.21**.

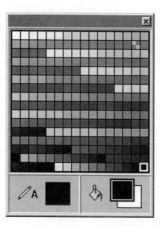

Figure 3.21
The Colors Inspector appears.

3. Click the type of fill color by selecting one of the three options at the bottom of the Colors Inspector window. The color chip on the bottom left is the text or stroke color. The color chip in the foreground on the bottom right is the foreground color. The color chip in the background on the bottom right is the background color.

A white highlight appears around the edge of the chip you selected.

4. Click a palette chip to select the color for the fill.

Authorware applies the color to the selected object.

TIP You also can apply color to one-bit graphics that you import into Authorware.

Often the graphics you want to use in a piece already exist (for example, a set of custom graphics designed by an artist, a collection of digitized photographs, or an archive of historical documents saved on CD-ROM). At other times you may want to use the power of a vector-based graphics tool such as Macromedia FreeHand to create original hand-drawn images or special text treatments and import them into Authorware.

You can import most of the common graphics formats available on the Internet into Authorware, including GIF and JPEG formats; so if you are creating graphics for a web site, you also can use them inside your Authorware piece. You can import and internally store graphics in Authorware on either platform, or you can create links to the external image files using the Link option when importing them. Whether you choose to import them into your piece or link to them, they show up in the Presentation window where you can position them on screen.

TIP When linking to external files, you now have the capability to point to an image's URL location, giving you the power of dynamic, web-based content inside your pieces. For an example of how to do this, see Chapter 6, "Managing Your Content."

Authorware supports the following graphics formats:

Microsoft DIB (.BMP, .RLE)
Macintosh PICT (.PCT)
FreeHand (.FH7, .FH5)
xRes LRG (.LRG)
Photoshop 3.0 (.PSD)
Encapsulated PostScript (.EPS)
GIF (.GIF)
JPEG (.JPG)
PNG (.PNG)
Targa (.TGA)
TIFF (.TIF)

TIP Windows users also can import Windows Metafile (.WMF) format graphics into their pieces. Although the metafile format isn't as commonly used as other formats, it's helpful when you need to export a slide from a Windows presentation tool like Microsoft PowerPoint, but still want to edit pieces of the graphic as individual objects.

Importing graphics involves selecting the graphics file, and then pasting it into the piece or linking to it. You can either import the image directly into a display or interaction icon, or add it to the flowline using the following steps:

1. Position the paste hand where you want to add the graphic.

2. Choose Import from the File menu.

The Import window appears, giving you a list of folders and files.

3. Select a file to import from the list of files available by clicking it.

4. Click Import to import the image into the display icon.

The graphic appears in the Presentation window.

When importing an image, the Import dialog box gives you three additional options, labeled for you in **Figure 3.22**:

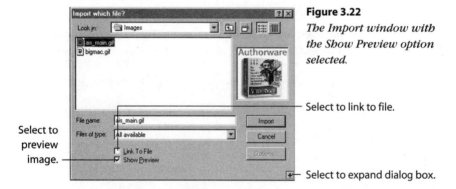

Figure 3.22
The Import window with the Show Preview option selected.

Select to link to file.

Select to preview image.

Select to expand dialog box.

- If you check the Show Preview option, a preview area appears in the dialog box. This option is useful when you have a long list of files without descriptive names.

- If you check the Link option, Authorware creates a link to the image file you selected to import. The image appears inside the Presentation window, but it's stored outside of the piece, allowing you to dynamically update it when the piece runs.

For more information about working with linked files, see Chapter 6, "Managing Your Content."

- Selecting the Expand (+) button at the lower right-hand corner of the dialog box allows you to import multiple images at the same time. (This option is also available to you when importing other types of files into Authorware.)

Importing multiple images

Using the expanded dialog box, you can quickly add multiple images to your piece all at the same time. If you import the files directly into the flowline, each image creates a separate display icon. If you want to add several images to the same display icon, open the display icon before you import them.

To import multiple images at the same time:

1. Choose Import from the File menu.

The Import dialog box appears.

2. Click the Expand (+) button at the lower right-hand corner of the dialog box.

The dialog box expands, as shown in Figure 3.23, showing two additional buttons, Add, and Add All, and an empty import list box.

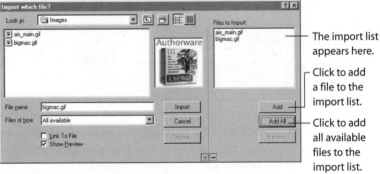

The import list appears here.

Click to add a file to the import list.

Click to add all available files to the import list.

Figure 3.23
The expanded dialog box allows you to import multiple files at the same time.

3. To add a file to the list, click on the name of the file and click the Add button.

The name of the file appears in the import list.

4. Add additional file names using the Add button; to add all available files in the folder, click the Add All button.

5. When you have added the files to the import list, click the Import button.

Authorware imports the files into the piece. If you choose to add them directly to the flowline, each image creates a separate display icon with the name of the imported file.

Setting Graphics Properties

Any time you import a graphic into Authorware, it centers automatically in the Presentation window. However, if you want to reposition your graphic on screen, or rearrange multiple graphics at the same time, you have several options (these also apply to graphics created in Authorware):

- You can drag the graphic to a new position with the arrow tool.

- You can align graphics vertically and horizontally by using the Align Objects palette.

- You can move graphics in front or in back of other objects in the same display or interaction icon by assigning them to a different layer, or by using the Bring To Front and Send To Back commands.

Dragging and grouping objects

Most of the time, you can reposition an object quickly by dragging it with the arrow tool.

To drag an object:

1. Select the object.

2. Drag the object to a new location.

To drag several objects at once and maintain their positions relative to each other:

1. Shift-click to select multiple objects and then drag them to their new position, or group them by selecting Group from the Modify menu.

Shortcut: To group several objects together, use Ctrl+G (Windows), or Command+G (Macintosh).

---

2. After you have grouped the objects, drag them to the new position. To ungroup them, select Ungroup from the Modify menu.

Shortcut: To ungroup a set of objects, use Ctrl+Shift+G (Windows), or Command+Shift+G (Macintosh).

Grouping objects saves time because you don't reselect the objects when you want to continue moving them as a group.

TIP To move an object straight up or down, left to right, or to a 45-degree angle, hold down the Shift key after you start dragging the object.

Shortcut: To select all objects in the current Presentation window, use Control+A (Windows), or Command+A (Macintosh). To deselect all objects in the current Presentation window, press the Spacebar.

Aligning objects

If you repositioned several objects on screen, and notice that their alignments have changed, you can quickly realign them by using the Align Objects palette. You might want to do this if you're creating a table layout of imported pictures, or if you're trying to align a set of buttons on screen. (See Chapter 7, "Creating Basic Interactivity," for details on creating buttons.)

To align several objects in the Presentation window:

1. Shift-click to select the objects you want to align.

2. Choose Align from the Modify menu.

Shortcut: To display the Align Objects palette, use Ctrl+Alt+K (Windows), or Command+Option+K (Macintosh).

The Align Objects palette appears, as shown in **Figure 3.24**.

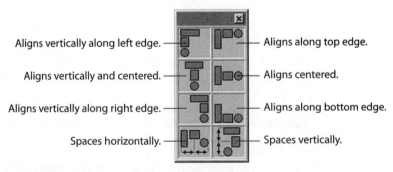

Aligns vertically along left edge. — Aligns along top edge.

Aligns vertically and centered. — Aligns centered.

Aligns vertically along right edge. — Aligns along bottom edge.

Spaces horizontally. — Spaces vertically.

Figure 3.24
The Align Objects palette has eight alignment options.

3. Click on the alignment option you want to apply to the selected objects.

The objects shift position in the display window to match the alignment you selected.

Shifting display order in a single icon

When you overlap objects inside a display or interaction icon, the objects appear in front of each other in the order in which you create or import them. However, you can change this order using the Bring To Front and Send To Back commands.

To move an object in front or in back of another object inside a display icon:

1. Select the object.

2. Choose Bring to Front or Send to Back from the Modify menu.

Shortcut: To bring an object to the front, use Ctrl+Shift+Up arrow (Windows), or Command+Shift+Up arrow (Macintosh). To send an object to the back, use Ctrl+Shift+Down arrow (Windows), or Command+Shift+Down arrow (Macintosh).

If you have selected Bring to Front, the object moves to the front layer inside the display icon and appears in front of any other object in the same location. If you have selected Send to Back, the object moves to the back layer inside the display icon and appears behind any other object in the same location.

Setting layer properties

Sometimes, however, you may need to change the layer order of multiple icons on the flowline. When more than one display icon is active at a time, the graphics can appear in the same area with some graphics in front of others. By default, Authorware stacks the display icons' contents from back to front in the order in which Authorware encounters the icons on the flowline.

Suppose that you want to rearrange the order in which display icons appear on top of each other. For example, you may want to keep an icon that contains the title or caption of a section on top and have the content of subsequent icons appear behind it. Setting the icon's layer property gives you the capability to control how other icons display relative to this icon.

An icon's default layer setting is 0. Higher layer numbers allow icons to appear closer to the front of the Presentation window. Adjusting icons' layer settings relative to each other allows you to control how graphics "stack" on top of each other in the Presentation window.

To set a display icon's layer property:

1. Select the icon in the flowline.

2. Choose Icon > Properties from the Modify menu.

Shortcut: To open the Properties dialog box for a display icon without using the menu bar, press the Ctrl key (Windows), or the Command key (Macintosh) while double-clicking the icon.

The Display Icon Properties dialog box appears, as shown in **Figure 3.25**. You can see that there are quite a number of options available to you. For now, all you need to do is modify the Layer field.

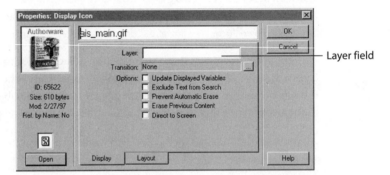
Layer field

Figure 3.25
The Display Icon Properties dialog box.

3. Type a number greater than 0 in the Layer field.

4. Click OK to close the dialog box.

The icon now has the layer number you specified. Giving other icons lower layer numbers makes them appear behind this icon; giving them higher layer settings makes them appear in front of this icon every time they display.

Before you go wild using layers, you need to carefully consider the alternatives first. Take a close look at how you have positioned the objects in the flowline and try to find an easier way to control object layering using the flowline rather than the layer properties.

If you've used layers everywhere in a file to control how the objects display, chances are you'll get to a point in development where a new type of layering issue is introduced, and you may have to go back through the entire file to reset many of the icons that use layers.

All warnings aside, layers are an effective way to troubleshoot a particular issue when something in the flowline doesn't display in the Presentation window. You may want to go in and assign a higher layer to the icon that doesn't display properly. This allows you to test whether or not the icon is making it to the Presentation window in the first place.

After you have determined that the icon isn't getting erased, go back and find a way to resolve the issue without depending on a layer to bring it to the front. In most cases, you can do this by changing the order in which the icons are presented on the flowline. However, if you can't get around an issue without using the layer property, then by all means take advantage of it.

Working with Linked Graphics

As mentioned earlier, you now have the option in Authorware 4 to link to any type of graphics file you import into your piece. (Actually, this applies to all types of files that you import into Authorware, except text files.)

Many developers will find this new feature a powerful addition to the Authorware stable of tools, for the simple reason that it gives you the capability to update a graphic, sound, or movie without reimporting it.

When you select the Link To File option during an import, Authorware displays the contents of the file in the Presentation window as if you imported it directly. However, the actual file isn't imported. It remains on the hard drive, and Authorware creates a link to it using the path where it's located.

Using linked graphics is very useful for improving content management. You'll learn more about some techniques you can use to create pieces that are better organized and more tightly structured in Chapter 6, "Managing Your Content."

Linking to an external file gives you several added benefits when authoring:

- You can quickly update any file imported as a linked file during run-time by replacing it with a new copy of the file without repackaging your run-time files. For more information on packaging, see Chapter 17, "Distributing Your Piece."

■ You can swap graphics and other types of content in the piece dynamically at run time by using variable pathnames that point to different locations where the files are stored.

This gives you the power to do such things as switching between 8-bit and 24-bit images, depending on the color depth of the machine on which the piece is running; or displaying multiple sets of graphics in the same place on screen, depending on user feedback. Chapter 6, "Managing Your Content," covers using variable filenames in more detail.

■ You can create a modular template that you can reuse for many types of situations. For instance, you might want to create a digital catalog application for a variety of different companies. Using linked files, you can create a master template that you can send to all your customers, who then can switch out a set of "placeholder" images you've used with the product images.

Controlling image properties with linked graphics

One problem with using linked graphics is that they *can* change during run time. This can affect the look and layout of your screens, especially if the new graphic is larger or smaller than the original file you linked to the piece. Authorware now has a separate Properties dialog box, the Image Properties dialog box, to help you with this issue.

After linking an image to a display icon, use the following steps to display the Image Properties dialog box:

1. Click on the image with the display icon open.

2. Select Image Properties from the Modify menu.

Shortcut: To display the Image Properties dialog box, use Ctrl+Shift+I (Windows), or Command+Shift+I (Macintosh).

The Image Properties dialog box displays, as shown in **Figure 3.26**.

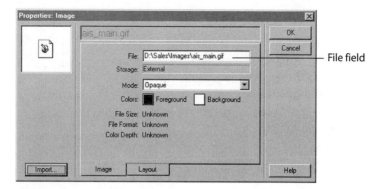

File field

Figure 3.26
The Image Properties dialog box with the Display properties tab active.

The two tabs at the bottom of the dialog box allow you to switch between the Display and Layout properties. When the Display properties are active, you should see the following options:

- The File field gives you a way to specify a path to the file that you want displayed. You can use a variable expression in this field to point to different locations that depend on a condition that's determined during run time.

  For instance, you may not know the exact drive path to an image file, but you may know its location relative to the Authorware application. This field gives you a way to specify a path without using a full pathname.

  You'll find an example of using variable pathnames with a linked image in Chapter 6, "Managing Your Content."

- The Mode option lets you select the same Opaque, Transparent, Matted, Erase, or Inverse settings available to you in the Modes Inspector, and applies them to the selected image in the Presentation window.

- The Colors option allows you to change the foreground and background color of a one-bit image you've imported, as you would if you were using the Colors Inspector.

- The Import button allows you to place a new image in the display icon, replacing the current image.

Switching to the Layout properties, as shown in **Figure 3.27**, you see several unique options that are available to you only in this dialog box. You need to use the Display drop-down list options to determine

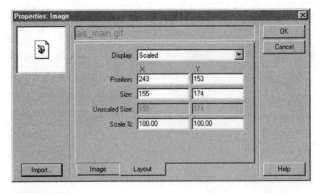

Figure 3.27
The Layout properties give you control over the placement of the imported image on screen.

how your linked image should always appear in the Presentation window. Three different methods of displaying the image are available to you: Scale, Crop, and As-Is.

NOTE Don't confuse the Image Properties Layout options with the Layout options available to you in the Display Properties dialog box. These are two different sets of options: the first controls positioning and cropping of a linked graphic; the second controls placement of all graphics contained inside the display icon.

Using the Scale option

Selecting the Scale option from the Display drop-down list allows you to size an image based on predefined dimensions, as shown in **Figure 3.28**.

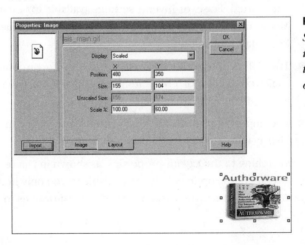

Figure 3.28
Sizing an image with the Scale option.

■ Entering X and Y values for the Position category specifies where Authorware will place the graphic in the Presentation window. The X and Y values you set here determine how far from the upper left-hand corner of the Presentation window the image displays.

For example, entering 100 for the X value and 200 for the Y value displays the image 100 pixels to the right and 200 pixels down from the upper left-hand corner of the Presentation window.

■ Underneath the Position category is the Size category, which shows the current dimensions of the image. If a linked image is larger than these pixel dimensions, the object scales to fit.

■ Underneath the Size category is the Scale category, which allows you to type in a horizontal and vertical scaling percentage to resize the graphic if it is a different size than the original linked image.

Using the Crop option

If the graphic you're scaling is much larger than the original linked graphic, you may want to use the Crop option, as shown in **Figure 3.29**. Otherwise, your graphic may look pixelated.

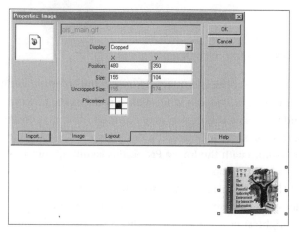

Figure 3.29
Cropping an image with the Crop option.

■ The Position and Size categories under the Crop option work the same way they do in the Scale option. The only difference here is that Authorware crops the new image to fit the dimensions that you specify in the Size category.

■ Below the Position and Size categories is the Placement guide. This lets you define how an image crops when Authorware brings it into the Presentation window. For example, selecting Placement in the upper left-hand corner crops extra pixels that overlap on the right and the bottom of the graphic. Selecting Placement in the center crops extra pixels around all edges of the image. This is very much like changing the size of the image canvas inside Adobe Photoshop.

Using the As Is option

If you don't want to resize or crop any linked images, you can select the As Is option, as shown in **Figure 3.30**.

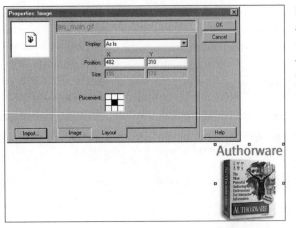

Figure 3.30
Displaying an image without scaling or cropping with the As Is option.

The As Is option displays the newly linked image without scaling or cropping it. This can work well in some cases; however, keep in mind that using this option may cover up other graphics or interface controls on screen. Depending on the type of piece you're creating, play around with the Image Properties layout options to see what works best for you.

However, this is a small price to pay for the capability to dynamically swap content in your piece. External linking is certainly one of the brightest new features in Authorware 4—a welcome addition for developers accustomed to using custom third-party functions to get the same results. This chapter only touched the surface of using this powerful new feature. You'll learn more about the intricacies of using linked files in Chapter 6, "Managing Your Content."

Looking Ahead...

This chapter explored how to integrate text and graphics into your Authorware piece. Using text and graphics, you have many ways to bring information directly to the user. You can maintain consistency of text styles and graphics when designing your piece. Using such tools as text styles and linked graphics, you can develop stylish applications that you can update quickly.

While text and graphics are an integral part of most pieces you create, you'll find that relying too heavily on them can sometimes limit the amount of interactivity in your piece. Most users enjoy seeing other elements present in your piece—particularly video, sound, and animation. The next chapter begins covering these elements, as you learn about the basic techniques used to add motion-based animation to the screen.

Chapter 4

Adding Motion

Animation can offer more than just surface-level entertainment for your piece. Motion can provide a valuable way to simulate the behavior of real-world objects, drawing attention to onscreen content or giving visual feedback.

Many authors shy away from using animation effects in a piece, believing them to be too difficult and time-consuming to set up properly. While this is certainly true when creating sophisticated character-based animation or 3D environments, not all animation is difficult to create.

If your piece needs an additional dose of realism, or if you want to produce short, animated segments that are interactive as well, you may want to incorporate Director movies into your Authorware piece. Most of the time, however, you'll find that you can achieve professional-looking end results by using animated segments created in Authorware.

This chapter covers the basic Authorware techniques for adding motion to your pieces by looking at transition effects and the motion icon.

Transitions are a quick and reliable way to add motion to a piece. Using the Director Transitions Xtra included with Authorware, you can access over 30 different animated effects that can provide additional emphasis for your piece (if used appropriately). The next few sections look at how to use the transitions that come with Authorware.

NOTE Use transitions with the framework icon to create transition effects between pages in your piece. Chapter 11, "Working with Pages," covers this in more detail.

Generally, you can use transitions to create fades between segments in your piece, or to animate a graphic onto the screen when it first appears. Like dissolves and wipes, you can apply transitions to graphic objects in the Presentation window. You also can apply transitions to remove objects from the screen using the erase icon.

The Director Transitions Xtra

Macromedia includes the Director Transitions Xtra with Authorware, along with several other third-party transitions Xtras. (Xtras are extensions that you can use with Authorware for additional functionality.) The Director Transitions Xtra gives you access to animated effects that you can apply to display, interaction, erase, or framework icons.

Applying a transition effect

You can apply a transition effect to an icon using the Transition dialog box, as shown in **Figure 4.1**. This dialog box contains the same type of options discussed in Chapter 2, "Getting Started," to apply a transition effect to your piece when jumping from one file to another.

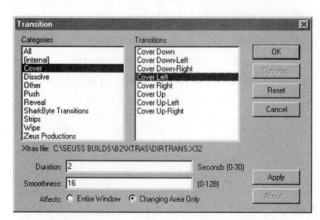

Figure 4.1
The Transition dialog box.

Before applying a transition to a display or interaction icon, make sure that you've placed one of these icons into the flowline and have added graphics or text to it. While there are many instances when you can use transitions, the process for applying the effect is the same for both types of icons.

To apply a transition effect to a display or interaction icon:

1. Select the icon in the flowline.

2. Choose Icon > Transitions from the Modify menu.

The Transition dialog box appears (see **Figure 4.1** above).

Shortcut: To apply a transition effect to a selected icon, use Ctrl+T (Windows), or Command+T (Macintosh).

---

3. Select a transition category from the left-hand side of the dialog box. If you want to view all the available transitions, select All from the list of categories.

The transitions for this category appear on the right-hand side of the dialog box.

4. Click on the name of a transition on the right-hand side of the dialog box to select it.

Use the Apply button to preview the transition in the open Presentation window; however, before you do this, make sure that you already have placed a graphic into the display or interaction icon.

5. Click OK to close the dialog box and to apply the transition to the icon.

When you run your piece, you should see the transition effect applied to the objects you've placed inside the icon. If it doesn't look quite right, apply a different transition. If the timing is off, you can adjust it using one of several techniques discussed below.

Timing transitions

You may find that timing your transitions is difficult at first—especially if you use several transitions with multiple icons in the flowline. There are a few basic ways you can improve the timing of your transitions.

First, you can adjust the duration and smoothness settings for the transition. These settings are active when you select a transition from the available list in the Transition dialog box. Keep in mind the following points when using the duration and smoothness options:

- The duration of the transition can be no longer than 30 seconds; however, you can use any number between 0 and 30, including decimal values like .5 (one-half second). This value is by no means absolute, however. It's very much dependent on the processor speed of the machine you're using—so test your piece on a variety of system configurations, not just on the machine you're using to develop the piece.

- The smoothness setting changes the size of the animated pixels. A higher setting causes fewer pixels to be animated on screen during the transition. You'll find that using a higher smoothness setting allows you to get more accurate control over transitions on multiple machine configurations.

After adjusting the duration and smoothness settings, you can reset the transition to its default settings by clicking the Reset button in the Transition dialog box. You also can adjust the timing of the transition using the Affects options, which are located at the bottom of the Transition dialog box. They work as follows:

- Selecting Entire Window applies the transition effect to everything currently displayed in the Presentation window.

- Selecting Changing Area Only limits the transition effect to just that portion of the screen where the icon that you applied the transition to displays.

TIP If you use a third-party transition effect, there may be additional options available to you, including timing options. To view these options, select the desired transition and press the Options button.

If the transition settings don't give you the effect you want, you may want to modify the icons on the flowline, change their positions, or apply separate transition effects to any display icons preceding the current icon. When you apply the same transition to icons that follow each other on the flowline, they display at the same time using the transition you selected.

However, if you would like the objects in the two icons to appear at different times, place a wait icon between them and set it to pause for a duration of less than one second, as shown in **Figure 4.2**.

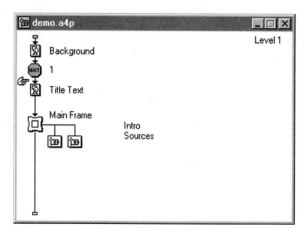

Figure 4.2

Inserting a wait icon between icons forces them to appear at different times in the Presentation window.

Distributing transition Xtras

Because Xtras are separate files, they require special handling during authoring and delivery. When developing your piece, you should place Xtras in the Xtras folder, which sits inside the Authorware folder. When you install Authorware, it copies the Director Transitions Xtra into the Xtras folder automatically so you can begin using it right away.

When delivering a piece, you'll need to also distribute any Xtras you're using with the piece. Depending on the platform and whether you're delivering your piece as a standalone or Shockwave file, you'll need to store these Xtras in different locations, as shown in the table below:

Platform...	*Xtra Name...*	*Where to place it...*
Windows 95, Windows NT	Dirtrans.x32	[Folder or CD containing the run-time program]\Xtras\
Windows 3.1	Dirtrans.x16	[Directory or CD containing the run-time program]\Xtras\
Macintosh	DirTransFat	[Folder or CD containing the run-time program]:Xtras
Shockwave	Same name for each platform	[Folder where the Shockwave Plug-In is installed]\Xtras This only applies to third-party transitions Xtras that you use. The Director Transitions Xtra is included with the Shockwave Plug-In for both the Windows and Macintosh platforms, so there is no need to distribute it separately.

NOTE If you use *only* the transitions listed under the [Internal] category in the Transition dialog box, you won't need to include transitions Xtras when you distribute your final piece.

Applying erase effects

A cross-fade between two screens is an example of a common effect used frequently when authoring. As one background disappears, the next background appears in its place, using the same transition effect. You can do this quite easily by placing an erase icon in the flowline. It removes the first background using the same transition effect that you applied to the second background's display icon.

To do this:

1. Place an Erase Icon immediately above the second background screen in the flowline.

2. Double-click the erase icon to open it.

The Erase Icon Properties dialog box appears on top of the Presentation window, as shown in **Figure 4.3**, along with any graphics that were previously displayed.

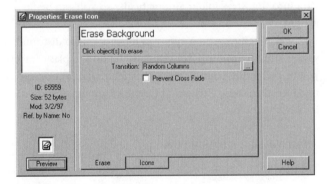

Figure 4.3
Select an erase transition in the Erase Icon Properties dialog box.

3. Click the [...] button and select a transition for the erase icon.

4. Click the graphic you want to erase. This erases the background from the Presentation window using the transition you've selected.

TIP You can continue to select transitions, even when the background isn't displayed in the Presentation window. When you run the piece, the Erase Icon Properties dialog box appears, prompting you to select the icons that you want to erase.

5. After selecting the transition and the graphic to erase, click OK to close the dialog box.

In order to make the cross-fade work, apply the same transition that you've selected in the erase icon to the display icon that follows it. Doing so results in a smooth change between the two screens. It's a simple, but useful visual trick.

TIP If you want to prevent two icons from cross-fading into each other, simply select the Prevent Cross-Fade checkbox option in the Erase Icon Properties dialog box.

Using Prevent Automatic Erase

By default, when Authorware exits framework, decision, or interaction icons, it automatically erases objects displayed in the Presentation window. This is an issue that you will encounter frequently when authoring—one that can sometimes cause problems.

There are several ways to work around this issue. Your best option is to take advantage of Authorware's control over automatic erasing for the different icons. Both the interaction and decision icons have built-in options for specifying when automatic erasing should happen on screen, so you can adjust these options to fit your needs. Chapter 7, "Creating Basic Interactivity," discusses how you can do this with interactions.

In the case of the framework icon, your best option is to create your piece using framework icons for all your major navigation structures. This allows you to take advantage of the framework icon's unique characteristics (i.e., its capability to apply transition effects between pages), discussed in greater detail in Chapter 11, "Working with Pages."

Nonetheless, erasing issues seem to be a recurring source of anxiety for most Authorware developers. If you've looked at the icon options, reorganized your flowline, and still have problems with an object disappearing on you, there's the Prevent Automatic Erase checkbox option that you can apply to any display, interaction, or digital movie icon to prevent Authorware from automatically erasing the icon.

Figure 4.4 shows you where you can locate this option for the display icon. The interaction and movie icons both have a similar checkbox option when you open their Properties dialog boxes.

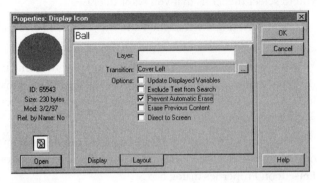

Figure 4.4
Using Prevent Automatic Erase for an icon prevents Authorware from erasing the icon automatically.

Learn to use this option carefully. If you get into the habit of using it whenever an erasing issue crops up, you'll find memory and speed performance will start to suffer in your piece. This is because you quickly accumulate a large number of objects on screen. The only way to get rid of them is to use an erase icon targeted specifically for each object displayed.

NOTE The DisplayIcon, DisplayIconNoErase, and EraseIcon system functions all give you additional control over displaying and erasing objects on screen. Chapter 15, "Controlling the Flowline through Scripting," discusses more about working with these functions.

Regardless of the size of your piece, you need to be acutely aware of erasing issues while developing your piece. Get into the habit of testing early and often to make sure that icons erase properly, because you will be better prepared if you run into problems when finishing your piece.

Using the Motion Icon

Transition effects can only go so far in giving your piece an animated quality. Like most developers, you will probably want to provide the user with more than simple screen transitions. If you want to make an object actually appear to move inside the Presentation window, use the motion icon.

The motion icon allows you to create both simple direct-to-point and complex path-based animation. For instance, you might want to move a rocket ship across the screen to simulate a blastoff; or you might have a graphic of a moon that needs to travel in a circular direction around a planet to simulate planetary orbits. You can easily create both animation types using the motion icon's options and properties.

The motion icon properties

Motion icons can move objects in different ways to imitate the motion of everyday objects. Some move objects along a straight line; others move objects along curved paths. You also can choose to move an object only part of the way along the path, making the motion dependent on some predefined condition.

You can select the type of motion you want in the Motion Icon Properties dialog box, shown in **Figure 4.5**. There are five types of motion effects available from this dialog box.

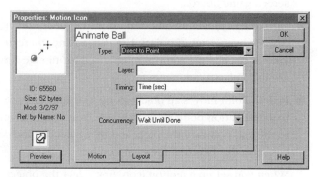

Figure 4.5
The Motion Icon Properties dialog box.

- Direct to Point moves an object along a straight line to a point that you set, regardless of the object's current location. Direct to Point is useful for moving objects quickly to a new place on screen. For example, use this type of motion if you want to show a rocket ship blasting off.

- Direct to Line moves an object in a straight line to a point that you assign on the destination line. By assigning values to the end points of the line, you define the object's range of movement. You can use variables to control where the object ends up on the line after it moves.

  Direct to Line is useful for moving objects within a given range. For instance, you could have an object on screen that simulates a thermometer and reacts to different conditions by moving up and down the temperature scale.

- Direct to Grid moves an object to a point on a defined grid of X and Y values in the Presentation window. By assigning an object different X and Y values, it can move to different positions within this grid.

  Direct to Grid is useful for creating full-screen movement based on a condition in the piece. You can specify the dimensions of the Presentation window as your positioning grid, and then animate an object from one position on screen to another. You could use this effect to animate chess or puzzle pieces on a full-screen game board.

- Path to End moves an object along a straight or curved path defined by a series of points. Use Path to End to create the kind of circular motion you might need to animate a moon around a planet.

- Path to Point moves an object along a straight or curved path to a destination point along the path. You simply assign values to the end points of the path, and then calculate the destination based on the values of these end points.

When you set up a motion icon, first select the object you want to move. Then choose the type of motion you want and the rate or speed of the motion. All the motion types require that you define a path for the moving object to use. Several motion types require that you define values for points on the path. The Path To Point type requires that you do both.

What is variable motion?

Before you get into the specific steps involved in creating animation using the motion icon, you may find it helpful to learn a bit more about the concept of variable motion.

Many of the examples above depend on variables to define how the object moves on screen. Variable motion moves an object to a point in the Presentation window that you define with a specific value. At any time, you can determine what this value is and apply it to the object's motion.

Variable motion is especially useful for creating motion that mimics a real-world condition. For instance, you could interactively simulate a basketball shot or a steel ball rolling within a magnetic field using variable motion settings. Although you might move the basketball or steel ball to a single destination when it initially moves, later in the piece you may want it to move to a different location that depends on a condition such as the strength of the magnetic field or the height of the basketball shot.

Variable motion paths are more complicated to set up simply because they require that you first understand how to use variables. However, they can provide a great deal of added realism to a piece; they are especially useful when creating a specialized effect or explaining a complex concept visually. Variables also allow the user to directly affect how an object moves on screen; this provides the piece with a more interactive "gaming" feel that the user—bored with the average point-and-click approach to multimedia—will appreciate.

TIP The system variables `Animating`, `Moving`, `DisplayX`, `DisplayY`, `PathPosition`, `PositionX`, and `PositionY` are helpful when creating sophisticated effects with motion icons. For a complete list of system variables, see *Using Authorware* or Authorware Help.

Number lines and grids

The Direct to Line, Direct to Grid, and Path to End motion icon types require that you define a range of points on a line or grid in order to control where the object moves on screen. You define the object's position on screen with the values you set for the motion icon's base point, end point, and a separate value for the object's destination. You can use either a specific numerical value or a variable expression.

NOTE While this chapter covers a few simple techniques for creating motion based on variable expressions, you may want to zoom ahead and take a look at Chapter 14, "Using Functions and Variables," to get a better idea of how you can use variables and variable expressions in a piece.

This may seem a little complex right now, especially if you are new to using variables. Simply, Authorware uses variables to store temporary values to use in your piece. In the case of the variable motion paths, they're used in the following ways:

- The start and end points of a path are numerical values that define a range of possible destination points for the object. The default range of this path is 0 to 100. This means that you can position the object on any point between these two values.

  It's helpful to visualize the path's end points as opposite ends of a numbered line, and the object's destination point somewhere on this line. After setting up a path animation in the Presentation window once, you will understand how it works.

- You define an area the same way you define a path, except that you use a two-dimensional range of values rather than the one-dimensional range specified by a path.

  Specify an area's range in terms of X and Y coordinates on a grid. The object's destination is a point somewhere inside this grid. If the dimensions of the grid are (0, 0) and (100, 100), then the object can move to any point inside the area defined by these dimensions. You always specify the object's destination in terms of X and Y point values.

Now that you have a better grasp on variable motion paths, the following sections explain how you can create each of the five types of animation using the motion icon.

Creating Direct to Point animation

In some situations, you may want an object to move to the same destination every time. Direct to Point animation moves objects from any position on screen to the location you choose. If an object is already at its destination, it ignores the motion icon.

Direct to Point animation is the easiest type of animation to set up using the motion icon. First, you need to create an object to animate.

To do this:

1. Drag a new display icon to the flowline and open it.

   The Presentation window and toolbox appear.

2. Using the ellipse tool, create a small circle.

3. When you have finished, close the display icon and return to the flowline.

You will use the motion icon to animate this circle to a position inside the Presentation window. The next step is to set up the motion icon for the type of animation you want to use.

To set up the motion icon:

1. Drag a motion icon to the flowline and place it below the display icon.

2. Run the piece by choosing Play from the Control menu.

As soon as Authorware encounters the motion icon, it opens the motion icon Properties dialog box. The dialog box has two tabs at the bottom labeled Motion and Layout, which contain different groups of settings. When the dialog box first opens, you see the Motion options displayed, as shown in **Figure 4.6**.

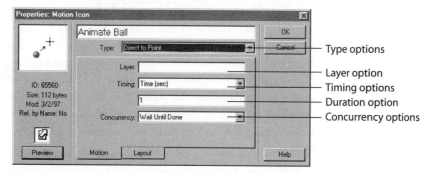

Figure 4.6
The Motion tab options.

A closer look at the Motion tab options reveals five options:

- The Type option allows you to specify the kind of animation you want. Direct to Point is the default selection.

- The Layer option allows you to specify on which layer the object will appear when it animates. The default is Layer 0. Changing this setting to Layer 1 or higher helps speed up the animation when other graphics display in the background.

- The Timing option allows you to select the duration of the animation in terms of Time (seconds) or Rate (seconds per inch).

- In the Duration option you enter a value in terms of seconds. If you select Rate as your Timing option, enter a relatively small value such as .1 or .2 seconds.

- The Concurrency option gives you control over when other actions happen while the animation plays. The Wait Until Done setting pauses presentation in the flowline until the object finishes moving; the Concurrent setting allows other animation or events to happen while the object moves; the Perpetual setting allows the object to move at any time in your piece.

NOTE The Perpetual setting isn't available when you use Direct to Point; however, some other animation types allow you to use Perpetual, and they can produce some very interesting results (as you'll see later in "Moving objects in an area").

- In some cases, you can exceed the range of motion that you assign to an object if the variable value you use is higher than the specified range. In this case, the Beyond Range option allows you to control how the object behaves.

Setting this option to Loop causes the object to "turn over" and loop around to the other end of the path. Stop At Ends does just what you might expect—it stops the object at either end of the defined path and doesn't let it continue. Go Past Ends allows the object to keep moving, but your object can quickly appear as if it is falling off the edge of the screen. In most cases, you probably will want to have Stop At Ends selected, unless you need a special effect.

The same Motion tab options are available for each of the five types of animation. However, the Layout tab has specific options for each type of animation. Go ahead and click on the Layout tab to view the options specific to the Direct to Point animation, as shown in **Figure 4.7**.

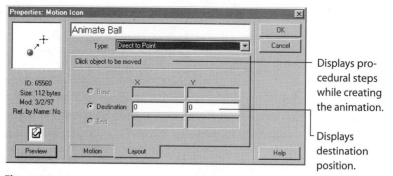

Displays pro-
cedural steps
while creating
the animation.

Displays
destination
position.

Figure 4.7
*Selecting the Layout tab displays its options for the
Direct to Point animation.*

Because you need to move the object to only one specific
point in the Presentation window, you see only one Layout option
available when you select Direct to Point as your animation type,
Destination.

Destination displays the object's current position using X and Y
values to specify the current position of the object in relation to the
size of the Presentation window. These values update each time you
move the object in the Presentation window.

NOTE Authorware calculates the current position of objects based
on the size (in pixels) of the current Presentation window. The
Presentation window's origin point (0,0) is in the upper left-hand
corner of the window. Point values increase from left to right, and
from top to bottom, so if your Presentation window size is 640 x 480
pixels (the standard VGA setting), the point located at the lower
right-hand corner of the Presentation window has the point value
(640, 480).

TIP The procedural steps for creating the animation appear underneath the Type drop-down list. Use this feature to keep track of what
you need to do to set up the animation type you want to create.

Now that you've checked out the options available in the Motion
Icon Properties dialog box, you can continue setting up the Direct to
Point animation example. If you've run the piece correctly, the circle
that you created should display inside the Presentation window.

To set up the animation:

1. Make sure that you select Time and Wait Until Done in the Motion options, and that you enter a value of 1 in the Duration field.

2. Switch to the Layout options by clicking the Layout tab.

3. Click on the circle in the Presentation window and drag it to a new location.

NOTE While animating an object, you can move the Motion Icon Properties dialog box to a different position on screen for a better view of the Presentation window and the animation path you're creating.

After you have finished moving the circle, look at the Destination values listed in the dialog box. They should reflect the current X and Y positions of the circle inside the Presentation window.

4. Click the Preview button located in the lower left-hand corner of the dialog box to preview the animation.

If you want to change the circle's destination point, simply drag it to a new location.

5. When you have finished, click OK to close the dialog box, and then run the piece to view it.

At some point, you may want to reposition the graphic inside the display icon and run the piece again. Notice that even though you have changed the initial location of the object in the Presentation window, it still moves to the same destination point that you defined using the motion icon. In Direct to Point animation, the motion icon moves the object in a straight line to the destination point you've set, regardless of the object's initial position inside the Presentation window.

Moving objects to a point on a line

Now that you've played around with the motion icon a bit, this section looks at a more difficult type of animation to set up—one that uses variable motion. Sometimes, rather than moving an object directly to a point or along a set path, you may want to move the object to a varying point on a line. For instance, if you're creating a thermometer simulation that shows the current temperature, you would need some control over positioning the thermometer's onscreen indicator.

Using the Direct to Line type of motion allows you to move objects to a specific point on a line. When the object already rests on the line, it appears to slide along the line as it changes position. If an object isn't already on the line, it will move toward the specified point and stop.

Moving objects to a point on a line requires that you set up the motion icon, define the base and end points for the line, and provide a variable expression that defines the object's position on the line.

To set up the Direct to Line motion:

1. Open a display icon and create a small circle using the ellipse tool; position it at the top of the screen.

2. Place a new motion icon on the flowline after the display icon; open the motion icon by choosing Play from the Control menu and running the piece.

   The Motion Icon Properties dialog box appears.

3. Select Direct to Line for your animation type.

4. Change the Concurrency option to concurrent. Leave all other settings the same.

Next, you need to define your base and end points for the line. To do this:

1. Click on the Layout tab at the bottom of the dialog box.

   The Layout tab options appear.

2. Click on the circle at the top of the Presentation window and drag it to the bottom of the screen, positioning it in the left-hand corner.

   Authorware creates a new point in the Presentation window at the spot where you dragged the object. This is the base point for your line.

3. Click the End radio button, as shown in **Figure 4.8**.

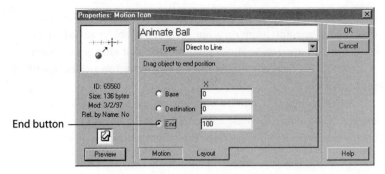

End button —

Figure 4.8
The End position defines the end of the range of motion for the object positioned on the line.

4. Keeping its vertical position the same, drag the circle to a new point along the right edge of the screen and release it. This creates your end point.

You now should see a line that connects the base point and end point on screen, as shown in **Figure 4.9**. This is the line of motion that controls where the object animates inside the Presentation window.

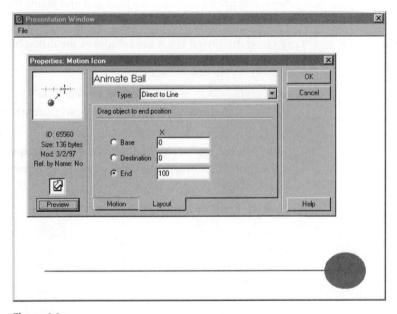

Figure 4.9
Setting up the line of motion for the object in a Direct to Line animation.

When you click the Base radio button, the object moves directly to the base point of the line. Then you need to define a Destination point for the object:

1. Click the Destination radio button to select it.

   When you select the Destination radio button, you can assign a value to the Destination field by clicking on the object and dragging it to a new position on the line of motion. Notice that the object's range of motion is constrained to this line, and that it stops at each end point.

   If you want, you can type a number into this field. Remember, however, that it must be a number somewhere between the base and end point values you've defined.

2. Go ahead and type **50** in the Destination field.

3. Click Preview to view the effect.

You now should see the circle move from its initial position at the top of the screen to a position halfway along the line of motion at the bottom of the screen, as shown in **Figure 4.10**.

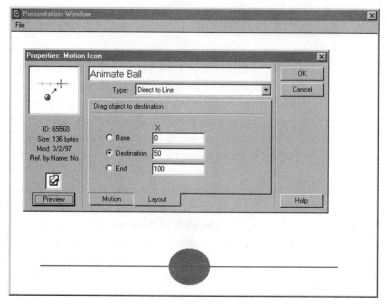

Figure 4.10
When you type in a new Destination value, the object repositions itself.

Unless you want the object to move to the same point each time, don't use a specific numerical value for the Destination point. Instead, use a variable expression that updates the position of the object on the line based on a changing condition in the piece (as you would if you were trying to simulate a thermometer that gives a temperature reading).

TIP By increasing or decreasing the value of your End range, you can create some interesting effects. For example, you can replace the End range value (100) with the variable expression `MediaLength@"My Movie"` (an expression that returns the total number of frames contained in the digital movie icon titled My Movie). You could then use a Direct to Line animation to update the position of a custom movie controller bar. Chapter 15, "Controlling the Flowline through Scripting," covers how to set up this type of custom control in greater detail.

 The CD accompanying this book includes a working example of the movie controller bar piece. To view it, go to the Chapter 15 examples folder and open the file MOVCNTRL.A4P.

Moving objects along a path

You may not want to move an object along a straight path. For instance, you may have a ball that needs to bounce erratically across the screen; or, as mentioned earlier, a moon that needs to orbit a planet. When you want to animate an object along a curved path, you need to use Path to End or Path to Point to set up your animation.

Setting up these points involves selecting the object you want to move, creating a path by dragging the object to points that define the path, and then previewing the effect. The Path to End and Path to Point animation types are similar to the Direct to Point and Direct to Line animation types. You can use Path to End to animate an object along a set path. Use Path to Point when you need to move the object to different points on the path, which depends on a condition in your piece.

To create the bouncing ball example, set up a Path to Point animation. Before you begin, however, you will need to set up a new display icon with a circle that you can animate.

To set up the Path to Point animation:

1. Drag a new motion icon onto the flowline, place it in front of the display icon you want to animate, and then run the piece.

The Motion Icon Properties dialog box appears.

2. Select Path to Point as your animation type.

3. Leave the timing and concurrency options default settings.

4. Click the Layout tab.

The Layout tab options for Path to Point are shown in **Figure 4.11**. You have some of the same basic options here that you did in the Direct to Line animation. Notice, though, that you have two additional buttons, Undo and Delete, which you can use to edit the points on your path.

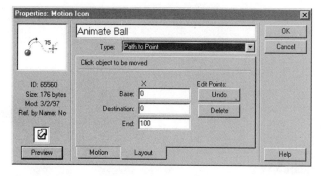

Figure 4.11
The Path to Point Layout tab options.

You can define points along the path by moving the object to different onscreen locations. Points can be modified later when adjusting the path.

To create the path for your object:

1. Click on the object in the Presentation window.

A triangle marker appears in the center of the object.

2. Drag the object to the first point on the path and release the mouse button. Make sure that you drag the object and not the triangle marker.

Another triangle marker appears where you released the mouse button. This becomes the first control point on the path.

3. Continue dragging the object and releasing the mouse button to create additional control points on the path.

Triangle markers appear at each point where you released the mouse button; lines that indicate the motion path appear between the markers. After you set up your path, it should look something like the example in **Figure 4.12**.

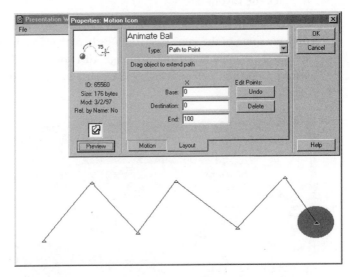

Figure 4.12
The path you've created displays as a series of lines with control points in between.

Try to create a zig-zag pattern across the screen. If you make a mistake, don't worry about it. You can readjust the points of the path by clicking on them, and then moving them to a different position inside the Presentation window.

You now need to select a destination point for the object (as you did when you created the Direct to Line animation).

4. In the Destination field, type a numerical value between the range of values defined for the path, or use a variable expression. Initially, when testing how the animation will play, you may want to type **100** in this field. This will animate the object to the end of the path.

TIP The Path to End animation type does not require you to define a Destination point. Authorware automatically animates the object to the End point of the path that you've defined. Therefore, you probably will want to use the Path to End type any time you need the object to move just once along a set path.

5. Click Preview to view the effect.

The object should move along the path you've defined. If it is moving too fast, try adjusting the value that you entered in the Duration field under the Motion options. Click Preview to see how the object now moves.

After you've define a path, there are several ways you can edit the path to adjust your animation:

- To adjust the path, click a control point and drag it to a new location inside the Presentation window.

- To add an additional control point, click the position on the path where you want the control point added. A new control point appears, which you can position where you want.

- To make a section of the path curved, double-click on the control points that define the section of the path you want to modify. The control point changes from a triangular marker to a circular marker and transforms the path into a curved path, as shown in **Figure 4.13**. If you want to undo these changes, double-click on the control points again to transform the path back to its original state.

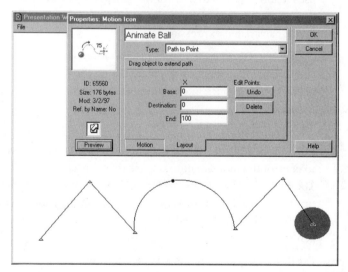

Figure 4.13
Double-clicking on a control point creates a curved path for the object.

- To remove a point from the path, click on the point you want to delete and click the Delete button.

- To undo a change you've made to the path, click the Undo button.

TIP To animate an object completely off screen, drag the object off the Presentation window when setting the end point of your path. If you want to animate an object off screen, make sure that you don't reset the Presentation window to a larger size. Animation paths that you set will not scale to this new size, so consequently your object may scurry off to the edge of the screen, and then stop without disappearing.

Moving objects in an area

Using the Direct to Grid motion type can sometimes save you a lot of hard work. It's one of the most under-used animation types; yet it provides a great deal of built-in control over objects that are otherwise very difficult to create in Authorware.

The Direct to Grid option moves objects to a specific horizontal and vertical coordinate on screen. You've experienced this already when setting up the Direct to Point animation type. Direct to Grid uses X and Y values to control the positioning of the object in the Presentation window. You can use either specific numerical values here or a variable expression.

NOTE The Direct to Grid options for placement are similar to defining an object's initial position in an area using the Display Icon Properties dialog box. For more information, see Chapter 9, "Using Movable Objects."

Because you can make Direct to Grid animation perpetual throughout a file, it may be helpful to use the Direct to Grid technique to control the movement of objects that constantly need updating. The best example of this is a virtual game board with pieces that need updating, based on moves the user selects in the game. Using several different motion icons and some custom variables, it is fairly easy to achieve this effect.

For those curious about how to set up game pieces that move on a board, the CD that accompanies this book includes an example of this type. You'll find it in the Chapter 4 examples folder in the file GAMEBRD.A4P.

To give you an overview of how Direct to Grid animation works in Authorware, the following example takes a look at how to use the motion icon to make an object follow your cursor anywhere on screen.

To set up the motion icon for Direct to Grid animation:

1. Place a motion icon on the flowline after the display icon that contains the object you want to move; run the piece by selecting Play from the Control menu.

The Motion Icon Properties dialog box appears.

2. Select Direct to Grid as your type.

3. Type .01 for your duration and select Perpetual for the concurrency option. Leave all other default settings.

NOTE It's important that you make the concurrency perpetual for this example, so the object continues to move after Authorware exits the motion icon.

4. Click the Layout tab when you have finished.

The Direct to Grid Layout tab options appear, as shown in **Figure 4.14**.

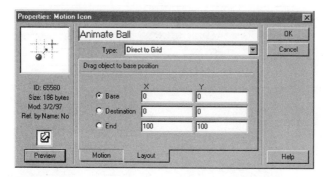

Figure 4.14
The Direct to Grid Layout tab options.

Define the area of motion by moving the object in the Presentation window to create a "grid." Because you want the object to follow the position of the cursor anywhere in the Presentation window, you need to define an area that covers the entire size of the Presentation window.

NOTE This example assumes that your Presentation window is set to a default size of 640 x 480 pixels. If it's not, you may want to adjust this setting inside the File Properties dialog box, and then resume this section.

To define the area of motion:

1. Click on the object and drag it to the upper left-hand corner of the screen to define the base point of the area. Make sure that you have the Base point radio button selected before you do this.

2. Click the End point radio button, then drag the object to the bottom right-hand corner of the screen.

You should see a rectangle in the Presentation window that shows you the size of the area you've defined, as shown in **Figure 4.15**. You may need to shift the area's Base and End point settings to define a grid that covers the entire screen. Because you define the Base and End points by the center point of the object when you drag it, you may want to move the object partially off screen to accomplish this.

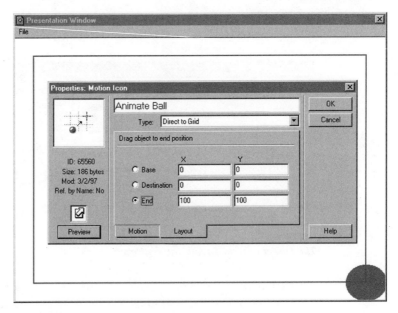

Figure 4.15
Defining the area of the grid in the Presentation window.

After you set up the grid, you can define how you will update the object's position. Because all that you need to do is update the object's position based on the position of the cursor, you can use two of Authorware's system variables, `CursorX` and `CursorY`, to define the Destination point of the object.

To define the object's variable position in the Presentation window:

1. Click the Destination point radio button.

2. In the Destination field, type `CursorX` for your X value and `CursorY` for your Y value.

NOTE Type in these values exactly as you see them; otherwise, you will get a dialog box that asks you to define a new custom variable, and you'll have to repeat this step.

By typing in these values, you set up the motion icon to update the object's X and Y positions based on the current position of the cursor. However, in order for our example to work correctly, you also need to define the entire range of values that the object can have when it updates. These values are the same as the dimensions of the Presentation window.

3. Click the End point radio button.

4. Type in **640** for your X value and **480** for your Y value. This defines a range of cursor movement that covers the entire Presentation window.

5. When you have finished, click OK to exit the dialog box, and then run the piece to test it.

Were you successful? If so, the object now moves in response to the position of your cursor. If not, you should go back and make sure that you've set the Concurrency option to Perpetual. Otherwise, the object doesn't move at all.

This is a pretty neat effect and one that isn't that complex to set up. Notice that when you move the cursor out of the Presentation window, the object stops. This is because you have gone beyond the area's defined range of values.

As you can see, animation in Authorware isn't limited to point-to-point animation. It can vary based on a wide range of events in your piece. Director has similar control over objects on screen, but to build the example above in Director would require using Lingo, the Director scripting language.

In this chapter, you learned how to utilize transition effects and the motion icon to add movement to your piece. While transitions provide a certain amount of visual appeal, use the motion icon if you're trying to create sophisticated onscreen movement. The motion icon is a great way to explain more complex ideas to your audience visually. You also can increase the level of interactivity in your pieces by taking advantage of variable motion when using the motion icon.

However, these techniques are really only a small part of what you need to create interactive software that captures the user's attention. In the chapter ahead, you will learn how to add greater realism to your piece by working with sound and video to communicate ideas quickly and effectively to your audience. Using the sound, movie, and video icons, you will have the tools and power to create content that teaches while it entertains.

Chapter 5

Adding Sound and Video

What you'll learn...

Using the sound icon

Using the movie icon

Using external video

While the animation techniques covered in the last chapter can make the screen come to life, you soon may find yourself wanting a bit more realism—especially when creating pieces that simulate real-world scenarios. As your multimedia pieces become more sophisticated, you will want to incorporate sound and video into your design. Once you work with these two media types, you will realize the power they provide to communicate ideas quickly and effectively to your audience.

Given the current high demand for digital audio and video content, you may be tempted to try to produce pieces that feel like a customized movie or television show. However, even with the current technologies on the market, most multimedia pieces don't yet offer the type of full-motion, audio-visual fluidity that you are accustomed to seeing on the big screen.

What multimedia does offer is a unique capability to create richly varied content that teaches while it entertains. You can achieve both results by learning how to take advantage of sound and video. This chapter introduces you to working with these types of media in Authorware.

Using the Sound Icon

Many people go to the movies expecting to be blown away by the latest in advanced special effects and cinematic wizardry. However, you would be disappointed if the theater happened to be missing its speakers and you were forced to watch the movie in complete silence. The visual imagery would seem strangely out of place without the soundtrack accompanying it.

While most multimedia pieces don't rely on sound alone, you nonetheless should consider using sound in your design. You can use sound as background narration, as an element that helps set the mood or tone of your piece, or as a transition between scenes. Sound may even become the focus or your entire piece if you're working on an educational or entertainment piece that teaches the audience about a particular musical artist or style of music.

Preparing to use sound in a piece

Any computer with a sound card can play digital audio. Because sound playback hardware is a pre-installed component on all Macintosh systems as well as most new Windows multimedia systems, you probably need not worry whether you can use sound in a piece.

However, when developing cross-platform applications for clients with older Windows machines, make sure that you have installed the proper sound hardware, or use a Windows system function to see if the sound driver is loaded. Chapter 20, "Developing with External Code," explains more about using custom functions.

When using sound in a piece, here are some general guidelines to follow:

- Edit the sound first to set the length of the sound and looping point (if appropriate) as you cannot edit the sound in Authorware. Authorware simply plays the imported sound files. You can pause and resume sound files using Authorware's media functions, but for the most part a sound plays as it was imported.

- For audio and narration tracks where you need to specify start and stop points, you may want to convert your sound into a sound-only QuickTime movie (for cross-platform playback). Using the movie icon, you can program your piece to play back different ranges of the sound (see "Playing a variable range of frames" later in this chapter).

- Some older systems only have hardware that supports playback of 8-bit sound. If you use 16-bit audio files, you may run into an error message when you try to play these sounds with an 8-bit audio card. If you don't know whether or not your audio hardware supports 16-bit sound, check the documentation that came with the sound card, or with the computer's manufacturer.

- Systems that don't have audio hardware installed will still run your piece; however, no sound will play. This may affect the timing of events in your piece, especially if you set up sound icons to control the movement of a piece between separate screens.

- Authorware can load both mono and stereo sounds that you have saved with a sample rate of 11 kHz, 22.050 kHz, or 44.1 kHz (CD-quality). The best sound quality is heard at 44.1 kHz stereo. However, this increases the size of your file, and it isn't recommended for pieces that you plan to deliver on CD-ROM or over a network. Most developers stick with 16-bit, 22.050 mono sound files. This gives you decent quality, but takes only a quarter of the memory space used by a 16-bit, 44.1 stereo sound file.

TIP There are many third-party sound utilities, including the Waves Audio Track Xtra for SoundEdit 16/Deck II, that can resample 16-bit audio files down to an 8-bit format while retaining the overall sound quality of the sample.

Sound formats

Adding sound to a piece is much like adding text, graphics, or animation. The Sound icon handles sound playback, shown in **Figure 5.1.** The sound icon enables you to define the properties associated with the sound and to control how it plays. You can use one-shot sounds or sound loops, and you can even integrate sounds into your buttons to give the user additional feedback.

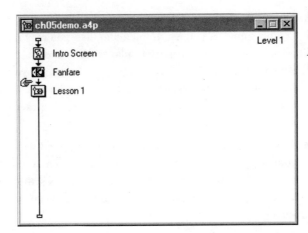

Figure 5.1
The sound icon positioned in the flowline.

The main sound type you use in Authorware is digital audio, which is sound that you record onto a computer disk and save in a digital format. When adding sound to a piece, make sure that you have your audio files saved in a format that Authorware recognizes. Authorware can import audio saved in WAVE (.WAV), AIFF (.AIF) files, or in PCM (.PCM) format. These are the most common digital audio formats that multimedia developers use.

TIP Authorware 4 now supports the Shockwave Audio (.SWA) format, a compressed digital audio format that is optimized for Internet and intranet delivery. Shockwave Audio files can be imported or linked to a piece in the same way as the other audio formats mentioned above. For more information on using Shockwave Audio files with a piece, see Appendix B, "Using Shockwave Audio."

Because Authorware doesn't have built-in editing or recording capabilities, you will need an editing tool when you start compiling sounds to use in your piece. Save your sound files using a commercial digital audio editing package, such as Macromedia's SoundEdit 16/ Deck II, or SoundForge XP from Sonic Foundry. Designed for editing and recording digital audio files, Macromedia includes these tools as part of the Macintosh and Windows versions of the Authorware Interactive Studio.

TIP Although the functionality isn't built into Authorware's sound icon, you have the capability to integrate other audio formats such as CD audio and MIDI files into your piece using a custom function. For more information about using custom functions, see Chapter 20, "Developing with External Code."

Importing and previewing sounds

Loading sounds involves placing a sound icon in the appropriate place on the flowline, opening the sound icon, and selecting a sound. When the sound icon is open you can preview the sound, choose how fast it plays, set the conditions under which it plays, and set the number of times it repeats.

Like graphics, you now can link to external files when importing sound into your piece. This is especially beneficial if you're developing a piece in which you want to continually update audio tracks without modifying the original packaged file. Using linked audio, you could create an audio jukebox application with a selection of tracks that updates monthly for subscribers. Remember, however, that if you have linked sound files in your piece, you must distribute the sound files in their original formats along with the piece.

NOTE If you have imported (rather than linked) a sound into the sound icon, you cannot export the sound from Authorware to edit. Keep all your original sources backed up so that you can make changes to a sound file if necessary, and then reimport the modified sound file into Authorware.

If you don't plan to change the sounds in your piece, import the sounds directly into the piece and store them internally. Keeping your audio stored internally makes it easier to distribute the piece, especially if you plan to deliver it over a network using Shockwave.

To load and play a sound:

1. Drag a sound icon onto the flowline where you want the sound to play.

2. Double-click the sound icon, or run the piece to open it.

   The Sound Icon Properties dialog box appears. Information about the audio file appears in this box after you import the file, as shown in **Figure 5.2**.

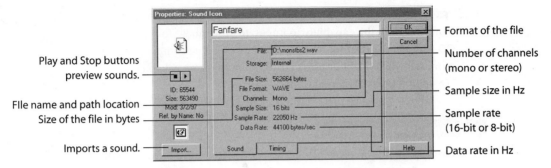

Play and Stop buttons preview sounds.

File name and path location
Size of the file in bytes

Imports a sound.

Format of the file

Number of channels (mono or stereo)

Sample size in Hz

Sample rate (16-bit or 8-bit)

Data rate in Hz

Figure 5.2
Information about the sound appears in the sound icon Properties dialog box.

TIP Authorware updates the sound icon's displayed information any time you replace the previously imported sound with another sound. This information is extremely helpful when making revisions, allowing you to check the sound formats that you have added to your piece.

Before assigning timing properties to the sound icon, you must import the sound file first.

3. Click Import.

4. Select a sound file to load and click OK. If you want to link to the external sound file, select the Link To File checkbox option before you import the sound.

The sound file now loads internally and the Sound Icon Properties dialog box appears again. You can use the Play and Stop buttons (see **Figure 5.2** above) to preview the sound you imported.

Shortcut: To preview a sound without opening the sound icon, right-click on the sound icon (Windows), or click on the sound icon while pressing the Control+Alt keys (Windows), or Command+Option keys (Macintosh).

Controlling timing of sounds

The Timing tab, shown in **Figure 5.3**, gives you a number of options that you can use to control how the sound plays in the piece. The Timing tab options also give you the capability to specify variable expressions, which you can use to stop and restart the sound after Authorware initially encounters it on the flowline.

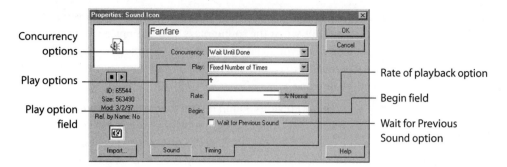

Concurrency options
Play options
Play option field
Rate of playback option
Begin field
Wait for Previous Sound option

Figure 5.3
The Timing tab options give you control over how the sound plays in Authorware.

The Timing options give you a variety of ways to control playback:

- The Concurrency option controls whether Authorware starts the sound and then continues to the next icon immediately, or waits until the sound plays completely before continuing.

  If you select Wait Until Done for this option, Authorware pauses presentation until the sound plays completely. If you select Concurrent, Authorware continues down the flowline while the sound plays.

  Use the Perpetual setting when you want to start and stop the sound many times throughout the piece. Use this option if you want background sound loops throughout the piece.

- The Play option controls whether the sound plays once, a fixed number of times, or until a variable condition is TRUE. In the Play option field, you specify the fixed number of times the sound should play, or a variable condition that stops playback.

- The Rate option controls the speed of playback. Setting this option to a higher value speeds up play of the sound. A lower value slows down the sound's speed of play. You also can assign a variable expression to this field to control the playback speed dynamically.

NOTE Some Windows sound cards don't have the capability to play back sound at variable speeds. Authorware ignores the Rate option if you have it set to something other than 100 percent and if you play the sound on a machine that doesn't support variable-speed playback.

- The Begin field enables you to specify a variable expression that controls when the sound plays. Use this option in instances when you need to skip the audio if the user turns off the sound, or to restart a perpetual sound from another place in the flowline.

- The Wait for Previous Sound option forces Authorware to wait for other sounds to finish playing before playback of the sound in the current icon occurs. Use this option when you don't want a narration to be prematurely cut off when moving from one screen or page to another.

Playing a sound once

When Authorware encounters a sound icon on the flowline, the sound plays using the properties you've assigned to it. In some cases, you may want to play the sound once and then move on to show the content of other icons. Use this technique when you want an audio track to introduce a segment of your piece, as shown in **Figure 5.4**.

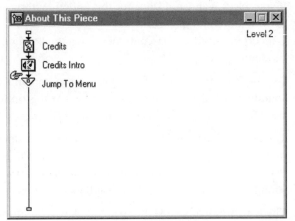

Figure 5.4
You can use the sound icon to begin a segment of your piece.

To play a sound only one time in a piece:

1. Drag a sound icon to a position on the flowline where you want the sound to play.

2. Import the sound.

3. In the Sound Icon Properties dialog box, switch to the Timing view.

4. For the Concurrency option, select Wait Until Done if you want the sound to play before showing additional icons. If you want to continue presentation while the sound plays, select Concurrent.

TIP If you selected Concurrent for one sound icon and a second sound icon appeared on the flowline, playback of the first sound stops and the second sound icon starts playing. You can get around this by using the Wait for Previous Sound option.

5. The Play option defaults to the Fixed Number of Times setting, and Authorware automatically enters a value of 1 in the Play option field. If you want to change the number of repetitions, you simply type in a new value.

6. Select the Wait for Previous Sound option, if you want the sound icon to wait for other sound icons to finish playing.

Go ahead and run the piece now. The sound that you imported plays only once in the segment of the piece where you placed the sound icon.

Managing sound resources is very important because sound consumes a lot of memory. If you plan to use a sound several times in a piece, consider moving the sound into a library. This allows you to create a library link to the sound when you need it. Chapter 6, "Managing Your Content," takes a closer look at using libraries.

Synchronizing events with sound

One of the most common uses of the sound icon is for synchronizing events in a piece. For instance, you might want a different screen to appear during different points in a narration. Splitting up your narration into separate sound icons and using the Wait Until Done Concurrency option, can create a "slide show"-style presentation that pauses while each section of narration finishes. **Figure 5.5** shows what this example might look like on the flowline.

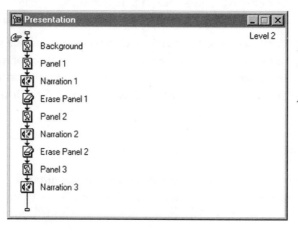

Figure 5.5
You can use the sound icon to create a simple "slide show" presentation.

Using the sound icon for synchronization of onscreen display elements usually requires trial-by-error testing and a lot of patience—especially if you want to synchronize display and motion icons at the same time. In this situation, it is usually better to use a combination of sound and wait icons to control the flowline tempo.

However, if you're using the sound icon and the wait icon to control synchronization and you don't get the desired effect, consider using a digital video file instead. You can use either a separate sound-only movie (if you're trying to synchronize sound with bitmap graphics displayed on screen); or, you can make both the animation and the sound a single digital video file. In addition to guaranteeing that the sound and images remain synchronized, a single digital video file typically results in smoother playback on slower machines because Authorware doesn't need to maintain two streams of data.

 If you would like to see an example of a sound-only movie that controls synchronization, look at the file MOVSYNC.A4P. It's included in the Chapter 5 examples folder on the CD accompanying this book.

The following additional techniques may help you solve timing issues in a piece:

- Use a sound editor to edit the sound's length. Remove any silent gaps at the beginning or end of the sound file. This results in better timing for a sound.

- Adjust the sound's speed by changing the Rate (% of Normal) setting, which affects the sound's pitch when it plays back.

- Use the SyncPoint and SyncWait system functions to set a delay to allow a sound icon additional time to play before going on to the next icon. For more information about the SyncPoint and SyncWait functions, see the list of system variables included in *Using Authorware* or Authorware Help.

- Create a Director movie for the segment of animation you want to use, and then play the audio through the Director movie. However, you need to take into consideration the extra memory needed to load the Director drivers (see Chapter 19, "Using Director Interactively").

Looping sounds

In some pieces, you may want sound in the background to establish a mood or to indicate a progression from one scene to another. The most efficient way to handle this is to use a short five- to 10-second sound set to loop in the background until the piece advances to the next screen.

While there isn't a built-in loop option for sound in Authorware, you can use a variable expression in the Play option field to make the sound repeat continuously:

1. Import a sound into the sound icon.

2. With the Sound Icon Properties dialog box open, click the Timing tab.

3. Set the sound to play Concurrent.

4. Select Until True as your Play option.

   In order to create the loop, you need to define a variable expression in the Play option field that controls when the sound stops playing.

5. Type **FALSE** in the Play option field, as shown in **Figure 5.6**.

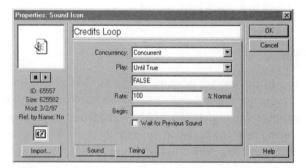

Figure 5.6
Enter the variable expression in the Play option field.

6. After you have finished, run the piece to test it.

Your sound now plays continuously. Since the variable expression you entered in the Play option field is never TRUE (because it always has a value of FALSE), the sound continues to play until another sound icon interrupts it.

If you want the sound loop to pop up again at a later point in the piece, you can do one of two things:

■ Set the sound's Concurrency option to Perpetual and add a variable expression to the Begin field, which restarts the sound.

- Leave all other settings the same, and simply restart the sound using the `MediaPlay` system function. This option is easier to set up, but requires that you understand how to work with Authorware's system functions. Chapter 15, "Controlling the Flowline through Scripting," takes a closer look at using this function.

If you're confused about how the variable expression works in this example, you may want to take a quick look at Chapter 14, "Using Functions and Variables." Variable expressions, which are part of Authorware's scripting language, give you a great deal more control over both sound and digital video in a piece. The next section explores how you can use variable expressions with digital video icons.

NOTE If you want to play two or more sounds simultaneously, remember that Authorware for Windows only supports playing one channel of audio at a time. On the Macintosh computer you can play two sounds simultaneously, but only if you have saved one of the sound files in a QuickTime format.

Using the Movie Icon

In the past three years, advances in digital video technology gradually have transformed multimedia from a page-turning metaphor into something more closely resembling video-based entertainment or video gaming. Many high-end multimedia PCs now have the capability to play back video clips at full-screen resolution, giving you the ability to deliver applications with an enhanced "cinematic" feel.

However, you still need to concern yourself with bandwidth issues any time you deliver your application from CD-ROM, a network, or the Internet. Video playback over a busy local network is a network administrator's nightmare, and it still isn't a feasible approach to delivering this type of content online. Nonetheless, technology is improving dramatically. If you explore this area now, you can prepare yourself for delivering interactive video-based content on a wide variety of platforms in the future.

Knowing your limitations

In practical terms, working with video requires a great deal of hard disk storage space and preproduction as you film, edit, and compress your digital video clips. Because digital video technology continues to progress at a lightning pace, you need to make informed decisions up front about the type of video content you want before you start creating it.

Consider the basic issues below when using video:

- How backward-compatible can you afford to be? Older systems with single-speed CD-ROM drives may not play video clips that are larger than the original 160 x 120 pixels "postage stamp" clips. Most new Power Macintosh and Pentium systems come fully-equipped to handle playback of full-screen, 15 frames-per-second video clips. As mentioned before, the key rule here is "test early, test often, and test on all target platforms."

- If you plan to deliver on the Windows and Macintosh platforms, then stick with the QuickTime format because the Windows AVI format isn't supported on Macintosh. Most developers also include the latest QuickTime for Windows drivers with their pieces for those Windows users who are either missing the required software or are using outdated versions.

- If you're developing for Windows specifically, then you need to think about whether to deliver your piece in the 16-bit Windows 3.1 environment, or the 32-bit Windows 95 and Windows NT environment. Although 32-bit system software includes AVI drivers, you need to provide an updated installer for those users still running Windows 3.1. You also may need to scale down the size and data rate of your video.

- The MPEG (Motion Picture Experts Group) format delivers the best overall quality because of its compression format. MPEG also can require expensive encoding equipment to create the movies and an MPEG playback card installed on the user's system to play the movies. However, as encoding becomes cheaper and software-based MPEG drivers become more widely standardized, this format seems poised to become the standard for delivering large, video-based pieces.

TIP For more information on using MPEG with Authorware, go to the Authorware technical notes area on Macromedia's web site: **http://www.macromedia.com/support/authorware/ts/documents/**.

- No matter what type of digital video you plan to use, you should take a few moments to study the two sides of the digital video equation: data rates and compression. These two elements affect the quality and performance of the digital video clips you produce. While this book can't go into all the details of how to use data rates and compression, you may want to look at some of the many web sites that cover working with digital video.

TIP You'll find some of this information available on the web sites listed in Appendix C, "Authorware Resources on the Internet."

- You cannot import some of the latest video and 3D animation formats directly into Authorware through the movie icon, including QuickTime VR and VRML (Virtual Reality Modeling Language). However, many third-party software developers have announced plans to create Xtra Plug-ins that you can use to incorporate these video and animation formats into your pieces.

TIP For the latest list of supported Authorware Xtras, go to the Xtras area on Macromedia's web site: **http://www.macromedia.com/software/Xtras/**.

- If you include digital video in a Shockwave piece designed for the web or an intranet, the entire video clip must download before the user can play it. You also need to include these files on the server in a "flattened" format, as well as the Authorware drivers required to play back the files. Chapter 17, "Distributing Your Piece," discusses this in more detail.

NOTE Several companies, including Progressive Solutions and Iterated Systems, are developing video streaming technologies that enable you to deliver video-based content over a network without requiring a long download time. While video streaming technology is still under development, it nonetheless makes delivering video-based Shockwave content much more feasible in the future.

Supported movie formats

As with the sound icon, you use the movie icon to control the movie's playback options. You simply place the movie icon on the flowline where you want the movie to play, as shown in **Figure 5.7**. Using variable expressions and system functions, you can achieve an even greater degree of control over how your movies play frame by frame.

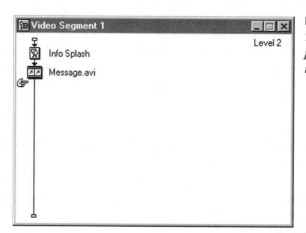

Figure 5.7
The movie icon positioned on the flowline.

There are two basic groups of "movies" that you can use with the movie icon. Movies that you can use fall into either the digital video formats (Video for Windows, QuickTime, MPEG), or the frame-based animation formats (Director, FLC/FLI, PICS, DIB sequences). The table below lists the formats that are compatible with each platform:

Platform...	*Supported movie formats...*
Windows	Video for Windows (AVI)
	QuickTime for Windows
	MPEG
	Director
	FLC/FLI
	DIB sequence
Macintosh	QuickTime
	Director
	PICS

Director, QuickTime, and AVI movies link externally to the movie icon. This means that you must distribute the movie files along with your piece, as well as the Authorware drivers required to run them. Director, QuickTime, and AVI movies all support sound as well as video or animation. As mentioned earlier, you can create sound-only external movies to more easily synchronize events in your piece.

TIP When using external movies, you should try to keep them in a single folder during development. This makes them much easier to manage when testing and distributing your piece. Because Authorware relies on the Search Path settings specified in the file to find linked content, you should include this folder location in the Search Path. For more detailed information on setting up the Search Path option, see Chapter 2, "Beginning a Piece."

The other animation movie formats supported by Authorware include the Macintosh PICS format, and the Autodesk FLC/FLI format. You can import both of these formats directly and Authorware stores them internally. Because Authorware converts the movie into internal image data when you import it, you can play these movies on both platforms without special drivers. However, these formats do not support audio.

On the Windows side, you also can import a series of Windows bitmaps (.BMP or .DIB format) into the movie icon. Simply place the sequence of images (or "frames") in a single folder; make sure that you name the frames sequentially with the same root name followed by four digits. For example:

```
ball0001.bmp, ball0002.bmp, ball0003.bmp,
ball0004.bmp
```

When you import the first file in the sequence, Authorware uses the remaining files in the sequence to build the movie. After you've imported the frames, you cannot change the sequence in which they appear. If you need to change this sequence, you must go back to the original files and rename them using a different sequence.

Importing and playing digital movies

Loading a digital movie involves placing a movie icon in the appropriate place on the flowline, opening the movie icon, and then importing the digital movie file you want to use. At any time, you can open the movie icon to preview the digital movie inside the Presentation window or set the movie's playback options.

To import a movie:

1. Drag a movie icon onto the flowline and place it where you would like the movie to play.

2. Open the movie icon by double-clicking it, or by running the piece until it reaches the empty icon.

The Movie Icon Properties dialog box opens, as shown in **Figure 5.8**.

Preview controls —

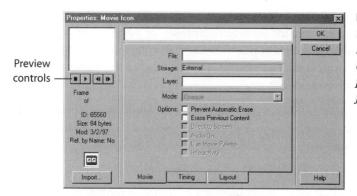

Figure 5.8
The Movie Icon Properties dialog box controls playback options for the movie.

3. Click the Import button.

The Import dialog box appears.

4. Select a movie file and click Import to import the movie into the movie icon. To preview the movie before importing it, select the Show Preview option, as shown in **Figure 5.9**.

Show Preview option. —

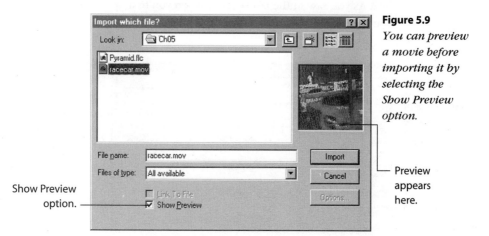

Figure 5.9
You can preview a movie before importing it by selecting the Show Preview option.

— Preview appears here.

If you don't have a digital movie handy, you can use the RACECAR.MOV file included in the Chapter 5 examples folder on the CD accompanying this book.

The movie you've imported now appears in the Presentation window.

5. Click OK to close the dialog box, and run the piece to view the movie.

Working with the movie icon is similar to working with the display icon. You can reposition a movie by dragging it to a new location when the presentation pauses, or you can edit the movie by double-clicking it. If you want to remove the movie from on screen, set up an erase icon to erase it as you would with graphics in a display or interaction icon.

Shortcut: To preview a movie without opening the movie icon, right-click the movie icon (Windows), or click on the movie icon while pressing the Control+Alt keys (Windows), or the Command+Option keys (Macintosh).

NOTE You cannot use Transition effects with digital movies. Even if you apply a transition effect to a movie icon, Authorware ignores it during playback of the piece.

Setting movie playback options

After importing a movie into a movie icon, you can specify different playback options for the movie using the Movie Icon Properties dialog box. As you saw in the last section, when you first open a movie icon you see the default Movie tab options, as shown in **Figure 5.10**.

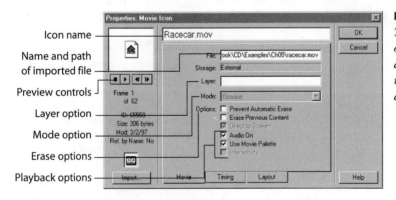

Icon name
Name and path of imported file
Preview controls
Layer option
Mode option
Erase options
Playback options

Figure 5.10
The Movie tab options display automatically when you open a movie icon.

Because the movie icon supports many digital movie formats, some of these options may not apply to the type of file you've imported into the movie icon. However, the options work as follows:

- The controls at the upper left-hand corner of the dialog box allow you to play, stop, or step frame-by-frame through the movie you've imported. Since the movie is playing inside the Presentation window, you may need to adjust the position of the dialog box for better viewing.

- The Layer field allows you to assign the movie to a specific layer. The Layer option has no affect on digital video files (AVI, QuickTime, or MPEG), which always play on top of any other graphics displayed in the Presentation window.

- The Modes option allows you to assign transparency modes to the movie using the Modes option. This option, however, is only available when using PICS or FLC files imported with a solid white or black background.

- There are two different Erase checkbox options available. Selecting Prevent Automatic Erase prevents Authorware from automatically erasing the movie. Selecting Erase Previous Contents automatically erases any graphics or movies that displayed prior to the movie icon from the Presentation window.

- The Direct to Screen option applies to PICS and FLC movies only. This option improves performance by displaying PICS and FLC movies on top of all other layers in the Presentation window. When you load an AVI, QuickTime, or MPEG movie, Authorware automatically selects this option and you can't change it.

- The Audio On option allows you to turn on or off the audio track of a digital movie. This option is not available if you've imported a PICS or FLC file into the movie icon.

- The Use Movie Palette option allows you to control whether the movie uses its internal palette or the palette loaded in Authorware. Selecting this option improves the look and performance of your movies when running in an 8-bit (256) color depth; however, it can cause a palette flash when the movie loads. This isn't noticeable when running at a higher color depth.

- The Interactivity option is available only when loading Director movies. It allows you to incorporate interactive Director movies into your piece where they will behave and respond as if they were built in Director with Lingo. Chapter 19, "Using Director Interactively," looks closely at using these types of movies with Authorware.

Setting timing and layout properties

The Movie Icon Properties dialog box has two other option tabs—Timing and Layout. These options give you complete control over timing the movie icon with other icons on the flowline and positioning the movie inside the Presentation window.

As with the sound icon, the movie icon's Timing options allow you to control how the movie stops and starts. You also can use these options to assign variable start and end frames for the movie. **Figure 5.11** shows you where to locate these specific options.

Duration
Frame rate value
Start frame value
End frame

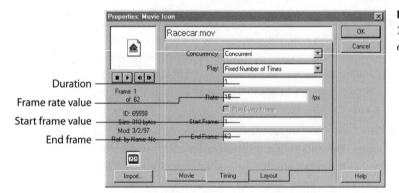

Figure 5.11
The Timing tab options.

You can use the Timing options in a variety of ways to either synchronize your video playback with other icons on the flowline, or provide the user with more control over playback of the movie.

- The Concurrency option uses the same Wait Until Done, Concurrent, or Perpetual settings that you have in the motion and sound icons.

- Using the Play options, you can choose whether to play a movie repeatedly, a fixed number of times, or until a specified variable condition occurs.

If you've imported a QuickTime movie, you can specify Under User Control for the Play option when the movie plays concurrently. This creates a QuickTime-style movie controller bar below the video clip in the Presentation window, as shown in **Figure 5.12**.

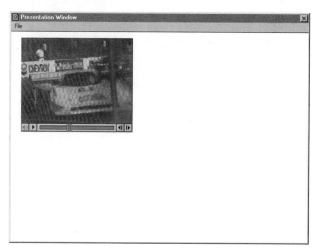

Figure 5.12
Playing a QuickTime movie under user control.

If you've imported a PICS or FLC movie, the Only While in Motion and Times/Cycle Play options are active. These options control playback of the movie when a motion icon animates it, or the user moves it on screen.

■ The Rate field controls the frame rate of playback for the movie. When you import a movie, Authorware assigns the original frame rate of the movie here. Entering a variable expression in this field allows you to dynamically adjust the speed of the movie by changing the value of the variable expression in the field.

■ The Start and End fields are set by default to the first and last frames of the movie you imported. Entering new values for either of these two fields allows you to play back a section of the movie without creating a different file; entering a variable expression in these fields enables you to play back different sections of the movie by changing the values of the variable expressions in the fields.

As with the display and motion icons, you can assign variable positioning options for a movie icon by modifying its Positioning options. Click the Layout tab to access these options, as shown in **Figure 5.13**.

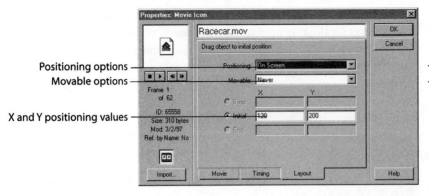

Positioning options ⎯⎯⎯
Movable options ⎯⎯⎯

X and Y positioning values ⎯⎯⎯

Figure 5.13
*The Layout tab
options allow
you to position
your movie in
different places
on screen.*

Working with Layout options is similar to using the motion icon to set up the initial positions of objects. These options for the most part define the movie's initial position on screen. Chapter 9, "Using Movable Objects," describes how to work with these options in more detail.

Creating matted or transparent movies

When you display a movie in the Presentation window, it occupies a rectangular area on the screen. At times, however, you may want the movie to display background objects that are underneath the movie so they appear to be in the same scene together. In movie effects shops, this technique is known as "matting" or "chroma keying." Generally, the movies you use in Authorware require that you composite the background elements of your piece into the digital video clip when you first create it.

If you use a PICS or FLC movie, you can create an animation with a matted or transparent background using the Modes settings. The Modes settings work in much the same way as the Modes palette works with display objects. The modes settings only work when you save the movie with either a white or black background.

- When you select Opaque, the movie's rectangular region completely covers any object(s) underneath it.

- When you select Matted, Authorware creates a series of matted frames for the movie. The matted frames mask out any pixels on the outside boundaries of the movie region that use the chroma key background color (white or black).

- When you select Transparent, Authorware removes all pixels from the movie region that use the chroma key background color.

- When you select Inverse, Authorware reverses colors in the movie region with the colors of the graphic or text objects displayed underneath the movie region.

You can specify the chroma key background color to use with a PICS or FLC file when you import the movie into Authorware. The Import dialog box has an Options button, as shown in **Figure 5.14**, which is active when you select one of these movie formats.

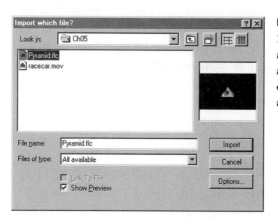

Figure 5.14

The Options button is active when importing a PICS or FLC file into the movie icon.

Selecting the Options button displays the Movie Import Options dialog box, as shown in **Figure 5.15**. Use the two checkbox options in this dialog box to control playback of the PICS or FLC movie.

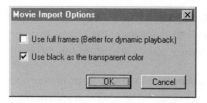

Figure 5.15

The Movie Import Options dialog box.

- When you select Use Full Frames, Authorware imports each complete frame of the movie into the movie icon and stores it internally. If you deselect this option, Authorware uses a technique called "frame differencing" to compare each frame to the previous frame and to import only those frames that have changed. If you need to play your movie in forward and reverse directions, you should select this option.

- When you select Use Black As Transparent Color, Authorware sets the chroma key background color for the movie to black. If you deselect this option, Authorware uses white as the chroma key background color.

Although most movies play once and then erase, you can take advantage of the Timing options to give you (or the user) more control over the movie. For instance, you can assign a different numerical value or variable expression to the Start Frame and End Frame fields of a movie to show different segments of the movie at different times.

Using this technique, you could include one movie with your piece that might have different views of the same scene or multiple views of a rendered 3D image. You can show these views at different points in the piece, depending on what view the user selects.

To try this technique, set up a movie icon and import a movie. Select a movie with more than 20 frames because you need to use different start and end values to create this technique.

To set the Start Frame and End Frame values:

1. Open the movie icon.

   The Movie Icon Properties dialog box appears.

2. Click the Timing tab.

   The Timing tab options appear.

3. Select Fixed Number of Times for your Play option.

4. Type **1** in the Play options field.

5. Type **10** in the Start Frame field.

6. Type **20** in the End Frame field. If your movie has more than 20 frames, you can type a higher value here. Just keep this value lower than the number of the last frame.

NOTE If you're unsure how many frames are in your movie, refer to the movie information listed on the left-hand side of the Movie Icon Properties dialog box.

7. Click OK to close the dialog box.

Go ahead and run the piece to see the results. The movie should begin playing on frame 10, and end shortly thereafter—at the end frame you specified.

This example used numerical values for the start and end fields. However, Authorware also allows you to specify start and end frames using a variable expression. By doing so, you could set up the movie icon once, and then copy and paste it to different parts of the flowline, thereby controlling the playback position of the movie, using a calculation icon.

NOTE If you are using a sound-only digital movie, start and end "frame" values are specified in terms of seconds rather than frames. For example, a start frame value of 5000 would start playing the sound at the 5-second mark.

You may want to play with this by assigning a variable expression to the start and end frames and running the piece. If you're not sure how to create variables and assign values, jump ahead to Chapter 14, "Using Functions and Variables."

Like the sound icon, you can take advantage of the digital video icon's different options to provide the user with different types of feedback and information. Because digital video is now cheaper and easier to integrate into a multimedia application, it's the preferred method of handling playback of video in both entertainment and instructional pieces.

Using External Video

Some larger companies and universities, however, continue to use analog video sources such as videodisc and videotape to provide employees and students with high-quality video footage. This chapter concludes by looking at the basic ways to integrate external video into your pieces.

Authorware gives you the ability to play back video from video-disc or videotape using the video icon, as shown in **Figure 5.16**.

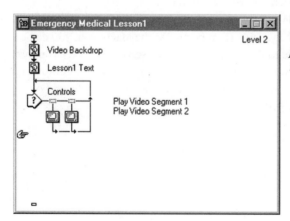

Figure 5.16
The video icon positioned on the flowline.

Using external video with a piece requires that you have the following hardware available:

- A videodisc or videotape player connected to the computer.
- A place for the image to appear—either an external monitor or a computer that contains a video overlay card.

The video icon's options are similar to those found in the sound and movie icons. You can specify many types of playback options. These options include:

- The segment's start and end frames;
- How fast the video plays;
- Which audio channels play; and
- Whether to provide an onscreen controller that lets the user control the video.

Configuring your computer for video

Video that you play through the video icon can appear on either an external monitor or on the main computer screen—depending on how you configure your computer. Setting up hardware involves installing the hardware (a video player and possibly a video overlay card) and the proper drivers, and then using the Preferences dialog box to tell Authorware your hardware type and how you have it connected to the computer.

In Windows, these devices connect to the computer through one of the available Com ports. On the Macintosh, you can connect the device to the modem or printer serial port. After you install the hardware and the appropriate drivers on your computer, continue setting up your piece using the Preferences dialog box, as shown in **Figure 5.17**.

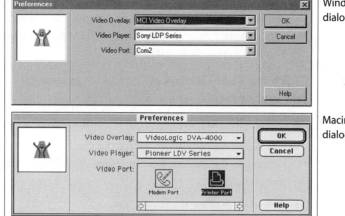

Windows Preferences
dialog box

Macintosh Preferences
dialog box

Figure 5.17
*The Preferences dialog boxes appear slightly different
on each platform.*

To tell Authorware which type of hardware you have installed:

1. Choose Preferences from the File menu.

Shortcut: To open the Preferences dialog box, use Control+U (Windows), or
Command+U (Macintosh).

The Preferences dialog box appears.

2. Select the Player option that matches your hardware settings.

Players appear in the list when their drivers are in the same
folder or directory as Authorware or the Authorware run time
application.

NOTE For more information on your specific hardware and driver
requirements, see the documentation included with your hardware.

3. Select a video overlay device if you plan to use video overlay to
display the video image on the computer screen rather than on
an external monitor.

If the driver you need is missing, you must install it in the folder
that contains the Authorware application or run-time application.
You need to quit Authorware, and then install the driver. Otherwise, Authorware does not recognize the driver.

As with players, video overlay cards appear in the list when their drivers are in the same folder or directory as Authorware or the Authorware run-time application. When the driver you need is missing, you must install it.

NOTE The Video Overlay option requires an installed video overlay card on the playback system.

4. Specify the port where you have connected the video player.

On Windows computers, select the Com port from the Port drop-down list. On Macintosh computers, click the icon that represents the serial port.

5. Click OK to close the dialog box.

Setting up the video icon

Use the video icon to specify playback options for the particular segment of video you want to play. As with the sound and movie icons, you define the point where the video plays by positioning the video icon on the flowline.

To set up the video icon:

1. Drag a Video Icon to the flowline.

2. Double-click it to open or run the piece from the flowline.

The video icon Properties dialog box appears, as shown in **Figure 5.18**.

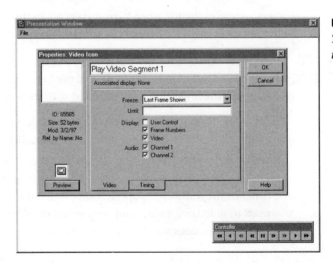

Figure 5.18
The Video tab options.

The Video Icon Properties dialog box includes options to control timing and playback of the video, as well as a floating control panel that allows you to preview the video. Two sets of options, Video and Timing, are available using the tabs at the bottom of the dialog box.

When you select the Video tab, you can choose from the following options:

■ The Freeze option lets you specify what remains on screen when the video stops. Last Frame leaves the last frame that played on screen. No Frame removes the video display completely. End Frame displays the frame specified in the End Frame field (see bullet below). If you want to leave the final frame of the video on screen until a specific condition occurs, you can type in a variable expression in the Until field.

■ The User Control checkbox option displays a set of buttons on screen that controls playback of the segment. These are the same buttons that appear in the floating video icon control panel.

■ The Frame Numbers checkbox option displays frame numbers on screen when the video plays.

■ The Video checkbox option allows you to turn the video image on or off, in cases where you want to use only the audio track.

■ The Audio Channel 1 and 2 checkbox options let you specify which audio channels to use in a piece. In some instances, this can allow you to switch between an English and a foreign language track contained on the videodisc.

When you select the Timing tab, as shown in **Figure 5.19**, you can choose from the following options:

Figure 5.19
The Timing tab options.

- The Concurrency option lets you specify Wait Until Done or Concurrent to play back the segment.

- The Rate option lets you assign one of six speeds to the video clip when it displays. These speeds range from pause to fastest.

NOTE The numbers in parentheses after each Playback choice represent the corresponding speed's value for the system function `VideoSpeed`. For more information on this function, see the list of system functions included in *Using Authorware* or Authorware Help.

- The Start Frame and End Frame fields enable you to specify the start and end points of the video segment you want to play. For frame-based video, the Set buttons to the right of each field let you specify the current frame as the start or end frame; the Jump To buttons move the video to either the start or end frame, depending on which button you click.

- The Stop at End Frame Or option gives you additional control over when to stop playback of the video segment. You can assign a variable expression to the When TRUE field, or use the Key Pressed checkbox option to stop playback when the user presses a key on the keyboard.

Using video overlay

Video overlay is one benefit of using an external video source. You can map the video into any onscreen display object that is filled with the chroma key color specified in the File Properties dialog box. In Authorware, the default color is magenta.

If you don't know the assigned chroma color, or if you have changed the default settings, you can find out quickly by either opening the File Properties dialog box or the Color Inspector. Authorware displays the chroma key color in the palette with two inverted squares located at the upper left-hand and lower right-hand corners, as shown in **Figure 5.20**.

The assigned chroma key color. —

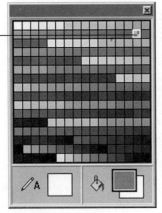

Figure 5.20
The active chroma key color displays with two inverted squares in its corners.

When using video overlay, you must select the area where the video will display in the Presentation window. You do this by creating an object in a display icon (which is set to the chroma key color), and then specifying this object as the display area in the Video Icon Properties dialog box.

When the piece runs, the video appears only when the display area is on screen. Authorware scales the video to the object's boundaries and displays video on all parts of the object set to the chroma key color.

NOTE Some video overlay cards, such as the IBM M-Motion overlay card, have limited choices for which colors can serve as chroma key colors. The M-Motion card requires that you use magenta—the default Authorware chroma key color. Check the documentation that comes with your hardware for more information.

To create a chroma key display area:

1. Place a display icon before the video icon on the flowline, as shown in **Figure 5.21**.

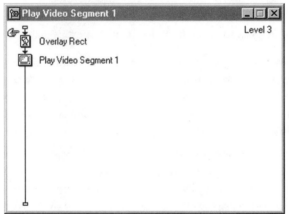

Figure 5.21
Creating the chroma key display area.

2. Open the display icon. In the Presentation window, draw a filled object to use as a display area.

NOTE Make sure that you use a filled object. When you use an unfilled object, the video appears only at the object's edge. While this can create some interesting effects, the most likely result is that you will wonder what's wrong with your video setup.

3. Using the Color Inspector, assign the chroma key color to the object's foreground and line fills.

4. After creating the object and assigning the chroma key color, switch back to the flowline to open the video icon. Make sure that the display object still displays in the Presentation window.

The Video Icon Properties dialog box appears.

5. In the Presentation window, click on the object.

This assigns the name of the display icon to the display area. The display icon's name appears in the Associated Display field at the top of the dialog box, as shown in **Figure 5.22**.

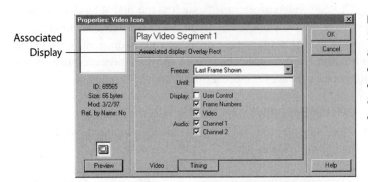

Associated
Display

Figure 5.22
The name of the associated display icon appears at the top of the dialog box.

6. Click OK to close the Video Icon Properties dialog box.

When you run the piece, the video appears in the display icon parts that use the chroma key color. You can, if you want, include other graphic objects in the display icon that you have not mapped to the chroma key color; however, these objects cannot display video.

Because Authorware maps video onto any part of the display where you have assigned the chroma key color, you may want to use this to your creative advantage in a piece by creating irregularly shaped video display objects such as circles or ovals. When you use a nonrectangular shape, Authorware scales the video to the rectangle that encompasses the entire object.

TIP You can assign a transition effect to the display area when using video overlay to get some interesting visual effects that aren't possible when using digital movies.

This chapter explored some basic techniques for using sound and video in your piece. Using these file types requires that you know their technical limitations; nonetheless, they offer many advantages over text- and graphic-based content.

The next chapter concludes your look at Authorware's basic features by discussing its tools for managing content. These tools include libraries, models, and a feature that is new to Authorware 4, the External Media Manager. Content management strategies can be as varied as your projects; the next chapter addresses the basic organizational issues that you confront on all projects.

Chapter 6

Managing Your Content

With each new project, you should set aside time to develop a content management plan that works for you. While your strategies may change from project to project, you will need to address the basic organizational issues that pertain to the types of media you use, and find methods of working in Authorware that can cut development time.

This chapter focuses on those aspects of developing a piece by introducing you to the Authorware tools that help you manage your work. These tools include models, libraries, and a new feature to Authorware 4, the External Media Browser, which allows you to manage external content linked to your piece.

Think of everything you create in Authorware as "reusable" content. If you think this sounds a little like "recycled" content, guess again. It doesn't mean simply taking graphics, sounds, and videos that you have used before and including them in a piece. It means taking the media or flowline structures of a piece that you use frequently and moving them to an external location so they are accessible at all times. When you create reusable content using Authorware's media management tools, you can see dramatic improvements not only in the size of your files (remember, small files are good!), but in the amount of time it takes you to develop a piece.

Managing file size is an important issue. Pieces tend to perform poorly when file size gets into the stratospheric 20–30 MB range. This happens because the computer running the file must work very hard to swap content in and out of memory to display everything on screen at the same time. When you factor in other considerations, such as using 16-bit audio or 24-bit graphics in a piece, a system can become overloaded quickly if you aren't careful.

As you become more familiar with Authorware, you will begin to recognize types of content and flowline logic that you can reuse in your pieces. You will reuse items like sounds and graphics because they can fit your design criteria for multiple projects. At other times, you will share some logical structures with other authors because they can help solve complex problems or standardize aspects of a piece.

What are models and libraries?

Models and libraries enable you to get more out of your development time and effort by allowing you to reuse flowline structures and content that you have created and tested already. Although they share a similar function in this respect, you use models and libraries in different situations:

- Use models to save and reuse portions of your flowline logic (the Authorware equivalent of "source code"), so you can quickly paste in pieces of logic that you find yourself creating frequently.

- Use libraries to store individual icons and their content so you can reuse them throughout a piece.

Authorware 4 extends its binary-compatible file format to include libraries and models. This means that now you can move libraries and models easily between platforms without first converting them. This also means that your packaged Macintosh and Windows files can share the same library content during run time, eliminating the need to deliver two complete sets of library files to accommodate both platforms. You can now deliver the same library content for both platforms, whether you're developing for CD-ROM or the Internet.

Authorware saves any model or library you create in a separate file so you can use it again. Because you paste models into a file, you can use an unlimited number of models when developing a piece. Models that you create also can include content that you have stored in a library file. Libraries, on the other hand, are a bit more limited. You can have up to 17 libraries attached to a piece at one time— although an unlimited number of pieces can access the libraries that you create.

With libraries you can avoid duplicating unnecessary tasks, like importing the same image ten different times when using it in multiple places in a piece. Models go the extra mile; they allow you to save parts of your flowline logic and paste it into a piece so you don't have to build a sequence of icons over and over again. In the next few sections, you'll learn how to take advantage of these tools when working in a piece.

Working with Models

A model is a flowline segment (a group of one or more icons with their connecting flowline and content intact) that you have saved so you can reuse it easily. Models provide a way to standardize your flowline icon structures and calculation scripting and to share them with your development team.

When you paste a model into a piece, it becomes part of the piece, and any content that you placed in the model when you created it is pasted into the file. Unless you've linked the icons in your model to a library, the content that you've added in the model is pasted into the piece, along with the icons, making your file larger. For this reason, most authors use models to create a generalized structure or "template" for a segment of empty flowline logic, and then add content to it later.

When you create a model, Authorware saves the icons you select—along with their content—in a separate model file on your hard disk. To use a model, you load it from your hard disk, and then paste it into the area in the flowline where you want to use it. This is similar to how you would add logic to the flowline by using the Copy and Paste commands. If you're unfamiliar with how to copy and paste in Authorware, you may want to go back to Chapter 1, "Getting Started," and take a moment to review the steps.

As mentioned earlier, you can paste a model into the piece and then edit its content to fit your needs. However, the original model remains unchanged because it is stored in a separate file. A model that you save is always available to you later when you need to paste it into other locations in the same piece or into a piece that you plan to create.

Unlike libraries, you cannot use a model to update multiple flowline segments at the same time. When you use a model, you modify each segment of the flowline separately by pasting in the model; then you can edit the separate segments to make changes.

When creating a model, it's important to plan ahead and think about how you might reuse it in a piece. As mentioned earlier, sometimes it's better to create a more generic model that you can use to create many variations of the same flowline logic. You can see an example of this in **Figure 6.1** below, where the same model was used to create two different interactions: one to play a movie; the other to advance the user to the next screen. If you would like to know more about how to create interactions, see Chapter 7, "Creating Basic Interactivity."

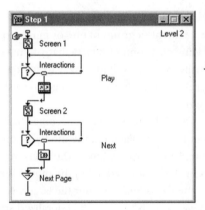

Figure 6.1
Both interactions shown here on the flowline were created from the same basic model.

Creating a model

Models are easy to create and use. You can turn any sequence of icons you've created into a model or you can create a new sequence of icons for the specific purpose of building and saving a model. After you've created and saved a model, load it into Authorware and it is available to use in any piece.

As mentioned in the last section, models provide a great way to standardize certain elements of your piece such as design elements like buttons and text styles. They also are useful when you need to share standard components among members of a development team. For example, you might want to create a model for a user logon routine that members of your development team can share to avoid duplicating work. You'll learn more about using logon routines in Chapter 16, "Tracking the User."

To see how to create a model, first add some content to the flowline that you can use as a model. Then, perform the following steps:

1. Select the icons you've added to the flowline by either clicking on them or drawing a selection area around them by dragging the mouse.

TIP If you're selecting a large segment of icons, it may be easier to group the icons into a single map icon, and then select the map icon itself. This allows you to paste a single map icon into a section of the flowline later, when using the model you've created.

2. After you've selected the icons that you want to add to the model, choose Create Model from the Insert menu.

The Model Description window appears, as shown in **Figure 6.2**.

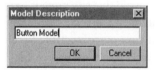

Figure 6.2

Enter a description for the model in the Model Description window.

3. Type in a description for the model. Authorware displays this description for you when you load the model into the piece later.

4. Click OK after you've entered the description.

The Create New Model dialog box appears, enabling you to save the model.

5. Select a folder where you want to save the model, enter a file name in the File name field, and click Save to save the model.

The model is saved as a separate file with an .A4D extension.

You may need to adjust the model you're creating, if you include the names of any custom variables in the model (either in a calculation icon or in an Icon Property field).

When this happens, Authorware displays the Variables Used In Model dialog box, as shown in **Figure 6.3**. Using this dialog box, you can select the custom variables you want to rename, if you paste the model into a new piece and find that you have two variables using the same name.

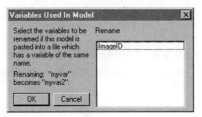

Figure 6.3
The Variables Used In Model dialog box lists any custom variables that you've included in the model.

For example, you may have included a variable named UserID in the model that is meant to store a name; when pasting the model into the new piece, however, you find that a variable you are using to store a password is using the same name. Renaming your custom variables can help you avoid this issue. To rename a variable that you want to paste into another piece, you simply click on the name of the variable you want to rename and click OK. The model is now saved with this information. Then you can make sure that your custom variables are used appropriately when you paste the model into another piece.

NOTE▸ While you can't always avoid this situation, it's wise to keep your custom variable names unique in a piece—especially if you're planning to make models from your piece available to others. For more information on working with variables, see Chapter 14, "Using Functions and Variables."

Loading and pasting a model

When you create a new model, Authorware automatically loads it into the current file. Since you've already created a model, you can see how this works by clicking on the Insert menu. The Unload Model and Paste Model options are now active, as shown in **Figure 6.4**.

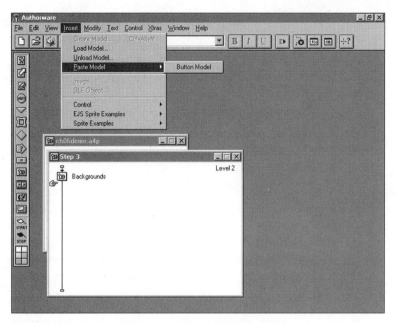

Figure 6.4
Additional model options become available after creating a model.

TIP If you create an interaction with custom buttons and save it as a
model, Authorware adds the buttons to the Button Library when you
paste the model into another file later. You'll learn more about using
the Button Library in Chapter 7, "Creating Basic Interactivity."

To view the description of the model you created in the previous
section, click on the Paste Model command in the Insert menu. You
now can paste this model into the flowline by selecting the model
description from the Paste Model submenu. You also can load the
model and paste it into a new piece by using the following steps:

1. Create a new file.

2. Choose Load Model from the Insert menu.

   The Load Model dialog box appears, as shown in **Figure 6.5**.

NOTE The Load Model dialog box on the Windows platform has an
Info button that enables you to look at the description of the model
before loading it.

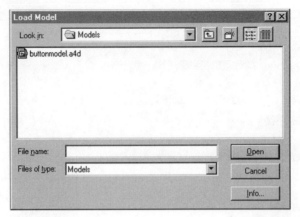

Figure 6.5
You can load a model through the Load Model dialog box.

3. Select the model you want to load by clicking on it in the list of available files. (Remember that models on both platforms are saved with an .A4D extension.)

4. Click Open to load it.

Again you can see the model included in the Paste Model submenu, indicating that it is now available to paste into your piece. You can paste it anywhere on the flowline, clicking in the Design window to place the paste hand where you want to insert the model into the flowline. Then you can choose Paste Models from the Insert menu and select the description of the model you want to paste. Authorware pastes the icons saved in the model into the flowline. You now can edit them as you would any other icons on the flowline.

Unloading a model

If you no longer need to use a model in a piece, you can unload it by choosing Unload Model from the Insert menu. This command displays the Unload Model dialog box, as shown in **Figure 6.6**.

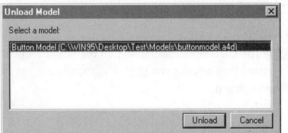

Figure 6.6
The Unload Model dialog box.

To unload a model, click on the name of the model to unload, and then click the Unload button. This unloads the model from the current piece. You will need to load the model again if you want to use it.

As you can see, models are fairly simple to use. Experiment with creating and pasting models into your piece to get a feel for the kind of things you can accomplish with models. Remember, you can save any type of icon in a model; this gives you an unlimited range of possibilities when figuring out creative ways to use them.

However, depending on the type of content contained in the icons you've added to the model, you may start to see the size of your file swell after using the same model four or five times in a piece. While you can't always get around this, you can better manage your memory resources by either using icons that you have linked to external content, or by selecting icons that you have already linked to a library. These options are explored in the sections ahead.

Working with Libraries

Multimedia developers have a tendency to go overboard on the sound, graphics, and video that they want to use in a piece; consequently, they go to great lengths to make it all fit. In some cases, using video, image, and sound compression is enough to get the job done. However, libraries are another way to manage this aspect of development.

A single CD-ROM title can contain 650 MB of data, which you must deliver at the same time. The Authorware 4 binary file compatibility can help you in this regard; however, you still need a way to manage all the data. Using libraries, you can keep better track of your information and update it quickly throughout the entire piece, using a few simple library options.

Shockwave pieces can be even more of a problem to manage because you need to keep your piece as small as possible so it's easier to deliver over the typical network connection. Libraries can be your best friend because they allow you to reuse the content stored in a single icon anywhere in a piece without taking up any additional real estate.

Some pieces you create may have only a few screens and a couple of sounds, totaling 1 or 2 MB. Using libraries in this situation may not be as crucial in meeting your delivery goals, but this isn't always the case. When you begin developing pieces that run from a web server or local area network, every single kilobyte matters in the end because file size affects how long users are forced to stare at an empty screen, waiting for your piece to download.

Creating a library

A library file contains individual icons and all content that is created in, or imported into, the icon (any linked content Authorware continues to store externally). Libraries can include display, interaction, calculation, movie, and sound icons. Unlike models, however, libraries don't preserve logic or relationships between icons on a flowline—meaning, you cannot store a map icon with nested logic in a library.

The first step toward using libraries with a piece is to create a new library file. Icons that you place in a library are called "linked" icons (as opposed to external files "linked" to an icon). Icons that you link to a library will be displayed on the flowline with an italicized title, as shown in **Figure 6.7**.

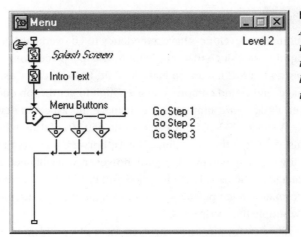

Figure 6.7
An italicized title indicates that you have linked an icon to a library.

When you create a new library or open an existing one, a separate Library window appears in the Authorware window, as shown in **Figure 6.8**.

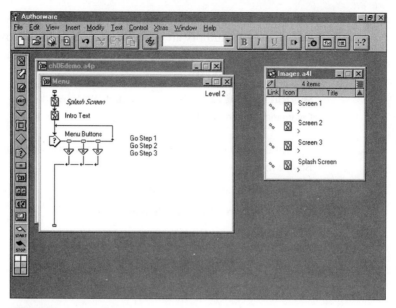

Figure 6.8
Library windows appear as a second open window in the
Authorware window.

You can drag icons on the flowline into the Library window,
creating a link and placing the icon's contents into the library.
Icons in the library that you have linked to your piece display with
a special link symbol to the left of the linked icon's name, as shown
in **Figure 6.9**.

Figure 6.9
Linked icons in the Library
window display with a link
symbol.

Creating a new library is similar to creating a new file. If you don't already have an Authorware file open in the Design window, go ahead and create a new file. Then choose New > Library from the File menu to create a new library.

Shortcut: To create a new library, use Control+Alt+N (Windows), or Command+Option+N (Macintosh).

An untitled Library window appears in the Design window. Before moving on, save the library so you can continue to use it:

1. Select the Library window.
2. Choose Save from the File Menu.

   The Save As dialog box appears.
3. Select a location where you want to save the library, and then enter a name for it in the File name field.
4. Click Save to save the library.

Shortcut: To save all libraries currently open, use Ctrl+Shift+S (Windows), or Command+Shift+S (Macintosh).

Authorware 4 saves libraries with an .A4L extension. They are saved separately from your main Authorware file so you can use them with other Authorware files during development.

TIP As mentioned earlier, you can use up to 17 libraries at a time with any given file, and you can have up to 20 libraries open at once in the Design window to copy content from one library to another. However, it's usually best to keep only four or five libraries linked to one piece at a time because you need to manage these files separately and distribute them with your final piece.

When you open a piece, Authorware automatically opens all attached libraries. Authorware attaches a library to a piece when the library contains an icon that you have linked to the flowline. If you previously saved the file with the Library windows closed, you can quickly open one of the attached Library windows by choosing Library from the Window menu and selecting the name of the Library window you want to display.

If Authorware can't find a library that you have attached to a piece, it displays the dialog box shown in **Figure 6.10**, and asks you to locate it on the hard disk. If the library is missing from your hard disk or deleted, you can open the piece but you cannot access the content you placed in the library file. Authorware preserves the library link information so you can relink your content later by placing the library file in a location where Authorware can find it.

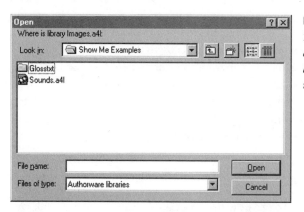

Figure 6.10
This dialog box appears when a linked library is missing.

NOTE Authorware does not use the search path settings you specified in the File Properties dialog box to locate attached libraries. Instead, it looks for the libraries in the same folder where you placed your piece. For more information about setting up the search path, see Chapter 2, "Beginning a Piece."

When you have finished using a library or want to close its window to create more space in the Design window, you can click on the Library window's close box; or, you can select the Library window you want to close, and then choose Close > Window from the File menu.

Shortcut: To close the active window, use Control+W (Windows), or Command+W (Macintosh).

Closing a library doesn't break the connections between the file and the library. All icons linked to the library in the Design window remain linked. You also can close all open libraries and the Authorware file you're working on by choosing Close > All from the File menu.

Shortcut: To close the current piece and all active libraries, use Control+Shift+W (Windows), or Command+Shift+W (Macintosh).

After you create or open a library, you can add existing content to it by dragging and dropping an icon from the flowline into the Library window. This replaces the icon on the flowline with a linked icon and moves the icon's contents into the library, where they are stored.

You also can create libraries filled with information ahead of time by adding new icons directly to the library itself. To do this, drag and drop a new icon from the icon palette into the Library window and then add your content. Add these icons to the flowline in the same way that you would add new icons from the icon palette. This is a convenient way to create libraries of content to distribute to others working on a large project.

NOTE As mentioned earlier in this chapter, you can only store display, interaction, sound, movie, and calculation icons in a library.

To see how the process of creating a simple link works, you can use the same library you created earlier. To create the link:

1. Open the library (if it isn't already open) by choosing Library from the Window menu and selecting the name of the library file.

    The Library window appears in the Design window.

2. Drag a new display icon into the library and name it.

3. Open it and draw a simple shape, using the oval or rectangle tool.

4. After you have finished, close the display icon.

5. Then select the display icon by clicking it, drag it from the library to the flowline, and place it where you want the display icon to appear.

When you do this, Authorware automatically creates a linked icon to the icon stored in the library. Each time Authorware encounters the linked display icon, it looks to the icon stored in the library and displays its content. You can easily create other links to the same library icon using the process you just learned.

Notice that the linked display icon on the flowline appears as if you had dragged it directly from the icon palette. It even uses the same name as the display icon you added to the library. However, as mentioned earlier, the title of the linked icon is italicized so you can quickly see which icons on the flowline are pointing to library content.

TIP You can rename any linked icon on the flowline the same way you rename a standard icon without affecting its link to the library.

If all this talk about linked icons has you confused, you might want to think of a linked icon on the flowline as a kind of "alias" or "shortcut." These are what you use on the Macintosh or Windows 95 desktop to create an icon that points to a folder or file stored in another location on your hard disk. Linked icons in Authorware are virtually the same thing. Although the linked icon on the flowline doesn't contain content itself, it points to the original source icon that you've stored in the library. When Authorware encounters a linked icon while running, it looks at the source icon and uses its content instead.

Editing a linked library icon

In most cases, you modify the original library icon itself if you want to change a linked icon's content. If you open a linked icon from the flowline, the icon's title appears in braces and Authorware dims the options available to edit this icon. For example, if you open a linked display icon to view its contents, you will see that the only active element of the toolbox is the pointer, as shown in **Figure 6.11**. The exception to this is the calculation icon. You can add or modify scripts in a linked calculation icon without opening the original library icon to do it. You'll learn more about the calculation icon in Chapter 14, "Using Functions and Variables."

Figure 6.11
When editing a linked icon, most editing options are unavailable to you.

If you still have your piece open, open the display icon on the flowline and try editing or deleting the graphic inside. What happens? If everything is set up correctly, nothing happens unless you drag the graphic to a new position.

Because you now have the icon stored in a library, you only can control the repositioning of the graphic in the Presentation window. If you want to edit the graphic, you must go to the source itself:

1. Double-click the display icon in the Library window.

The Presentation window opens, displaying the toolbar. You now can make any changes you want to the graphic.

2. Modify the icon by adding a graphic, or changing its color. When you have finished, close the display icon to return to the Library window.

3. To test your changes and see them reflected in the flowline, run the piece.

Authorware updates the linked icon on the flowline to reflect the content changes you made.

You can change some icon properties directly in the flowline. However, there are some very specific rules about what types of changes you can make to a linked icon, and what types of changes you can make to the original source icon. The following table summarizes these rules:

Icon type...	Edited in library icons only...	Edited in icons linked to a library...
Display	Content	Object's position on screen
	Color, fill, line, shape properties	Layers, erasing, and transition effects
	Displayed variables	Attached calculations
Interaction	Content, including display objects	Object's position on screen
	Color, fill, line, shape properties	Layers, erasing, and transition effects
	Displayed variables	Interaction properties settings
		Attached calculations
Movie	Linked or imported movies	Movie properties settings
	Mode settings for PICS and FLC files	Attached calculations
Sound	Linked or imported sounds	Sound Options settings
	Attached calculations	Attached calculations

NOTE Compared to other icons, the calculation icon follows its own set of rules when used in a library. You can continue to modify a script in a linked calculation icon after you have added it to the flowline. You also can modify the original script in the library without affecting the edited script on the flowline.

Updating a library icon

To demonstrate these rules for you, take a look at the display icon in the piece you've been working with in this chapter. When you make the following types of changes to the display icon in the library, the changes are visible the next time you run the piece:

- Change the color, shape, size, or fill of the graphic.

- Import additional graphics into the display icon.

- Delete the graphic from the display icon.

Other property changes you've made, including layer, erasing, or transition effects settings, don't show up automatically in the piece until you update the linked icons to reflect this change.

To see how to update the linked icons on the flowline after modifying the original source icon:

1. Select the display icon stored in the library you created earlier.

2. Apply a new transition to the display icon by choosing Icon > Transitions from the Modify menu. When you have finished, click OK to close the Transitions dialog box.

3. With the display icon still highlighted, choose Icon > Library Links from the Modify menu.

Shortcut: To update links to a library icon, use Ctrl+Alt+L (Windows), or Command+Option+L (Macintosh).

The Update Links dialog box appears, as shown in **Figure 6.12**.

Figure 6.12
You can update linked icons on the flowline via the Update Links dialog box.

Several options are available to you in this dialog box:

■ The list field on the lower left-hand side of the dialog box displays the titles of all the current icons on the flowline that you have linked to the selected library icon. Since you've only created one link so far, you should see just one icon title listed here.

■ The Select All button selects all the titles of icons displayed in this dialog box.

■ The Show Icon button brings up the Presentation window, showing you the flowline location of the currently selected icon. (This button is dimmed when you have selected multiple linked icons.)

■ The Preview button enables you to preview the content stored in the original source icon.

In order to see the transition effect you just applied to the display icon when running the piece, use this dialog box to update the linked icon on the flowline.

To do this:

1. Click on the title of the linked display icon, and then click the Update button.

A confirmation dialog box displays, asking if you want to update the selected linked icon using its associated library icon.

2. Select Update to continue updating the linked icon.

3. When you have finished, click the Close button to close the Update Links dialog box, and then run the piece to test it.

As you can see, the transition effect is applied to the linked display icon on the flowline. Actually, if you want to, you can apply a separate transition effect to each linked display icon that appears on the flowline. Other properties, including the Layer and Prevent Automatic Erase properties, can be applied separately to each linked icon as well.

This feature gives you an added amount of flexibility when reusing content in specific parts of the flowline. However, it makes it more difficult to troubleshoot a problem in your piece when you've applied separate property settings to each linked icon because they retain these settings even if you try to update them using the Update Links dialog box.

TIP To quickly update a link without using the Update Links dialog box, simply drag the original source icon from the Library window and drop it onto the linked icon you want to update. For any type of linked icon (except a calculation icon), this resets all the properties of the linked icon to those of the original source icon.

Finding the original library icon

At times you may need to change the name of the linked icon on the flowline, especially if you want to reference it using an Authorware variable expression. (Remember, Authorware requires unique names for icons when variable expressions reference them.) If you have changed the name of a linked icon on the flowline, and can't seem to remember where you have stored the original source icon, here is a quick trick to help you find it:

1. Select the linked icon on the flowline.

2. Choose Icon > Library Links from the Modify menu.

Shortcut: To find the original library icon for a linked icon, use Ctrl+Alt+L (Windows), or Command+Option+L (Macintosh).

This command displays the Find Original dialog box, as shown in **Figure 6.13**. This dialog box, which contains information about the linked icon, can be used to point you directly to the linked icon's original source icon.

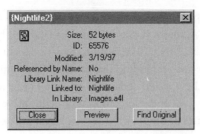

Figure 6.13
The Find Original dialog box.

3. To quickly point to the original source icon, click the Find Original button.

This displays the library window with the source icon highlighted for you, as shown in **Figure 6.14**. Knowing how to use this dialog box is helpful when working in a large piece—especially if you have moved source icons from one library to another.

Source icon ——————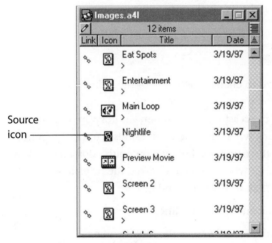

Figure 6.14
Using the Find Original option points you to the linked icon's source icon in the library.

Using the Library window

In addition to the Library Links dialog box, you can use the Library window to help track links and sort through content. The Library window provides several basic ways to sort the icons stored in a library. These options, shown in **Figure 6.15**, are explained in more detail below.

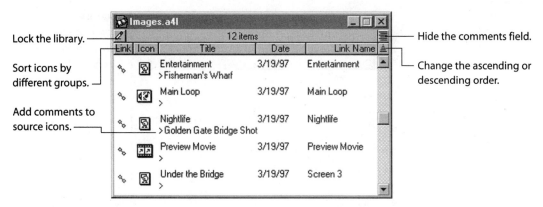

Lock the library.

Sort icons by different groups.

Add comments to source icons.

Hide the comments field.

Change the ascending or descending order.

Figure 6.15
The viewing options in the Library window help you find icons.

■ With the Sort bar, you can sort icons by linked and unlinked status, icon type, title, date, or link name. The Sort bar is located at the top of the window, above the icons.

■ Using the Ascending/Descending order button, located to the left of the Sort bar, you can sort icons in the library alphabetically in either ascending (A-to-Z) or descending (Z-to-A) order. The direction of the arrow on the button shows you which order you've chosen.

■ You can add comments to your linked icons in the comments field, located below the title of the icon. This field enables you to provide additional information with the icon for content management.

■ If you need to create more room in the window, you can hide the comments field by clicking the Comments button, located above the Ascending/Descending order button.

■ If you would like to prevent changes to a library, you can lock it by clicking the Read-Only button. This is the button located in the upper left-hand corner of the window, marked by a yellow pencil. When the library is locked, the pencil appears with a red line through it, as shown in **Figure 6.16**. To unlock the library, click the button a second time and the file opens to allow edits.

NOTE If you're storing a library on a local network drive, multiple authors can share it at the same time. However, you must make the library Read-Only before doing so.

Figure 6.16
You can lock libraries to prevent changes.

You might want to consider locking your libraries during the final stages of development, so that nothing unexpected happens to your piece. The next few pages focus on other preventive measures that you can take to keep your libraries and hours of work safe from harm.

Moving linked library icons

Working on large files with many icons stored in libraries can be troublesome if you've renamed icons and need to reference multiple sources in the same library that are similarly named. Keep this in mind when developing a piece and try to consolidate your icons based on how you are using them. You might try creating a separate library for each main section of your piece. Another method is to divide your libraries based on the type of content they contain.

This is usually the best way to organize your icons because it narrows your search to a selected library. If you need to edit a sound, you can go immediately to the sound library and find the icon that you want to modify. However, if you've started a piece without a plan for organizing your content and then decide that you want to reshuffle your icons, you can do so by moving an icon from one library to another.

To move an icon from one library to another:

1. Open both libraries so that both Library windows display together.

2. Select the icon you want to move; drag and drop it from its current library to the new library.

This displays a confirmation dialog box, shown in **Figure 6.17**.

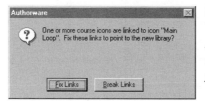

Figure 6.17
When moving an icon, Authorware prompts you to fix all links to the icon you're moving.

3. Click Fix Links so Authorware points all associated linked icons to the source icon's new library.

Authorware moves the icon, and all of its associated links are still intact.

NOTE Don't select the other option, Break Links, unless you want to rebuild the file and have no need to maintain the current links to this icon.

4. Make sure that you save both libraries.

Copying library icons

At times, you also may need to copy an icon from one library to another without affecting its links in the piece. For example, you may want to create a smaller demo version of your piece, and don't want to include the entire library of content with the demo. You can quickly make a copy of a library icon using one of the following methods:

■ Drag and drop the icon from its location to a new library while pressing Control+Alt (Windows), or Command+Option (Macintosh).

■ Copy the icon and paste it into the new library using the Copy and Paste commands from the Edit menu.

If you delete an icon from a library, either by accident or on purpose, Authorware breaks the links to all its attached icons on the flowline. Authorware prompts you to confirm the delete one time; however, after you have deleted an icon from a library, its associated linked icons no longer display content, and the icon appears on the flowline with a broken link symbol next to it, as shown in **Figure 6.18**.

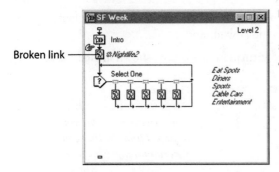

Broken link

Figure 6.18
*When a link breaks, the attached
icon appears on the flowline with
a broken link symbol.*

Fixing broken library links

Actually, breaking links to libraries is not as uncommon as you might
expect. Usually it happens when you decide to replace an icon and
delete it from the library first, rather than import new content into
it and update its links. While you should try to avoid doing this,
sometimes you can't help it.

If you delete an icon from a library that has attached icons,
you can quickly find out how many icons in the piece are affected
by opening the Library Links dialog box and viewing the list of broken
links. This list contains the names of all attached icons in the piece
with broken links.

To view this information, choose Library Links from the Xtras
menu. The Library Links dialog box appears, as shown in **Figure 6.19**.
At the top are two radio button options for viewing current links in
the piece: Unbroken Links and Broken Links. Select the Broken Links
option to show all the icons in the piece with broken links.

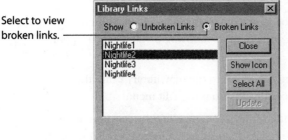

Select to view
broken links.

Figure 6.19
The Library Links dialog box.

While rare, links also can be broken when you open a piece and
Authorware can't find a library to open. In this case, it's best to close
your piece without saving changes, figure out where you've placed the
library on your hard disk, and then move it to the same folder as your
piece. Otherwise, you need to repair the links that are broken.

To repair a broken link in a piece, you can drag the original source icon from the library and drop it on top of the unlinked icon you want to repair. The icon is relinked to the source icon, and the broken link symbol disappears from the flowline and the Library window.

NOTE You also can drag the unlinked icon and drop it on top of the original source icon to repair a broken link.

Final considerations

Libraries are really an effective way to manage the content in a piece. They provide many benefits that usually outweigh the headaches you can get when using them. Repairing broken links can be tricky, but redesigning your piece at the last minute because you've exceeded your file size limitations is a much more difficult and time-consuming task.

The main issue to consider up front when using libraries is whether or not you need to use them. If you're not planning to reuse any of your content, then it may be easier in the long run to forego using libraries and store your content internally. Your piece will be easier to manage and entirely self-contained. You will also have fewer files to worry about when you start packaging your piece for delivery.

NOTE You can package libraries as part of the final run-time file, eliminating the need to distribute multiple files when delivering your piece. However, because this increases the size of the final run-time file, you may run into performance issues when doing so. For more information about packaging libraries, see Chapter 17, "Distributing Your Piece."

However, choosing to design your piece this way means that you must make all changes to content at the ground level by going into each of the icons you want to modify and updating them one at a time. This can be difficult in projects where your content goes through many revision cycles. One way to minimize the impact this may have on your development time is to use external content that you have linked to your icons. In the next section, you'll learn some techniques for managing external content.

What's the best way to utilize external content? The answer primarily depends on two issues: how often you need to update your content, and how you plan to distribute your final application. You need to consider both of these issues up front, as they help determine the direction you take during development.

To give you an example, consider a promotional marketing piece you might design for a recreational clothing company that gives customers a preview of each season's upcoming styles. If you distribute your piece on CD-ROM, and you have plenty of time to update it every three months, you might decide to make changes directly to the library files you've created. Because you've come up with a standardized interface for displaying the ordering information and images, you can make updates quickly by importing the new images into your libraries and then repackaging your files.

However, if you need to update the information more quickly, and you don't want to repackage your piece each time you update it, you should consider using linked images rather than imported images. Using linked images, you can quickly update the piece by replacing the current folder where you have your images stored with a new folder of images. As long as you keep the file names of the linked images the same when you replace them, Authorware automatically updates your piece to reflect the content changes that you have made.

 For an example of this type of piece, take a look at the example file named CATALOG.A4P. You'll find this file in the Chapter 6 examples folder on the CD-ROM accompanying this book.

This example helps point out one of the most challenging aspects of developing with external content—keeping on top of simultaneously managing many files. Libraries in which you've used imported content are less problematic because you only need to make sure that the library is in the same location as your piece. When you use external content, you not only need to keep track of all the external files that you've linked to your icons, but you also have to maintain separate file and path information for each file linked to your piece. (When you use digital movies in your piece, you will have to deal with this issue because they too are stored externally.)

This—in and of itself—is not a difficult task; you simply have to be careful how you store and update your content. Learning when and how to use external content in a piece can be tricky; once you figure it out, you'll begin to recognize ways of improving how you handle the process of managing the content in your piece.

Using the External Media Browser

When you decide to use external content, make sure that you maintain links to your content by keeping the file and path information for your links intact. One of the best methods of organizing and maintaining your links to external files is using the new External Media Browser, which is built into Authorware 4.

NOTE You can link any image, sound, or digital movie file that Authorware supports to an icon. In addition, third-party Xtras are being developed that will allow you to create links to additional types of files in your piece. For the latest list of Xtras that you can use with Authorware, go to the Xtras section of the Macromedia web site (**http://www.macromedia.com/software/Xtras/**).

The External Media Browser is a separate window that eases the process of keeping track of the file and path information for your external content. You can use it to create variable paths to your files so you can quickly update content in your piece based on a changing condition. This might be a path pointing to the current location of the piece—or even a standard Internet URL (Uniform Resource Locator) address that points to an external file stored on a web server.

At any time you can open the External Media Browser to edit an icon linked to an external file by choosing the External Media Browser from the Window menu. The External Media Browser window appears, as shown in **Figure 6.20**.

Changes the type of links to view. ———

Sorts icons by link, icon, title, or file name. ———

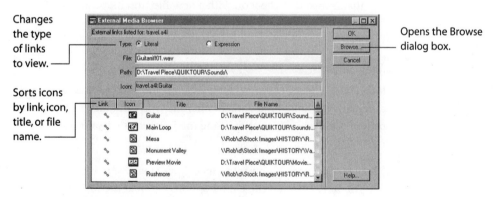

Opens the Browse dialog box.

Figure 6.20
The External Media Browser shows you all the icons linked to external files.

At the bottom of this window, you can see a list of every icon in your piece that you have linked to an external file. For example, in the figure above, the sound icon named Guitar is linked to a WAV file stored on a local hard disk.

If you have multiple files linked to your piece, you can use the Link, Icon, Title, and File Name sort bars at the top of the icon list to help you find the icon for which you're searching. If you want to view the information for one of the icons listed, click on the icon or the name of the file. Authorware displays both in the list of linked icons inside this window.

NOTE Because you can import more than one linked image into a display or interaction icon, you may see several linked file names appearing with the same icon in the External Media Browser window.

When you have selected an icon, use the button options in this window to modify the icon link (labeled above in **Figure 6.20**):

■ The two Type button options, Literal and Expression, enable you to switch between using a hard-coded (literal) path to your external file, or using a variable expression to point to the file. (You'll learn more about these in a moment.)

■ The Browse button allows you to select a new file to link to the icon. This option is similar to the Import button found in the Properties dialog box for the display, interaction, sound, and movie icons. It allows you to quickly replace the current file that is linked to the icon with a new file, and it updates the file and path information displayed in the External Media Browser.

Modifying or replacing linked content

If you've linked an external file to an icon, and you find that you need to replace the linked file with another file, you can quickly change the path or file name information using the External Media Browser:

1. Open the External Media Browser window.

2. Select the icon you want to modify and make sure that you have selected the Literal option button at the top of the window.

3. Type in the new file name in the File field, or type in the new path in the Path field.

4. When you have finished, click OK to close the window.

The file name and path information for a linked icon is also stored in the Image Properties dialog box (when updating a display or interaction icon), or in the Icon Properties dialog box (when updating a sound or movie icon). When you use the Import command to add a linked file to the flowline, Authorware adds the file name and path in the File field, as shown in **Figure 6.21**. You can modify the link to a file by typing in a new file name or path in the File field of the Properties dialog box, whichever applies to the type of icon you want to update.

The
File field

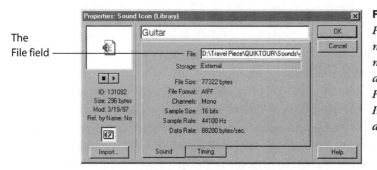

Figure 6.21
Path and file name infor- mation as it appears in the File field of the Image Properties dialog box.

Similarly, you can use the Browse button on the right-hand side of the External Media Browser window to open the Browse dialog box, as shown in **Figure 6.22**; there you can select a new external file to link to the icon. After you've selected the new file, Authorware updates the information in the External Media Browser window (and the Properties dialog box for the icon) to reflect the new location of the selected file.

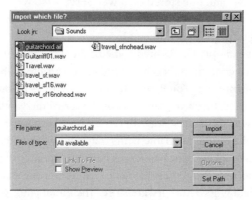

Figure 6.22
Opening the Browse dialog box.

TIP As mentioned earlier, you also can use the Import button inside the icon's Properties dialog box to quickly replace the content you've linked to the icon.

If you're working with a sound, display, or interaction icon, Authorware 4 allows you to type in a URL in this field that points to a file you've stored on a web server. However, you must have an active web connection open, or Authorware cannot link to the file specified in the URL.

NOTE Movie icons cannot link directly to a file stored on a web server. While you can use digital movies with Shockwave pieces, you must download the movie first using options specified in the Shockwave piece's map file before you can play it. For more information on editing map files, see Chapter 17, "Distributing Your Piece."

Using the Expression field

One of the advantages to using external content is that you can use a variable expression created in Authorware to point to it. This allows you to change the image, movie, or sound being displayed or played by an icon; the changes are based on information updated by Authorware, or through a custom script created using the calculation icon. For more information about using the calculation icon, see Chapter 14, "Using Functions and Variables."

Variable paths are a powerful way to build dynamic content management into your piece. For example, you can use a variable expression to point to a folder location that may change when you deliver your final run-time application. Better yet, you can use a calculation script to control a variable expression that automatically chooses between two versions of the same file—one stored locally on your hard drive, and one stored on a web server—so when you deliver the piece as a Shockwave file, you can provide the correct path information to retrieve the linked file.

The last example highlighted some of the difficulties involved in using external content in pieces you plan to distribute on both CD-ROM and the Internet. You'll need to use a few tricks if you want to make sure that Authorware can find your external media when the piece runs. One of the best ways to ensure that Authorware can locate external media is to use variable paths that point to linked files.

You can quickly change an icon's path to a variable expression by opening the icon's Properties dialog box, and inserting an expression in the File field where Authorware stores the literal path. When you do this, make sure that you type an equal (=) sign before the expression, as shown in **Figure 6.23**.

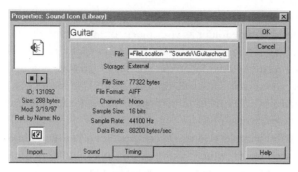

Figure 6.23
A variable expression can be quickly added to the File field inside the icon's Properties dialog box.

In most cases, however, you'll keep track of your linked path information using the External Media Browser because you can quickly set up a variable expression that points to the location of an external file for any icon in your piece. After you've added linked content to the flowline, you can open the External Media Browser window, and select the icon you want to modify. Then select the Expression radio button option at the top of the window. The window changes to display an Expression path field for the icon, as shown in **Figure 6.24**.

The Expression field

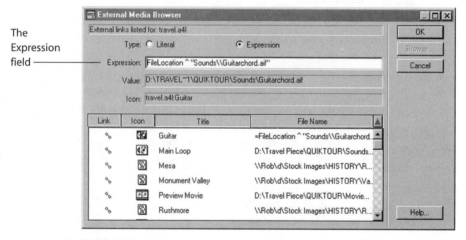

Figure 6.24
Switching to the Expression path option.

You can specify any type of variable expression in the Expression field of the External Media Browser window. For instance, you might want to use a custom or system variable to point to the path location of your file using the same file name each time so that you can maintain your links when moving your piece to a different machine or delivery platform.

One quick way to do this is to place all your external media in either the same folder as your piece, or in a subfolder of the current piece. (See Chapter 2, "Beginning a Piece" for more information on using relative folder locations.) If you set up your content this way, you can conveniently use Authorware's `FileLocation` system variable in an expression that points to the location of each external file linked to your piece.

For example, you might create a link to a sound file named Guitarchord.aif, which you've placed in a subfolder called Sounds, and then later realize that you need to copy your project to another drive. Rather than type in a new literal path for your linked file each time you move the piece to a different drive, simply use the following expression in the Expression field to do the work for you:

`FileLocation ^ "Sounds\Guitarchord.aif"`

In this expression, a concatenation symbol (^) is used to join the system variable with the folder name and file name of your external content. You can omit the folder name if you've placed the external file in the same folder as your piece:

`FileLocation ^ "Guitarchord.aif"`

Because `FileLocation` always contains the current path to the piece you're working on, you can use this type of expression for each file that you've linked to your piece. The `FileLocation` system variable maintains the same type of information when you distribute your piece, so you can use it if you plan to deliver your final piece from a LAN network, CD-ROM, or as a stand-alone application.

If you plan to use variable paths with your content, you will need to assign a variable path to each icon listed in the External Media Browser window. There is no quick-and-easy way to do this, other than modifying each icon's path separately.

Using variable paths with Shockwave

Unfortunately, the `FileLocation` trick doesn't work very well with Shockwave pieces that contain linked external content. When you deliver a Shockwave piece, the `FileLocation` system variable points to the folder where you have the Shockwave Plug-In installed. Because you probably have all your content stored on a web server, you first must download all your content to the Plug-In location so that your piece can find it.

NOTE Take a close look at Chapter 17, "Distributing Your Piece;" it covers many of the finer details for delivering a Shockwave piece.

You can use a similar approach to point to the web server location where your piece resides when the piece plays back as a Shockwave piece by including the system variable `NetLocation` in your variable path expression. The `NetLocation` system variable contains the web location where you have your Shockwave piece stored. Authorware specifies the path using the standard URL format:

```
http://[server name]/[folder name]/[file name]
```

Using NetLocation in the expression field, you might create an expression that is similar to the expression you created when using `FileLocation`, as shown below:

```
NetLocation ^ "Sounds/guitar.aif"
```

Note, however, that you must use the forward slash character (/) as opposed to the backslash character (\) when separating the folder name and the file name. If you don't use the correct syntax here, Authorware cannot find the linked file you've specified.

The only inherent problem with using `NetLocation` is that it only works when you deliver the piece as a Shockwave document. This means that in order to test your links, you must package the piece, convert it to a Shockwave document, and then test it using a web browser (see Chapter 17, "Distributing Your Piece").

Variable expressions are useful if you need to anticipate folder and file name changes. However, if you want to avoid the hassles of using expressions to point to your files, and you don't anticipate folder and file name changes, you can simply point to the file using the following relative path format:

```
.\Sounds\guitar.aif
```

Unlike the previous examples, Authorware treats this type of path as a literal path rather than an expression. It is the default format used by Authorware if you import a file into a piece that is stored in a folder location relative to the location of your piece. You can use this type of relative path for any type of piece, whether it's delivered on a Windows system, a Macintosh system, or from a web server because Authorware dynamically adjusts the path format to fit all these different delivery situations. This type of relative path is covered in more detail in Chapter 17, "Distributing Your Piece."

Needless to say, you need to be acutely aware of file name and path issues when creating more complex pieces that you want to run on a variety of platforms. While the binary-compatible file format makes developing for Windows and Macintosh much easier, carefully think about how you plan to optimize your piece for the Internet when designing it, if you plan to use external content.

Looking Ahead...

This chapter explored the Authorware tools that help you manage your content better. Libraries and models provide a powerful way to manage different aspects of your piece, including standardizing your flowline structures, and streamlining the file size of your piece. However, if you want a fast way to update content, you also can take a look at using the External Media Browser to manage files that you've linked to the icons in your piece.

Authorware's content management tools bring you a step closer to the goal of delivering sophisticated applications quickly to a variety of different platforms. Now that you've become familiar with working with content in Authorware, it's time to focus on increasing the amount of interactivity in your piece. The chapter ahead covers the types of controls that you can create for user input from the mouse or keyboard. These may include custom buttons, dials or sliders, or text entry fields where the user types in a word or phrase. At other times, you can set up automatic types of controls that branch to a location or provide feedback automatically to the user. You'll learn the techniques for creating interactivity in the next part of this book.

Developing Interactivity

If you design a multimedia piece with interactivity in mind, it not only provides users with enrichment through words, images, and sounds, it also enriches through involvement with the learning process. Whether you develop high-level interactivity that simulates a real-world environment, or low-level interactivity that a simple click or keypress initiates, you can make a more lasting impression if you add a dimension of interactivity to your pieces.

These are the types of design issues that you will want to consider when designing your piece. However, because Authorware handles both types of interactivity well, this makes it much more possible to deliver dynamic content that responds to a user's needs. Part II, "Developing Interactivity," focuses on the techniques you can use to provide a new level of depth to the multimedia pieces you create that allows users to become participants rather than just a member of the audience.

Creating Basic Interactivity

When designing a project, you'll want to consider methods of injecting life into your piece through interactivity. Authorware handles interactivity through the interaction icon and the types of responses that you can create to help guide the user through your piece. Using the interaction icon, you can engage the user in the content you're delivering—improving learning retention and adding a great deal of fun to the process.

Authorware enables you to create many types of sophisticated interactions using the interaction icon. This chapter teaches you how to create basic interactions in Authorware, and along the way it introduces you to the three most common types of interaction responses used in a piece: buttons, hot spots, and hot objects.

Most of us are accustomed to working in a program by selecting options from a menu, or clicking an onscreen button using the mouse. In this type of limited "interactivity," a pull-down menu might appear on screen, giving you several options or a set of commands. When you click on one of the options, the application does what it is told to do and you get feedback on screen. If the option is available to you, then you might see a progress bar that animates across the screen while the program performs the action. If the option is not available, you might hear a sharp beep and see an error message that tells you to select something else.

All interactions in Authorware are similarly designed to facilitate a dialog between the user and the computer. As the author, you can define the possible paths that a user might encounter in your piece at any given time. The user sees only an onscreen button to click—not all the elements of a particular interaction. What you create on the flowline is a bit more complex and usually includes several responses for an interaction.

For instance, you might have several types of mouse responses on screen for a single interaction. Each response is set up to track a different event. If you were to create a menu screen, you might have several buttons that navigate to different areas of your piece; you might have another button that quits the application; and you might have a hot spot defined that covers the entire screen, so if the user clicks in an undefined area, you can provide a prompt that asks the user to click one of the navigation buttons to continue.

As you start building pieces in Authorware, it's important to have a thorough understanding of what is happening in the flowline so you can design interactions that are effective. You can use any type of icon—including display, sound, or movie icons—in the flowline to create feedback in an interaction. Interactions also are used with framework icons to set up paging and navigational controls. Chapter 11, "Working with Pages," discusses how you set up these types of controls.

Any interaction you create in Authorware is made up of four main components: the interaction icon, the response type, the response feedback, and the response branching. These four components work together to create an interaction "loop," a series of steps that help define the "action" behind each interaction.

In **Figure 7.1**, you can see the structure of a typical interaction in Authorware. After you place the interaction icon on the flowline, you can define the type of interaction by dragging another icon to the right of the interaction icon (in this case, a display icon); then select the response type, add the response feedback, and choose how the interaction will branch after the user or computer matches the response.

The inter-
action icon

The response
type

The response
feedback

The response
branching

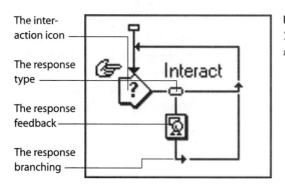

Figure 7.1
The interaction loop has four main components.

The example in **Figure 7.1** is a simple button interaction. The response type symbol in the flowline indicates that this is a button response (the default response type created by Authorware when building a new interaction). The button displays in the Presentation window when the piece runs, as shown in **Figure 7.2**.

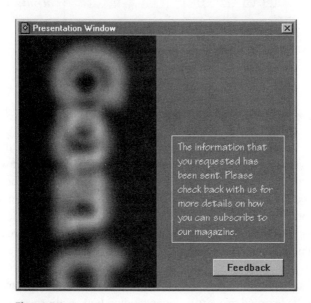

The information that you requested has been sent. Please check back with us for more details on how you can subscribe to our magazine.

Feedback

Figure 7.2
The button response, as it appears in the Presentation window.

The arrows below the button response indicate the path that Authorware will take during this interaction. After the button is clicked, Authorware displays the contents of the display icon attached to the button, and then exits the interaction. This is indicated by the branching arrow, which continues down from the display icon and then rejoins the main flowline path below the interaction icon.

In the second example, shown in **Figure 7.3**, you can see a more complex interaction—the type you might use for a screen that has several active hot spots where the user can click to see or hear additional information about a topic. This interaction uses two types of responses: the button response, which controls exiting the interaction, and the hot spot response, which controls the display of additional help graphics or a sound. All these responses are active at the same time.

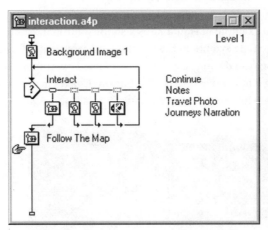

Figure 7.3
Additional hot spot responses in this interaction give the user specific feedback about a topic.

Notice that when the hot spot responses are clicked, the user never actually leaves the interaction. If you follow the arrows, the branching paths that you have set up for the hot spot responses loop around again to continue presentation from the original interaction icon. At times, however, you may want to create an interaction response that loops around each time and takes the user back to the same position in the piece.

Recognizing Authorware's visual representations of the flow of actions within interactions helps you become a better author. Part of the learning process is understanding how Authorware displays the paths of your interactions inside the Design window. Once you understand this, you begin to recognize how the flowline translates into what the user sees or hears while the piece runs.

When creating interactions in Authorware, you can use the flowline to quickly scan your interactions to see how they are set up. Later, you'll see how you also can modify some interaction options—namely, the branching path and the automatic judging options—by clicking directly in the flowline. For more information on setting up automatic judging for a response, see Chapter 16, "Tracking the User."

Types of responses

When you create a new interaction response, you have a set of 11 possible response types from which you can choose. These response types define the type of action that guides the user along the flowline. When creating a new interaction response, Authorware creates a button response by default. However, at any time you can quickly change the default button response type to one of the other options listed below:

Response symbol...	Type of response...	How it is used...
	Button	Creates system or custom buttons that the user can click.
	Hot Spot	Creates a rectangular area on the screen that the user can click.
	Hot Object	Creates a hot spot out of a display object that the user can click.
	Target Area	Creates a rectangular area that the user can drag a movable object into.
	Pull-Down Menu	Creates a custom pull-down menu choice.
	Conditional	Creates a response that is controlled by a variable expression.
	Text Entry	Creates a field that enables the user to enter text.
	Keypress	Creates a response that checks for a single key typed by the user.
	Time Limit	Creates a response that becomes active after a specified amount of time elapses.
	Tries Limit	Creates a response that becomes active after a specified number of failed attempts by the user.
E	Event	Creates a response that is controlled by a scripting or event Xtra.

NOTE When you create a new interaction, you may use as many response types as necessary to control the logic at that point. It's easy to set up multiple responses for the same interaction (e.g., when you want to display several different buttons on screen at the same time, or create a combination of two or more types of responses).

Keep in mind that Authorware follows a specific set of steps each time it encounters an interaction icon in the flowline:

- Authorware displays any graphics inside the interaction icon and its associated responses in the Presentation window.

- Authorware waits until the user or the computer matches one of the responses.

- If you have multiple responses attached to an interaction icon, and more than one is active, Authorware gives priority to the first response to the left of the interaction icon when looking for a match; if no match is made, it continues to the next response on the right and does the same process.

- If the user matches a response, Authorware disregards all other responses while it displays the response's associated feedback, except where you have applied a perpetual response to an interaction icon. Chapter 8, "Keyboard and Menu Responses," covers perpetual response types in more detail later.

- After Authorware presents the response feedback, it follows the branching option you selected for the response—continuing presentation of the flowline.

TIP While there really is no limit to the number of responses that you may attach to a single interaction icon, you rarely need to use more than 10–15 responses at a time. If you find yourself going above this number of responses, you may want to rethink the way you're approaching the interaction, or consider using Authorware's system functions and variables to simplify your design. You will learn more about this in Chapter 15, "Controlling the Flowline through Scripting."

Now that you're more comfortable with how interactions work, the best way to learn more is to start working with them. In the next section, you'll see how this is done by creating a simple button response.

Setting Up a Button Response

Working with the interaction and display icons is very similar. You can import graphics and text into an interaction icon, or create them using the same tools found in the graphics toolbox. However, there are several other options available when editing an interaction icon, which controls the interaction itself. Using these options, you can set up automatic erasure of response feedback, define response branching paths, or display a wait button on screen after the user completes the interaction.

To set up a simple interaction, begin by creating the button interaction you saw in **Figure 7.1**. First, build the interaction, and then investigate the options associated with the interaction icon.

1. Drag an interaction icon to the flowline and name it.

2. Double-click on the interaction icon. The Presentation window and toolbox appear.

3. Create or import a graphic into the Presentation window; click the close box to close the Presentation window and return to the flowline.

When you run a piece, Authorware displays the content of the current interaction icon along with any graphics or movies placed in the flowline before the interaction icon. If you want to edit the contents of the interaction icon while viewing the contents of previous icons, run your piece from the start flag (positioned above the interaction), and then pause it when the content of the interaction icon displays.

The interaction icon is a good place to put text that only the current interaction needs, or other objects that the current interaction doesn't need after the interaction finishes. Place the text for the current question in the interaction icon so that it erases when the user moves on to the next question.

TIP If you plan to reuse a graphic or a text field in other places in a piece, try to store it in a library within a clearly labeled separate display icon. This makes your display content easier to locate and manage when working with a large piece, and also allows you to use your graphics as separate hot objects when creating interactivity. (You'll learn more about this later in the chapter.)

The interaction icon options enable you to control how Authorware displays interaction content inside the Presentation window. As mentioned earlier, the interaction icon also has several options that control erasing and branching. All these options are located in the Interaction Icon Properties dialog box.

To view these options:

1. Select the interaction icon by clicking on it.

2. Choose Modify > Icon > Properties from the menu bar.

Shortcut: To open the Icon Properties dialog box without opening the Presentation window, double-click on the icon while holding down the Control key (Windows), or the Command key (Macintosh).

The Interaction Icon Properties dialog box appears. When you first open the dialog box, the Interaction tab options display. These options, as shown in **Figure 7.4**, are explained in more detail below:

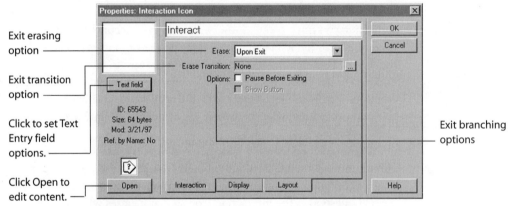

Exit erasing option

Exit transition option

Click to set Text Entry field options.

Click Open to edit content.

Exit branching options

Figure 7.4
The Interaction Icon Properties dialog box displays interaction options.

- The Erase option controls when the content of the interaction icon erases, including any button responses or text entry fields used in the interaction. The settings available in this option are After Next Entry, Upon Exit, and Don't Erase. (You'll learn more about these options later in the chapter in "Modifying erasing and branching options.")

- The Erase Transition option allows you to select a transition to use when the interaction icon content erases from the screen.

- The Options area contains two selections. When you select Pause Before Exiting, Authorware pauses presentation when a response matches and waits for a mouse click. If you've selected Pause Before Exiting, the Show Button option becomes active, allowing you to display a standard Wait button on screen that the user can click.

- Use the Text Field button at the upper left-hand corner of the dialog box to set up a text field when creating a text entry response. You will learn more about this in Chapter 8, "Keyboard and Menu Responses."

- Clicking the Open button in the lower left-hand corner of the dialog box opens the Presentation window, allowing you to edit the content stored in the interaction icon.

When editing an interaction icon's properties, you see two additional sets of tab options that you can select: Display and Layout. The Display options control such features as layer positioning, erasing behavior, and transition effects. These are the same options you learned about when editing display icons in Chapter 3, "Working with Text and Graphics;" if you're unsure how to use them, you may want to refer to this chapter later.

As with display and movie icons, the Layout options for the interaction icon allow you to control onscreen positioning of the graphic elements stored inside the icon. You will learn more about how to use these options later in Chapter 9, "Using Movable Objects."

Creating the button response

Now that you've added an interaction icon to the flowline, you can continue building your first interaction by adding a button response. Simply select the type of icon you want to use as the response feedback, drag it to the flowline, and drop it to the right of the interaction icon.

In this example, add a display icon to the button response to give the user some simple text feedback. However, when creating your own interactions, you can use almost any type of icon for the response feedback, including sound icons, movie icons, or a map icon that contains another segment of flowline logic.

TIP Map icons are irreplaceable when you need to build complex feedback for a response. For instance, you cannot use a single decision, framework, or interaction icon when creating your response feedback. However, by attaching a map icon to the interaction response, you can include these types of icons inside the map icon when building your feedback.

To set up the button response and text feedback:

1. Drag and drop a new display icon to the right of the interaction icon you just created.

The Response Type dialog box appears as soon as you release the icon, as shown in **Figure 7.5**.

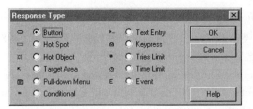

Figure 7.5

Selecting the button response type from the Response Type dialog box.

The Response Type dialog box appears each time you create the first response for an interaction. However, when you add additional responses to the interaction icon, Authorware creates the new response using the settings you specified previously when creating the first response.

2. Click OK to accept the default button response setting and close the dialog box.

An untitled button response symbol appears on the flowline above the display icon, as shown in **Figure 7.6**. Authorware automatically sets the response branching to Try Again. (Later you'll see how to modify this for your response.)

3. Before you continue, give the button a name by clicking on the icon title that appears to the right of the response and by typing in a new name. This name appears as the button's label when you run the piece later, as shown in **Figure 7.7**.

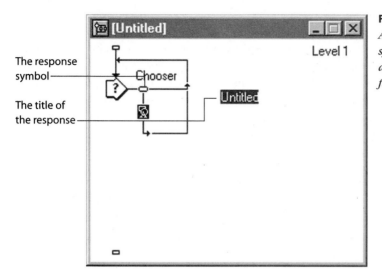

Figure 7.6
A button response symbol and title appear on the flowline.

The response symbol

The title of the response

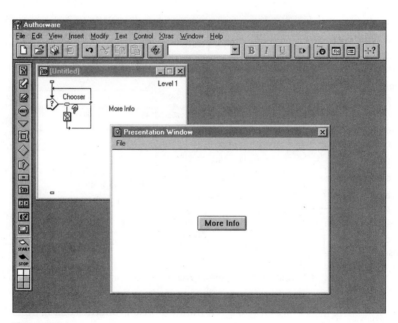

Figure 7.7
The title of the button response appears as the button's label.

After you've created a response, you can edit it by double-clicking on the response type symbol on the flowline. For instance, you may want to change the type of response from a button to a hot spot. You also can quickly edit the properties of the response—in the same way you would change the appearance of the button you're using. (You'll see how to do this later in this chapter.)

To edit the response:

1. Double-click the response symbol for your button. (As mentioned earlier, it's located directly above the display icon you're using as response feedback.)

The Response Properties dialog box appears, as shown in **Figure 7.8**.

Changes response type.———

Changes button's size.———

Changes button's onscreen location.———

Changes button's label. ———

Adds an optional key.———

Adds a custom cursor.———

Selects a different button style.———

Opens feedback icon attached to the response.———

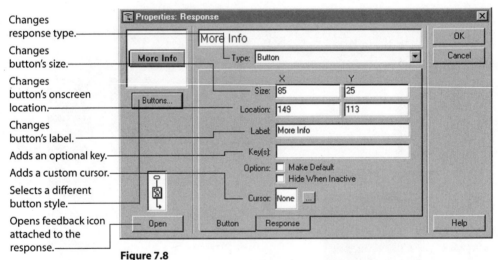

Figure 7.8
Change button options inside the Response Properties dialog box.

When you open the Response Properties dialog box, notice that the button you've created appears inside the Presentation window, along with any graphic objects you've placed inside the interaction icon. Inside the dialog box, the Button tab options display by default. You can use these options to modify the button response you've created:

■ To change the response type from Button to another type, choose a setting from the Type drop-down list. This also changes the initial options displayed in the Response Properties dialog box.

- To change the appearance of the button, click the Button option at the top left-hand corner of the dialog box. This displays the Button library window, allowing you to choose a new button to use with the response. See "Using the Button library," for more information on adding custom buttons to your piece.

- To change the size of the button, specify new X and Y values in the Size fields. X and Y represent the button's width and height in pixels. You also can resize the button by clicking it inside the Presentation window and adjusting the dimensions with the selection handles that appear.

- To change the location of the button in the Presentation window, specify new X and Y values in the Location fields. You also can reposition the button by clicking it while inside the Presentation window and dragging it to a new location.

- To change the button label, type in a new word or phrase in the Label category. This label will be displayed with the button in the Presentation window.

- To add an optional key that triggers the button, type in a value in the Key(s) category. Use the letter (e.g., "a" or "A") if it's a single key, or the modifier key followed by the key letter if you want to use a key combination (e.g., "Ctrla" or "Alta").

- Check the Make Default option to make the button display as a default system button. This applies only to the Macintosh or Windows system buttons available in the Button library. When you select this option, the button displays with a solid black outline around it, as shown in **Figure 7.9**.

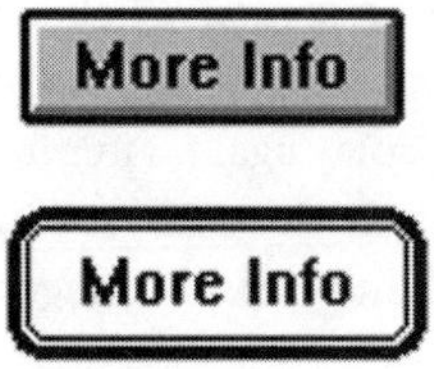

Figure 7.9
Windows and Macintosh system buttons set to the Make Default option.

- Select Hide When Inactive to hide the button when another response matches or when a condition is True. Otherwise, the button appears on screen in its dimmed state when it's inactive, as shown in **Figure 7.10**.

Figure 7.10
When a button is inactive, it appears in a dimmed state.

NOTE If you're using a custom button, make sure that you include a dimmed state when importing the button into the Button library. (For more information on how to do this, see "Using the Button Library," later in this chapter.)

■ Use the Cursor option to open the Cursor library window and select a custom cursor that displays when the mouse is over the button. (You'll work with this option later in this chapter in "Setting Up a Hot Spot Response.")

Adding response feedback content

Although you've created the button response, it does no good to run the piece since you have added no content to the display icon attached to the response. Because you already have the Response Properties dialog box open, you can quickly add some content to your response feedback icon by doing the following:

1. Click the Open button at the lower left-hand corner of the Response Properties dialog box.

This closes the dialog box and displays an empty Presentation window, along with the toolbox.

2. Create new text field using the text tool, and add some text that reads: **You clicked, didn't you?**

3. When you have finished, close the Presentation window and run the piece to test it.

You should see the button appear on screen. Clicking it displays the text for you inside the Presentation window. If you continue clicking the button, the graphic will display again, after it erases. You've just created a simple button interaction. The sections below take a look at some other ways you might want to change your button interaction.

Setting Response options

Every response type also has a set of Response options, which display in the Response Properties dialog box when you select the Response tab, as shown in **Figure 7.11**. These options remain unchanged between response types, and retain their settings even when you change your response to a different type.

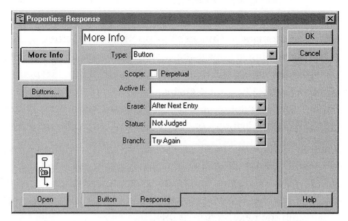

Figure 7.11
The Response options control erasing, judging, and branching options for a response.

When you click the Response tab, the following options are available:

■ The Scope checkbox option enables you to set your response to perpetual throughout the piece. You need to know how to work with this option if you want to create more complex interactions or custom menu responses. You will learn more about working with perpetual menu responses in Chapter 8, "Keyboard and Menu Responses."

NOTE You also can use perpetual responses when creating custom paging and navigation controls inside a framework icon. For more information on using the framework icon, see Chapter 11, "Working with Pages."

■ The Active If field enables you to type in a variable expression that turns the response on or off depending on a condition. For instance, typing the variable expression MouseDown into this field activates the response only when the user clicks the mouse; otherwise, it remains inactive. For more information on creating variable expressions, see Chapter 14, "Using Functions and Variables."

- The Erase drop-down list allows you to select how the response feedback icons will erase. This option affects the interaction differently than the erase options available to you in the Interaction Icon Properties dialog box. (You'll see how to use both erase options together in the next section of this chapter.)

- With the Status drop-down list, you can select how Authorware automatically judges the response when setting up data tracking in your piece. The default setting for this option is Not Judged. Changing this option to Wrong Response or Correct Response enables Authorware to keep track internally of the number of user responses marked wrong and right in a piece. Chapter 16, "Tracking the User," talks more about using automatic response tracking in a piece.

- Using the Branch drop-down list, you can select the type of branching you want Authorware to use when the response matches. (You'll see some examples of how to use this option in the next section of this chapter.)

Modifying erasing options

One of the unique features of interaction icons and interaction responses is the way in which you can control the erasing of elements displayed on screen. While you can use an erase icon as part of your response feedback to control erasing of elements on screen, it's usually better to stick with the automatic erasing options of the interaction icon so you don't have to manually select the objects you want erased. The interaction icon controls two types of erasing:

- Erasing of the display elements contained inside the interaction icon. This includes buttons attached to the interaction icon because they appear inside the Presentation window when the interaction icon first displays.

- Erasing of the display elements that you're using as feedback for a response. These are the elements that appear when a user matches a particular response that you've set up.

Knowing how these two erasing options work together can save you a lot of headaches in the future. This section takes a quick look at how to set up each of the options. Be prepared to spend some time working with them to get a better feel for the effects that you can produce when using them.

The erasing option for the interaction display elements is set inside the Interaction Icon Properties dialog box. You may remember this from the previous section, where you learned how to import graphics into the interaction icon and how to set up its display properties.

To access the interaction icon's erase options:

1. Select the interaction icon and choose Icon > Properties from the Modify menu.

The Interaction Icon Properties dialog box appears, as shown in **Figure 7.12**.

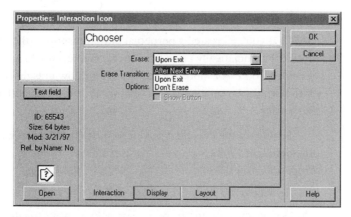

Figure 7.12
Setting up erase options for an interaction icon.

2. Select the Interaction tab at the bottom, and then select an erase option using the Erase drop-down list.

3. If you want to apply a transition effect when erasing the icon's display elements from the screen, click the [...] button next to the Erase Transition option and select an erase transition.

4. When you have finished, click OK to close the dialog box.

When setting erase options in the interaction icon, there are three options available to you:

■ Choosing the After Next Entry option erases any display elements contained in the interaction icon whenever the user matches a response, including buttons that appear on screen. If you use Try Again branching for the response, the interaction

icon display elements appear again when the user exits
the feedback response icon and returns to the start of the
interaction.

■ Choosing the On Exit option only erases the display elements
contained in the interaction icon when the user exits the
interaction. Otherwise, they remain displayed in the Presentation window.

■ Choosing the Don't Erase option prevents the display elements
in the interaction icon from being erased when the user exits
the interaction. This is a useful option—especially when you
need to gradually build display elements on screen during a
series of interactions. However, Authorware still erases all
buttons attached to the interaction when exiting the interaction.

NOTE If you've created a perpetual button response, the button
does not automatically erase from the screen, even when you exit
the interaction. For more information about how erasing is handled
with perpetual interactions, see Chapter 8, "Keyboard and Menu
Responses."

Setting up the erasing behavior for response feedback in an
interaction is a similar process that is handled through the Response
Properties dialog box.

To access the response erasing options:

1. Double-click on the response symbol you want to edit.

The Response Properties dialog box appears.

2. Click the Response tab at the bottom of the dialog box
to display the Response options.

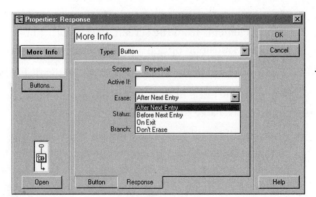

Figure 7.13
*Setting up
erase options
for a response.*

The Response options display, as shown in **Figure 7.13**.

3. Select an erase option from the Erase drop-down list.

4. When you have finished, click OK to close the dialog box.

NOTE You cannot use transition effects when using automatic response feedback erasing.

The options for erasing response feedback in an interaction are similar to the options available for erasing interaction icon display elements. These options are explained in more detail below:

- Choosing Before Next Entry erases the feedback as soon as the user matches the response—unless you've set up a pause using another interaction icon or a wait icon as part of your response feedback.

NOTE If you're using Try Again branching for the response (and you haven't included any type of pause in your response feedback), when you select this erase option, any feedback (including sound) erases automatically as soon as the response matches.

- Choosing After Next Entry erases the feedback after another response matches. This is the default selection.

- Choosing On Exit erases the feedback as soon as the user leaves the interaction.

- Choosing Don't Erase prevents the feedback from erasing, even after the user leaves the interaction.

If you're working with display elements that erase at the wrong time and you cannot correct the problem using the automatic erasing options, use the Prevent Automatic Erase option with these icons (provided you're working with a display or movie icon). However, the Prevent Automatic Erase option can cause you problems down the road (as mentioned in Chapter 3). You usually begin to run into performance speed issues as elements start piling up on screen.

TIP If you use a sound icon as response feedback and it stops immediately when the response matches, chances are that you have your response erase option set to Before Next Entry, which cuts off the sound quickly. Changing the erase option to Don't Erase prevents the sound from cutting off prematurely.

When setting up a response, think about the type of branching you want to use with each response you create. Response branching completes the interaction "loop" that is created when all four elements of an interaction (interaction icon, response, response feedback, and response branching) are in place on the flowline.

If an interaction is like a "fork in the road," then branching is the route you take after you've made your decision about which way to go. You can quickly see which type of branching option you've selected for each response by taking a quick glance at the flowline, as shown in **Figure 7.14**.

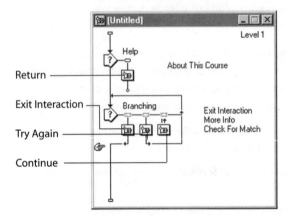

Figure 7.14
The four types of interaction branching appear differently in the flowline.

Like erasing options, you set response branching options in the Response tab options area of the Response Properties dialog box. You have four different branching options from which to choose:

■ Try Again branching for a response returns the user to the same interaction, starting the interaction loop again after the response feedback displays.

■ Continue branching for a response works like a continuous check point. If the response matches, the feedback attached to the response displays. Authorware then continues looking for other possible matches from the list of other responses attached to the interaction icon.

■ Exit Interaction branching for a response displays the response feedback first, and then exits the interaction and continues down the flowline.

■ Return branching for a response returns the user to the same point in the piece where he or she was before matching the response. Return branching is in the "special case" category because you can only use it with perpetual interactions. Chapter 8, "Keyboard and Menu Responses," describes how to use this type of branching.

The branching options, along with the erasing options, are generally the most difficult aspects of working with interactions. As you learn more about different types of interactions in the chapters ahead, you will begin to feel more comfortable with using these options to control your interactions. After you learn how to work with these options, you can create more difficult types of interactions that use a variety of response types.

However, buttons are still the easiest type of response to work with in most cases, and this makes them the most commonly used interface element in most pieces. Using the options available in Authorware's Button Library, you can easily create the customized look and feel that you want in your piece.

Using the Button Library

You can use Authorware's Button Library to create a custom button that is available whenever you want to use a button in an interaction. A button is also the simplest and most straightforward way to display a control that the user can either select or deselect, such as a radio button or a checkbox.

When you begin using buttons, you may want to work with the standard system buttons included with Authorware. You can quickly take a look at these by opening the Button Library window and scrolling through the list of buttons included with Authorware.

To open the Button Library window:

1. Choose Buttons… from the Window menu.

The Button Library window appears, as shown in **Figure 7.15**.

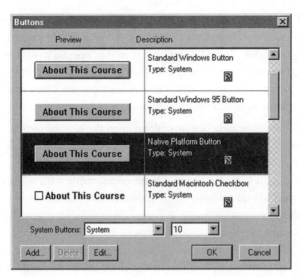

Figure 7.15
*The Button
Library window.*

NOTE You also see the default framework paging control buttons when you open the Button Library window. Authorware saves them as part of the default framework model, and adds them to the framework icon when you create a new framework. For more information on using frameworks, see Chapter 11, "Working with Pages."

If you have the window open, take a look at the buttons included. These include Macintosh, Windows 3.1, and Windows 95-style system buttons, as well as standard radio buttons and checkboxes for each platform. **Figure 7.16** shows you the difference in appearance between these types of system buttons when including them in your piece.

Macintosh system button set ——————

Windows 3.1 system button set ——————

Windows 95 system button set ——————

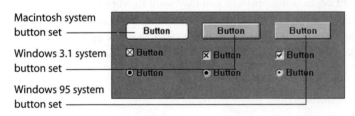

Figure 7.16
System buttons for each specific platform.

If you plan to include system buttons in a piece to be delivered on both the Macintosh and Windows platforms, make sure that the correct type of system buttons are displayed on each platform by choosing one of the system buttons labeled Native Platform from the Button Library. Authorware automatically selects the correct type of button to display for each platform.

Using the System Buttons font and size selection options in the Button Library window, you can change the appearance of the label used with all system buttons in your piece.

To modify the system button font:

1. Open the Button Library window.

2. Select a new font from the System Buttons font drop-down list.

3. Select a new size from the System Buttons size drop-down list.

Authorware modifies all system buttons in the Button Library window to reflect the changes you have made. These changes also apply to any Wait buttons you've included in the flowline.

TIP You can edit system buttons the same way that you edit custom buttons. However, Authorware creates a copy of the button before you can modify it. (See "Creating a custom button," below for information on how to modify a button in the Button Library.)

While you probably will not include system-style buttons in every piece you create, they are extremely helpful when developing a piece that models real-world software. However, most designers try to choose a button style that fits with the rest of the piece, which means creating a custom button.

Creating a custom button

If you don't want to use one of the standard system buttons in your piece, create your own custom button using graphics and sounds that you import into the Button Library.

To add a custom button to your piece:

1. Choose Buttons… from the Window menu to open the Button Library window, if you do not already have it open.

The Button Library window appears.

2. Click Add.

The Button Editor dialog box appears, as shown in **Figure 7.17**.

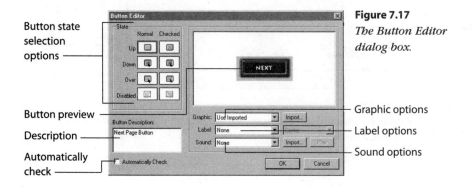

Button state selection options

Button preview

Description

Automatically check

Graphic options

Label options

Sound options

Figure 7.17
The Button Editor dialog box.

Take a look at the buttons in the State area of the Button Editor dialog box. Use these to select the state you want to create or modify. Two groups are listed: Normal and Checked. Each group has four states: Up, Down, Over, and Disabled.

3. Choose a state to edit by clicking a button in the State area.

The four normal states are standard for every button you create:

■ Use the Up state when the custom button is enabled.

■ Use the Down state when the cursor is over the button and the user presses the mouse button.

■ Use the Over state when the cursor is over the button, but the user hasn't pressed the mouse button.

■ Use the Inactive state when the button is disabled or dimmed.

In addition, you can add checked states for each of the four states, which you can use to create more complex button interactions. Use checked states when you want to indicate that a button has been previously selected or deselected.

A common way to do this is to create answer buttons on a multiple choice exam that allows users to return to previously answered questions, and select or deselect current answer choices. An example of this is shown in **Figure 7.18**.

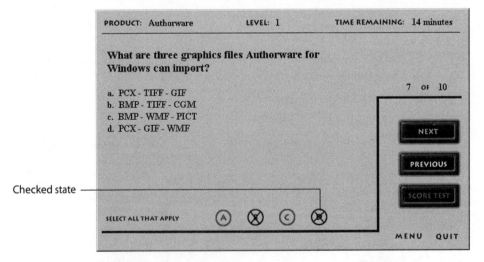

Figure 7.18
Checked states are a convenient way to create a button that the user can select or deselect.

To see an example of using checked button states, open the file named CHECKED.A4P. It's included in the Chapter 7 examples folder on the CD accompanying this book.

NOTE When you select the Automatically Check checkbox option in the Button Editor dialog box for the state you're editing, Authorware uses the checked state rather than the normal state when the button displays in the Presentation window. You should leave this option checked if you plan to assign separate graphics to the checked states of your button

When editing a button, you can see a preview of the button in the preview area of the Button Editor dialog box. As you import new graphics for each state, you can switch between the state selection buttons to see if your graphics align properly. You must edit each button state independently. To do this, use the options in the Graphic, Sound, and Label areas of the Button Editor dialog box.

TIP It's important when creating states for your buttons that you keep the pixel dimensions of the buttons exactly the same. Otherwise, you see a shift in the screen position of each button state when it displays in the Presentation window.

Adding graphics and sounds

The Graphic and Sound areas consist of an Import button that allows you to select a graphic or sound to import for the current state you're editing, and a drop-down list that enables you to modify or delete the current button state setting.

To import a graphic for the state you're editing:

1. Select the button state.

2. Click the graphic Import button.

   The Import dialog box appears.

3. Select the graphic file you want to import and click Import to add the element to the button state.

After you add the graphic, it appears in the preview area of the Button Editor dialog box, and the Graphic setting changes from None to Use Imported. Use this graphic for each button state; you can repeat this same procedure to add a different graphic for the states you want to customize.

Adding sounds to a button state is a similar process. You simply select the state you want to add the sound to, and then click the sound Import button. The Import dialog box appears. Select the sound file you want to import and click Import to add the sound to the button state. After you add the sound, the Play button becomes active so you can preview the sound. In addition, the Sound setting for the state changes from None to Use Imported.

NOTE Although you can assign separate sounds to each button state, you probably will import a sound for only the down state (when the mouse is clicked) because sounds take up a great deal of storage space.

At any time, you can delete a graphic or sound that you've imported using the following steps:

1. Select the state you want to edit.

2. Change the Graphic or Sound setting from Use Imported to None.

   A confirmation dialog box appears and asks you whether or not you want to delete the imported graphic or sound.

3. Click Yes to delete the graphic or sound.

Because Authorware stores custom buttons inside your piece, you cannot link to external files when importing graphics or sounds into a custom button. Because of this, custom buttons can considerably add to your total file size. Try to keep your sound and graphics files as small as possible when using them in a custom button state—especially if you plan to distribute your piece over a network using Shockwave.

In addition, keep the following information in mind when you start working with custom buttons:

- Authorware imports button graphics into the Button Library at the color depth at which you currently have your monitor set. If you save your button states in 8-bit, reset your display to 256-color before importing the graphics into Authorware. Otherwise, they resample to the current color depth.

- If you don't import a graphic for a particular state, Authorware automatically uses the graphic you imported for the normal state. You must, however, import a graphic for the Up state in order for the button to appear correctly in the Presentation window.

■ Test your piece out carefully if you are using sounds in a custom button. If you click a button with a sound attached to it while a sound icon plays, the sound icon stops to allow the button sound to play.

How can I manage file size when using custom buttons?

One of the best ways to manage your file-size limitations while using custom buttons with Shockwave pieces is to create a button with a single imported graphic for the Up state, and then use a button label that changes for each of the other states.

When creating a button, you can use a text label by turning on the Show Label option for the selected state. Authorware displays Text labels inside the preview window of the Button Editor dialog box, as shown in **Figure 7.19**, so you can see how they will appear when the piece runs.

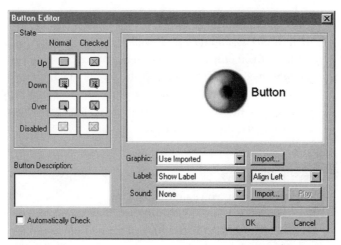

Figure 7.19
Previewing a custom button with the Show Label option turned on.

You can control the positioning of the label by either selecting a new setting from the Alignment drop-down list next to the Show Label option, or by clicking on the text label inside the preview window of the Button Editor dialog box and dragging it to a new location.

Because a text label is simply a text field attached to a button state, you can use the options in the Text menu to change the font, size, or style of the text. If you want to quickly create multiple states for your button that are easily visible, use the Colors Inspector to apply a different color to the label.

To do this:

1. Select the state you want to edit, and make sure that you have turned on the Show Label option.

2. Click on the text label inside the preview window of the Button Editor dialog box.

3. Choose Inspectors > Colors from the Window menu.

   The Colors Inspector appears.

4. Select a color to apply to the label state and click OK to close the Colors Inspector window.

   The label state now appears with a new color inside the preview window.

   If you decide to use a label for a button, Authorware shows the title you give to the button response. The label also appears in the title field of the button's Response Properties dialog box. If you want to change the label, you need to change the title of the response or the text in the title field.

Custom buttons provide the type of interactivity that you find in most pieces, and they do it well. However, limitations are quickly reached if you only use buttons in a piece because they limit you to a single small rectangular area of the screen in which the user must click. When you need to open the screen to additional types of clicking, use hot spots and hot objects, which are discussed in the next two sections of this chapter.

Setting Up a Hot Spot Response

Using a hot spot, you can make any rectangular area in the Presentation window clickable to trigger a sound, video clip, or graphic. Hot spots are ideal for making part of a custom background graphic interactive, and also for setting up catch-all feedback areas. A catch-all area—usually a hot spot set up to accommodate the entire Presentation window—lets you respond to users when they click near (but not on) the buttons or hot spots you've set up.

Using the hot spot response type, you can make any rectangular area on screen a hot spot. The benefit to using a hot spot is that the clickable area doesn't have to be a discrete graphic or button. This means that you can turn any image that's part of a background into a clickable area without worrying about importing additional graphics into your piece, or making sure that the region around the graphic is composed entirely of white pixels to mask out the edges.

To create a simple hot spot:

1. Set up an interaction icon if you haven't already done so.

2. Drag a display icon to the right of the interaction icon.

As soon as you release the icon, the Response Type dialog box appears automatically.

3. Select Hot Spot and click OK.

The response type symbol on the interaction flowline changes to the hot spot symbol.

4. Give the response a name.

To position the hot spot on the screen and change its size, you need to edit the hot spot response:

1. Double-click on the hot spot response symbol.

The Response Properties dialog box appears on top of the Presentation window, as shown in **Figure 7.20**. Move the Response Properties dialog box to the side so you can see the hot spot, which appears as a dotted rectangular area in the Presentation window.

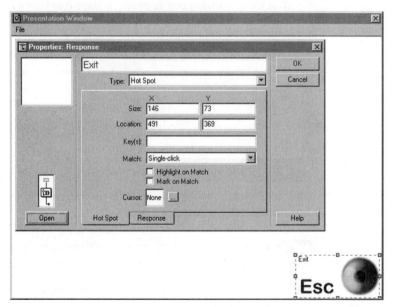

Figure 7.20
The hot spot Response Properties dialog box.

The hot spot Response Properties dialog box has two unique options: the Highlight on Match checkbox and the Mark on Match checkbox. Use these options to provide additional visual onscreen feedback to the user:

■ When you select Highlight on Match, the hot spot inverts the background when the user clicks it. This can be effective visually, but sometimes plays havoc with carefully designed backgrounds, so use it with caution.

■ When you select Mark on Match, a small checkbox in the upper right-hand corner of the hot spot appears. When the user clicks the hot spot response, the box is checked. While this may be useful in certain cases, it's not used frequently because it rarely fits with design schemes. Nevertheless, if you want a quick way to mark a matched question response, you can use this option.

Now, back to creating the hot spot:

2. Set the Match option to Single-click.

3. Click the Cursor button.

The Cursors dialog box appears, as shown in **Figure 7.21**.

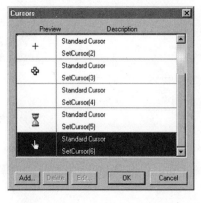

Figure 7.21
Use the Cursors dialog box to select a custom cursor.

NOTE To get rid of a custom cursor you're using with a response, select the cursor labeled None in the Cursors dialog box.

4. Select the pointing hand cursor, and then click OK to close the Cursors dialog box.

5. Click the Open button in the Response Properties dialog box to open the display icon and create a small test graphic in the empty display icon. When you have finished, close the display icon.

6. Run the piece to see what happens.

Because there isn't a background, it will be hard to locate the hot spot. However, because you selected a custom cursor, you can move the mouse around to find the hot spot. When you find it, click on the hot spot to display the graphic.

Now that you've created the hot spot, it's easy to adjust its size and location directly in the Presentation window, as follows:

1. Pause the piece if it is running, or restart the piece and then pause it.

The hot spot appears in the Presentation window.

2. Select the hot spot by clicking on it.

Selection handles appear, to enable you to resize the hot spot and reposition it.

3. Change the size and location of the hot spot. When you have finished, restart the piece to see the results.

TIP To more accurately reposition a hot spot, button, or a hot object, use the arrow keys on the keyboard. They move the object one pixel in the direction you've selected.

A trick you can use with hot spots is to create the same type of Over state you saw when using custom buttons. (Actually, you can use this trick with hot objects as well.) Using the Cursor in Area response option for the hot spot (for hot objects, this is Cursor on Object), you can display a graphic on screen when the cursor moves over the hot spot area. This is commonly referred to as a "rollover."

Cursor in Area rollovers are especially useful in situations where you need to show some type of onscreen cue, but don't want to create a custom button. For instance, you might want to simulate Windows- or Macintosh-style help balloons that don't appear on top of the button. Using two responses—a button response for your toolbar button and a hot spot response for your help balloon—you can build software simulations that look like the real thing.

To create a hot spot rollover:

1. Take the hot spot interaction you've just created and double-click on the response symbol.

The Response Properties dialog box appears.

2. Select Cursor in Area from the Match drop-down list.

TIP One of the trickier aspects of this type of response is deciding when to erase your feedback. My personal preference is to mimic most mouse rollovers by setting the feedback erase option to erase Before Next Entry. This displays the graphic when the mouse is over the hot spot, and erases it as soon as the mouse leaves the region.

3. Switch to the Response options by clicking on the tab.

4. Choose Before Next Entry from the Erase drop-down list.

5. Click OK to close the Response Properties dialog box.

6. Run the piece to see the results.

If you set up everything correctly, your graphic now displays whenever the cursor enters the hot spot area, and erases as soon as the cursor moves out of the hot spot area.

TIP To improve performance of Cursor in Area rollovers, you can do two things: set the display icon you're using as response feedback to a higher layer, and position all Cursor in Area responses to the left of any other responses attached to the interaction icon.

Hot spots provide hidden benefits. For one, you can use them to track mouse activity inside the entire Presentation window. Second, they come in handy when you need to keep file size smaller. Additionally, you can use graphic elements built into your backgrounds to draw users into active regions that don't take up additional storage space as custom buttons do.

However, at times you may need to either create irregularly shaped (read: non-rectangular) regions that the user can click, or you may want the user to be able to click on a moving object. To accommodate these types of situations, you can set up a hot object response.

Setting Up a Hot Object Response

Generally, you use hot objects less often in a piece than buttons or hot spots. This is because you must place the target object in a separate display or movie icon. The benefit to using hot objects, however, is that you can create regions of interactivity in your piece that aren't rectangular. They are also useful if an object moves around the screen and you want the object to remain interactive—no matter where it's located.

The most important rule to remember when setting up a hot object is to make sure that the object is in a separate display icon.

Authorware actually makes the contents of the entire display icon hot. So if there are several objects in the same display icon, they all become hot and react the same way. (You don't have this problem with a movie icon because it can contain only one object at a time.)

Although somewhat more difficult to set up, hot objects can get you out of a sticky jam in a hurry. Take a map of the United States, for example. You might want to set up each state as a different clickable region so that you can display facts about each state or jump to a blow-up image of the state map. However, as you're working, you soon realize that all of the states in the Northeast have irregularly shaped borders that are impossible to conform to the hot-spot standard rectangle. A hot spot simply doesn't give you the kind of interactivity you need.

 To see an example of how you can use hot objects in this situation, take a look at the file called MAP.A4P. It's located in the Chapter 7 examples folder on the CD accompanying this book.

However, you can use the polygon tool to create a solid outline of any object that you've included in a separate display icon. This becomes your clickable object, which you can use in a hot object response.

To create the polygon region:

1. Drag a new display icon to the flowline and open it.

The Presentation window and toolbox appear.

2. Select the polygon tool from the toolbox.

3. Click once inside the Presentation window to create the first point of your polygon. Continuing clicking to create a multi-sided polygon that matches the size and shape of the object you're outlining. When you reach the first point, double-click to close the polygon. You should end up with something like the shape shown in **Figure 7.22**.

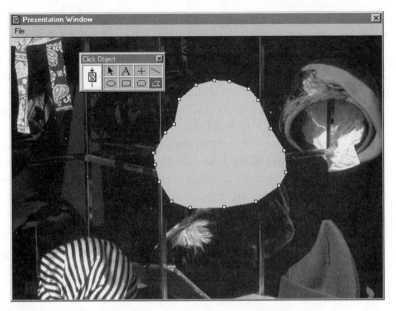

Figure 7.22
Creating the polygon outline of the background object.

Although you want the hot object active when the cursor is over the region you have outlined, you probably don't want it to appear in the Presentation window. In a situation like this, you need to modify the fill and mode options:

1. With the polygon selected in the Presentation window, open the Fill Inspector and click on the solid white fill selection, as shown in **Figure 7.23**.

   The polygon region you've created now appears solid white in the window.

   TIP If you can't see your object inside the Presentation window, you may want to change the background color of the piece, using the options in the File Properties dialog box.

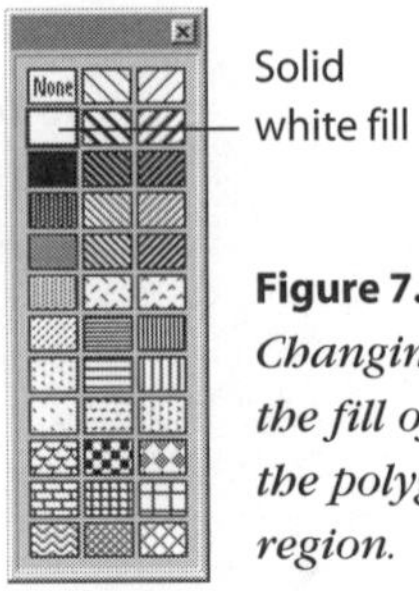

2. After the object is solid white, open the Modes Inspector and change the mode from Opaque to Transparent.

   The polygon region you've created now appears transparent, allowing the background image you've outlined to show through.

Solid
white fill

Figure 7.23
Changing the fill of the polygon region.

You can still see the outline of the object, however.

3. Open the Lines Inspector and select the "dotted line" option at the top of the Lines Inspector window. This removes the outline from the object.

After you've created the hot object, you need to set up the hot object interaction so the user can click the region, as follows:

1. Drag an interaction icon to the flowline, place it below the display icon that contains your polygon, and give the interaction icon a name.

2. Drag a new display icon to the right of the interaction icon and release it.

The Response Options dialog box appears.

3. Choose Hot Object, and then click OK.

The response type symbol on the interaction flowline changes to the hot object symbol.

4. Give the response a name, and then double-click on the hot object response symbol.

The Response Properties dialog box appears with the options for the hot object response, as shown in **Figure 7.24**.

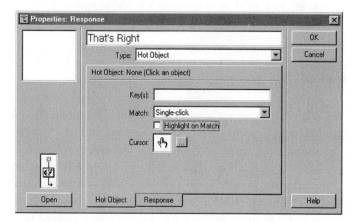

Figure 7.24
The hot object options as they appear inside the Response Properties dialog box.

At the top of the dialog box, you should see "None (Click an object)" next to the Hot Object field. You need to define the object to use for the hot object response and set up any additional options you want for the response:

1. Click the area where the transparent polygon is located.

   The name of the display icon that contains the polygon is now listed as the target object at the top of the Response Properties dialog box.

2. Select the hand cursor for your custom cursor.

3. Click the Open button and add some content to the display icon you've attached to the response.

4. When you have finished, run the piece and test your hot object.

You now can click anywhere on the hot object to make your feedback appear. Take a look at how the cursor changes from an arrow to a hand when the cursor moves off the region you defined as a hot object. You can use this technique in many situations to provide interactivity to areas of the screen that a custom button or a rectangular hot spot cannot access.

NOTE While there isn't enough time to cover using movable objects as hot objects, the technique for defining them as a hot object is the same. You will learn more about working with movable objects in Chapter 9, "Using Movable Objects."

Looking Ahead...

In this chapter, you learned the basic techniques for building interactions using custom buttons, hot spots, and hot objects—only three of the ways in which you can add elements of interactivity to the screen. Buttons, hot spots, and hot objects are, however, the most common types of interaction responses, so you are now ready to start designing pieces that provide some direct hands-on contact for the user.

The next chapter continues to look at adding interactivity to your piece by focusing on the ways in which you can use keyboard and menu responses to create more sophisticated types of interactions for the user.

Chapter 8

Keyboard and Menu Responses

When you begin developing sophisticated training applications with Authorware, you probably will want to add functionality that emulates real-world software. The primary components of most real-world software are the keyboard entry and menu systems that applications use. Most software relies on combinations of these two elements to perform different tasks. Even game titles tend to rely on some type of keyboard input from the user—especially if it's a simulation or role-playing environment.

To create these types of interactions, you can use Authorware's built-in text handling and menu responses. They are assigned to an interaction in the same way that you created buttons, hot spots, and hot objects. However, because these types of responses are not mouse-driven, you should spend some time determining the best method to integrate them into your pieces. This chapter covers the basic ways you can create keyboard and menu responses in Authorware.

Setting up a response to look for a single keypress is useful in a piece. Take the Spacebar for example. You might want to use interactions that require the user to hit the Spacebar to continue through a series of screens that explain a procedure. At times, this type of interaction response is the easiest way for a user to interact with your content. This would not be possible if you simply used the wait icon to pause presentation until the user clicks any key. At other times, you may want to use the keypress response in more complicated ways—to simulate a piece of software, or to create a custom password field that echoes an asterisk rather than the letter the user types.

You can set up a keypress response type symbol to react to a single key, or to a key combination such as Ctrl+A or Command+P. You also can set up a single keypress response to react to several different keys or key combinations—although it can react to only one key or key combination at a time. And you can set up a keypress response to respond to a "wildcard"— meaning that it matches regardless of which key the user presses. In this case, the keypress really is behaving like the wait icon. However, because you're using an interaction response, you can have other responses such as buttons, hot spots, or time limits active at the same time to match other types of conditions in the piece.

NOTE A common mistake new authors make is to use the keypress in combination with a button to create an optional key for a button. This isn't necessary because all other types of mouse responses (including menu responses) have their own Optional Key(s) field in the Response Properties dialog box.

To create a simple keypress response:

1. Drag a new interaction icon to the flowline and name it.

2. Drag a calculation icon to the right of the interaction icon.

   When you release the calculation icon, the Response Type dialog box appears.

3. Select Keypress and click OK.

   The response type symbol on the flowline changes to the keypress symbol, as shown in **Figure 8.1**.

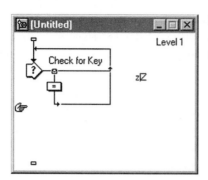

Figure 8.1
The Keypress response, as it appears in the flowline.

When you use a keypress response, you don't have to name the response feedback icon attached to the response (as you do when you create buttons, hot spots, or hot objects). Authorware automatically does this for you when you assign the key for the keypress response.

To assign the key or keys that you want to use with the keypress response you're creating:

1. Double-click on the keypress response symbol.

The Response Properties dialog box appears, as shown in **Figure 8.2**.

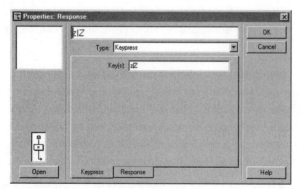

Figure 8.2
The Response Properties dialog box.

2. In the Key(s) field, type: **z|Z**.

After entering the key names, they will appear in the flowline as the title of the response feedback icon. If you want to edit the Key(s) field for a keypress response, change the title of the response in the flowline.

Because keypress responses are case-sensitive, the value you enter in the Key(s) field needs to contain both a lowercase and uppercase character if you want to anticipate the fact that some users may have their Caps Lock key active. You should separate any key names you type in by the logical "or" (|) character—sometimes referred to as the "pipe" character. (It's located above the backslash character (\) on all QWERTY keyboards.)

To test that the keypress response matches, add some simple audio feedback using Authorware's `Beep` system function. To do this, you modify the calculation icon attached to the keypress response you just created:

1. Click the Open in the Response Properties dialog box to open the response feedback icon attached to the response.

The Response Properties dialog box closes, and the calculation icon window appears.

2. To add the `Beep` function to the calculation icon, type in: **Beep()**.

NOTE Make sure that you include the set of parentheses after the name of the function, otherwise Authorware prompts you to create a new custom variable. You will learn more about working with the calculation icon window in Chapter 14, "Using Functions and Variables."

3. When you have finished typing in the function, press the Enter key on the numeric keypad to close the calculation window.

4. Run the piece to test it.

Now that you've created the interaction, you hear a system beep when you type **z** or **Z** on the keyboard. Using the `Beep` system function in a calculation script is a quick and simple way to test your response without creating additional response feedback. Of course, you always can go back and modify this later, replacing the calculation icon with a display, sound, or movie icon.

NOTE Authorware deletes an interaction response if you delete the response feedback icon attached to it. If you want to modify a response feedback icon, first select it, and then choose Group from the Modify menu. This places the response feedback icon into a map icon that you can edit without deleting its associated response.

Any time you create a keypress response, you need to consider all the possible combinations that you might want to match. If different keys need different types of feedback, use several keypress responses in the same interaction. Otherwise, you can specify as many valid key names as you want for each keypress, as long as they're separated by the (|) character. (For a list of valid key names that Authorware accepts, see "Checking for key combinations," later in this chapter.)

Checking for any key pressed

If you are setting up a keypress response to match any key typed, simply use a single question mark (?). The question mark character is also referred to as a single-character "wildcard." When you use this character in a keypress response, Authorware accepts any key pressed as a valid match.

Make sure that when you use this character in a keypress response, you place the response to the right of any other keypress responses that you've assigned specific keys, as shown in **Figure 8.3**. As mentioned in the last chapter, Authorware works from left to right when matching a response in an interaction. By positioning the wildcard response at the far right of the interaction, you force Authorware to check the key the user presses against all other keypress responses in the interaction.

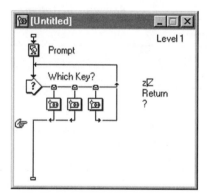

Figure 8.3
Place the wildcard response to the right of any other keypress responses in an interaction.

Using the question mark character in a keypress response introduces a problem, however. If Authorware uses this wildcard character to recognize any key pressed as valid, how do you create a keypress response that tests for the question mark character itself?

To do so you need to use the backslash character (\) in front of the question mark. The backslash character indicates that the character it precedes should be interpreted literally by Authorware—in other words, Authorware disregards its "special character" status and views it as a normal question mark.

TIP You also can use the question mark (?) character in text entry responses to set up a single-character wildcard for a word or phrase you want to match. (This is covered below in the section, "Setting Up Text Entry Responses.")

Checking for key combinations

When setting up a keypress response to check for a key combination (e.g., Ctrl+Q on the Windows side, or Command+Q on the Macintosh side), you need to first type the name of the modifier key and then type in the letter of the other key in the combination.

For example, say that you are creating a tutorial piece, and you want to simulate selecting all files in a directory. You can type in either **Ctrla** or **CtrlA** in the Key(s) field of the Response Properties dialog box. Keyboard combinations are case *insensitive*, so either value is correct. Authorware allows you to use multiple modifiers with a key, so you can also type in values like **CtrlAltF** and **CmdOptC** in the Key(s) field. The table below lists specifically how Authorware recognizes the names of the modifier keys.

Modifier key...	Platform...	Keyname in Authorware...
Alt key	Windows	Alt
Command (Apple) key	Macintosh	Cmd
Ctrl key	Windows	Ctrl, Cmd, Control
Ctrl key	Macintosh	Ctrl
Option key	Macintosh	Opt
Shift	Both	Shift

In some cases, you don't need to specify the modifier key, only the character the key combination creates. This is true when using a Shift-[letter] or Option-[letter] combination. If you are unsure which combination to use to ensure Authorware recognizes it, you can refer to the Key system variable to see how Authorware recognizes the combination you want to use.

To do this:

1. Type in a key combination you want to use.

2. Open the Variables window by choosing Variables from the Window menu or by clicking the Variables Window button on the toolbar.

Shortcut: To open the Variables window, press Ctrl+Shift+V (Windows), or Command+Shift+V (Macintosh).

The Variables window appears.

3. Scroll through the list of General variables in the window until you find the one named Key. When you find it, click it.

The current value of Key displays in the Current Value field. Check this against the key value you type in the Key(s) field of the keypress response to make sure that you're checking for the correct value in your interaction.

NOTE Because Key is a character variable, its current value appears inside quotation marks when you look at it in the Variables window. You don't need to enclose this key value in quotation marks when you assign it to the keypress response.

At times you may want to create an interaction where the keypress response is perpetual. For example, you may want to give the user the ability to exit the course at any time if the Escape key is pressed. Although you can't make a keypress response perpetual, you can get around this issue by entering a key value in the Optional Key(s) field of the button, hot spot, or pull-down menu Response Properties dialog box, as shown in **Figure 8.4**. Use the same key value in this field that you would use creating a keypress response.

Insert the Optional key value here. ————

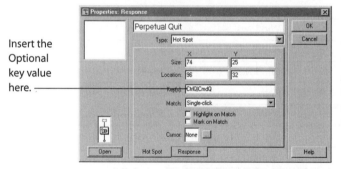

Figure 8.4

You can assign a key value to a perpetual button, hot spot, or pull-down menu interaction response by entering it in the Key(s) field.

You can use an optional key for any response that accepts it, and the response does not necessarily have to be perpetual to use it. However, in special cases where you want the keypress active—but you do not want to display a button or a pull-down menu—you can include an optional key value for a perpetual hot spot response and then position the hot spot so it is not visible inside the Presentation window by dragging it to the side of the screen. This allows you, in effect, to set up a perpetual keypress response that is always active in the background while your piece runs.

Other valid keypress entries

You also can set up special keys such as Escape, Delete, Home, and Backspace as valid keypress values. Like the modifier keys, you need to type these keys a specific way so Authorware can recognize them. The following table lists the special keys that Authorware recognizes.

Special key...	*Platform...*	*Keyname in Authorware...*
Backspace key	Windows	Backspace
Break key	Windows	Break
Clear key	Macintosh	Clear
Delete key	Windows	Delete
Delete key	Macintosh	Backspace
Down Arrow key	Both	DownArrow
End key	Both	End
Enter key	Windows	Return
Enter key (on numeric keypad)	Windows	Enter
Enter key	Macintosh	Enter
Esc key	Both	Esc
F1, F2, ... F15 key	Both	F1, F2, ... F15
Help key	Windows	Help
Home key	Both	Home
Insert or Ins key	Windows	Insert
Left Arrow key	Both	LeftArrow
Page Down key	Both	PageDown
Page Up key	Both	PageUp
Pause key	Windows	Pause
Return key	Macintosh	Return
Right Arrow key	Both	RightArrow
Shift key	Both	Shift
Tab key	Both	Tab
Up Arrow key	Both	UpArrow

TIP To specify the Spacebar as a key value, type a single space in the Key(s) field.

If you're developing a cross-platform piece and you include a platform-specific key name in the keypress response, Authorware recognizes the key on the host platform and ignores it on the other platform during authoring and playback.

For the most part, this only applies to responses that check for a special key name or key combination. Remember to include both platform-specific modifier key names in the Key(s) field of the keypress response if you plan to deliver your piece on both platforms.

NOTE The same theory applies to responses in which you've assigned an Optional Key(s) value.

While the keypress is easy to set up, it doesn't give you as much control as the text entry response—especially if you want to check for keyboard input from the user. The next section looks at how you can create interactions that require the user to type in a complete word or set of words using the text entry response.

Setting Up Text Entry Responses

Authorware's capability to handle multiple types of text entry make it a useful tool when designing any type of interactive application that requires the user to type in a word or a phrase to receive appropriate feedback. However, what if you want to create an online catalog? Here, the text entry tool becomes a powerful way to handle form-related orders or subscriptions. Although you can accomplish this with an HTML page, you wouldn't have access to Authorware's set of custom multimedia features that give the user additional information.

While the text entry response is more difficult to set up than the keypress response, Authorware and its set of system variables handles most of the programming aspects of text entry behind the scenes.

Most programming tools require that you write a long set of instructions to tell the program how to parse (read in and evaluate) each line of text the user enters. However, with Authorware, most of the text handling properties are checkbox items that you simply turn on or off. Coupled with Authorware's capability to judge interaction responses automatically, the text entry response can be a powerful tool in training pieces that you create.

To get a better feel for the basic text entry response options, go ahead and set up a new text entry field using the following steps:

1. After creating a new file, drag an interaction icon to the flowline and name it.

2. Drag an icon to the right of the interaction icon. (If you're unsure what type of feedback you want to give, use a map icon and fill in the contents later.)

   The Response Type dialog box appears.

3. Select Text Entry and click OK.

   The response type symbol on the interaction flowline changes to the text entry symbol, as shown in **Figure 8.5**.

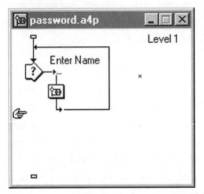

Figure 8.5
A text entry interaction, as it appears on the flowline.

4. For this example, make sure that you have the branching option for this response set to Try Again. If it isn't, you can quickly change this by double-clicking on the response and changing the Branching option inside the Response tab options to Try Again.

Shortcut: To cycle through the branching options of an interaction response, click once below the response feedback icon attached to the response while pressing the Ctrl key (Windows), or Command key (Macintosh).

The next few sections describe the different options available for this type of response.

Moving and resizing the text entry field

You can move and resize the text entry field without opening the response type by editing in the Presentation window. When moving or resizing a field in the Presentation window, you don't have full control over the text entry field properties. However, you usually can make location and size changes while running the piece, and then go back later and customize the field's appearance.

To adjust the size and position of the text-entry field you just created:

1. Place the start flag above the interaction you just created.

2. Run the piece from the flag by choosing Restart From Flag from the Control menu, or by clicking the Restart From Flag button on the toolbar.

Shortcut: To restart a piece from the flag, press Ctrl+Alt+R (Windows), or Command+Option+R (Macintosh).

The text entry field appears in the Presentation window, next to the text entry marker, as shown in **Figure 8.6**.

Figure 8.6

The text entry field and text entry marker display in the Presentation window.

3. Choose Pause from the Control menu to pause the piece.

Shortcut: To pause a piece, press Ctrl+P (Windows), or Command+P (Macintosh) while the piece runs.

When the piece pauses, the text entry field appears in the Presentation window as a dotted outline.

4. Select the text entry field by clicking on the center of it.

Selection handles appear around the field, as shown in **Figure 8.7**.

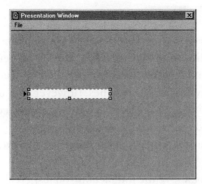

Figure 8.7
Selection handles allow you to resize the text entry field.

5. To resize the field, click on one of the selection handles and drag it.

The text entry field is resized in the Presentation window.

NOTE Resizing the field limits or expands the number of characters a user can type. As soon as the user reaches the bottom of the field, no more characters may be entered.

6. To reposition the text entry field, click on the its center and drag it to a new location inside the Presentation window.

TIP You can use the arrow keys to move the field one pixel at a time.

After you have resized and repositioned the field, you may want to make other changes to the field to customize its appearance. For instance, you might want the text or background of the field to be a different color to fit in with the style of a graphic. The next section looks at the built-in text field customizing options available.

Customizing the appearance of the text entry field

Unlike the keypress response, the text entry response displays what the user types in the Presentation window. Each interaction icon contains a separate text entry field that you can modify using the Interaction Icon Properties dialog box. This dialog box gives you additional control over the look and behavior of the text field you've created.

To edit the options available for customizing the appearance of a text entry field:

1. Select the interaction icon and open its Properties dialog box by double-clicking on it while pressing the Ctrl key (Windows), or Command key (Macintosh).

The Interaction Icon Properties dialog box appears.

2. Click the Text Field button in the upper right-hand corner of the dialog box.

The Text Field Properties dialog box appears, as shown in **Figure 8.8**. This dialog box contains the options you can use to customize the way your text entry field appears in the Presentation window. (In a moment you'll learn more about these options.)

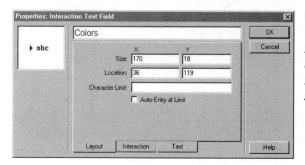

Figure 8.8
The Text Field Properties dialog box with the Layout tab selected.

3. With the Layout tab selected, go ahead and modify the size or font you're using by changing the Font or Size option settings. When you have finished, click OK to close the Text Field Properties dialog box.

4. Click OK to close the Interaction Icon Properties dialog box.

The Text Field Properties dialog box has three sets of options tabs available: Layout, Interaction, and Text. You use these tabs to customize the look and feel of the text entry field as it displays in the Presentation window. When the Text Field Properties dialog box first opens, you can see the Layout tab options, which control such things as size, location, and the number of characters that the user can type into the field.

You can modify the Layout options in the following ways:

- You can change the size and location of the text entry field by typing in new X and Y values for the Size and Location fields. After you make these changes, the text entry field's position and size update in the Presentation window.

- Typing in a value for the Character Limit field sets a limit on the number of characters the user can type into the field. You can enter either an integer value (1, 2, 3...) or a variable expression in this field to determine the character limit. If the field is empty, Authorware uses the size of the field to determine the limit.

- Selecting the Auto-Entry at Limit checkbox option sets the field to automatically accept an entry as soon as the user reaches the character limit specified in the Character Limit field.

Clicking the Interaction tab brings up the options shown in **Figure 8.9**. These options modify how the interaction processes user input. You can modify these options in the following ways:

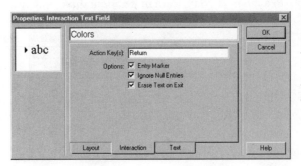

Figure 8.9
The Text Entry Properties dialog box with the Interaction tab selected.

- Typing a key name in the Action Key(s) field sets the key that the user must press for Authorware to accept the user's entry. If you want to use more than one valid key (for example, Enter or Tab), enter all the key values in this field, separated by the (|) character, as you did with a keypress response.

- Selecting the Entry Marker checkbox option displays the entry text marker in the Presentation window (see **Figure 8.6** above). Authorware selects this option for you by default.

- Selecting the Ignore Null Tries checkbox option requires the user to type in a character before Authorware attempts to match the response. Authorware selects this option for you by default. Use this option in cases where you require the user to enter something into the field (as you would if you were to create a password text entry response).

- Selecting Erase Text on Exit erases the text the user entered from the screen when the user exits the interaction. If you're creating a screen with multiple text entry fields, turn this option off so each text entry field remains displayed when the user shifts to another field.

NOTE You can use the system function `SetKeyboardFocus` to change the focus of the current text entry field to another specified interaction icon. For a description of this function, see Appendix A, "New Authorware 4 Functions and Variables."

You can see an example of a piece that uses multiple text entry fields by opening the file named COOLFORM.A4P. It's included in the Chapter 8 examples folder on the CD accompanying this book.

Clicking the Text tab displays the options shown in **Figure 8.10**. Use these options to modify how the text entry field appears in the Presentation window.

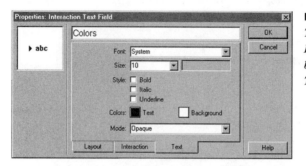

Figure 8.10
The Text Entry Properties dialog box with the Text tab selected.

You can modify these options in the following ways:

■ Change the font that displays in the field by selecting a new font from the Font drop-down list.

■ Change the point size of the font by selecting a new size from the Size drop-down list. The default point size of the text entry field font is 10. If you select Other as your size option, you can type in a new point size in the Size field next to the drop-down list.

■ Modify the style of text (Bold, Italic, or Underline) by selecting one of the Style checkbox options.

■ Change the text color by clicking on the Text color chip and selecting a color from the palette that appears. The default text color is black.

■ Change the background color of the text entry field by clicking on the Background color chip and selecting a color from the palette. The default background color is white.

■ Change the mode setting of the text entry field by selecting Transparent, Matted, or Inverse from the Text Mode drop-down list. The default mode is Opaque. These settings work the same way that the settings in the Modes Inspector window work.

NOTE You cannot place a text entry field on a higher layer in the Presentation window. You must use a layer setting of 0.

While making modifications to the Layout, Interaction, and Text options, you can view changes in the Preview window in the upper left-hand corner of the Text Entry Properties dialog box. You also can use the text entry field displayed in the Presentation window behind the dialog box to preview changes you make, as shown in **Figure 8.11**.

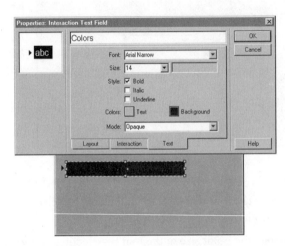

Figure 8.11
Changes you make to the text entry field are visible in the Preview window, as well as the Presentation window.

Play around with some of these options before continuing to the next section, where you will learn how to define the text that the user needs to enter to match the text entry response successfully.

Defining a correct text match

After you set up the response, position, and size of the text entry field, and you make any changes you want to the appearance of the field, your next step is to define the correct text that the user should enter into the text entry field. You define this text value in the text entry Response Properties dialog box.

To open the text entry Response Properties dialog box, double-click on the text entry response symbol next to the interaction icon. The text entry Response Properties dialog box appears, as shown in **Figure 8.12**.

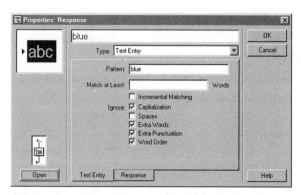

Figure 8.12
*Editing the
properties for
a text entry
response.*

In a moment, you will work with these properties to modify
your text entry response. First, however, you should know a bit
more about how to use them:

- The Pattern field enables you to specify a set of characters to
correctly match. Authorware ignores all other entries that don't
match what you specified. Because this field becomes the title
of the response feedback icon, you can edit it later directly in
the flowline without opening the dialog box.

  You can use up to 400 characters in this field, although
  Authorware only displays the first 160 in the flowline. Like the
  keypress response, you have the option to use the (|) character
  to specify two or more correct responses. For example, if you
  want to accept both moon and satellite as the correct words for
  a match, you would type "moon|satellite" into the Pattern field.

- The Match At Least field allows you to specify the number of
words that the user must enter correctly for Authorware to
match the response and display the result feedback. For
example, if you type the value 2 in this field, and the Pattern
field contains the phrase "moon, satellite, star," then the user
only needs to enter two of these words for the match.

NOTE Authorware treats any set of characters separated by a space
as a word. For instance, "blue" and "blu4" are both treated as words
when matching a response.

- When you check the Incremental Matching option, Authorware
does not require that you enter all the words of the Pattern
field at the same time. They can be entered one after the other,
and the match still is made. For example, if the Pattern field
contains the phrase "system software," the user can enter

"software" the first time, press the action key, and then enter "system" the second time. As long as you have checked this option, the match is made.

- The Ignore options let you specify what Authorware can disregard from the user's entry when attempting to match the response. You can ignore capitalization, spaces inside the word, extra words, extra punctuation, and word order. With all these options checked, you can give the user more flexibility when entering an interaction response.

Now that you know more about the Text Entry Response Properties dialog box, go ahead and set up the correct text for the response:

1. With the Response Properties dialog box open, type **blue** in the Pattern field, and then click OK to close the dialog box.

   The word "blue" appears in the flowline as the title of the response feedback icon.

2. If you haven't added feedback to your response, do so now.

3. When you've set up your response feedback, run the piece by choosing Restart From Flag from the Control menu, or by clicking the Restart From Flag button on the toolbar.

4. Type **red** in the text entry field that is displayed, and press the Return key to enter the text you've just typed.

   Because "red" is not a valid match, Authorware highlights the text and allows you to reenter it without displaying the response feedback.

5. Now type **blue** in the field, and press Return.

   Your response feedback now appears.

A text entry response set to Try Again branching is useful when you need to set up a "catch-all" text entry response that provides feedback when the user enters the wrong text. The next section explains how to do this.

Setting up a catch-all response

In most cases, you will set up two text entry responses in the same interaction: one that reacts to any text, and one that reacts only to an exact match. As mentioned earlier, you can use several text entry responses with the same text entry field in an interaction. This allows you to set up one response that looks for the correct match and another that acts as a catch-all response for any other characters typed into the field.

To create the catch-all response, type an asterisk (∗) in the Pattern field for your text entry response. Like the question mark (?), the asterisk is another type of wildcard character; it tells Authorware to accept any text a user enters—a letter, a number, a word, a phrase, or even a paragraph. Place the catch-all response that you've created to the right of any other text entry responses in the interaction for the correct response to match, as shown in **Figure 8.13**.

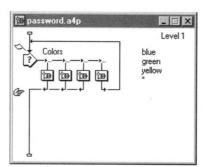

Figure 8.13
Setting up the catch-all response.

However, in cases where you simply are gathering information such as the user's name, address, or email address, use only one response and create it as a catch-all response.

Can you store values entered in a text entry field?

Because Authorware tracks the information the user enters in a system variable called EntryText, you can store the user's information for later use; to do this, attach a calculation icon script to the text entry response that assigns the value of EntryText to another variable.

For instance, if you have a text entry response that requires the user to type in a name, you can store the user's name by including the following expression in a calculation icon attached to the response:

```
UserName := EntryText
```

This is a convenient way to store the user's name because Authorware already has created the system variable UserName for this purpose. However, you can assign the value of EntryText to any custom variable that you create. See Chapter 14, "Using Functions and Variables," if you would like to find out more about creating your own custom variables.

If you include several text entry interactions in your piece, you can specify the value of `EntryText` at a specific interaction by including the interaction icon's title in the expression added to the calculation icon.

For example, if you have an interaction named Enter Address that asks the user to type in a current mailing address, you could access the value entered in this interaction by including the following expression in a calculation icon elsewhere on the flowline:

```
Mail_Address := EntryText@"Enter Address"
```

This example assumes that you already have created a custom variable named `Mail_Address` to store the current mailing address information. In general, keep user-entered information stored in separate custom variables so you can quickly access it. Chapter 16, "Tracking the User," gives you many additional tips on how you can better manage the information you're using in a piece.

Accepting variant spellings

Because there is such a wide range of characters the user can type into a text entry field, Authorware allows you to use wildcard characters to accept variant spellings of a word or phrase. Authorware can do this because it allows you to combine the use of the asterisk (*), which acts as a catch-all wildcard for words or phrases, and the question mark (?), which acts as a single-character wildcard.

TIP If there's an asterisk (*) or a question mark (?) in the text you want to match, type * or \? rather than an asterisk or a question mark by itself.

If you're setting up a word or phrase that might have multiple valid spellings, you can use a catch-all wildcard in the value you type into the Pattern field. For example, if you want to accept either satellite, sattelite, or satelite as the correct entry, type: **sat*el*ite**

However, in some cases you only need a wildcard for one character; in such a case, you would use the question mark. For example, if you want to accept either Rome or Roma as a correct entry, type: **Rom?**. Any character typed in after Rom is considered correct, but the user still must enter four characters for Authorware to match the response.

As you can see, there are many ways to set up the text entry field to handle anything the user inputs. The best way to learn which options work best is to map out all the possible combinations before you begin building your piece.

Defining default text for a field

While running the example piece you set up earlier, you may have noticed that the text entry field was empty the first time you entered the interaction. However, in some cases, you may want to fill in this field with a default text value so the user has an idea what to enter into the field.

In order to set this up, use a calculation icon to set a value for the system variable `PresetEntry`. You can use this system variable to "populate" the field with a default word or phrase, including information the user previously entered in another text entry interaction (see "Can you store values entered in a text entry field?").

To set up your text entry field with a default entry already displayed, you can modify the interaction you have been working with:

1. Drag a new calculation icon into the flowline, place it above the interaction icon, and name it **Set default text**.

2. Double-click the calculation icon to edit it.

   The calculation window appears.

3. In the empty Calculation window, type:
   PresetEntry := "Type in your favorite color".

4. Close the Calculation window by pressing the Enter key on the numeric keypad.

5. Run the piece to see what happens.

The text entry field appears with the phrase "Type in your favorite color" already entered in the field, as shown in **Figure 8.14**. This only appears the first time the interaction displays. You can type your favorite color into the field, press the Return key to overwrite the preset entry, and then continue through the interaction.

Figure 8.14

The text entry field now appears initially filled with text.

The example above demonstrates how to use one of the most common text entry system variables, but it's only one of many ways you can use Authorware's system variables to control what happens inside a text entry response. You will learn more about some of these in the chapters ahead. In addition, you can find descriptions of them in *Using Authorware* or Authorware Help.

As you can see, it isn't difficult to create sophisticated pieces that resemble commercial software in the way they function. However, in most cases, you also will need to set up custom menus that function similar to a real-world application. The next section discusses how to work with this type of response.

Setting Up Menu Responses

Pull-down menus are ideal for providing users with options without taking up real estate on screen. Pull-down menus are best for options that need to be available throughout the entire application, such as a set of menus that include Quit, Print Screen, and Help commands. Although menus aren't always the best solution when designing a custom interface for your piece, they nevertheless are easy to set up and can provide a standard Windows or Macintosh user interface appearance if that is what you want.

NOTE Make sure that when you use menu responses, you have the User Menus option turned on in the File Properties dialog box. Access the File Properties dialog box by choosing File > Properties from the Modify menu.

You probably have noticed that your Authorware pieces already display a File menu with a Quit command at the top of the Presentation window. However, you may want to replace this with a custom File menu that has several other options available, as well as a custom quit dialog box. You can do this very easily using a few simple techniques. In the process, you will learn more about using perpetual responses and menu interactions.

1. Create a new file.

2. Drag a new interaction icon to the flowline and name it **File**.

Authorware uses the title you give the interaction icon as the title of the pull-down menu that appears across the top of the Presentation window. In order to replace the default File menu with one of your own, create a new File menu interaction.

TIP Place your custom menu interactions near the top of the flowline so they display immediately when the piece first launches.

Now that you've created the menu interaction, you need to create a separate response for the Quit menu command:

1. Drag a map icon to the right of the interaction icon.

The Response Type dialog box appears.

2. Select Pull-down Menu as your response type and click OK.

The response type symbol on the interaction flowline changes to the pull-down menu symbol, as shown in **Figure 8.15**.

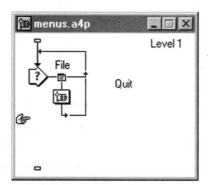

Figure 8.15
Setting up a custom File pull-down menu.

3. Click on the map icon attached to the pull-down menu and name it **Quit**.

Authorware displays this name in the menu bar under the menu defined by the interaction icon.

The most important part of this interaction is the response feedback that appears when the user chooses Quit from the File menu. You could simply exit the application, but you probably will want to add a dialog box that gives the user the option of quitting:

1. Double-click the map icon to open it.

A separate panel of the Design window opens, as shown in **Figure 8.16**.

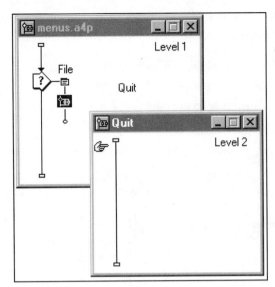

Figure 8.16
Opening the map icon attached to the Quit menu response.

2. Add a display icon and an interaction icon to the flowline.

3. Open the display icon and create an opaque box using the rectangle tool. Apply a color to it using the Colors Inspector.

4. Select the text tool and add the words **Do you want to quit?** on top of the box, as shown in **Figure 8.17**. You may need to change the color and mode of the text field using the Modes Inspector and the Colors Inspector. When you have finished, close the display icon.

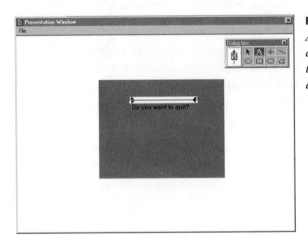

Figure 8.17
Adding the quit dialog box and text to the display icon.

Now that you've created the quit dialog box, you can add two buttons to this interaction to allow the user to quit the piece:

1. Drag an erase icon to the right of the interaction icon and create a new button response for the interaction. Label the button **No**, and change the response's branching option to Exit Interaction.

2. Drag a calculation icon to the right of the erase icon, creating a second Button response for the interaction. Label this button **Yes**, and change the response's branching option to Exit Interaction.

Your interaction now appears, as shown in **Figure 8.18**.

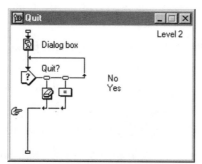

Figure 8.18
The completed quit dialog box interaction.

3. To finish setting up this interaction, double-click the calculation icon to open it and type in: **Quit()**.

Use the Quit system function to quit a piece that's running. While authoring, calling this function simply returns you to the Design window. In a packaged piece, calling this function closes the piece and returns the user to the Macintosh or Windows desktop.

4. Close the calculation window when you have finished.

Run the piece from the flag to quickly edit the position of your buttons and to select the object to erase from the screen when you click the No button in the quit interaction:

1. Click the start flag icon on the icon palette to grab the start flag, and then place it in the flowline above the display icon inside the second panel of the Design window.

NOTE If the start flag is already in another part of the flowline, you won't see the start flag in the icon palette. However, you can click above the words "start flag" in the icon palette to quickly grab it.

2. Run the piece from the flag by choosing Restart From Flag from the Control menu, or by clicking the Restart From Flag button on the toolbar.

   The quit dialog box you just created appears in the Presentation window. Pause the piece and reposition the buttons.

3. Choose Pause from the Control menu to pause the piece, and reposition both buttons so they are aligned next to each other inside the quit dialog box.

4. When you have finished, choose Play from the Control menu to restart the piece and click the No button.

   The Erase Icon Properties dialog box appears, prompting you to select the object to erase.

5. Click on the quit dialog box in the Presentation window.

   The quit dialog box erases from the screen.

6. Click OK to close the Erase Icon Properties Dialog box.

7. Now that you've set up the dialog box interaction, you can run the piece from the beginning by choosing Restart from the Control menu.

As you can see, the File menu displays along with the Quit command. When you choose Quit, the dialog box is displayed, along with the two buttons you created, as shown in **Figure 8.19**. Clicking the No button erases the box from the screen. Clicking Yes quits the piece and returns you to the Design window.

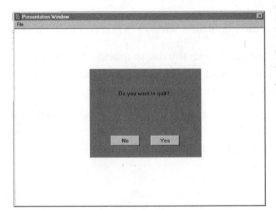

Figure 8.19
The completed quit dialog box interaction, as it appears in the Presentation window.

NOTE There are additional options available for the Quit function
that control how Authorware exits the piece. To learn more about
these options, see *Using Authorware* or Authorware Help.

If you saw the results described above, congratulations. You've
just set up your first piece using an interaction within an interaction—
a technique worth knowing so you can build more complex logic into
your pieces. However, there are a couple of things you can do to make
your File menu interaction behave more like the menu in a commercial
software application such as Authorware.

Modifying pull-down menu properties

Because users need to access most menus at any time, you usually
make all of your pull-down menu responses perpetual. You also may
want to add a keypress option that the user can use to access the
menu at any time. You control these through the options in the pull-
down menu Response Properties dialog box.

To modify the menu response properties, you double-click on
the Quit pull-down menu response symbol in the flowline and the
Response Properties dialog box appears, as shown in **Figure 8.20**.

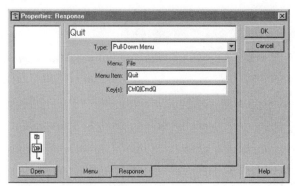

Figure 8.20
*The pull-down
menu Response
Properties
dialog box.*

There are two sets of response options available to you, Menu
and Response, which are accessible using the tabs at the bottom of the
dialog box. You can make modifications to both sets of options before
closing the dialog box.

As you can see, File and Quit are listed already under Menu and
Menu Item and don't need to be modified. As with other response
types you've seen, there is also a Key(s) field option, where you
can enter the name of a key that activates the response.

To add an optional key for the Quit menu response, you can type **CtrlQ|CmdQ** in the Key(s) field of the dialog box. The Key(s) field is located in the Menu tab options, which displays when the dialog box first opens.

Notice that you've specified both a Windows and Macintosh key shortcut for the menu. This sets up our Quit menu item to respond to either the Window-standard keyboard quit command, or the Macintosh-standard keyboard quit command. (Do this if you plan to deliver your piece on both platforms.)

Now that you've set up a key shortcut for the Quit response, you can set up the response as perpetual:

1. Click the Response tab at the bottom of the dialog box.

   The Response options appear.

2. Select the Perpetual checkbox option to make the response perpetual.

3. For your branching option, select Return using the drop-down list. When you have finished, click OK to close the dialog box.

   You should now see that your interaction response appears in the flowline using Return branching, as shown in **Figure 8.21**.

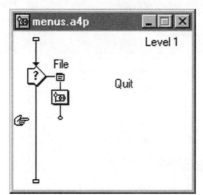

Figure 8.21
The Quit menu response set to Perpetual and Return branching.

4. Run the piece to see what happens now.

   If you were successful, everything should work exactly as it did before. However, because the menu is now perpetual, you can add additional icons to the flowline and still access the menu at any time. Try building some simple interactions below the File menu interaction to see what happens.

Because the File menu is now perpetual, you can choose Quit at any time and the dialog box appears on top of any other graphics displayed in the Presentation window. Clicking No erases the quit dialog box and returns you to the place in the flowline where you were previously.

You now see how you can use perpetual interactions and return branching in a piece to create interactions that are always available. Perpetual responses can control other aspects of your piece as well, including responding automatically to conditions that change in a piece. You will continue to work with perpetual responses and learn more about them in Chapter 10, "Responding Automatically to Events."

Looking Ahead...

Using keyboard and menu interactions, you can create sophisticated interactive applications that begin to resemble the software programs that you use every day in the real world. While these types of interactions are useful in all types of multimedia content, they can be of significant advantage to you when you begin to develop interactive training and educational pieces that are teaching users step-by-step procedures about using software.

By now, you should be much more comfortable with the process of creating interactions and working with interaction responses in the flowline. The next chapter, "Using Movable Objects," focuses on a different type of interaction—the target area interaction, which you can use when you want to provide the user with a way to pick up objects and move them on screen.

Chapter 9

Using Movable Objects

What you'll learn...

Making objects movable

Creating a target area response

While some pieces may require the user to press a button, key, or hot spot, type in text, or choose a command from a custom menu, in some cases you may want to integrate movable object interactions into your content. Movable object interactions provide a hands-on approach to solving problems or learning about a particular subject.

There are many ways you can utilize movable objects in Authorware. For instance, you might be developing a foreign language training piece and want to provide words or phrases that the user can drag into place to form a complete sentence; or, perhaps you want to simulate a laboratory environment by having the user put together pieces of a telescope or other piece of machinery with parts you provide on screen. You also can quickly adapt movable objects into quizzes and lesson reviews to increase the "playability" factor of the pieces you're creating. This chapter teaches you how to create these kinds of interactions.

Graphics and movies normally appear where you position them in the Presentation window while editing the display, interaction, or movie icon in which they're contained. However, by setting the Positioning and Motion options of the icon inside the Icon Properties dialog box, you can create a movable object that the user can drag and reposition on screen when the piece runs, or an object that repositions automatically in response to an event or a changing condition in the piece (such as a value the user enters, an amount of time that passes, or the screen position of other objects).

NOTE Keep in mind that you never actually reposition or move the icon itself. The Positioning and Motion options only apply to the content that displays in the Presentation window.

Before you begin working with movable objects, it's important to understand the distinction between using the Positioning and Motion options of an icon. You commonly use these two sets of options in tandem; however, you are not required to use one when using the other.

The Positioning options allow you to define an initial position for a graphic or movie when it displays in the Presentation window. You can use initial positioning for any display, interaction, or movie icon, whether or not you use it as a movable object. The Motion options have no effect on the initial position of an object in the Presentation window—they simply enable the user to move the object on screen when the piece runs.

Usually, you can set an initial position for a movable object so the object can move back to its original location after the user drags it to a new position. For example, you would need an initial position in a situation where the user moves an object, jumps to a different screen in the piece, and then returns again to the screen that contained the movable object. If you haven't assigned an initial position for the movable object, it remains in the location where the user last dragged it each time you return to the screen.

When working with display and interaction icons, it's also important to understand that Positioning and Moving options apply to all graphics and text that you've added to the icon (these include graphic and text files you have imported, linked to, or created in Authorware). Although the display icon may contain three or four imported objects, Authorware treats the entire set of images as a single, self-contained "object" when applying Positioning or Motion settings to the icon.

TIP If you recall, you also can set an initial position for a single graphic that you have linked to a display or interaction icon. See Chapter 3, "Working with Text and Graphics," for a complete review.

Using the Positioning options

The options that you use to set the initial positioning of an object are located in the Layout tab of the Icon Properties dialog box. Although these options were briefly mentioned in previous chapters, you haven't actually used them yet. Now it's time to take a closer look at how the set of Layout tab options affect the display, interaction, or movie icon you're editing:

1. Create a new file.

2. Drag a display icon to the flowline and give it a name.

3. Double-click the display icon to open it.

4. Create or import a graphic so you have something to play around with in this example.

5. When you have finished, choose Icon > Properties from the Modify menu.

Shortcut: To open the Icon Properties dialog box while editing a display or interaction icon, use Ctrl+I (Windows), or Command+I (Macintosh).

The Display Icon Properties dialog box appears.

6. Click the Layout tab at the bottom of the dialog box.

The Layout options appear in the dialog box, as shown in **Figure 9.1**.

Positioning options —

Movable options —

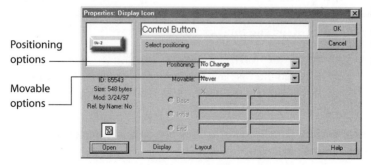

Figure 9.1

The Layout options for a display icon.

If you want to modify the object's default position, choose an option listed under the Positioning drop-down list. There are four options available to reposition the graphic you've just added to the display icon:

- The No Change option (default) sets the position of the object to the last place you moved it on screen while editing the icon.

- Using the On Screen option, you can position the object anywhere inside the Presentation window.

- Using the In Area option, you can position the object anywhere inside a rectangular area you define inside the Presentation window.

- Using the On Path option positions the object anywhere along a path you define inside the Presentation window.

NOTE Always load a graphic or movie into a display or movie icon before changing the Positioning options. This is especially true with In Area and On Path settings because you need to select the object in the Presentation window to define its area or path.

TIP The Positioning options for a display, interaction, or movie icon (On Screen, On Path, In Area) are very similar to the Positioning options you used when animating an icon by using the motion icon (Direct to Point, Direct to Line, Direct to Grid). Before you continue, you might want to take another look at the techniques used to define paths and areas, which are covered in Chapter 4, "Adding Motion."

The next few sections take a look at how these options differ.

On Screen positioning

The simplest and quickest way to position an object is to use the On Screen option because it doesn't require a separate area or path for the object. You simply specify the position of the object in relation to the size (in pixels) of the current Presentation window.

To set up On Screen positioning for your icon:

1. If you've closed the Display Icon Properties dialog box, open it by double-clicking on the display icon while pressing the Alt key (Windows), or Option key (Macintosh).

   The Display Icon Properties dialog box appears, along with the Presentation window.

2. Click the Layout tab at the bottom of the dialog box.

The Layout options appear.

3. Select On Screen from the Positioning drop-down list.

The Icon Properties dialog box changes to display the On Screen positioning settings, as shown in **Figure 9.2**. The Current fields display the current X and Y positions of the object in relation to the Presentation window.

Initial position of the object ———

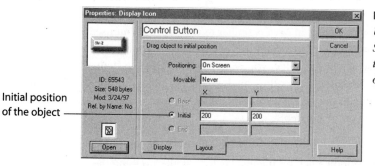

Figure 9.2
Using the On Screen settings to position an object.

4. To set the initial position of the object, you can either type new X and Y values into the Current fields, or drag the object in the Presentation window to reposition it. You also can use a variable expression in these fields so you can change the initial position of the object any time through a calculation icon script.

5. Click OK to close the Display Icon Properties dialog box, and then run the piece.

When you run the piece, the object appears in the location you specified. For instance, if you type in 10 for the X value and 20 for the Y value, the object positions 10 pixels to the right and 20 pixels down from the upper left-hand corner of the Presentation window.

If you're using a single icon stored in a library and need to reposition it from time to time in a piece, use the On Screen setting as a quick and easy way to move the object around. You might want to create two custom variables (one for the X value, and one for the Y value) to update the object's position more easily.

However, using variables to set an object's initial position and assigning new values to these variables while the object displays, means you have to erase the object and redisplay it to see the variable positioning changes take effect. You can do this quickly by using the

EraseIcon and DisplayIcon system functions. Chapter 15, "Controlling the Flowline through Scripting," discusses using these functions in more detail.

In Area positioning

If you need to keep your object confined to a smaller area than the Presentation window, use the In Area positioning option. This option is helpful when creating evenly spaced arrangements of onscreen graphics that the user can reposition when the piece runs.

Specifying In Area is similar to the process you used when animating a target object to a point in an area using the motion icon. First, select the object you want to position. Then define the area in the Presentation window by dragging the object to the base and end points of the area. Position the object in relation to the size of the area you've created.

To set up this type of positioning:

1. Double-click on the display icon while pressing the Alt key (Windows), or Option key (Macintosh).

The Display Icon Properties dialog box appears, along with the Presentation window.

2. Click the Layout tab at the bottom of the dialog box.

The Layout options appear.

3. Select In Area from the Positioning drop-down list.

The In Area positioning settings appear, as shown in **Figure 9.3**.

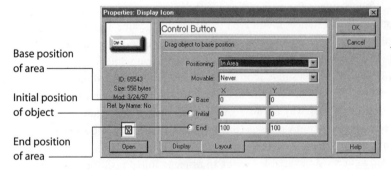

Base position of area ——

Initial position of object ——

End position of area ——

Figure 9.3
Using the In Area settings to position an object.

Next, you define the area for your object:

1. Click the Base radio button, and then drag the object to a new position in the Presentation window to set the base point of the area.

2. Click the End radio button, and then drag the object to a new
position in the Presentation window to set the end point of
the area.

A dotted outline appears, defining the area where you can
position the object, as shown in **Figure 9.4**.

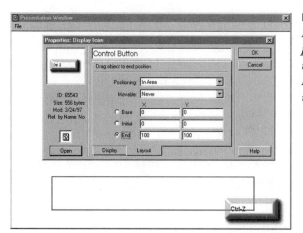

Figure 9.4
*Defining the
positioning area
inside the
Presentation
window.*

After you've defined the positioning area, set the object's initial
position inside this area:

1. Click the Initial radio button.

2. Insert the X and Y numerical values or variables that you want
to use to set the object's initial position. You also can drag the
object to a position in the Presentation window to set these
values.

NOTE Make sure that the values you specify for the object's initial
position are within the range of X and Y values defined by the base
and end points of the area.

3. Click OK to close the Display Icon Properties dialog box, and
then run the piece.

Once again, Authorware places the object in the initial position
you specified. In Area positioning probably doesn't look all that
much different from the On Screen positioning option you just
used. However, In Area positioning is helpful when designing more
complex interactions.

If you open the Display Icon Properties dialog box again, notice
that the value 100 is in both the X and Y End fields. You can replace

the value 100 in each of these fields with a different numerical value or variable expression to define the object's position based on an X and Y scale that you've defined elsewhere in your piece.

For example, you could use this to show someone the buying power of the dollar over the past 20 years. To do this you would use 100 for your X value (showing how much a dollar gets you these days), and 20 for your Y value (the number of years you're plotting). It is much easier to position your carefully scanned thumbnail portrait of George Washington somewhere on this graph because you don't have to use a separate ratio calculation to convert the year value into a fractional value based on 100.

On Path positioning

On Screen and In Area positioning are the most common positioning types. However, if you have an object that you want to position at different points along a path (e.g., a gauge or slider that moves to a specific point on the path depending on the value of a variable), use the On Path positioning option.

Defining an object's path here is similar to creating a path-to-point or path-to-end animation with the motion icon. You specify the base- and end-point values for the path and insert a numerical or variable expression that determines the object's position on this path.

To set up On Path positioning:

1. Double-click the display icon while pressing the Alt key (Windows), or Option key (Macintosh).

The Display Icon Properties dialog box appears.

2. Switch to the Layout options and select On Path from the Positioning drop-down list.

The Positioning options appear, as shown in **Figure 9.5**.

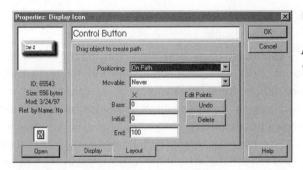

Figure 9.5
Using On Path positioning with an object.

3. Click on the object in the Presentation window then drag and drop it to create new points on the path you're defining. To create a loop, simply overlap the two end points. If you make a mistake while defining your path, click the Undo button. If you want to delete a point, click on the point once, and then click the Delete button.

TIP To create a circular path, double-click on each of the points. The square point marker changes to a circle point marker to show that it's now a circular path.

4. To define the object's initial position on the path, either drag it to a new location on the path, or type in a numerical value or variable expression in the Initial field.

5. After you've defined the initial position value, click OK to close the dialog box, and then run the piece.

The object repositions itself at the point you defined in the Initial field.

Making an object static

Try this simple test. What happens if you click on the display object in the last example and try to move it in the Presentation window? If you try it, notice that you can move it anywhere on screen—even though you haven't yet made the object movable.

While this is a good thing sometimes, many times it's not—especially if you have carefully positioned your object where you want it to display, and then accidentally drag it to a new location while trying to reposition another graphic or movie in the Presentation window.

To safeguard against this, you can use a simple trick that forces your display objects to remain static inside the Presentation window:

1. Select the display icon by clicking on it.

TIP You can use this technique with interaction and movie icons as well.

2. Choose Icon > Calculation from the Modify menu.

The Calculation window opens.

Shortcut: To open the Calculation window while you have an icon selected, use Ctrl+= (Windows), or Command+= (Macintosh).

---

3. Type in the following expression: **Movable := FALSE.**

4. Press the Enter key on the numerical keypad to close the Calculation window.

Notice that a small calculation symbol appears attached to the display icon, as shown in **Figure 9.6**. This indicates that a calculation script is attached to the icon. You'll learn more about this in Chapter 15, "Controlling the Flowline through Scripting."

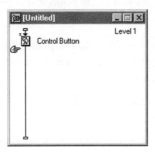

Figure 9.6
The display icon with a calculation script attached to it.

5. Go ahead and run the piece.

You now can move the display icon content when you click on it in the Presentation window. This is because you've turned off the icon's Movable property using the above expression. Remember this trick while authoring because it can cut down the amount of time you spend rearranging objects in the Presentation window. For more information about attaching calculation scripts to icons, see Chapter 15, "Controlling the Flowline through Scripting."

Fortunately, you don't have to worry about this problem when delivering your final piece because Authorware makes all display objects static when you package your piece. Chapter 17, "Distributing Your Piece," covers packaging a piece in more detail. However, when you really want the user to have the capability to move the object in the final piece, create a movable object using the techniques discussed in the next section.

Making an object movable

Suppose you've created a test in which the user moves tiles and places them in a specific order on screen (e.g., a jigsaw puzzle). Creating this type of interaction requires several steps:

■ Defining the object's initial position in an area of the screen. (You already know how to do this from the previous examples.)

- Making the object movable so the user can drag it to the correct location.

- Setting up the target area where the user can drag the object (covered below in "Creating a Target Area Response").

Authorware has four ways to make an object movable, which correspond to the four Positioning options you just learned about above:

- The No Change option is the default option for a display object. It enables you to move the object in the Presentation window, but only while authoring (unless you've turned off the icon's Movable property using the technique you learned in the last example). Your end users cannot move the object in the final packaged piece.

- Selecting the On Screen option enables the user to move the object anywhere in the Presentation window. You probably will use this option the most when creating movable objects.

- Selecting the On Path option enables the user to move the object anywhere along the path you define when setting up the object's initial position on a path. This option is available only when you've selected On Path in the Positioning options for the icon you're editing.

- Selecting In Area enables the user to move the object anywhere in the area you define when setting up the object's initial position in an area. This option is available only when you select In Area in the Positioning options for the icon you're editing.

To see how these options differ, go back to the example file and change the Movable options for the display icon:

1. Double-click the display icon while pressing the Alt key (Windows), or Option key (Macintosh).

The Display Icon Properties dialog box appears, along with the Presentation window.

2. Click the Layout tab.

The Layout options appear.

3. Select On Path from the Movable drop-down list, and click OK to close the dialog box.

Before you can run the piece, remove the expression you attached earlier to the display icon; otherwise, you cannot move the object.

To do this:

1. Click on the display icon and choose Icon > Calculation from the Modify menu.

The Calculation window appears.

2. Delete the expression from this window, and then press Enter on the numeric keypad to close the Calculation window.

3. Go ahead and run the piece.

Notice that when you now select the object and drag it in the Presentation window, it is constrained to the path you created earlier. This may be useful, for instance, when creating a custom paging controller that flips pages depending on the position of the graphic moving along the path.

TIP At any time, you can track the current location of an object along a movable path you've set up using the `PathPosition` system variable. For a description of this variable, see *Using Authorware* or Authorware Help.

To see how the other Movable options affect how you can drag and reposition an object, open the Icon Properties dialog box again and switch to another option:

1. Select the display icon, open the Display Icon Properties dialog box, and click on the Layout tab.

2. Select No Change from the Positioning drop-down list, and select On Screen from the Movable drop-down list.

3. Click OK to close the dialog box, and then run the piece.

Now the object can move anywhere—except off screen. This is a useful setting when you want to keep the user from accidentally dragging the object off screen (which can happen if you've selected Anywhere as your Movable setting).

Before moving on, try playing around with the other two Movable options. Remember if you select In Area as your Movable setting, you first must define the area using the In Area Positioning option. Get a good feel for using movable objects so you can integrate them into interactions using the target area response type.

Creating a Target Area Response

Use movable objects when you want the user to interact with your piece by dragging an object to a specific location. In Authorware, you can set up many types of interactions that integrate movable objects using the target area response.

For instance, you might have a screen where the user drags the names of cities to specific areas on a map to test his or her knowledge of a particular country. Or you might create a lab piece for an astronomy class where the user drags parts of a telescope to a location in the Presentation window to build it on screen. These types of interactions allow you to check the user's knowledge of a particular subject using a hands-on approach—which can't be done by simply answering multiple-choice questions or filling in blanks with a particular word.

In order to set up interactions like this, you need to create a movable object first (as you did in the section above, "Making an object movable"), and then create a target area response for the movable object.

In the following example, you set up this type of interaction by creating a simple name-matching game using the techniques you learned earlier in this chapter and in previous chapters. In the process, you will learn how to create movable object interactions that can perform several actions:

- Give the proper feedback if the user drops the object in its correct place.

- Give negative feedback if the user drops the object anywhere else on screen.

- Freeze the object after the user positions it correctly, so the user can't move it.

To see a more complex working example of this type of interaction, take a look at the file named DRAGIT.A4P. It's included in the Chapter 9 examples folder on the CD accompanying this book.

Each time you create a target response interaction, you first must create the movable object. If you want the user to match multiple items, place each one of your movable objects in a separate display icon.

To create a movable object:

1. Drag a new display icon to the flowline and name it **Last Name**.

2. Open the display icon, select the text tool, and type in: **Monroe**.

3. Change the text field's mode to transparent using the Modes Inspector. You also can change the font, size, or color of the text.

4. With the Presentation window still open, choose Icon > Properties from the Modify menu.

   The Display Icon Properties dialog box appears.

5. Click the Layout tab and change the Movable option to On Screen. When you have finished, click OK to close the dialog box, and then close the display icon to return to the Design window.

   Now that you've set up your movable object, you need to create the interaction and define the target area response for this example.

Setting up the target area response

The target area response tests whether or not the user is dragging the text object to its proper location. In this example, you want to match the correct last name with the correct first name, as you might do in a simple practice lesson of a piece.

First, set up the interaction icon:

1. Drag a new interaction icon to the flowline, position it below the display icon you just edited, and title it **Drag Example**.

2. Double-click the interaction icon, select the text tool, and add the following text to the Presentation window: **Marilyn**.

3. Select the rectangle tool and create a box next to the word Marilyn, as shown in **Figure 9.7**. (You'll use this in a moment when setting up the target area response.)

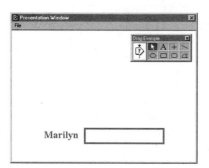

Figure 9.7
*Setting up the target area
interaction.*

4. When you have finished, click the close box on the toolbox
to close the Presentation window and return to the Design
window.

Now that you've set up the interaction, you can create the
target area response:

1. Drag a map icon to the right of the interaction icon, creating a
new response.

The Response Type dialog box appears.

2. Select Target Area and click OK.

A target area symbol appears in the flowline next to the interaction icon, as shown in **Figure 9.8**.

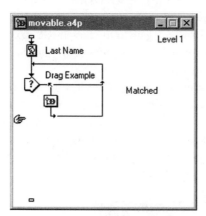

Figure 9.8
*The target area response, as
it appears in the flowline.*

3. Double-click the response symbol.

The Response Properties dialog box appears, showing you
the options available for a target area response, as shown in
Figure 9.9.

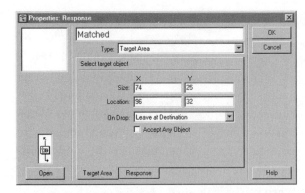

Figure 9.9
The Response Properties dialog box, with the target area options displayed.

4. In the title field at the top of the dialog box, type in the following title: **Matched**.

This title appears on the flowline next to the map icon attached to the response. (Remember that you refer to this as the response feedback icon.)

In most cases, it's a good idea to use a map icon for the response feedback icon so you can add content for the feedback later. Notice that Authorware automatically sets up the target area response to use Try Again branching. Because you're creating the correct response to the interaction, change the setting to Exit Interaction branching so the user exits the interaction when the correct answer matches. To do this, you click once below the map icon while pressing the Ctrl key (Windows), or Command key (Macintosh). The branching option for the response changes to Try Again in the flowline. You can use this technique to cycle through all the branching options that apply to the response you're setting up.

When creating target area interactions in your own piece, create additional target area responses for each object that you need to match. You also may want to create a target area response that looks for a wrong match. You'll see how to do this in a moment. First, however, you must assign the movable object to the target area response you just created.

Connecting a movable object with its target area

Because you already created the movable object, you now need to link it to the area where the user should drag it. Authorware uses automatic prompting to help you do this. You place the target area over the target box you created earlier in the interaction icon, and then select the text in the display icon as your movable object for the response.

To connect a movable object with its target area:

1. Run the piece from the beginning by choosing Restart from the Control menu, or by clicking the Restart button on the toolbar.

Because you haven't defined a movable object for the target area response you just created, the Response Properties dialog box appears again, prompting you to select the target object. There is also a small, dotted, rectangular area in the Presentation window, as shown in **Figure 9.10**. This is the target area for the response (which you'll position in a moment).

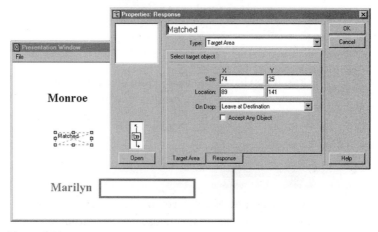

Figure 9.10
The target area appears in the Presentation window, allowing you to drag it into position.

2. Click once on the word Monroe, which appears in the Presentation window. This is the text you want to use as the target object for this response.

The Response Properties dialog box now prompts you to drag the object to the target position in the Presentation window.

3. Select the object by clicking on it in the Presentation window, and then move it to the center of the target box, next to the word Marilyn.

The target area snaps to the location where you released the target object, as shown in **Figure 9.11**.

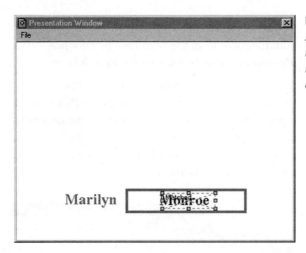

Figure 9.11
Positioning the target area over the box that was created.

Presentation Window
File

Marilyn Monroe

TIP If you have trouble selecting the target object with the cursor, simply use the selection handles attached to the target area to reposition the target area over the box. This works the same as moving the target object itself.

Setting up the target area

When a user drags an object to its target area, Authorware only matches the object if the mouse cursor is inside the area when the user releases the object. Otherwise, Authorware ignores the object and the interaction continues.

There are several options in the Response Properties dialog box that allow you to customize the target area and the way Authorware handles a match. After linking the target area to the object, you can resize or reposition it by dragging its size handles, or by dragging the entire target area to a new location. You also can type in exact values for the target area using the Size and Location fields in the Response Properties dialog box.

By selecting one of the options from the On Drop drop-down list, you can customize the way Authorware handles repositioning the target object once the user releases it. The following options are available:

■ Leave At Destination (the default option) leaves the object at the location where the user releases it.

■ Put Back moves the object back to its previous position in the Presentation window. You generally want to use this option only if you're creating a "safety net" target area for incorrect matches.

■ Snap To Center snaps the object to the center of the target area. This is a good option to select when you want to give the user immediate visual feedback, indicating that a target area response matches correctly.

NOTE In the Response Properties dialog box for a target area response, you have access to the same judging, erasing, and branching options used with other types of responses. (However, you don't need to modify any of these options for this example.)

To finish setting up the target area response, select Snap to Center from the On Drop drop-down list, and then click OK to close the dialog box. Before you run the piece, add some feedback to the response so you know the response matches correctly:

1. Open the Match map icon attached to the response by double-clicking it.

2. Drag a new display icon to the flowline and add some feedback text that indicates the response matches correctly. When you have finished, close the display icon and click the Restart button on the toolbar to run the piece from the beginning.

Your feedback text should appear when you drag and drop the word Monroe into the box next to the word Marilyn. Because you selected Snap to Center for the On Drop option, the target object snaps to the center of the target area.

Setting up a safety net

You already defined the correct target area for your object; but what happens if you drag it to the wrong location and release it? As it stands now, the object stays where you drop it in the Presentation window. Since there's no drama, it doesn't make for a very exciting game.

Instead, you can set up a "safety net" target area response that sends the object back to its original location when someone makes a wrong move:

1. Drag a new map icon to the right of the Matched icon and name it **Safety Net**, as shown in **Figure 9.12**.

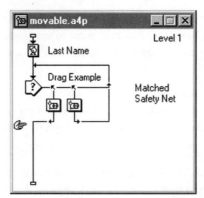

Figure 9.12
Setting up the safety net.

Because you already defined one response for the interaction, Authorware creates the new safety net response using the same settings. All you do now is open the safety net response symbol and edit it. Because you want the safety net to catch all incorrect matches, set it to use the entire Presentation window as its defined area.

2. Double-click the Safety Net response symbol. The Response Properties dialog box appears.

3. In the Size fields, type in 640 for the X value and 480 for the Y value. This sets the target area's size to the entire Presentation window.

4. In the Location fields, type in 0 for the X value and 0 for the Y value. This places the upper left-hand corner of the target area at the upper left-hand corner of the Presentation window.

5. Select Put Back from the On Drop drop-down list.

6. Select the Accept Any Object checkbox option so the safety net response matches any object dragged in the Presentation window.

7. Click the Response tab at the bottom of the dialog box, and set the response's branching to Try Again so the user isn't forced to exit the interaction if a wrong response is made.

8. When you have finished, close the dialog box and run the piece to see what happens.

Now, when you drop the object anywhere else in the Presentation window, it immediately moves back to its original location. Because you have the safety net response positioned to the right of the correct match response in the flowline, the user can drag the object to its correct location and get the appropriate feedback.

However, notice what happens when you try to move the object after it drops into the correct area. The object is still movable. It would be better if it froze in-place, so the user could not move it around after it dropped in the correct area. To do this, use the services of the `Movable` system variable—as you did when you learned about making objects static in the Presentation window.

Freezing the object after a match

Remember the example earlier in this chapter, where you made a display object static using the following expression attached to the display icon itself:

```
Movable := FALSE
```

Because this expression was attached to the icon itself, you were not required to specify the name of the icon to make it static. However, in a target area response interaction, you don't want to make the object static until the user makes a match. To do this, you could use a similar expression in a calculation icon that you have placed into the map icon attached to the correct target area response:

```
Movable@"Last Name" := FALSE
```

Here, you tell Authorware which icon to make static by including the title of the icon inside the expression. This type of expression is referred to as a "referenced variable" expression because it refers to a specific icon in the flowline. For more information about using referenced variables, see Chapter 15, "Controlling the Flowline through Scripting."

In the target area example you just created, including the title of the icon in the expression isn't too much of a problem because you only have to worry about one display icon. In the real world, however, you might be tracking five to 20 movable objects on screen at the same time when creating a target area interaction. That's a lot of icon titles to sort through—especially if you have more than one target area interaction in your piece. Fortunately, there's an easier solution.

To freeze any object that the target area response happens to match, you can use another Authorware internal system variable named `ObjectMatched` in your calculation script. Because this system variable contains the icon title of the last icon matched in a target area response, you don't need to include icon titles when you type in your expression.

To freeze any object that a response matches:

1. Click on the Match map icon, and open the Calculation window.

   The Calculation window appears.

2. Type in the following expression:
   Movable@ObjectMatched := FALSE.

TIP When creating expressions in Authorware 4, you can use a variable name after the @ symbol when working with any referenced system variable or function that requires an icon title. You'll learn more about using this feature in Chapter 15, "Controlling the Flowline through Scripting."

3. When you have finished typing in the expression, close the calculation window and run the piece.

As you can see, your target object now freezes when it matches correctly. Because you didn't place the same calculation script into the response feedback for the safety net response, the object still should move when the match is wrong.

This demonstrates the type of power that calculation scripting gives you when creating more complex interactions. Most Authorware pieces can benefit from your knowledge of a few simple scripting techniques like the one in the example above. While you cannot solve all problems this way, you can solve most of them if you learn to integrate scripting into the flowline.

Looking Ahead...

In this chapter, you learned how to work with movable objects and target area interactions. Including movable objects in a piece can do wonders to improve the interactivity in a piece. You can use them for many situations where you want to give the user a more "hands-on" approach to working through specific interactions.

You also saw how quickly scripting can improve your handling of difficult interactions—particularly when you must keep track of many things happening simultaneously. In the next chapter, you'll learn more about setting up complex interactivity in your pieces by taking a look at the time limit, tries limit, conditional, and event response types. You can integrate these event response types into an interaction to automatically respond to processes that are happening in the background while your piece runs.

Chapter 10

Responding Automatically to Events

As your pieces become more complex, you will want to think about ways to enhance how you provide feedback to users. While the interaction types discussed in the last three chapters are the most common ways to add interactivity to your pieces, they don't provide solutions for every situation. Most Authorware developers tend to combine user-controlled interactions and automatic feedback (which other types of interaction responses handle while running in the background of a piece).

This chapter introduces you to some powerful ways of building more robust applications that don't require user input to control branching and response feedback. Primarily, you accomplish this in Authorware with the time limit, tries limit, conditional, and event response types. Using these types of interaction responses, your piece can react automatically to internal Authorware system events, variable conditions, or any number of other events processed by scripting and sprite Xtras that you have integrated into your piece.

One of the easiest ways to manage a testing environment in Authorware is to set a time limit for each question. Using the time limit response, you can give the user a warning when time is running out for answering a question, or you can have the piece automatically move on to the next question. You also can use the time limit response to display the correct answer when the time limit expires in an interaction.

When you use a time limit response in an interaction, you set up the interaction to time out after a specified amount of time passes. Authorware stores the seconds-limit for the interaction in the system variable TimeRemaining. Authorware also records the amount of time a user spends in an interaction using the system variable TimeInInteraction. These system variables are always available— regardless of whether or not you use a time limit response. However, the time limit response is an easy way to take advantage of these system variables to give your piece automatic handling of time-out events.

You can set up a simple time limit response to see how it works by doing the following:

1. Drag an interaction icon to the flowline and title it.

2. Drag a new map icon to the right of the interaction to create the response.

The Response Type dialog box appears.

3. Select Time Limit, and then click OK.

The response symbol in the flowline changes to the time limit response symbol, as shown in **Figure 10.1**.

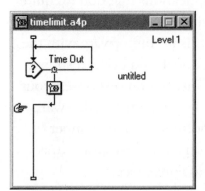

Figure 10.1
Setting up a time limit response.

4. Click on the map icon attached to the time limit response and change its title to **Time Out**.

Notice that when you first create a time limit response, the branching option is set automatically to Exit Interaction. This setting allows the user to exit the interaction when time expires. In cases where you want to simply display feedback when a time-out occurs, change the response's branching option to Try Again.

When setting up a time limit response, you should create another response for the interaction (either to the right or left of the time limit response). You usually place the time limit response to the right of other responses to allow the other responses to match while the time limit response runs in the background.

To continue setting up the time limit interaction:

1. Drag another map icon to the flowline and place it to the left of the time limit response. The Response Type dialog box appears.

2. Select Button (for now) and click OK to close the dialog box.

3. Name the button and change its branching to Exit Interaction (like the time limit response). This way, the user continues down the flowline if either response matches (e.g., if the button is clicked, or if the time limit is reached).

You now should have your time limit interaction set up correctly. In the future, you can use this example as a basic model for a question/time limit response; however, you may want to add additional buttons or hot spots for each answer you give the user, as shown in **Figure 10.2**.

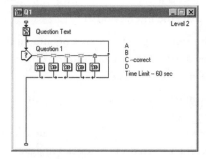

Figure 10.2
A typical question/answer model that uses a time limit response.

TIP You also can use the automatic judging option for each interaction response to improve data tracking. You'll learn more about this option in Chapter 16, "Tracking the User."

After the interaction is set up properly, the next step is to open the time limit response and define the amount of time (in seconds) that Authorware can use for the time limit in the interaction.

To set the amount of time a user gets to match a response:

1. Double-click the time limit response symbol.

The Response Properties dialog box appears, as shown in **Figure 10.3**. This lists the options you can set for the time limit response.

Time Limit field

Interruption options

Show Time
Remaining option

Restart for
Each Try option

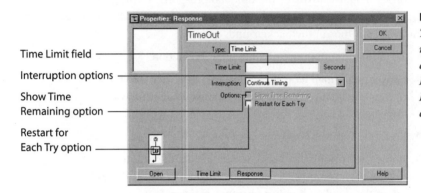

Figure 10.3
*The time limit
response options
appear in the
Response
Properties
dialog box.*

2. Type the number of seconds you want to give a user to answer the question in the Time Limit field. For this example, use **3** seconds (in the real world, though, this may make it very difficult to respond to the question).

3. Click the Response tab at the bottom of the dialog box and change the Erase option to Don't Erase. This allows the feedback response to stay on screen after the time limit expires and Authorware exits the interaction.

4. Click the Open button to open the map icon attached to the response and drag a new display icon into the flowline to create some feedback for the user.

Remember, you can use any type of icon inside the map icon—even an additional interaction icon. For instance, you might want to create a response interaction that prompts the user to make one of two choices: try to answer the question again, or move to the next question.

TIP To do this, you place each question of your test on a separate page of a framework so it is easier to navigate from one question to another. You'll learn more about using frameworks in Chapter 11, "Working with Pages."

5. To set up the feedback, open the display icon and add some text that says, **Sorry, you're not fast enough!** When you have finished, close the display icon.

6. Now run the piece to see what happens.

After the interaction starts, the time limit response activates almost immediately, displaying the feedback text you set up in the Presentation window.

Three seconds isn't all that much time. In most testing environments, you probably will use a value between 60 and 90 seconds—although it's fairly easy to adjust the time limit when testing your piece. One easy way is to adjust your time limit value globally (throughout the entire piece at the same time). You use a custom variable (called something like `TestSeconds`) in the Time Limit field of all time limit responses in your piece, as shown in **Figure 10.4**.

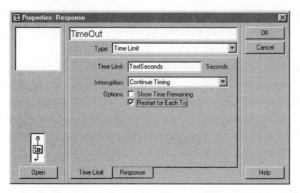

Figure 10.4
Including a custom variable in the Time Limit field allows you to update the time limit value quickly.

When the piece starts, you can quickly set the time limit value for every interaction in the piece by assigning a number of seconds to a custom variable. Use the following variable expression typed into a calculation icon:

```
TestSeconds := 60
```

The expression above assigns the value of 60 seconds to the custom variable `TestSeconds`. This is the same variable that Authorware uses to time each interaction in your piece that uses a time limit response. If you find that 60 seconds is too little or too much time, you can quickly change it by replacing the value 60 with a new value in the expression. This expression automatically updates every time limit response you've used in the piece. You'll learn more about creating and working with custom variables in Chapter 14, "Using Functions and Variables."

Controlling the timer options

Using the Interruption options listed in the time limit Response Properties dialog box (see **Figure 10.3** above), you can determine what happens when a perpetual response interrupts a time limit response while the piece runs. You can use this, for example, to control what happens when the user clicks on a perpetual button to look up a glossary term while a time-out response runs in an interaction.

When selecting an option from the Interruption drop-down list, there are four options available:

- Continue Timing (default)—Select this option to continue timing when jumping to the perpetual interaction.

- Pause, Resume on Return—Select this option to stop timing when jumping to the perpetual interaction. When Authorware returns to the timed interaction, it resumes counting from the time that already has expired.

- Pause, Restart on Return—Select this option to stop timing when executing the perpetual interaction. When Authorware returns to the timed interaction, it resets the time remaining in the interaction to the full value you've entered in the Time Limit field. Authorware restarts the timing, even if the time limit has not already expired before jumping to the perpetual interaction.

- Pause, Restart If Running—This option works the same as the Pause, Restart on Return option except that when Authorware returns to the timed interaction, it resets the time remaining in the interaction to the full value you've entered in the Time Limit field, but only if the time limit has not expired before jumping to the perpetual interaction.

If you take a closer look at the time limit options available in the Response Properties dialog box, you will see two other checkbox options at the bottom of the dialog box that you can use to customize the response (see **Figure 10.3** above):

- Selecting the Show Time Remaining option displays a small clock-shaped timer on screen, as shown in **Figure 10.5**, which shows the user how much time is left in the interaction. However, it is small and rather unobtrusive, so you may have trouble seeing it displayed on dark backgrounds.

Figure 10.5

The Show Time Remaining option displays an onscreen animated timer that counts down the seconds remaining in the interaction.

- Selecting the Restart for Each Try option resets the amount of time remaining in the interaction to the full value you've entered in the Time Limit field each time the user matches another response in the interaction. This applies to any type of response that you're using in the interaction (other than the time limit response).

Creating a perpetual time limit

You can't make a time limit response perpetual in a piece because it is unavailable when editing the time limit response options. However, there may be times when you want to limit the amount of time the user has to complete an entire section of the piece—especially if you're creating a test. At other times, you may want to display a separate screen when there has been no mouse or keyboard activity for a long period of time (as may happen in a kiosk piece that runs constantly).

Both types of perpetual time limits are fairly easy to set up in Authorware—but, you must handle them differently. The second type of time limit, a perpetual time-out after no user activity, is easier to set up because you can do so directly in a calculation icon. To create this kind of time limit, you need to be familiar with working with system functions and variables, which Chapter 14, "Using Functions and Variables," will cover in more detail.

The system variable `TimeOutLimit` and the system function `TimeOutGoTo` are used to set up a perpetual time-out event in Authorware. Use them together to jump to an icon or set of icons whenever there is no mouse or keyboard activity for a specified amount of time. This action is much like a screen-saver application that you might have running in the background on your computer.

To set up this type of perpetual time limit, simply include a script in a calculation icon at the start of your piece that uses both the `TimeOutLimit` system variable and the `TimeOutGoTo` system function. An example of this type of script is shown below:

```
TimeOutLimit := 300

TimeOutGoTo(@"Time Out")
```

In this example, the first line of the script sets the time limit to 300 seconds (or 5 minutes). You will always specify the value you assign to `TimeOutLimit` in seconds. The second line of the script calls the `TimeOutGoTo` system function, and specifies the icon named Time Out as the icon that Authorware should jump to if the time limit expires. **Figure 10.6** shows an example of how you might set this up in the flowline.

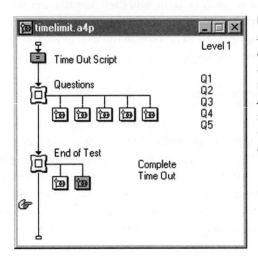

Figure 10.6
In this figure, the time limit script is placed in the calculation icon named Time Out Script. Authorware jumps to the map icon named Time Out when the time limit expires.

TIP For more information on using `TimeOutLimit` and `TimeOutGoTo` together in a piece, see the system variable and function descriptions included in *Using Authorware* or Authorware Help.

The value of `TimeOutLimit` resets whenever Authorware detects mouse or keyboard activity. Because of this, you cannot use this type of time limit to set up a time limit for a particular section of your piece where the user must click buttons, or use any other type of interaction.

In this case, use a custom variable to keep track of the amount of elapsed time in a particular section of your piece, and include a perpetual conditional response that matches when time expires.

You'll look more closely at this type of perpetual time limit interaction later in this chapter in "Using Conditional Responses."

Using time limits is an effective way to move the user through a sequence of questions or steps. However, you may want to think about other less obtrusive ways of guiding the user through an interaction than using a time limit. Another approach to creating automatic branching through an interaction is to use a tries limit response that branches after a set number of tries by the user. The next section looks at this type of response.

Using Tries Limit Responses

Examples of interactions in previous chapters have not taken into consideration how many times the user matches a response in the interaction. For example, if a button response is set to Try Again branching, the user could feasibly continue clicking the button, displaying the same response feedback each time.

In most cases, you won't need to prevent this from happening—unless you want to give the user only a few chances to match a response (as you might if you were creating some kind of performance evaluation or test). The tries limit response gives you a bit more control over how your interaction behaves; you also can use it to provide automatic feedback to the user, or as a way to move the user forward through your piece.

Setting up the tries limit response

The tries limit response allows you to create an interaction that tests for the number of times a user matches any response in an interaction. Authorware records the number of matched responses in the system variable Tries. When you set up a tries limit response, Authorware compares the value of Tries to the value you've specified for your tries limit each time the user matches a response. When this value exceeds the tries limit that you've specified in the tries limit response, Authorware automatically displays the response feedback attached to the tries limit response.

You can see an example of how this works by setting up a simple interaction:

1. Create a new file.

2. Place a new interaction icon in the flowline and name it.

3. Place a new map icon to the right of the interaction icon.

The Response Type dialog box appears.

4. Select Button for your response type and click OK.

5. Change the map icon's name to **Click Three Times**.

If you run the piece, you'll see that you can continue clicking on the button indefinitely. Because the button response is set to Try Again branching, you can't exit the interaction. However, by adding a tries limit response to the interaction, you can limit the number of response matches that can occur within the interaction.

To set up the tries limit response:

1. Place a new map icon to the right of the button response you just created and name it **Time Out**.

This creates a new button response in the flowline.

2. Double-click on the response symbol for the new button response.

The Response Properties dialog box appears.

3. Select Tries Limit from the Type drop-down list.

The tries limit response options now appear, as shown in **Figure 10.7**.

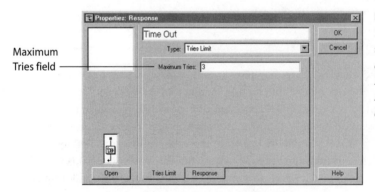

Maximum
Tries field

Figure 10.7
The tries limit response options appear in the Response Properties dialog box.

4. In the Maximum Tries field, type in **3**.

This sets the tries limit for the interaction to 3 tries. As with all other response property fields, you can use either a numerical value here or a variable expression.

5. Click the Response tab and change the Branch option to Exit Interaction. Change the Erase option to Don't Erase.

6. Click the Open button to modify the feedback response. Change the text in the display icon to say: **You clicked three times.**

7. When you have finished, close the display icon, and then close the map icon window to return to the main level of the flowline, as shown in **Figure 10.8**.

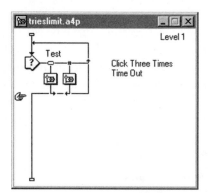

Figure 10.8
Adding the tries limit response to the interaction.

8. Go ahead and run the piece to test out the tries limit.

As you can see, if you continue clicking the button, the tries limit you've set up automatically matches, displays the feedback you've set up, and then exits the interaction. Because the Erase option for the response is set to Don't Erase, the text that you created remains on screen after you exit the interaction.

You won't always want to exit the interaction when using a tries limit response. You can use it to simply display additional help for the user, or you can use the tries limit response to navigate to a help screen using a navigate icon as part of your response feedback. Chapter 11, "Working with Pages," talks more about using the navigate icon to jump to other sections of a piece.

Using Conditional Responses

Time limit and tries limit responses respond to a specific internal event in a piece—namely, the elapsed number of seconds, or the total number of responses matched in an interaction. However, there is a great deal more happening in the background of a piece that Authorware's system variables track.

You can take advantage of this by creating automatic branching using the conditional response. Because conditional responses react to changes that occur in system or custom variables, you can set up a conditional response to automatically branch, navigate, or display feedback based on the value of the variable expression you're using in the response.

The main benefit of using a conditional response is that you have more control over your interactions. For example, you can manage a text entry interaction better by using a conditional response that tests if the password the user enters matches the user's logon name. To do this, you set up an interaction with both a text entry field for entering the password, and a conditional response that checks the user's entry and displays the appropriate feedback.

Conditional responses require that you set up an expression that evaluates to either True or False. In Authorware, simple expressions are created using system or custom variables. More complex expressions can include functions that return a specific value. In order to create an expression that evaluates as either True or False, you have to know the type of data you're comparing in the expression.

When creating expressions in Authorware, you normally will compare variables that contain one of three types of values:

- Numerical values, represented by an integer or decimal number.

- Text (or character string) values, represented by a set of alpha-numeric characters placed inside quotation marks.

- Logical (or Boolean) values, represented as either TRUE (1) or FALSE (0).

Although you can set up a conditional response to match any type of value, you need to know ahead of time which type of value the expression contains so the conditional response matches correctly.

NOTE You also can store lists and symbols in a variable that you create. These are a powerful addition to the Authorware scripting language. For more information on using these data types, see Chapter 16, "Tracking the User."

Structuring conditional expressions

One of the difficulties in using conditional responses is learning how to structure your condition so that Authorware evaluates it as either True or False. As mentioned earlier, you need to try to structure your condition so the two values you're comparing contain the same type of data (e.g., numerical, character, or logical values).

Setting up a conditional response can be complicated if you are working with variables that contain different data types. Authorware does have a set of data-comparison rules that it uses to compare the values of variables that contain different types of data. (These are explained in more detail in Chapter 14, "Using Functions and Variables.") In general, however, the rule of thumb is to create conditions that compare two variables that contain the same type of data. In addition, try to follow these general guidelines:

- When you want the conditional response to match when the value of a variable is True, you can substitute the name of the variable in place of a complete expression. For example, `MouseDown` and `MouseDown=TRUE` are both evaluated as True when the user presses the mouse button.

- In cases where you want the conditional response to match when the value of the variable is False, you must use the entire expression (e.g., `MouseDown=FALSE`).

- When comparing the value of a character string with character string variables, you always must place the character string inside quotation marks. Quotes aren't necessary when comparing a numerical value with a numerical variable.

- Never use the assignment (:=) operator in place of the equal sign in a conditional response. If you do, you will change the value of the left-hand side of the expression to the value you placed on the right-hand side of the expression.

NOTE You'll see an example of this issue in Chapter 18, "Debugging Your Piece."

The list below shows some examples of how Authorware evaluates conditional expressions to help you when using different types of variable expressions in a conditional response.

Expression...	How Authorware evaluates it...
`AllCorrectMatched`	True when the variable contains a value of True, 1, or On. False when the variable contains a value of False, 0, or Off.
`AllCorrectMatched=TRUE`	True when the variable contains a value of True, 1, or On. False when the variable contains a value of False, 0, or Off.
`AllCorrectMatched=FALSE`	True when the variable contains a value of False, 0, or Off. False when the variable contains a value of True, 1, or On.
`FirstTryCorrect<10`	True when the variable contains a numerical value less than 10. False when the variable contains a numerical value greater than or equal to 10.
`FirstTryCorrect`	Never True because this variable is a system variable that contains only numerical data.
`IconTitle`	Never True because IconTitle is a system variable that contains only character data.
`FirstTryCorrect:=10`	Never True because this expression assigns the variable a value of 10.
`FirstTryCorrect=10`	True when the variable contains the numerical value 10. False when the variable contains any other numerical value.
`EntryText="dollars"`	True only when the variable contains the character string "dollars." False when the variable contains any other characters.
`EntryText`	Never True because this is a system variable that contains only character data.
`EntryText=dollars`	True only when dollars is a custom variable, and contains the same character string contained in the system variable EntryText.

Some of this may not make much sense to you right now. That's okay. You'll learn a great deal more about working with variables and functions in Chapter 14, "Using Functions and Variables." For now, you can get a feel for how conditional responses work by creating the type of password-checking interaction described above. In the next example, you'll create an interaction that requires the user to enter the correct four-digit password to continue.

Setting up the conditional response

To create the conditional response, start by creating a new interaction in which the user types in characters from the keyboard. This is the "password entry" field. By now you should be comfortable setting up a new interaction to handle text entry input from the user. Remember from Chapter 8, "Keyboard and Menu Responses," you need to define only one type of response to do this.

To set up the new interaction:

1. Create a new file.

2. Drag a new interaction icon to the flowline and name it **Password**.

3. Drag a map icon to the right of it to create the text entry response.

4. Set up the text entry response to use Continue branching and to accept any text the user enters. Remember, you want to use the asterisk (*) character in the Pattern field of the response so the user can enter any character into the field.

5. Double-click the interaction icon to open it.

   The toolbox and Presentation window appear.

6. Draw a box in the Presentation window and add some text above it that says: **Please enter your password in the field below.** Close the interaction icon when you have finished.

7. Run the piece by clicking the Restart button on the toolbar.

8. When the text entry field appears, pause the piece and reposition the field so that it fits neatly inside the box you just created, as shown in **Figure 10.9**.

Figure 10.9
Reposition the text entry field so that it fits inside the password entry box.

So far, so good. Although you can type anything into the field, you shouldn't see any feedback right now. Because you are using a conditional response to provide the correct feedback to the user, you don't need to place anything in the map response icon attached to the text entry response.

At this point, you may be wondering why you set up the text entry response to use Continue branching. This is because you want Authorware to continue looking for other possible matches in the interaction—namely, the conditional response you will set up next. Using Try Again branching would cause Authorware to skip over the conditional response because it loops back to the start of the interaction when the text is entered.

Now that you've set up the text entry interaction, go ahead and add the conditional responses you need to check the user's input. You will add two different conditionals: one that matches if the password is valid, and one that matches if the password is invalid.

To set up the first conditional response that checks for the valid password:

1. Drag a new map icon to the right of the text entry response.

   Authorware creates a new text entry response, using the same settings as the first response. You will need to edit this response to create a conditional response.

2. Double-click on the response symbol of the second text entry response.

   The Response Properties dialog box appears.

3. Select Conditional from the Type drop-down list.

   The Response Properties dialog box changes to reflect the properties of the conditional response type, as shown in **Figure 10.10**.

Condition field ⎯

Automatic
matching option ⎯

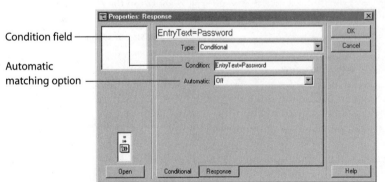

Figure 10.10
The conditional response type properties are displayed in the Response Properties dialog box.

4. In the Condition field, type in: **EntryText=Password**.

When this expression evaluates as True (i.e., when the two variables equal each other), Authorware matches the conditional response. In a moment, you'll set up the second conditional response, which matches when the two variables are not equal to each other.

Before you do this, however, you need to make modifications to the first response and create a new custom variable called Password.

1. Click the Response tab and change the Branch option to Exit Interaction so that Authorware automatically leaves the interaction when this conditional response matches. Change the Erase option to Don't Erase so that your feedback remains on screen.

2. When you have finished, click OK to close the Response Properties dialog box.

The New Variable dialog box appears.

3. In the Initial Value field, type in: "".

This defines the custom variable Password as an empty character variable. (In a moment, you'll assign a set of characters—a "dummy" password—to this custom variable by using a calculation icon.)

4. Select OK to create the Password custom variable.

You should see that the expression you typed into the Condition field of the conditional response appears in the flowline as the title of the response feedback icon, as shown in **Figure 10.11**. At any time, you can change the condition in a conditional response by editing the response feedback icon's title directly in the flowline.

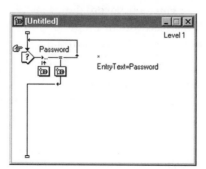

Figure 10.11

The conditional response, as it appears in the flowline.

In review, when you use a conditional response, you enter an expression in the Condition field to set up a match for the response. In this example, you set up an expression that compares the value of the Authorware system variable EntryText with a custom variable you created, Password.

If you remember, EntryText stores the characters the user types into the text entry field. You can use this information to check the user's entry against a previously entered password value you assigned. In a moment, you'll set up the custom variable Password to store the valid user password, use the conditional response to compare the two, and then either display a message to users if they entered an incorrect password, or exit the interaction if they entered it correctly.

Now that you've created the first conditional response, you need to assign a value to Password so that Authorware can check it against the value of EntryText.

1. Place a calculation icon above the Password interaction and name it **Set Password**.

2. Double-click the calculation icon to open it.

   The calculation window appears.

3. In the calculation window, type in: **Password := "1234"**.

4. When you have finished, close the calculation window.

The calculation icon that you just added to the flowline assigns the value "1234" to the custom variable Password each time you run the piece. This gives you a convenient way to test the conditional response to make sure that it's working properly when the correct password is entered in the text entry field.

In a real piece, you would most likely handle this differently. You would have the user enter a password during an initial logon session and then store this password in a separate user record file so that you can access it each time the user runs the piece. Chapter 16, "Tracking the User," explores logon routines in more detail.

To finish setting up the current example, you'll need to add another conditional response that checks for an invalid password:

1. Place a new map icon to the right of the first conditional response.

   This creates a new conditional response and displays a text cursor within the new conditional response's title.

2. Type in: **EntryText<>Password**.

   The "<>" symbol means "is not equal to." When this expression evaluates to True (i.e., when these variables are not equal to each other), Authorware matches the conditional response.

3. Change the second conditional response's branching to Try Again by clicking on the branching symbol in the flowline while pressing the Ctrl key (Windows) or Command key (Macintosh).

4. Double-click the map icon attached to the new conditional response.

   This opens a second panel of the Design window.

5. Add a display icon to the map icon's Design window, double-click the display icon, and add some text that says: **Sorry, that isn't the correct password**. Place this text near the bottom of the Presentation window so that it's not obscured by the text entry field you created earlier.

6. When you have finished, close the display icon, and then close the map icon's Design window panel.

   After performing these steps, your interaction should now appear as shown in **Figure 10.12**. Go ahead and run the piece to see how it works.

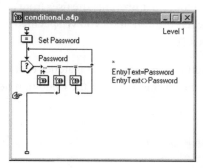

Figure 10.12
The flowline structure for the finished password interaction.

You should now see two things happen—depending on what you entered into the text entry field. If you entered the correct password (1234), Authorware matches the first conditional response, erases the interaction, and continues down the flowline. If you typed in anything else, you see feedback that tells you that you've entered the password incorrectly.

If nothing happens, go back and double-check the expressions you've entered for each conditional response. You also can open the calculation icon where you set up the initial value of `Password` to make sure that you typed in the expression in this calculation icon correctly.

Using auto-matching

The auto-matching option is a special feature of conditional responses. Auto-matching enables a conditional response to react to the target condition in an interaction without user input. The Automatic drop-down list options are located in the Response Properties dialog box when editing a conditional response (see **Figure 10.10** above).

The default value for this option is Off. If you want to turn on auto-matching, you can use one of two settings:

- Selecting On False To True sets the conditional response to match automatically as soon as the target condition changes from False to True. As soon as the condition is True, Authorware no longer matches the conditional response.

- Selecting When True sets the conditional response to match automatically when the condition is True. You want to avoid using When True auto-matching with a conditional response that uses Try Again or Continue branching because this can create a perpetual loop that prevents the user from exiting the interaction when the condition you've specified for the response becomes True.

TIP To set up a conditional response that matches every time in an interaction, use the logical value `True` in the Condition field of the response.

Using a perpetual conditional response

You can use a conditional response's auto-matching capabilities to create perpetual conditional responses that are triggered automatically when a variable condition changes in a piece. Perpetual conditional responses are particularly useful when you need to add automatic branching and feedback control to your piece, and you want it to be active throughout an entire section of the piece. An example of this type of response was mentioned earlier in this chapter when you looked at creating a perpetual time limit for a section of your piece.

To do this, include a simple script at the beginning of the section you're timing that assigns a time-out value to a custom variable based on the value of `SessionTime`—a system variable that contains the number of minutes that the user has ran the piece. An example of this type of script is shown below:

```
TimeOut := SessionTime + 5
```

In the example above, the expression adds an additional 5 minutes to the current value of `SessionTime`, and then assigns the new value to the custom variable `TimeOut`. Because Authorware constantly updates the value of `SessionTime` while the piece runs, you can predict that the value of `SessionTime` eventually will equal the value that you've assigned to `TimeOut`. In the example above, this happens after the piece continues to run for another 5 minutes.

NOTE If you want to use the same perpetual conditional response to time other sections of your piece, remember to reassign a new value to your custom variable each time the user enters a different section of the piece.

Because you now have a numerical value that you can use as your time limit, simply set up a perpetual conditional expression that compares the values of `SessionTime` and `TimeOut`, and then displays feedback when the two values equal each other (i.e., when 5 minutes have elapsed in the piece).

To do this, include the following expression in the Condition field of the conditional response:

```
SessionTime=TimeOut
```

After setting up your condition, change its auto-matching option to On False To True. This enables you to display the appropriate feedback as soon as the time limit expires. You also need to make the response perpetual so you can continue timing the user after Authorware exits the interaction that contains the conditional response. In **Figure 10.13**, you can see an example of how the flowline logic for this type of piece might appear.

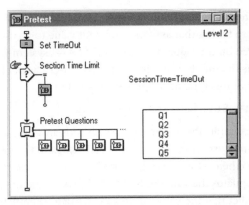

Figure 10.13
The perpetual conditional response appears above the rest of the flowline logic.

 To see an example of a piece that uses a perpetual time limit, look at the example file named TIMEOUT.A4P. This file is located in the Chapter 10 examples folder on the CD-ROM accompanying this book.

Using Event Responses

While time limit, tries limit, and conditional responses are ideal for responding automatically to Authorware system events, you may not always have these options if you are developing interactivity that goes beyond the scope of Authorware's internal functions and variables. In some cases, the better option may be to use a third-party Xtra that provides the type of functionality you need to create a more complex interaction.

For example, because many programs now adhere to open-ended design specifications defined by such technologies as Microsoft's ActiveX and Apple's OpenDoc and AppleScript, you now can hook directly into these types of applications as if you were using an application developed in a language such as C++. To do so, you need to work with a custom Xtra like the ActiveX Xtra included with the Windows version of Authorware. Chapter 20, "Developing with External Code," covers the new custom Xtras included with Authorware in more detail.

Two types of Xtras—scripting and sprite Xtras—allow you to integrate components into a piece that Authorware doesn't directly control. A new response type is now included with Authorware that enables you to respond to any event that is handled by scripting or a sprite Xtra. This is called the event response.

The underlying difference between using the event response and another response such as the button response is that when using an event response, Authorware does not directly track events like a mouse click or a change in a variable condition. Instead, Authorware waits for the Xtra to tell it that something has happened in the piece. In the case of sprite extras, this process is initiated when the user begins to interact with the object created by the Xtra.

NOTE When using Xtras with a piece, remember to distribute them with your final packaged piece. For more information on distributing Xtras with your Authorware piece, see Chapter 17, "Distributing Your Piece."

A powerful example of this is the type of custom web browser interface you can create using the ActiveX Xtra. If you're working with the ActiveX Xtra and have Microsoft's Internet Explorer 3 installed, you can integrate the ActiveX web browser control into your piece to display live HTML documents inside the Authorware Presentation window, as shown in **Figure 10.14**.

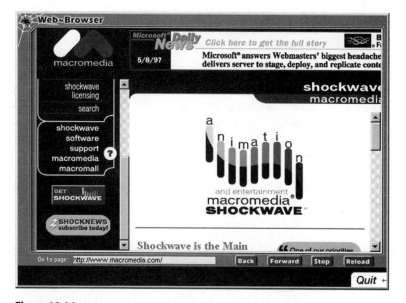

Figure 10.14
Using the ActiveX Xtra, you can display an HTML document in the Presentation window of your piece.

You may even experiment with creating complex interactions that combine Authorware-controlled interactivity with event-related information generated by the Xtra you're using. For example, you might create a text entry field that allows the user to view a web page by typing in the URL. You can use the event response to notify your piece when a new HTML document loads in the Presentation window, or to update onscreen information like the title or URL address of the document when this happens.

 To view a working example of this type of interactivity, take a look at the example file named BROWSER.A4P. It's included in the Chapter 20 examples folder on the CD accompanying this book. In order to view this example file, you must be running Authorware 4 on a Windows machine that has both the Macromedia ActiveX components and Microsoft's Internet Explorer 3 already installed. For information on installing these components, see the documentation included with each of them.

Using a sprite Xtra

The ActiveX Xtra is just one example of the kinds of sprite Xtras that you can integrate into your piece. The term "sprite" is used with these types of Xtras because they create a new object that is displayed in the Presentation window—in this case, the field that displays the HTML document.

NOTE While scripting Xtras don't display objects in the Presentation window, they too can be used with the event response to respond to events handled by the Xtra. Scripting Xtras (such as the FILEIO Xtra included with Authorware) are controlled through the calculation icon. You'll learn more about working with scripting Xtras in Chapter 20, "Developing with External Code."

TIP Several third-party Xtras have been included in the 3RDPARTY folder on the CD accompanying this book. Take a look at them to see what other types of Xtras you can include in your piece.

To use a sprite Xtra with a piece, use the Insert menu to insert a new sprite Xtra icon into the flowline. The sprite Xtra icon contains the type of object created by the sprite Xtra. In many cases, you can double-click the sprite Xtra icon to modify the appearance or behavior of the object and to get more information about the Xtra.

 In the next example, you'll learn more about using a sprite Xtra and the event response in a piece by looking at a sample sprite Xtra included on the CD-ROM accompanying this book. Look in the Chapter 10 examples folder, and you'll find an Xtra named Newoval.x32 (Windows) or OvalSpriteFat (Macintosh). Before going through the next series of steps, copy this Xtra to the Xtras folder inside the folder where you've installed Authorware 4. You must close Authorware, and then reopen it after you've copied the Xtra into the Xtras folder.

In this example, you will work with an Xtra that creates a small oval object that changes shape each time you click on it. First, use the Insert menu to insert the sprite Xtra icon into the flowline:

1. Position the paste hand in the flowline where you want to insert the sprite Xtra icon.

2. Click on the Insert menu.

The categories and names of any sprite Xtras that have been placed in the Authorware Xtras folder are listed under the Insert menu for you, as shown in **Figure 10.15**.

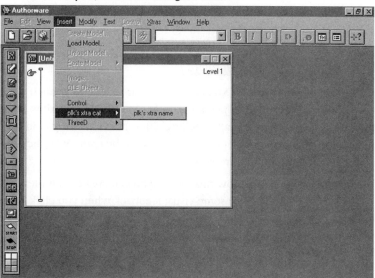

Figure 10.15
Sprite Xtras that you can add to your piece appear in the Insert menu.

3. For this example, choose the sprite Xtra category named Plk's Xtra Cat and then choose the sprite Xtra named Plk's Xtra Name from the submenu that appears.

After choosing the name of the sprite Xtra to insert, a new sprite Xtra icon named PLK's Xtra Name appears in the flowline, as shown in **Figure 10.16**.

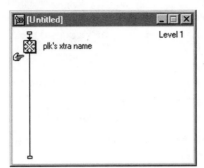

Figure 10.16
The new sprite Xtra icon appears in the flowline.

4. Go ahead and run the piece to see what happens.

You should see the oval-shaped sprite getting larger and then shrinking again. If you click on it once, the sprite changes to an X and holds its position. You can continue clicking on it to see other variations.

Setting up the event response

Although the Xtra doesn't appear to be doing much except changing the sprite's appearance in the Presentation window when you click on it, it's actually tracking different events for you in the background. For instance, it can tell you when the sprite was clicked on by notifying Authorware with an event.

To see how this works, you can create a simple event response that gives you some visual feedback when you click on the sprite in the Presentation window. You use the same type of procedure that you would use to create any other type of response:

1. Place a new interaction icon below the sprite Xtra icon, and give it a name.

2. Drag a new display icon to the right of the interaction icon and drop it into the flowline.

The Response Type dialog box appears.

3. Choose Event from the list of responses and click OK to close the dialog box.

A new event response symbol appears in the flowline, as shown in **Figure 10.17**.

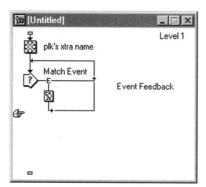

Figure 10.17
The event response, as it appears in the flowline.

4. Change the icon title of the display icon to **Event Feedback**, and then double-click it to open it.

5. Select the text tool and add the following text: **That was a double-click.** When you have finished, close the display icon.

Now that you've created the event response and added some response feedback, select the type of event that you want Authorware to use to match the response by editing the properties for the event response.

1. Double-click on the event response symbol.

The Response Properties dialog box appears, as shown in **Figure 10.18**.

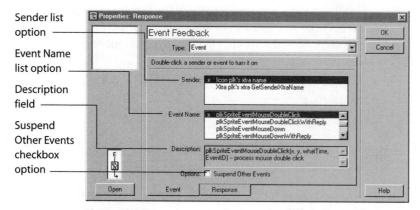

Figure 10.18
The Response Properties dialog box lists the event response properties available.

The name of the sprite Xtra icon appears as Icon PLK's Xtra Name in the Sender option's scrolling list. You should also see the name of the Xtra appear as well, listed as Xtra PLK's Xtra Name. When working with sprite Xtras, you need to select the name of the specific sprite Xtra icon to target when setting up the event response.

NOTE When using an event response with scripting Xtras, you select the name of the Xtra that appears in the Sender list rather than the name of the Sprite Xtra icon.

2. Double-click on the Sender named Icon PLK's Xtra Name.

NOTE This is the same icon title that appears for the sprite Xtra icon in the flowline of your piece.

Selecting the sender name targets the sprite Xtra icon as the sender of the event, and places an x next to the name of the sprite Xtra icon. You'll also see a list of events associated with the sender you've selected. These appear in the Event Name scrolling list.

TIP If you have trouble viewing the entire event name, you can resize the Response Properties dialog box by dragging the bottom left-hand corner of the dialog box.

In order for the event response to match in the interaction, you'll need to select one or more of the events that appear in the Event Name scrolling list. In this example, select the event that is triggered when the sprite is double-clicked in the Presentation window.

3. Double-click on the event named "plkSpriteEventMouse DoubleClick."

An x appears next to the selected event.

NOTE Deselecting a sender also deselects any associated event names that you've selected.

4. When you have finished, click OK to close the Response Properties dialog box.

5. Run the piece to test it.

As you should see, you can now double-click on the sprite object in the Presentation window and see your feedback appear on screen. Because you've selected a double-click event for the response, the text does not appear if you single-click the sprite object. Try changing the event name selected in the Response Properties dialog box to see how this affects the way you interact with the sprite.

Processing multiple events in a piece

When setting up the event response in this example, you saw many other events listed for the sprite Xtra icon. Because each type of sprite or scripting Xtra you use in a piece may contain different kinds of events, you can use the same event response to keep track of multiple events that are being handled by a sprite or scripting Xtra.

Authorware manages multiple events using a constantly updated internal list of events that are being processed. Authorware stores this list in the system variable `EventQueue`. As soon as the Xtra notifies Authorware that an event has occurred (e.g., when the user clicks on the sprite), Authorware places the name of this event and its associated icon into the `EventQueue` list so it can continue processing multiple matched event responses one at a time.

TIP Additional system variables and functions are available when working with an event response. For example, if you need to clear the event queue, you can use the `FlushEventQueue` system function in a calculation icon script. Descriptions of the new event system functions and variables are included in Appendix A, "New Authorware 4 System Functions and Variables."

If you're working with multiple event responses, you may want to select the Suspend Other Events checkbox option for the response. This effectively puts a hold on processing other incoming events when Authorware matches the current event in an event response and displays the appropriate feedback.

If the Suspend Other Events option is not checked, and additional events are in the `EventQueue` list, Authorware continues to look for additional event responses in the current interaction that it can match. This includes all event responses that you've made perpetual in your piece. When responding to Xtra events, Authorware attempts to match any perpetual event responses that you've created before it matches event responses that are not perpetual. However, perpetual event responses are a convenient way to respond to an Xtra event that you want to track throughout the entire piece.

TIP Using the `EventLastMatched` system variable, you can retrieve specific information about the event after it is processed by Authorware. This system variable contains a property list that stores information about the last event matched in an event response. To access this information, you'll need to use the set of system functions that are available for working with lists. These are covered in more detail in Chapter 16, "Tracking the User."

Overall, event responses are an extremely powerful addition to the set of tools you can use in Authorware. They allow you to integrate custom controls into your piece while maintaining a consistency in how you handle user interactivity. When used in combination with other types of responses, they can provide an unlimited range of possibilities for creating sophisticated multimedia applications.

TIP If you would like to see more examples of how to use event responses in a piece, take a look at the Show Me example files included on the Authorware 4 CD-ROM.

Looking Ahead...

In this chapter, you saw the ways in which you can use automatic event handling when creating more sophisticated types of interactivity in your piece. Time limit, tries limit, conditional, and event responses are necessary when monitoring what is happening in the background of your piece while the user works with other types of interaction responses or sprite Xtras that you've inserted into the flowline.

As you can see, your choices are relatively open-ended when structuring the interactivity in an Authorware piece. At times you may want to create several variations of the same interaction, and then base your final design decision on the one that provides the best performance during testing. Hopefully, you can integrate many of the ideas explored in the last several chapters into the interactions that you add to your own pieces.

Interactivity is extremely important in keeping the user involved in what is happening on screen—but no matter how well-designed your interactivity is, the user can't appreciate it unless you also provide a well-designed system of navigation that guides the user through your content. In the next part of this book, you will learn about using the framework and navigate icons—the primary tools for building a system of navigation into your piece.

Controlling Navigation

You probably have encountered this scenario: a CD-ROM or instructional media piece that was too frustrating to use because the layout of the piece and the navigation tools did not allow you to explore the content intuitively. Users coming to a multimedia piece for the first time recognize this problem as soon as they begin clicking on areas that appear to take them nowhere—or worse, lose them in a maze of screens without providing any contextual help to get out of the maze. In these situations, users are inclined to press the eject button rather than stick around for more frustration.

While the navigational structure of a piece may seem apparent to the team designing the application, it is not always clear to the end user. User interface design plays a significant part in helping users understand how to navigate through a piece. However, user interface design is often dictated by the content and the types of navigation that you're using to guide users through the piece.

Consequently, it is very important to focus on developing a solid navigational structure at the start of a piece because it affects not only the structure of the flowline, but the way you design your screens and user interface. In Part III, "Controlling Navigation," you begin to learn how to create the types of navigational structures that are used consistently in Authorware to bring depth and clarity to the various types of content included in a piece.

Working with Pages

What you'll learn...

Designing navigation

Using default navigation controls

Creating pages

Creating a paging structure

How the user will navigate through your content is one of the most challenging tasks that you face when designing an application. If the user has no way of moving through the content, then all you really have accomplished is building a collection of beautifully designed images, sounds, and movies that the user can't explore. It would be like visiting an art museum that contains several levels of priceless antiquities, only to discover that once you're inside, there are no stairways or elevators to take you past the first floor.

Fortunately, Authorware's toolset gives you a great deal of flexibility when designing the various pathways through your application. Authorware can accommodate practically any kind of navigation—whether it's moving from one page to another, jumping between related sections, navigating to a quick help screen, or calling up an image or a sound from another portion of the file that relates in some way to the information currently being displayed.

This chapter discusses navigational concepts by introducing you to the framework and navigate icon, the primary navigation tools in Authorware. You begin by looking at the techniques for creating simple paging structures using these icons.

Complexity often gets in the way of designing the navigational interface for a piece. Remember that complicated user interfaces, for the most part, are exactly that—extremely complicated to use for the person coming to the program for the first time. Before you start developing the navigation for your piece, you may want to ask yourself the following general questions to guide the design process and to focus on the critical aspects of the piece:

- Who is the audience?
- What is the message that you want to convey?
- What essential information do you want the user to take away from this piece?

After you've answered these and similar questions, you can begin working on how to organize the content in your piece. It helps to ask yourself some important content-related design questions, such as the ones listed below:

- What types of media (e.g., text, graphics, sound, video) will I use?
- Do I have areas of content that overlap? If so, will I need to cross-reference them?
- Into how many separate categories does the content fit?
- Can I simplify these categories, or narrow them down at all?
- What kinds of navigation is the user most familiar with?
- How much time will the user have available to view the material in the piece?

Asking yourself questions like these helps you create a visual picture of how you need to organize the piece. Eventually, you'll need to come up with a navigation scheme that fits the criteria you've defined by answering the questions above.

Integrating navigation into a piece

If you've looked at many of the multimedia applications on the market today, you probably have noticed similarities in how they handle navigation. There are two common types of navigation: the standard paging structure that, like a book, lets the user flip back and forth between consecutive pages; and the menu/subtopic structure that enables you to jump from a main level menu to various subtopics and back again.

These navigational structures (or templates) are used frequently, providing two directions of movement through an application—horizontal and vertical. In general, these types of navigation also contain different sets of navigation controls. Paging structures provide the user with at least two controls—a page forward button and a page backward button. Menu/subtopic structures usually offer various controls to jump to a specific section, as well as a control in each section that allows the user to return to the main menu.

Frequently, these types of navigational structures are used together in a piece. For example, if you're creating a multimedia travel guide, the first set of navigation controls that you would set up would be a main menu with choices such as Sights, Hotels, Restaurants, and Shops. Each of these sections might be a collection of pages that contains more information about the topics. In each section, you would set up navigation controls that allow the user to page back and forth through the information.

There are, however, other types of navigation that you may add to this mix. Perhaps you want to set up a navigational control that enables a user to find information by entering a word, such as the name of a museum, a type of cuisine, or an item the user wants to buy. And to make it even easier for the user to return to information that has been displayed already, you would set up two more controls: one to take the user back to the last page that was on screen, and another to list all the pages that have been displayed most recently, and then allow the user to jump to any one of them.

All of these types of navigation are possible using Authorware's framework and navigate icon. You can build many more types of structures that aren't mentioned in the example above. For instance, if you're distributing your piece as a Shockwave piece, you also might include a hypertext link that points the user to a travel-based web site to make hotel reservations online.

As you can see, your choices of navigation in Authorware are extremely open-ended. You have the flexibility of designing the type of navigation for your piece that best suits the content. This is the best approach to designing your piece—creating content that's logically organized and easy to find, and making your navigation controls intuitive.

When creating a navigational structure in Authorware, you can do most of your work using the navigate and framework icons. **Figure 11.1** shows you what these icons look like when placed on the flowline. The navigate and framework icons provide the main options necessary for controlling the flow of navigation in your piece, guiding the user from one area of the piece to another.

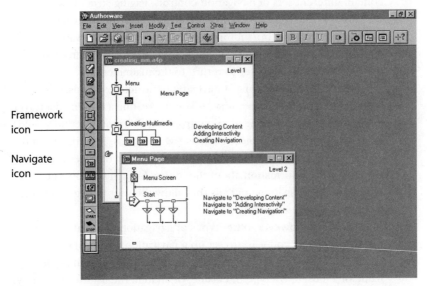

Framework icon

Navigate icon

Figure 11.1
The framework and navigate icons are used together to create navigational structures in Authorware.

The navigate icon

The navigate icon works by jumping presentation on the flowline from one location to another. You can place the navigate icon anywhere in the flowline, just as you can any other icon; however, the destination that the navigate icon points to must always be attached to a framework.

Any icon (or group of icons) attached to a framework is called a "page" in Authorware. Because so many of the techniques for designing navigation revolve around pages and frameworks, you should become familiar with the term and begin using it to describe the navigation in your own piece. As you move forward in this chapter, you'll become more familiar with how frameworks, navigate icons, and pages are used together to create accessible content.

When working with the navigate icon, you'll find it has several specific uses:

- Jumping to any specific page in a framework.

- Jumping to the first or last page in a framework.

- Jumping to a page in a framework that immediately precedes or follows the current page.

- Jumping to the last page viewed in the piece.

- Displaying the Recent Pages dialog box, which contains a list of all the pages recently viewed in the piece.

- Displaying the Find dialog box, which enables the user to do a keyword or full-text search of all the pages in a piece, and then navigate to a specific page found in the search.

Keep in mind that the navigate icon must always point to another page attached to a framework—whether it's the current framework, or one that's located in another part of the piece. Some make the mistake of thinking that "navigate" means navigating to any icon in the file; you'll quickly find that this is not so. When developing your application, try to structure your content around a system of frameworks that take advantage of Authorware's built-in navigational features.

Here are some other points to keep in mind when working with the navigate icon:

- A navigate icon can jump to any framework page in the current open file, but it can't jump to a framework page that is inside another Authorware file.

- A navigate icon only jumps to framework pages; it can't jump directly to a single icon in the flowline (unless it's attached to a framework page). **Figure 11.2**, for example, shows you a framework in which all of its pages are single movie icons.

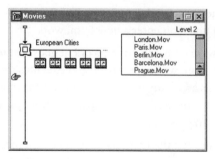

Figure 11.2
You can use different types of icons as pages of a framework.

TIP The navigate icon is a better way of creating navigational paths than using Authorware's GoTo system function to jump to another icon on the flowline. In general, you should try to avoid using the GoTo function when authoring because it can make debugging your flowline logic much more difficult. This is especially true in larger files where you are navigating to nested content.

The framework icon

Think of the framework icon as the container around which you can build your navigational structure. It helps organize groups of icons into related sets (pages), and provides a convenient way of building levels and sublevels of logic within your file automatically.

The framework icon really has three separate components: the framework entry pane, a set of default navigation controls, and the framework exit pane. These three components are visible when you open a framework icon, as shown in **Figure 11.3**. Knowing how these components fit together can help you build navigational structures that are easy to maintain, update, and debug when you run into a problem while testing your piece.

The framework entry pane —

The framework exit pane —

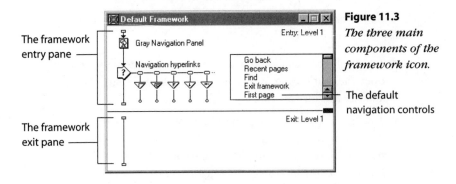

Figure 11.3
The three main components of the framework icon.

The default navigation controls

When using the framework icon in the flowline, the following actions occur each time you enter a new framework:

■ When Authorware enters the framework, it goes first to the flowline in the framework entry pane and executes the logic contained in this area. Any graphics or buttons that you placed inside the entry pane continue to display on every page attached to the framework.

■ After moving through the entry pane, Authorware then navigates by default to the first page attached to the frame-work. If this is a single display icon, it simply displays whatever is in the icon. If this page is a map icon, it executes whatever logic you have set up inside the map icon. You also can navigate directly to other pages in the framework using the navigate icon, as mentioned earlier.

- When Authorware exits the framework, it executes any logic contained in the exit pane. This happens each time Authorware leaves the framework to navigate to another location in the file. When exiting a framework, Authorware erases everything in the framework not set to Prevent Automatic Erase. This may include text, graphics, movies, or sounds that you've added to a page of the framework or to the framework entry pane.

NOTE For information on working with the entry and exit panes of the framework icon, see Chapter 12, "Creating Links and Hyperlinks."

The framework icon has its own set of features that you should know about to help you make decisions regarding the design of your flowline logic. These are explained in more detail below:

- You can use almost any type of icon as a page, except framework, decision, and interaction icons. If you want to include one of these icons, you must place them inside a map icon attached to the framework.

- Frameworks placed in a map icon and attached to another framework are called "nested" frameworks. You can see an example of how a nested framework appears in the flowline in **Figure 11.4**.

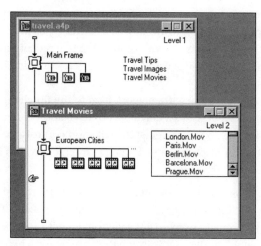

Figure 11.4

A nested framework placed inside the page of another framework.

- If you're using a nested framework, you can point to any one of its pages when setting up a link with the navigate icon. Furthermore, you can create multiple levels of nested frameworks if you are developing more complex navigation for your piece.

NOTE You can use nested frameworks in many different ways. You can see some examples of how to work with nested frameworks in Chapter 12, "Creating Links and Hyperlinks."

The framework and navigate icons work together to provide a quick and easy method of setting up navigation structures in your piece. The framework icon is particularly important, since you cannot create a link with a navigate icon without already having pages attached to frameworks in the flowline.

Another useful feature of the framework icon is its set of default navigation controls that Authorware creates automatically when you drag a new framework icon to the flowline. In the next section, you'll learn how to work with these controls and modify them to fit your own needs.

Using Default Navigation Controls

Navigation controls provide a way of moving around the file. Think of them as a kind of instant menu of traveling options—one that is constantly available in the background to enable you to jump to any framework page from any other location in the piece. You can use them to move forward and backward in a framework, or to point to a specific page in a framework, as well as other types of navigation— including finding a specific word or jumping to a recent page. These types of navigation are discussed in Chapter 12, "Creating Links and Hyperlinks."

When you drag a new framework icon to the flowline, Authorware automatically creates a default set of navigation controls. As you saw in **Figure 11.3** above, the default navigation controls are a set of perpetual button responses attached to an interaction icon in the entry pane of the framework icon.

NOTE All navigation control interaction responses created in the entry pane of a framework are set to perpetual by default. They do not, however, remain perpetual throughout an entire piece; they only are perpetual when the user is inside the framework where they have been placed.

The default navigation controls are comprised of eight custom buttons and a gray panel graphic displayed behind them. To see how they appear when a piece runs, try the following:

1. Create a new file.

2. Drag a framework icon to the flowline and name it.

3. Place several map icons to the right of the framework icon, creating three or four empty pages.

4. Run the piece by clicking the Restart button on the toolbar.

When the piece runs, the default navigation controls for the framework you've created immediately appear in the Presentation window, as shown in **Figure 11.5**. These are the basic set of controls that are stored in the default framework icon model and added to each new framework. The functions of each button have been labeled for you in **Figure 11.5**.

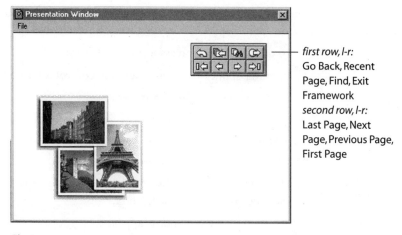

first row, l-r:
Go Back, Recent Page, Find, Exit Framework
second row, l-r:
Last Page, Next Page, Previous Page, First Page

Figure 11.5
The default navigation controls appear in the Presentation window.

Notice that if you've followed the example above and now try to page forward or backward, you don't see anything change inside the Presentation window. This is because all your pages are empty.

To see a change in the way the pages display:

1. Open each map icon one at a time, and add a unique graphic or a text item to each page using new display icons.

2. Run the piece to see how this changes what you see on screen.

Now you see that you can move from one page to another using the default navigation controls. Each page continues to display the navigation controls for you, so you always have the option of moving to another page.

TIP Place navigation controls in the entry pane of the framework icon so they are available on each page of the framework.

This example demonstrates how quickly you can add paging structures to your piece without creating custom templates. At any time, however, you can customize these controls to fit the types of navigation you're creating by using the techniques in the next several sections.

Editing a control button

You can select a new type of button for each control by using the Button Library window or by modifying the original button by creating a copy of it. For more information on working with the Button Library window, see Chapter 7, "Creating Basic Interactivity."

To change the button associated with a control:

1. Open the framework icon where the control is located.

   The Framework window appears.

2. Double-click the button response of the control you want to edit.

   The Response Properties dialog box appears.

3. Click the preview graphic of the button in the upper left-hand corner of the dialog box.

   The Button Library window appears.

4. Select the new button you want to use and click OK.

   The Button Library window closes, and the new button is displayed in the preview area of the Response Properties dialog box.

5. Click OK to close the Response Properties dialog box.

   In some cases, you may want to use the same control button and modify one of its button states (e.g., you might want to add a custom sound to it).

To modify the original button instead of selecting a new button:

1. Open the framework icon where the control is located.

   The Framework window appears.

2. Double-click the button response of the control you want to edit.

   The Response Properties dialog box appears.

3. Click the preview graphic of the button in the upper left-hand corner of the dialog box.

   The Button Library window appears.

4. With the original button selected, click Edit.

   The Button Editor dialog box appears.

5. Select the button state you want to make the change to and then import the new graphic or sound.

NOTE For more information on using the Button Editor, see Chapter 7, "Creating Basic Interactivity."

6. When you have finished, click OK to close the Button Editor, and then click OK again to close the Button Library window.

   The Button Library window closes.

7. Click OK to close the Response Properties dialog box.

Modifying the control button response settings

You can change the way each control behaves by modifying the settings in the Response Properties dialog box of each button response. For example, you can add a variable expression in the Active If True field, or you can add a value in the Optional Key(s) field so that a user can press a key instead of clicking the button each time.

TIP A good example of this is assigning the key named LeftArrow to the Previous Page button, and the key named RightArrow to the Next Page button. This is particularly important when delivering a piece to users who may not always have access to a mouse (e.g., field technicians who only use laptops).

To change the button response settings for a control:

1. Open the framework icon where the control is located.

   The Framework window appears.

2. Double-click the button response of the control you want to edit.

   The Response Properties dialog box appears.

3. Modify the response property settings, and then click OK to close the Response Properties dialog box.

NOTE The third type of change you can make to a default navigation control is to change how Authorware navigates when the control button is clicked. You'll look at some of the ways to do this later in "Setting up custom paging controls."

Repositioning the navigation controls

When running a piece, you may find that the placement of the default navigation controls interferes with other objects you want to display in the upper right-hand corner of the Presentation window. At any time, you can reposition the controls on the screen by using the following steps:

1. Run the piece. If you don't want to run the piece from the beginning, you can use the start flag to start from anywhere before the framework icon's flowline position.

2. When Authorware reaches the first page of the framework, pause the piece by choosing Pause from the Control menu.

3. While holding down the Shift key, click the navigation controls you want to reposition, including the controls background (this is the gray graphic that displays behind the set of buttons).

4. After releasing the Shift key, drag the navigation controls to the part of the screen where you want them to appear.

5. Choose Play from the Control menu to resume play of the piece from where you've paused it.

The controls now appear in this new position on every page in the current framework.

TIP You also can modify the position of the controls by opening the interaction icon in the entry pane of the framework icon and moving the buttons to a new location.

Why don't my navigation controls appear?

In most cases, you'll use buttons to create your navigation controls. If you find that they do not appear on every page of your framework, it is possible that they are hidden by another display object that is set to a layer value higher than 1.

If this is the case, you can set the buttons to a higher layer in the Presentation window:

1. Open the framework icon where you have the buttons located.

2. Select the interaction icon that the buttons are attached to and choose Icon > Properties from the Modify menu.

NOTE If these are the default navigation controls, the icon is named Navigation Hyperlinks.

The Interaction Icon Properties dialog box appears.

3. Click the Display tab at the bottom of the dialog box to display the Layer setting.

4. Type in a new value in the Layer field that is greater than the layer value used with other display objects in the framework.

NOTE The default navigation controls are automatically set to a layer of 1 inside a new framework icon.

5. When you have finished, click OK to close the dialog box.

This technique only works if you want to display the buttons on top of other graphics or text. Remember that buttons, like other display objects, are hidden from view if they are displayed in the same area of the Presentation window as digital video or Director movies you've placed in a page of the framework. Keep this in mind as you continue to design the screen layout of the elements of your piece.

Replacing the default navigation controls

Both the default navigation controls and the framework icon that contain the controls are stored in a model that is located in the folder where you have installed Authorware. Whenever you drag a new framework icon from the icon palette to the flowline, Authorware uses this model to create the new framework icon on the flowline.

If you find yourself frequently using the same set of custom navigation controls, you may want to replace Authorware's default framework model with your own framework model. Remember, however, that any model you create needs to contain both the navigation controls and the framework icon that contains them.

When creating a new default framework model, you don't need to limit yourself to just the navigation controls and the framework icon. You also can include other icons in the entry pane and exit pane of the framework that you want to appear every time you drag a new framework icon to the flowline.

For example, maybe you have a screen layout template with a fixed-size text field and positioning guides that you regularly use to help position other objects on screen. In this case, you would include this display icon in the entry pane of the framework before creating the model, as shown in **Figure 11.6**.

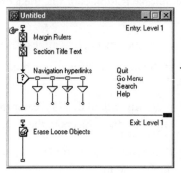

Figure 11.6
You can place icons in both the entry and exit pane of the framework before saving it as a model.

To make a framework icon the default model, create a backup copy of the current default model by renaming it. (This allows you to switch back to the original model at any time.) Then set up a new framework icon with the new default controls and save the framework icon as a model in the same folder where you have Authorware installed.

You can use the following steps to rename the current default model:

1. Go to the folder where you have the Authorware application installed and find the default framework icon model. The file name that you need to find depends on the platform you are using:

Windows   Find the model file named Framewrk.a4d.

Macintosh   Find the model file named Default Framework Icon.

2. Rename this file so that it's not erased when you save the ncw default model into the same location.

Next, set up the new framework icon:

1. Drag a framework icon to the flowline. Leave it untitled.

2. Double-click the framework icon to display the framework window.

3. Set up the navigation controls inside the entry pane of the framework.

4. Set up any other icons that you want to be part of the default icon in the entry and exit panes.

5. Close the framework window.

Now you need to turn the icon into a model:

1. Select the framework icon by clicking on it.

2. Choose Create Model from the Insert menu.

The Model Description dialog box appears.

3. Type a short description of the model, and then click OK.

The Create New Model dialog box appears, asking you to name the new model and save it.

4. For the name of the model, type **Framewrk.a4d** if you are working on the Windows platform. Type **Default Framework Icon** if you are working on the Macintosh platform.

5. Click Save. Remember to save the model in the same folder where Authorware is installed.

NOTE If the navigation controls appear on the flowline instead of the framework icon, you've saved the navigation controls as a model—not the framework icon that contains the navigation controls.

Each time you begin a new piece, plan the types of navigation controls you will need, and then decide whether to create a default set that you can add to the piece using the technique described above.

In many cases, it may make sense to create a custom framework model separate from the default framework model so you have the default controls to work with if you need them. Using the same technique, you can create a custom framework model that you can paste into your piece, as you would any other model that you've created. For more information on using models, see Chapter 6, "Managing Your Content."

There are obviously a great many ways to integrate navigation controls into your piece. You'll find that while each piece may contain different types of content, you'll frequently return to the same types of navigation controls—particularly paging controls—even though the appearance of these controls will change depending on how you design the look and feel of your interface. After you've decided on the type of controls for your piece, you can start adding content to the flowline. In the next section, you'll learn the basic ways to create pages by using the framework icon.

Creating Pages

Although any icon attached to a framework icon is referred to as a page, a framework page doesn't necessarily have to be a display icon filled with text or graphics. It can be a movie icon, a sound icon, or even a map icon that contains a complex sequence of icons. You can use almost any icon as a separate page (as mentioned earlier, this doesn't work with framework, decision, or interaction icons), or you can add more complex icon structures to a page, as long as you place them inside a map icon.

Here are some examples of how you might use pages in your piece:

- Suppose that you're creating an annotated version of Chopin's waltzes. You could set up each page to play a recording of one of the waltzes, accompanied by a text commentary.

- If you're explaining the process of editing a film, you could set up the first page in a framework to show an unedited scene, the second page to show the scene after it's been cut, the third to show the scene with special effects, the fourth with sound effects, the fifth with music, and the sixth with the final cut. (You might even add a seventh page that shows the "Special Director's Cut" of the scene, with restored footage.)

- Frameworks pages aren't always used to display a sequence of content. You also can use them to work around tricky issues, like creating a text form with multiple fields. Using the framework icon, you could set up each of the fields as a separate page with a text-entry interaction. Instead of using the default navigation controls, you could create custom controls that use the Tab key to move from the current page to the next one and Shift-Tab to move from the current page to the previous one.

For an example of setting up this type of multiple-field form using a framework icon, see the example file named COOLFORM.A4P. It's located in the Chapter 8 examples folder on the CD accompanying this book.

You can use pages in many unique ways, and each application that you design will probably use them a bit differently. Because of the way pages and frameworks work together, you have a great deal of flexibility designing the structure of your application. The structure that you finally decide to use should depend primarily on the type of content that you plan to deliver.

You've already worked with pages a bit when you learned about the default navigation controls earlier in this chapter. As you now know, when you create the pages of a framework, you follow these three basic steps:

1. Add a new framework icon to the flowline and name it.

2. Drag the icon you want to use as a page to the right of the framework icon and name it.

3. Add the appropriate content to the icon.

If you have similar content in each page, you can save a lot of time by adding some preliminary content to the first page, and then copying and pasting this icon or group of icons as new pages on the same framework. Each page retains the properties and icons of the first page, so you don't have to reinvent the wheel each time you add a new page to the framework.

NOTE This technique is especially important if you want to keep text in the same position on screen between pages.

Of course, if your piece contains a great deal of content, adding each page to the frameworks in your piece quickly becomes time-consuming. Fortunately, there are several techniques that allow you to create pages for frameworks very easily. You'll look at these in the next two sections.

Creating pages using drag and drop

You can quickly add new pages to a framework by using the mouse to drag and drop a group of files from the Macintosh or Windows desktop directly into the Authorware application window. This works not only with graphics, but with sound, video, and text files as well.

NOTE Drag-and-drop support is only included for the file types supported by Authorware. For a list of the files that Authorware supports, see Chapter 3, "Working with Text and Graphics" and Chapter 5, "Adding Sound and Video."

To create a set of pages using drag and drop:

1. Add a new framework icon to the flowline and position the paste hand to the right of the framework icon.

2. Switch to the desktop while Authorware is running and open the folder that contains the items you want to add to the framework.

3. Switch back to Authorware using the taskbar (Windows), or use the application menu (Macintosh) and position the Authorware window so the desktop and folder that contain the items display in the background.

NOTE You may have to temporarily resize the Authorware window while importing files this way.

4. Using the cursor, select the items in the folder that you want to import, drag them from the desktop into the Authorware window, and then drop them onto the flowline.

After Authorware imports the files, a new series of pages attached to the framework display with the names of the files you've imported. The type of icon that Authorware uses to create the page depends on the type of files you're importing. For example, dragging and dropping a set of PICT images adds a series of display icons to the framework.

TIP When importing sounds and graphics this way, Authorware stores them internally by default. You can create links to the external files you're adding to the framework by holding down the Shift key while you drag and drop the files.

Creating pages with RTF files

Authorware gives you one other option for creating pages. When you create, edit, and save a multipage document inside a word processor as an RTF (Rich Text Format) document, you can import it directly into your file and have Authorware create pages for it automatically. When you import the file into Authorware, each page of your file can be placed into a new display icon and attached to the framework.

NOTE When using this technique, you must make sure that any pages you create inside the RTF file are separated with hard page breaks. Otherwise, Authorware assumes that the RTF file is a single-page text file and imports the entire document into one display icon.

To import an RTF file and have Authorware create a separate icon for each page in the file:

1. Drag a new framework icon to the flowline.

2. Position the paste hand to the right of the framework icon.

3. Choose Import from the File menu.

The Import dialog box appears.

4. Select the name of the RTF file you want to import and click Import.

The RTF Import dialog box appears, as shown in **Figure 11.7**.

Hard
Page Break
options —

Figure 11.7
The RTF Import dialog box.

Text
Object
options

5. In the RTF Import dialog box, you have several options for importing the pages into Authorware. Selecting Create New Display Icon from the Hard Page Break options area creates a new page each time Authorware encounters a hard page break in the file. Use the Ignore option if you want to ignore the hard page breaks.

In addition, you can choose whether or not to use standard or scrolling text for each page by selecting one of the two options (Standard or Scrolling) listed in the Text Object options area.

NOTE If you don't know whether or not your pages are larger than a single screen, select the Scrolling option.

6. After selecting how you want to import the text file, click OK to import the file.

After Authorware finishes importing the RTF document, you can see multiple display icons (one for each page of your document) attached to the framework. Authorware creates a new name for each page, based on the page number and the name of the file. For example, if your document is named TRAVEL.RTF and contains four pages, the flowline will appear as shown in **Figure 11.8** after importing this document.

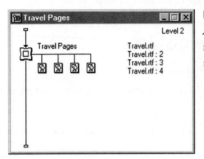

Figure 11.8

A four-page RTF document added to a framework.

TIP You also can use the drag-and-drop technique discussed earlier to import an RTF document into a piece.

The RTF import method is a great way to save time when working on a piece. It also allows you to tackle the formidable task of text editing and formatting in a word-processor environment, which is familiar to most people. This is especially important for those of you who have existing electronic documents that you want to repurpose for new interactive applications.

NOTE When importing RTF files, Authorware retains any text formatting characteristics that you have applied to the text before saving the document. It also retains the names of any styles you used to create the document. It does not, however, support such things as table formatting or OLE objects that have been inserted into the document.

As mentioned earlier, paging structures are used frequently, and are fairly easy to set up. However, there are many techniques that you haven't learned yet that can make navigating through pages in your piece a bit easier. In the next section, you'll get a feel for the ways in which you can work with the framework icon and navigate icon to set up custom navigation control over your piece.

Creating a Paging Structure

When creating pages and then testing your piece, the default navigation controls appear unless you've modified them first or you've created a new default framework model. Sometimes, you may need to create your own custom paging buttons for a particular framework rather than rely on the default navigation controls.

You can see an example of this by creating a simple paging structure that has only two buttons: a Previous Page and a Next Page button.

To create this paging structure, you need to create a new framework first:

1. Create a new file in Authorware.

2. Drag a new framework icon to the flowline and name it **Content Frame**.

3. Use one of the techniques described in the sections above to add several new pages to your framework.

Before you begin setting up your custom set of navigation controls for the paging structure, the next section takes a quick look at some of the options that are available to you with the framework to control how pages display inside the Presentation window.

Creating a transition between pages

The first thing you may want to do after creating a new framework is to assign a transition to the framework icon. The transition controls how pages of a framework are erased and displayed when moving from page to page.

To set a transition between pages in a framework:

1. Click once on the framework icon to select it.

2. Choose Icon > Properties from the Modify menu.

Shortcut: To open the Icon Properties dialog box, double-click on the icon while pressing the Ctrl key (Windows), or Command key (Macintosh).

The Framework Icon Properties dialog box appears, as shown in **Figure 11.9**. As you can see, the page transition is set to Smooth Change by default.

Page
Transition
option —

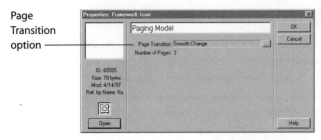

Figure 11.9
*The Framework Icon
Properties dialog box.*

3. To select a different page transition, click the button labeled
[...] next to the Page Transitions description field.

The Page Transition dialog box appears.

4. Select a transition from those listed in the dialog box. Transitions are listed by category. If you want the transition to
happen at a different rate, you can modify the Duration and
Smoothness settings at this time.

5. After selecting a transition, click OK.

The Page Transition description field is updated to show the page
transition you've selected.

6. Click OK to close the Framework Icon Properties dialog box.

You can apply a transition effect to a framework at any time;
however, if you're working with multiple frameworks with similar
content, it's usually a good idea to create one instance of the framework with the transition already applied to it. Then copy and paste
this icon to other parts of the file so that you can keep better track
of which transition effects you're using.

TIP You can preset your page transitions by including this setting
in the framework icon saved with the default framework model.

If you've already applied a transition to a specific page, the page's
transition is displayed rather than the framework transition, but only
when navigating to that page. For instance, a display icon already may
have a dissolve transition applied to it. If you're using this display icon
as a single page, and you've selected a wipe transition for the framework, you'll see the dissolve transition rather than the wipe transition
when you go to the page of the display icon. If you've placed the
display icon inside a map icon with other logic, you will see the
framework transition first, and then the display icon transition.

NOTE Using transitions can sometimes slow down performance on systems with slower processor speeds because it requires more processing power to animate the transition effect. If you are developing for multiple machine configurations, it's wise to use the Smooth Change transition effect because unlike the dissolve and wipe effects, it doesn't require the computer to move as many pixels on the screen.

Setting up the new controls

Now that you've created a new framework icon and selected a transition for your pages, you're ready to create a new set of buttons to control how the user moves between pages.

Begin by deleting the existing paging controls:

1. Double-click the framework icon that contains the controls you want to replace.

   The framework window appears.

2. Select all icons in the entry pane of the framework window by dragging a selection area around them with the mouse; then press the Delete key to clear them, or use the Clear command from the Edit menu.

Shortcut: You can select all icons in the current framework window by using Ctrl+A (Windows), or Command+A (Macintosh).

To set up new Next and Previous buttons, create the new controls by using the button response type for each control and select the navigation options you want to use:

1. Drag an interaction icon from the icon palette to the entry pane of the framework window and name the interaction icon **Page Buttons**.

2. Create the Previous button by dragging a navigate icon from the icon palette to the right of the interaction icon.

   The Response Type dialog box appears.

3. Since the Button response type is already selected for you, click OK.

   You'll see a new button response appear next to the interaction icon. Because you have not assigned a destination for the navigate icon you're using for the button response icon, it appears with the title Unlinked in the framework window.

4. Change the navigate icon's title from Unlinked to **Previous Page**.

5. Create the Next button by dragging another navigate icon to the right of the one you just created. Title this navigate icon **Next Page**. Your custom navigation controls should now appear in the framework window as shown in **Figure 11.10**.

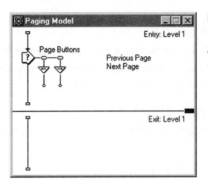

Figure 11.10
The modified navigation controls, as they appear in the framework window.

When creating the two controls, you may have noticed how Authorware handles creating new responses in a framework window. When you add a new response type to an interaction icon that is inside the entry pane of a framework icon, Authorware automatically makes it perpetual and sets its exit branching to Return. It does this for each additional response that you have added to the interaction icon.

While you're working with buttons in this example, the response type for navigation controls isn't limited to just buttons. You can use any type of response that you can set to Perpetual in the Response Properties dialog box. For example, you can use a hot spot response, but you can't use a keypress response because it cannot be made perpetual in an interaction.

Now that you've created your two navigation buttons, you need to assign the proper navigation options to each of them by doing the following:

1. Double-click the navigate icon attached to the response named Previous Page.

The Navigate Icon Properties dialog box appears, displaying the default set of destination options. You can use these options to target a specific page anywhere in your piece. You'll learn more about using these options in Chapter 12, "Creating Links and Hyperlinks."

In this example, you're creating controls that navigate either to the next or the previous page in the framework. To do this, you'll need to change your Destination setting for the navigate icon.

2. Select Nearby from the Destination drop-down list.

The Navigate Icon Properties dialog box changes to display the options for the Nearby destination type, as shown in **Figure 11.11**. The Page options area is where you select the destination page for the navigate icon.

Destination
option ——

Navigate
icon
preview ——

Page
options area ——

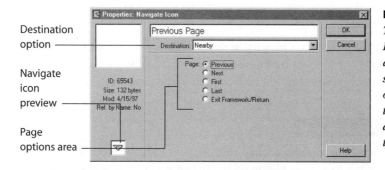

Figure 11.11
The Navigate Icon Properties dialog box, showing the options for the Nearby destination type.

You'll see that Previous has already been selected for you. This is the option that you need to use for your Previous Page button. However, notice that if you select any of the other Page options, the navigate icon preview area updates to show you how the navigate icon will appear on the flowline (see **Figure 11.11**). This is covered in more detail in Chapter 12, "Creating Links and Hyperlinks."

TIP You can quickly determine what type of navigation you're using in a particular section of a piece by learning how the navigate icons appear when they're in the flowline.

3. If you've selected a different Page option for the button, switch it back to Previous, and then click OK to close the dialog box.

You can set up the Next Page button using the same type of procedure:

1. Double-click the navigate icon named Next Page.

2. Repeat steps 2 and 3 in the above procedure, this time selecting Next as the Page option.

Go ahead and test your new paging structure. If you have performed everything correctly, you should now see two buttons on your screen when you run the piece. One is labeled Previous Page and the other one is labeled Next Page. Clicking on the Previous Page button takes you to the previous page in the framework. Clicking on the Next Page button takes you to the next page in the framework.

If you did not see anything change on screen, chances are you either have just one icon attached to your framework, or each page is displaying the same text or graphic on screen. You need to create several different pages of text or graphics to see a change between screens.

TIP If you haven't planned in detail what you want your pages to contain, it's usually best to use a map icon to build the navigation structure so you can add new content to the page at any time.

Closing the paging "loop"

You may have noticed when running your example piece, if you click the Next Page button on the last page of the framework, you can return to the first page in the framework. When clicking the Previous Page button on the first page of the framework, you're sent back around to the last page of the framework.

In Authorware, pages automatically loop around like this—that is, unless you modify the way your navigation controls work by disabling them when you're at either end of the paging structure. You can do this easily by placing variable expressions in the Active If fields of both buttons.

To modify the Next Page button so that it doesn't loop around to the first page:

1. Double-click on the Next Page button response.

   The Response Properties dialog box appears.

2. Click the Response tab at the bottom of the dialog box, and add the following expression in the Active If field: `CurrentPageNum < PageCount`.

3. When you have finished entering the expression, click OK to close the dialog box.

To modify the Previous Page button so that it doesn't loop around to the last page:

1. Double-click on the Previous Page button response.

The Response Properties dialog box appears.

2. Click the Response tab at the bottom of the dialog box, and add the following expression in the Active If field: `CurrentPageNum > 1`.

3. Click OK to close the dialog box.

4. Go ahead and run the piece to test it.

When you run the piece, you should now see that on page one of the framework, the Previous Page button is dimmed, and on the last page, the Next Page button is dimmed. To understand how this works, you need to know a bit more about the two system variables, `CurrentPageNum` and `PageCount`, that you used in the expressions in the example above.

The system variable `CurrentPageNum` contains the number of the page that is currently displaying. The system variable `PageCount` contains the total number of pages attached to the current framework. These system variables are specific to the framework icon, and you can use them for many different purposes. For the most part, however, they are useful in situations where you need to keep track of what page you're on and adjust the piece based on this information.

Because you are trying to avoid wraparound pages, you should disable the Next Page button whenever you're on the last page of the framework. The expression, `CurrentPageNum<PageCount`, compares the current page number with the total number of pages attached to the current framework icon. As long as this expression is True (i.e., as long as you're not on the last page), the button remains active.

Likewise, the expression typed in for the Previous Page button, `CurrentPageNum>1`, compares the value of the current page number with 1 (the first page of the framework). When you reach the first page, the Previous Page button is made inactive.

NOTE Use these expressions carefully when working with nested frameworks because they may produce the results that you least expect. For instance, a button that you set to inactive on the last page of the parent framework will become inactive when the user goes to the last page of a nested framework.

This is a simple example of how you can use Authorware system variables and variable expressions to control how navigation happens in your file.

Looking Ahead...

Not every piece requires that you use the framework icon and navigate icon to control how the user explores your piece. However, you'll find that these two tools are indispensable when you need to develop fully functioning navigation quickly. They also improve your capability to work within the Authorware Design window, since they help you to organize your content and develop paths through it that you can easily update and troubleshoot if you run into problems.

You can improve navigation in your piece by simply learning how the navigate and framework icons work together. In this chapter, you learned a few of the basic techniques for integrating navigation controls into a piece, including ways of importing content and creating custom paging controls. In Chapter 12, "Creating Links and Hyperlinks," you'll continue exploring ways of navigating through a piece—including search and hypertext functionality—by looking at Authorware's set of navigation tools in more detail.

Creating Links and Hyperlinks

While paging structures allow the user to browse specific sections of content, most pieces tend to combine paging with other kinds of navigation that enable the user to approach the content from many angles. This is especially important when designing comprehensive pieces that link many channels of information together by using links between related sections. In such a case, it may be desirable to provide navigational tools that help do the data-mining for the user, such as a search window or a window that enables navigation to previously viewed sections of a piece.

As your content grows larger and more information-dense, you may want to develop other types of navigational controls, such as hypertext links and icon cross-referencing, because they provide the best approach to connect related areas of information to one another in a meaningful way. This chapter focuses on adding all of these types of navigational elements to your piece by using the navigate and framework icons.

When you set up a navigation link in your piece, you make it possible for the user to jump from Authorware's current location—that is, a page on a framework—to another destination page. Because Authorware handles the jump itself, your job as author is to decide the appropriate types of links to use and where to place them.

Consequently, when building navigation into your piece, you need to think about the types of links that you want to use before you begin adding frameworks and navigate icons to the flowline. While you can continue to refine a navigation structure as you get further into a project, you already should have preliminary specifications outlined in your design plan that indicate how you plan to link content together.

You might recall that this is essentially the crux of creating a good flowchart for your piece, as discussed in Chapter 1, "Getting Started." After you begin working on larger projects in Authorware, you will realize how important it is to have a preliminary navigational structure worked out either on paper or in your head before you begin creating your piece. The navigational structure of a piece affects not only the way you create your flowline logic, but also how you design your screen layout and user interface. It's wise to take some time to plan your navigation before you hit the flowline.

Chapter 11, "Working with Pages," mentioned that you should design every Authorware piece around a set of frameworks. This is because the framework icon along with the navigate icon are the components that you use to build all types of navigation in a piece, whether you simply use paging structures or you use embedded content links between sections and other types of hypermedia elements.

Designing your piece around frameworks makes it easier for you control display elements like buttons and text between sections of a piece, as well as control the erasure of these elements when you leave a section. These reasons alone make using frameworks an extremely valuable and time-saving way of designing the structure of your piece. The added advantage of being able to create instant links between any section of your piece makes frameworks essential when structuring your navigation.

Types of links

When using the framework icon and navigate icon to create links between sections of a piece, you have two basic options:

■ You can create one-way links or "jumps" that take the user to another page of the piece.

■ You can create call-and-return links that jump the user to another page of the piece, and then immediately return them to the originating page.

One-way links are used mostly when designing navigation in Authorware. A one-way link jumps the user directly to another page of a framework, continuing presentation from the flowline inside this page. To get back to the originating page, you must set up another one-way link elsewhere in the flowline.

A call-and-return link, on the other hand, is the "boomerang" approach to creating a link. Call-and-return links jump to a page temporarily, and then return the user to the page previously visited automatically. They are particularly useful, for instance, when you want to set up a help screen that is accessible at any time in the piece, and you also want the user to be able to jump back immediately to the same page after looking at the help screen.

NOTE Call-and-return links are covered in more detail later in this chapter, in "Calling a page."

To understand how simple links are used, take a look in the next section at the easiest type of link to build—one that jumps the user to a specific page in the piece.

Linking to any page

You can add links to your piece in many ways. In some cases, you might set up a link inside an interaction to respond to the user clicking a button or a hot spot. This is used commonly when setting up the type of menu/subtopic navigational structure discussed in Chapter 11, "Working with Pages." **Figure 12.1** shows you what a typical menu/subtopic navigational structure looks like in the flowline.

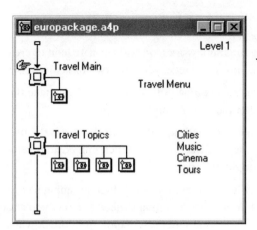

Figure 12.1
A typical menu/subtopic flowline structure.

In the example above, the menu screen is contained inside a page of another framework in the flowline. If you open up the page named Travel Menu, as shown in **Figure 12.2**, you can see the one-way links that are being used to navigate the user to a particular page of the framework named Travel Topics.

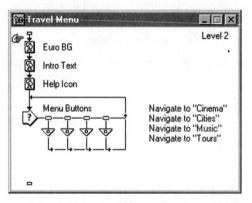

Figure 12.2
One-way links are used inside the menu page.

This is a useful way to set up this type of structure because it allows you to immediately return to the menu at any time by including a one-way link that points to the menu page.

To set up the type of one-way links used in the menu navigation example above, first you need to create a page attached to a framework. Then add an additional framework and pages to the flowline so that you can specify a destination. You can create your menu navigation controls by using an interaction icon and several button responses in the entry pane of the menu framework (replacing the default navigation controls), or you can place them directly on the flowline inside the page of the menu framework (see **Figure 12.2** above).

After setting up your basic flowline structure, you can use the following steps to create your links to specific pages (i.e. sections) of the destination framework:

1. Double-click the navigate icon in which you want to create the link.

   The Navigate Icon Properties dialog box appears, as shown in **Figure 12.3**.

Select Jump or Call-and-Return link.

Select current framework pages to view.

Select destination page.

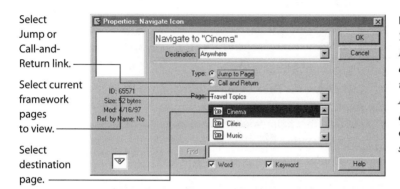

Figure 12.3

The Navigate Icon Properties dialog box with the Anywhere destination option selected.

As you can see, the navigate icon's destination option is set by default to Anywhere. You will learn more about the other destination options later in this chapter.

2. Click on the Page drop-down list.

   This displays a list of all the frameworks in the current file.

3. Select the framework that contains the target page to which you want to link.

   Authorware lists the pages for the selected framework in the display field below the Page drop-down list.

4. To create the link, click on the name of the page displayed in this field.

   This creates a link to the page you've selected. The name of the page remains highlighted in the scrolling list, even after you close the dialog box and open it again.

   NOTE If your navigate icon is Untitled, Authorware replaces its title with the title Navigate to "[name of page selected]." For example if you've selected a page named Solar System, the navigate icon's title changes from Untitled to Navigate to "Solar System."

5. When you have finished creating the link, click OK to close the dialog box.

If you're creating a link to a specific page, but are not sure which framework contains the page that you want to select, you have two options:

■ You can select Entire File from the Page drop-down list, which displays all pages for every framework in the piece. However, since these are not listed alphabetically, it may be difficult to find the page you're looking for, especially in a piece with many frameworks.

TIP Be careful about using the same names for pages. This makes it much harder to find a specific page in a large piece when using the Entire File selection method.

■ You can use the Find button to search for the page. When using the Find button, you can type a word or keyword into the Find field that helps you locate the page. You can search for a page using either the Word or Keyword options or both. These options are labeled for you in **Figure 12.4**.

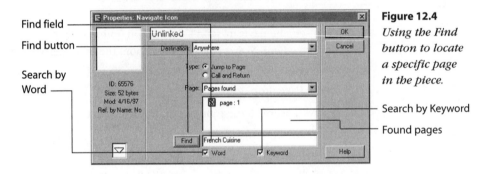

Find field

Find button

Search by Word

Figure 12.4
Using the Find button to locate a specific page in the piece.

Search by Keyword

Found pages

To use the Find button to set up a link:

1. Select either the name of the framework or EntireFile from the Page drop-down list.

2. Type in the word or keyword you want to search for in the Find field and set your Word and Keyword options.

The Find button becomes active.

3. Click the Find button.

Authorware displays the pages found in the Page field.

4. Click on the name of the page to which you want to link.

When using the Word option to find a page, Authorware displays all pages in the piece that contain the text you've entered in the Find field. The text may be inside either a display icon or an interaction icon, depending on the type of icons you've placed inside the pages of your frameworks.

When using the Keyword option, Authorware displays any pages in the piece that have been marked with the keyword you've entered in the Find field. For more information on setting up keywords for pages, see "Searching for a page" later in this chapter.

You can use both of these find options at the same time to facilitate the process of finding a page. You also can use the "and" (&) and "or" (|) characters to do a Boolean search for a page. For example, if you want to find all pages in a piece that contain the word "optical" or "mathematics," you would type the following into the Find field: **optical | mathematics**.

NOTE If you already have searched for a page and want to change the text you're looking for, first reselect the name of the framework or Entire File from the Page drop-down list before clicking the Find button again. Otherwise, Authorware does not update the list of found pages.

TIP The Find button functionality is similar to the functionality of the Find window, which displays when you've set up a navigate icon to use the Search destination type. You'll learn more about this later in the chapter in "Searching for a page."

These are the basic techniques you need to know to get started adding navigation links and cross-referencing to your piece. You can use one-way links to pages in any number of ways to guide the user from one section to another. However, what happens if the user clicks on a link you've set up and gets lost? The next section takes a look at this issue.

Returning to a previous page

When designing your navigational structure, think about how you use a web browser such as Netscape Navigator or Microsoft Internet Explorer. For example, when browsing the web, you always can return to the previously loaded document. This is extremely helpful if you happen to be nodding off while clicking links included and eventually want to return to the page that offered the most entertainment.

You'll find that this type of "backtracking" is very useful when setting up the navigation in your piece. It's always important to give users an easy way to return to places they've visited before. The travel guide described earlier in this chapter is a good example. After paging through descriptions of dozens of hotels, a user is likely to want to return to one or two hotels and get more detailed information. Likewise, a user who is searching for something specific—skipping around, rather than going from one page to the next—occasionally is going to want to jump back to the last page before looking for other relevant information.

When you have selected Recent for your destination option in the Navigate Icon Properties dialog box, there are two Return settings available that enable you to create both types of backtracking described above:

■ The Go Back setting returns to the last page Authorware displayed. This works differently than the Previous and Next settings that are available when using the Nearby destination option. The Previous setting takes the user to the page to the immediate left of the current page in the framework; the Next setting takes the user to the page to the immediate right of the current page. The Go Back setting takes the user to the last page displayed, regardless of which framework to which it is attached.

■ The List Recent Page setting displays the Recent Page window, showing the pages the user has visited most recently. When you create this type of link, the Recent Page window displays on top of the Presentation window, as shown in **Figure 12.5**. The most recent page is displayed at the top of the list of pages. The user can select any page from the list and return to it by double-clicking the name of the page.

Figure 12.5
The Recent Page window.

NOTE Authorware displays the icon title of each page in the Recent Page window, so it's a good idea to give your pages clear, descriptive names. For example, if you've titled a page of a framework Stories-0021, then "Stories-0021" appears in the Recent Page window if the user has visited this page. This is also true when using Authorware's Find window, as you will learn in "Searching for a page," later in this chapter.

To set up a link that allows the user to backtrack:

1. Double-click on the navigate icon in which you want to create the link.

   The Navigate Icon Properties dialog box appears.

2. Select Recent from the Destination drop-down list.

   When you select Recent, the dialog box changes appearance and displays the two Recent destination settings: Go Back, and List Recent Pages, as shown in **Figure 12.6**.

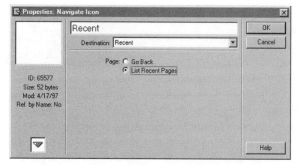

Figure 12.6
The Navigate Icon Properties dialog box with the Recent destination option selected.

3. Select Go Back if you want to take users back to the page from which they just came. Select List Recent Pages if you want to display a list of the pages that users have visited most recently.

4. When you have finished, click OK to close the dialog box.

When using these types of navigation links in a piece, it's common to make them part of a navigation button control inside the framework entry pane. In general, you only need to include them in one place in the piece—in the entry pane of the first framework the user enters. (This is usually referred to as the "parent" framework.) This makes them available on every page of the piece, whether or not you're using nested frameworks.

TIP Go Back and Recent Pages buttons are included in the set of default navigation controls that Authorware creates when you drag a new framework icon to the flowline. At times, it may be easier to use these rather than create your own custom controls, or you can modify the appearance of the default buttons if you like.

Customizing the Recent Page window

When you set up a link to display the Recent Page window, you may want to customize the window by changing its title, limiting the number of pages that it displays at one time, or having it automatically close when the user clicks on a page. You can quickly change these options inside the Navigation Setup dialog box.

To customize the Recent Page window:

1. Choose File > Navigation Setup from the Modify menu.

The Navigation Setup dialog box appears, as shown in **Figure 12.7**.

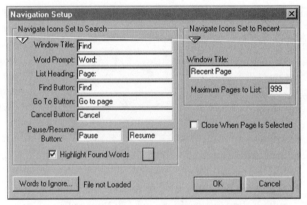

Figure 12.7
The Navigation Setup dialog box.

There are three options (labeled for you in **Figure 12.7**) that affect the way the Recent Page window works:

- If you want to change the title of the Recent Page window, enter a new title in the Window Title field. (The default title is Recent Page.)

- You can limit the number of pages displayed by entering a number in the Maximum Pages to List field. (The default maximum is 999 pages.)

- Check the Close When Page Is Selected option if you want to close the Recent Page window as soon as a user selects a page from the list.

2. After modifying these options, click OK to close the Navigation Setup dialog box.

Including backtracking navigation controls in a piece, particularly the Recent Page window, can help make users feel more comfortable exploring a piece because it gives them a way to return to a screen if they've found it useful or interesting. However, backtracking doesn't give them the capability to jump directly to a page with information that they haven't yet explored. To create this type of navigation, you need to set up a navigation control to search for a page.

How do I create a link to a web page?

Authorware doesn't allow you to create a link to a web page using the navigate icon. However, there is a quick way to provide this type of functionality in a Shockwave piece that you're building, using the network system function `GoToNetPage`.

NOTE This function works only when the piece is running using the Shockwave Plug-In.

When running a Shockwave piece within the browser window, you can include this function in a calculation icon script attached to an interaction response in order to open a separate browser window and display a web page. You can use this with buttons, hot spots, or any other type of interaction response.

To create the web page link:

1. Open the calculation icon you've placed inside the interaction response for the web link.

The Calculation window appears.

2. Type in the following expression, replacing MyWebAddress with the URL of the web page you want to open:
GoToNetPage("MyWebAddress", "_blank")

3. Close the calculation window.

In order to test this link, you'll need to save your piece as a Shockwave piece by using Afterburner. However, when you run the piece within a Shockwave-compatible browser such as Netscape Navigator or Microsoft Internet Explorer, you will see the specified web page displayed in a separate browser window on top of the window where the Shockwave piece is running.

NOTE If you do not include the optional argument `"_blank"` when using the `GoToNetPage` function, the Shockwave piece will quit, and the web page specified inside your script will be displayed in the browser window where the Shockwave piece was running previously.

For more information on testing and distributing Shockwave pieces, see Chapter 17, "Distributing Your Piece."

Searching for a Page

Authorware was designed to increase your productivity and to deliver large amounts of information to the user. One of Authorware's key strengths is its full-text searching capabilities, accessed through the navigate icon. Search navigation enables the user to search through the text contained in display and interaction icons, search for keywords that have been assigned to specific icons, or both at the same time.

TIP Keyword searches are particularly useful because you can attach keywords to any type of icon that you have included in a piece. For more information on using keywords, see "Assigning keywords to icons," later in this chapter.

You can add search functionality to your piece by using a navigate icon set to the Search destination option. Creating this kind of navigation link allows users to search for a word, phrase, or keyword, and then jump directly to the page.

To set up a navigate icon to search for a word or a keyword:

1. Add a navigate icon to the piece and double-click it to open it.

The Navigate Icon Properties dialog box appears.

2. Select Search from the Destination drop-down list.

The appearance of the dialog box changes to show you the Search destination options, as shown in **Figure 12.8**. You'll see how to use these options in a moment.

3. After selecting the Search options you want to use, click OK to close the dialog box.

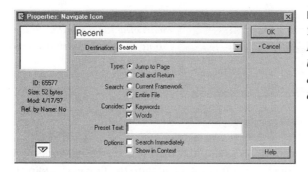

Figure 12.8
*The Navigate Icon
Properties dialog
box with the Search
destination options
displayed.*

Several options are available when setting up a navigate icon
to search for a word or keyword:

- The Search option allows you to define the scope of the search.
  You can select to search the entire file or just the current
  framework for text that is entered in the Find window.

- The Consider option allows you to search not only for words in
  text fields that are inside display and interaction icons, but also
  for keywords assigned to icons. Searching for keywords makes
  it possible for users to locate icons that don't display text, such
  as digital movie or sound icons. This is explained in more detail
  in "Assigning keywords to an icon" below.

- The Preset Text field allows you to enter a word or phrase that
  appears automatically in the Word field of the Find dialog box.

- You can check the Search Immediately option to have
  Authorware do an immediate search without the user clicking
  the Find button in the Find window.

NOTE In order to use the Search Immediately option, you must
include a character string or a variable expression in the Preset Text
field. For more information, see "Using automatic searching," later in
this chapter.

- You can select the Show In Context option to display the
  search results in context inside the Find window. Checking this
  option displays the names of all pages that contain the text for
  which the user is searching, as well as any words that appear
  beside it in the text field. **Figure 12.9** shows you how this
  appears in the Find window.

Figure 12.9
*Searching for a word with the
Show In Context option selected.*

Using the Find window

You can see an example of how text searching works in Authorware
by adding a new framework icon to the flowline, adding some pages
and text to the framework, and then running the piece. When you
click on the default Find button that appears in the Presentation
window, you see the Find window displayed, as shown in **Figure 12.10**.

Figure 12.10
*The Find window enables you to search
for words or keywords in a piece.*

The Find window works as follows:

■ Users can find specific pages that contain the text they're
looking for by typing in a word, phrase, or keyword in the
Word/Phrase field.

TIP As with the Find button inside the Navigate Icon Properties
dialog box, the user can use the "and" (&) and "or" (|) characters to
expand or limit the search as needed. If you are using this type of
navigation link, you might want to include this in the help documentation so that the user is aware of it.

■ After the user has entered text in the Word/Phrase field,
clicking the Find button starts the search.

■ While Authorware continues searching for pages, the user can
click the Pause button or the Cancel button to pause or stop
the search.

■ Authorware displays all pages that contain the text in the Page
field. To navigate to a specific page that Authorware has found,
the user selects the name of the page and clicks the Go To Page
button.

NOTE Authorware displays pages as it finds them. In large pieces with a great deal of text content, a search can take much longer if you are searching the entire file. You can speed up a search by limiting the text search to the current framework (see below).

As with the Recent Pages window, you can customize the Find window to fit the type of piece you are creating by changing the default text that appears for its fields and buttons. You can do this quickly by using the following steps:

1. Choose File > Navigation Setup from the Modify menu.

The Navigation Setup dialog box appears, as shown in **Figure 12.11**. It shows you several option fields where you can insert new labels for each field or button in the Find window. Several other options are also available that allow you to customize its functionality. You'll learn about these in a moment.

Highlight
Found
Words
option

Words To
Ignore
button

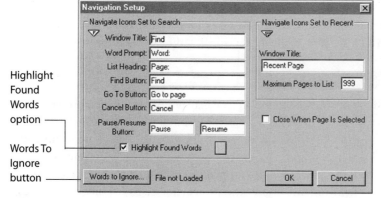

Figure 12.11
The Navigation Setup dialog box.

2. After making the necessary modifications to these options, click OK to close the dialog box.

Aside from changing the button and field labels in the Find window, you can use the Navigation Setup dialog box to customize how Authorware handles searching for a word, phrase, or keyword. These options, labeled in **Figure 12.11**, are explained in more detail below:

■ By default, Authorware checks the Highlight Found Words option so that the word or phrase being searched for is highlighted on the result page (i.e., the page the user jumps to after clicking the Go To Page button). If you don't want highlighted words, deselect this option.

- When the Highlight Found Words option is checked, Authorware highlights the found word or phrase on the result page using the color displayed to the right of the Highlight Found Words option. This color is green by default, but you can change the color of highlighted words by clicking on the color selection chip and selecting a new color from the current palette.

- Clicking the Words To Ignore button opens a dialog box that you can use to load a text file into your piece that contains words Authorware should ignore when searching the piece.

NOTE If you use the Words To Ignore option, compile your word list in a word processor or text editor by listing each word on a separate line and saving it as a plain text file.

The Find window gives the user a great deal more control over finding information in your piece. By specifying the option of keyword searching, you can give the user the capability to look for pages that contain information in all types of formats, including sound and video. You'll see how to create keywords in the next section.

Assigning a keyword to an icon

Much of your content in a piece may not be text, which presents a problem when including search capabilities in your piece. However, using the Keywords dialog box, you can assign a keyword to any icon. This allows you to let the user search not only for occurrences of words in a piece, but also for related content that is not text-based.

Keywords are useful when you include a large number of images, videos, and sounds that contain valuable information. For example, say that you are creating a piece on George Gershwin's compositions, and you want to allow the user to search for all occurrences in the piece of "Porgy and Bess," including segments of the musical composition. Using keywords, the user can do a search for this information and jump to any page that references this composition, including pages on which you've specifically included sound icons.

NOTE You can assign keywords to any type of icon, including map icons. However, in order for Authorware to find keyword-related content, it must be attached to either a framework or included inside the page of a framework.

To assign a keyword to an icon:

1. Select the icon you want to assign a keyword to.

2. Choose Icon > Keywords from the Modify menu.

   The Keywords dialog box appears, as shown in **Figure 12.12**.

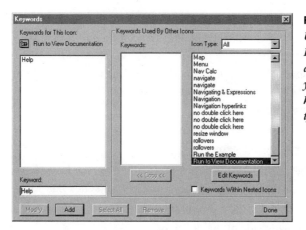

Figure 12.12
Using the Keywords dialog box, you can assign keywords to any type of icon.

3. Type in the keyword you want to add in the Keyword field. A keyword must be a single word without any spaces. If you enter several words, Authorware assigns the first word as the keyword.

4. Click Add to add the keyword to the keywords list of the icon you are editing.

   The keyword now appears in the list of keywords on the left of the dialog box (see **Figure 12.12** above).

   You can assign as many keywords to an icon as you want. You can continue adding them one at a time using the procedure above. However, in some cases, it is easier to copy keywords from other icons listed in the Keywords dialog box.

   To copy keywords from one icon to another:

1. Select the icon from the icon list on the right-hand side of the dialog box that has the keywords you want to copy.

   After you've selected an icon, the keywords you've assigned to it appear in the list under Keywords in the middle of the dialog box.

   TIP If you select a map, decision, framework, or interaction icon, click the checkbox next to Keywords Within Nested Icons to display the keywords assigned to any icon inside of, or attached to the icon.

2. Select the keywords that you want to copy by shift-clicking on them. If you want to copy all the keywords listed, click Select All.

3. After selecting the keywords you want to copy to the current icon, click Copy.

   Authorware copies the keywords you've selected to the list on the left-hand side of the dialog box.

   At times, you may need to edit keywords for a different icon, especially if you find out while copying a set of keywords that you haven't completely updated all icons in the piece that should share these keywords.

   You can edit or remove a keyword from an icon any time using the following steps:

1. Select the icon you want to edit from the list of icons on the right-hand side of the dialog box and click Edit Keywords.

   The list of keywords for this icon appears in the list on the left-hand side of the dialog box.

2. Click on the keyword you want to edit in the keywords list on the left-hand side of the dialog box.

3. Change the keyword in the Keyword field and click Modify. If you want to remove it, click Remove.

   Authorware replaces the keyword in the list with the edited version or removes it from the list.

   Using keywords and text searching, the Find window is a useful way to give the user control over searching for a reoccurring item. However, there may be times when you simply want to use Authorware's search functionality without having the user enter a word in the Find window. To do this, you will need to work with the navigate icon's automatic searching option.

Using automatic searching

You might recall from earlier in this chapter that you can set up the navigate icon to search immediately for a particular word or phrase. This is triggered by selecting the Search Immediately option listed inside the Navigate Icon Properties dialog box when the navigate icon is set to the Search destination option (see **Figure 12.8** above).

In order to use the Search Immediately option, you need to include a value in the Preset Entry field. The Present Entry field gives Authorware something to search for as soon as the navigate icon is executed in the flowline. If this field is left blank, the automatic search displays the Find window, but without any pages listed.

If you want Authorware to search for a particular word or keyword automatically, simply type a character string enclosed in quotation marks into the Preset Entry field. For instance, if you want the piece to immediately search for all instances of the word oxygen, you would type **"oxygen"** in the Preset Entry field.

You also can include a variable name or a variable expression in the Preset Entry field. This is a far more flexible method when creating an automatic search because it allows the value of the Preset Entry field to change depending on conditions in the piece.

For example, using the system variable `WordClicked` in the Preset Entry field creates a list of all occurrences of the last word clicked by the user in the Presentation window. Including a custom variable in the Preset Entry field (such as `CurrentSearchTopic`) allows you to change the automatic search topic from section to section by using a calculation icon script inside the entry pane of each framework, as shown below:

```
CurrentSearchTopic := "ghosts"
```

If you want Authorware to automatically search for more than one word, include the proper syntax inside the quotation marks when assigning the value of the search variable:

```
CurrentSearchTopic := "ghosts & goblins"
```

In the above example, Authorware displays only those pages (or keywords) in which both these words are used because the "and" (&) symbol is included in the character string assigned to the variable.

NOTE When using variable names in the Preset Entry field, don't enclose them in quotation marks. For more information about working with character strings and variables, see Chapter 14, "Using Functions and Variables."

Techniques like automatic searching are useful in instances where you want to predefine a list of terms, and then provide a way for the user to call them up and navigate to the pages immediately. Creating this type of functionality with a variable expression is an excellent example of how you can control navigation by using conditions in a piece. The next section takes a look at some other ways of controlling navigation dynamically by using variable expressions.

At times you may not know which page to select when setting up a link. This is especially true when you're developing more sophisticated navigation that allows the user to "bookmark" specific pages. You could build a specific button into your interface that enables the user to bookmark a page or navigate to a page that was marked already.

 For a look at how to create this type of functionality in a piece, see the file BOOKMARK.A4P. It's included in the Chapter 12 examples folder on the CD accompanying this book.

While this isn't too complicated to set up, it requires that you know a few things about using functions and variables in Authorware. As with the automatic search functionality described in the last section, the bookmarking example demonstrates one of the typical situations you might find yourself in when you start working on a piece.

This type of navigation requires that you create a navigation link that changes based on the current value of a variable expression. In the bookmarking example, the pages a user can navigate to depend on the names of the pages that the user added to the list of bookmarks stored inside the piece.

Using Page ID expressions

Before creating a calculated link like this, it is important to understand how Authorware navigates to pages in a piece. Authorware maintains a unique numerical value for each page in a piece. This is referred to in Authorware's scripting language as a Page ID. When setting up a calculated link, you need to use an expression that contains a Page ID; otherwise the calculated link goes nowhere.

One simple example of using a calculated link is an expression that takes the user to the last page displayed. This is the equivalent of using the Go Back setting when setting up a navigate icon to use the Recent destination type. To do this, you simply include the following expression in the Icon Expression field of the Navigate Icon Properties dialog box:

```
PageHistoryID(1)
```

The `PageHistoryID` function enables you to access the internal list that Authorware maintains of all pages that the user visits. This is called the "page history list." When using the `PageHistoryID` function, you simply provide Authorware with the number of the page that you want to find from the page history list, and Authorware returns the Page ID of the page. Using a value of 1 in this case returns the user to the previously displayed page, since using a value of 0 returns the Page ID of the currently displayed page.

NOTE For more information on using the `PageHistoryID` function, see *Using Authorware* or Authorware Help.

Creating the calculated link

When creating a calculated link in a piece, you need to use the Calculated destination option. This option is included in the list of destination options found inside the Navigation Icon Properties dialog box.

To create a calculated link:

1. Double-click the navigate icon in which you want to add the calculated link.

The Navigate Icon Properties dialog box appears.

2. Select Calculate from the Destination drop-down list.

The Navigate Icon Properties dialog box displays the Calculate navigation options, as shown in **Figure 12.13**.

Icon
Expression
field

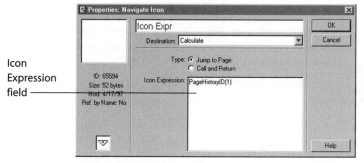

Figure 12.13
The Navigate Icon Properties dialog box with the Calculate destination options displayed.

3. In the Icon Expression field, add a variable expression that contains a Page ID value. For this example, you can use the variable expression `PageHistoryID(1)` if you want to return to the previous page displayed.

4. When you have finished, click OK to close the dialog box.

Assigning Page IDs to a calculated link is not as difficult as it sounds. It requires that you take some time to become familiar with the framework system functions and system variables included with Authorware. For a complete list of these functions and variables, as well as descriptions of how they are used, see *Using Authorware* or Authorware Help.

Calculated links round out the types of one-way links that you can create in the flowline using the navigate icon. In some cases, however, you may not want to include separate navigation controls on screen. You may just want the user to jump to a page when a word is clicked. To do this, you'll need to learn how to create hypertext links using a hot-text style.

Creating Hypertext Links

Text in Authorware can be interactive—that is, you can set up a text style to respond to a user click and then jump to a specific page. In many ways, this is like creating a hypertext link in an HTML editing tool. Using the Define Styles dialog box, you can even make the text appear underlined and highlighted in a different color, as it would if you were creating a hypertext link for a web page.

The benefit of using a hypertext link in a text field is that you can add interactivity to the screen without creating additional buttons or graphics. Hypertext links also add depth to a piece, and they are a convenient way to include cross-referencing to related topics because they don't take up additional space in the Presentation window.

Authorware's method of handling hypertext is very straightforward. You simply create a hot-text style in the Define Styles dialog box; then assign this style to a piece of text, selecting the page to jump to in the process.

To set up a hot-text style:

1. Choose Define Styles from the Text menu.

The Define Styles dialog box appears, as shown in **Figure 12.14**.

2. Create a new style. Make sure that you give it a unique name so that it shows up in the Apply Styles palette.

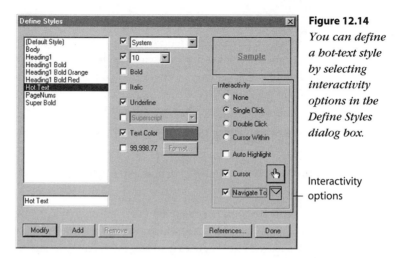

Figure 12.14
*You can define
a hot-text style
by selecting
interactivity
options in the
Define Styles
dialog box.*

Interactivity
options

TIP When creating a hot-text style, you probably should use a unique color so that the user can identify it quickly from anywhere in the piece.

3. In the Interactivity section on the right side of the dialog box, select the type of interactivity that you want to use with the style. You have three options to choose from: Single Click, Double Click, and Cursor Within.

4. Check the Auto Highlight option if you want the text to highlight on screen when the user clicks the hypertext link. Authorware highlights the hypertext link by changing the hot-text to its inverse color.

5. If you want the cursor to change when the user passes over the hypertext link, check the Cursor option and click on the cursor field to display the Cursors dialog box. (These are the same custom cursors available for interaction responses.)

The custom cursor you selected appears in the cursor field.

After you've set up the interactivity options for the hot-text style, define the type of navigation that you want to use.

To change the style to hot-text that can navigate to any page in the piece:

1. Check the Navigate To option.

Notice that the navigate icon field shows an unlinked navigate icon. This is because you haven't yet defined how you want the hot-text style to navigate.

If you want to define a single destination for the style, you can click on the navigate icon field. This displays the Navigate Icon Properties dialog box, allowing you to create a link using one of the destination types. However, if you set up the style this way, you'll navigate to the same page each time you set up a hypertext link using this style.

Leave the navigation undefined for right now. In a moment, you'll see why.

2. When you've finished defining the style, click OK to close the dialog box.

Now that you have defined the hypertext style, it appears in the Apply Styles palette along with any other text styles you've created. This makes it extremely easy to add interactivity to any text that you've created or imported into Authorware. However, you still need to define the type of navigation for your text.

To apply the hypertext style:

1. Open the display icon or interaction icon where the text appears.

2. Select the text tool and select the text you want to style as hot-text.

3. Choose Apply Styles from the Text menu. The Apply Styles palette appears.

4. Click the name of the hot-text style in the Apply Styles palette to apply it to the text you've selected.

The Navigate Icon Properties dialog box appears.

5. Select a Destination option and then set up the navigation options for the Destination options you've selected.

6. When you have finished, click OK to close the dialog box.

You can use hypertext links (as with links created with the navigate icon) to jump to a specific page. However, in some cases, you may want to display the page briefly and then return to the previous page—especially if you are creating an online help system. In the next section, you'll look at some ways of creating this type of call-and-return linking.

Calling a Page

Whenever you create a one-way link from one framework to another, Authorware exits the first framework before it enters the second, erasing everything displayed in the first framework. However, there is another type of navigation that you can use in Authorware to display the contents of the page you're navigating to without erasing the first page: a call-and-return navigation link.

There's one restriction when using a call that doesn't apply to a jump. Although you can jump between pages within the same framework, you cannot do this with a call-and-return link. Anytime you use call-and-return linking, you need to set the navigate icon to call a page outside the current framework.

Keep the following in mind when using call-and-return linking:

- If you attach a map icon to a framework and then set up a navigate icon inside it to call another page, Authorware returns to the place in the map where it left—not the top of the map flowline.

- Unlike a jump, you can set up a navigate icon that's on the flowline outside a framework to call a page. Authorware returns to the flowline even though it's outside a framework.

Any time you set up a call, you need to use two navigate icons: one to take Authorware to the destination, and another at the destination page to return Authorware to the page that originated the call. (You also can replace either navigate icon with a hypertext link.) At the destination page, the navigate icon that sends Authorware on its return trip must be set to Exit Framework/Return.

To set up the calling link:

1. Open the navigate icon you're using to make the call.

The Navigate Icon Properties dialog box appears.

2. Select a Destination option.

NOTE You can only use call-and-return linking with a navigate icon or hot-text style when you've selected Anywhere, Calculated, or Search for your Destination option.

3. Assign the page you want to call, and make sure that you've selected Call and Return as your Type option, as shown in **Figure 12.15**.

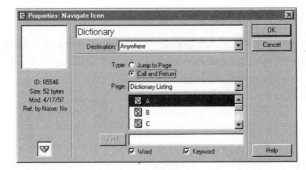

Figure 12.15
Make sure that you've defined the link as a call-and-return link.

4. Click OK to close the dialog box.

Continue by going to the destination framework to add a navigate icon set to exit the framework and return the user to the calling page.

To set up the return navigation control:

1. Double-click the framework icon to open it.

The framework window appears.

2. Add a navigate icon to the far right of the interaction icon that contains the navigation controls.

3. Double-click the navigate icon.

The Navigate Icon Properties dialog box appears.

4. Select Nearby for your Destination option.

The Nearby options appear, as shown in **Figure 12.16**.

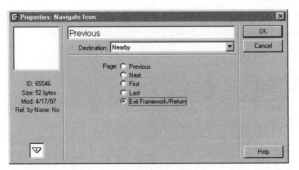

Figure 12.16
Creating the return link.

5. Select Exit Framework/Return.

6. Click OK to close the dialog box.

NOTE It's recommended that you use an interaction to control the return link; otherwise, if you place the return navigate icon in the flowline directly after the page's content, the page erases immediately, and the user never knows that the page was called.

Call-and-return linking offers the advantage of having Authorware keep track of the return page. Because of this, you can set up more complicated types of call-and-return links that display a series of referenced pages. These are known as nested calls. You'll learn about them in the next section.

Using nested calls

When you set up a call, you don't have to return immediately. For example, you can call one page, and from that page call a second, and from the second page call a third, and so on. What you're doing is nesting calls—that is, allowing pages to reference other pages that reference other pages.

However, it's really not as complicated as it sounds. In **Figure 12.17**, you can see how you might use this type of structure to gradually narrow down a set of glossary terms in a foreign language piece. Clicking on a call-and-return link in the framework named Main Lessons takes the user to the Dictionary Listing framework, where the words appear on separate pages alphabetically. Clicking on a hypertext link on one of the dictionary pages takes the user to the definition of the word included in the Definitions framework. Each framework contains a Previous button that is set up to return the user to the previously called page.

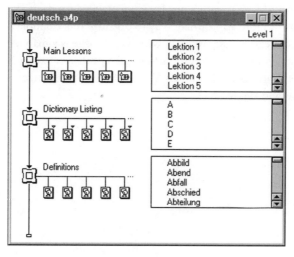

Figure 12.17
Setting up a dictionary of terms by using nested calls.

At times, you may create nested calls by accident—especially if you are using several perpetual navigate buttons set to make calls to other pages. In this case, just remember to place a return control in every destination page you call. That way, Authorware can always find its way back to the original page.

NOTE If you're on a called page, and you click on a link that navigates directly to another page without using call-and-return, Authorware erases both the previous page and the called page.

When you nest calls, it's important to remember that the navigate icon that returns Authorware to the place it came from isn't linked to a specific icon. It simply tells Authorware to return, and it assumes that Authorware knows from where it came. Authorware keeps track of called pages in the page history list you learned about in "Navigating with expressions," above.

Using Nested Frameworks

You can make designing navigation for a piece easier by learning how to take advantage of nested navigation frameworks. Nested navigation frameworks are simply frameworks that you place into a map icon attached to another framework. Using nested frameworks, you can build complex navigation rather easily, complete with all the linking functionality you find when working with the navigate icon and the framework icon.

To explain the concept of nested frameworks better, take a look at this book and then try to think about how you would design it if it were an Authorware piece. One way is to set it up by using a single framework icon with a display icon attached for every page in the book. A more appropriate way to organize this example piece might be to create a framework in which each page is a map icon that contains an entire chapter; inside each of these chapter "pages" is another framework with the pages of the chapter attached to it, as shown in **Figure 12.18**.

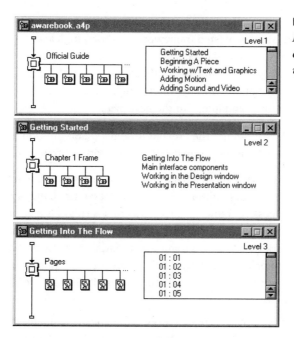

Figure 12.18
Nested frameworks contain sets of pages within pages.

Organizing the piece this way enables users to jump directly from the beginning of chapter 1 to the beginning of chapter 2, 3, or any other chapter, without clicking through all the intermediary pages. Another advantage to using nested frameworks is the capability to share common buttons and navigational controls. Since any object displayed in the entry pane of a framework icon displays on all pages attached to the framework, you can place common controls like a Quit or a Help button inside the entry pane of the parent framework so that they are visible on the pages of every nested framework.

When using nested frameworks, keep in mind these general rules:

- When using navigation controls set to one of the Nearby destination options (i.e., Previous, Next, First, Last), you will want to be careful because they jump users only to pages in the framework in which you've placed them.

  For example, if you have a Next Page button in a parent framework that is visible in a nested framework, clicking it jumps you to the next page in the parent framework. If you want to jump to the next page in the nested framework, include a Next Page button in the nested framework.

- When you jump from a nested framework page to another page outside the nested framework, Authorware leaves the nested framework and executes the icons inside the nested framework's exit pane. It then erases everything from the Presentation window—including text, graphics, movies, and sounds—and jumps to the new page.

NOTE You can use the Prevent Automatic Erase option to prevent icons from erasing automatically when exiting a framework.

- If you navigate to a page embedded inside multiple nested frameworks, Authorware executes the entry pane of each successive framework icon before it displays the destination page. Likewise, if you navigate from a page in a nested frame-work to a page in a framework somewhere else in the piece, Authorware executes the exit pane of each framework that is part of the nested structure before it displays the destination page.

Because nested frameworks automatically maintain the display contents of each framework entry pane in the Presentation window, you may find that your piece runs more slowly as you continue to add more nested frameworks. When developing your piece, look closely at your navigational structure. If you find yourself using more than five or six nested levels of frameworks, you may want to think about redesigning your logic to help improve performance when jumping between sections. You also may want to look at how you are using the entry and exit panes of each framework to control display elements on screen.

Using entry and exit logic

Until the framework icon was added to Authorware, it was very difficult to control what happened each time you entered or exited a specific group of icons. However, this is precisely what the entry pane and exit pane of the framework window now enable you to do.

As mentioned in Chapter 11, "Working with Pages," Authorware executes all icons located inside the framework entry pane each time it enters a framework. This happens regardless of which attached page is your destination. If Authorware is navigating from somewhere outside the framework directly to the third page attached to the framework, Authorware still executes the logic inside the entry pane before it proceeds to the page.

This helps you design onscreen navigational controls, because you can assume that Authorware will continue to display controls or any other display objects placed in the entry pane of a framework on every page attached to the framework. For example, the entry pane is the best location to use when setting up a quit button for the entire piece, or a display icon that displays the current page number or a content topic heading. It's also invaluable when tracking data using custom variables, since they can be updated quickly whenever the user enters a particular location of the file by including a calculation icon in the entry pane of the section framework.

Likewise, the exit pane gives you a convenient way to perform simple "clean-up" routines that enable you to erase any stray graphics, sounds, or videos, and update variables on your way out of a framework. For instance, you can track whether or not the user completes a section by including a calculation icon script in the exit pane of each section framework. The example below shows a common way to handle this:

```
if NavFrom = IconLastChild(@"Section 1 ¬
Questions") then
    Section1Complete := True
end if
```

In this example, the system function `IconLastChild` is used to get the value of the Page ID of the last page attached to the framework named Section 1 Questions. It is compared to the value stored in the system variable `NavFrom`. The `NavFrom` variable is one that you can use only in the exit pane of a framework. It is useful, however, as it is constantly updated to contain the Page ID of the page that you were on before leaving the current framework.

The end result is that this script (using an If-Then statement) can determine whether or not the user is navigating from the last page of the framework specified in the `IconLastChild` function (in this case, the framework named Section 1 Questions). If the user leaves the framework from this page, then the section is completed, and the script assigns a value of True to the custom variable `Section1Complete`.

TIP By placing the system variable `NavTo` in a calculation icon script in the entry pane of a framework, you can find out what page the user jumped from to get to the current framework.

As the example above indicates, tracking what is happening at any given moment in a piece becomes much easier as you work with the framework and navigate icons. You'll see additional ways of handling data tracking by using system functions and variables in Chapter 16, "Tracking the User."

Looking Ahead...

This chapter concludes your look at using the framework and navigate icon together to create navigation structures for your piece. These two icons are the primary tools available to you when you begin deciding how to create navigation in your piece. In particular, the navigate icon options provide you with the most accessible means for creating links, and they provide the user with hypertext referencing.

This chapter also explored how to use calculated links and automatic searching to create more customized navigation, which can change depending on information generated while a piece runs. In Chapter 13, "Creating Decision Paths," you will learn about the ways to handle flowline branching in a similar way by using the decision icon.

Creating Decision Paths

When working with the flowline, you may encounter situations where you want a particular section of the flowline to repeat a series of actions. For example, you might want to display and erase a sequence of images, or you might want to set up a sequence of screens that must be navigated before the user can continue. While you can set up some flowline structures like this using the techniques discussed earlier in the book, the decision icon is a far more useful tool when trying to set up sequential branching in the flowline.

Decision paths are useful for handling dynamic branching that occurs often as a result of the inter-action responses made by the user. For instance, if you are developing a training piece, you may want the user to automatically navigate to one of two framework pages based on the user's test score; or, you might want to set up a button that plays one of several sounds randomly so that you can add an element of surprise.

This chapter continues to look at how to control branching on the flowline by focusing on the ways you can work with the decision icon and the decision paths. This will help you not only with controlling the flowline, but also with automating tasks that you frequently repeat.

The decision icon uniquely enables you to set up multiple paths to flow logic quickly and to control this type of path branching automatically. You can present multiple paths in sequence, branch to them using a random selection process, or determine the path to take dynamically by using a variable expression. In each case, Authorware passes through the decision icon, takes a look at how you've defined the path options for the decision icon, and then determines how to pass through each of the paths attached to the decision icon.

You can create decision paths by attaching a series of path icons to the decision icon, as shown in **Figure 13.1**. This adds a decision path symbol to the flowline, which is similar to the symbol that appears in the flowline for interaction responses. You'll learn how to edit the options associated with the decision path symbol later in this chapter, in "Using sequential paths."

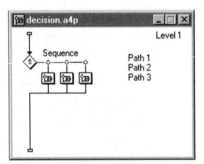

Figure 13.1
The main components of a decision path as they appear in the flowline.

In most cases, you'll use a map icon as your path icon so that you can place additional flowline logic inside each decision path. When creating decision paths with decision icons, you can place them anywhere in the flowline. They are particularly useful when placed inside the feedback response icon of an interaction response, since this allows you to set up multiple branching options for a single button, hot spot, or any other type of response.

There are three basic types of decision branching that you can create in Authorware:

■ Sequential branching enters and exits each path attached to the decision icon. Authorware repeats this action until all paths have been used, or until a condition is met. Sequential branching is useful for branching through a sequence of icons.

Using the decision icon's repeat option, you can continue branching through the path sequence a set number of times or until a variable condition is met.

■ Random branching selects a decision icon path randomly. As with sequential branching, you have control over repeating through the sequence of paths until all of the paths have been used, or until a variable condition is met. Random branching is useful for randomizing questions in a test; you also can use it to choose randomly from a selection of sound or video clips in a piece, or to control random display of graphic elements in the Presentation window.

■ Calculated branching enters a specific decision icon path based on the value of a variable expression. Calculated branching is useful for determining automatically how to navigate to another screen—depending on how a user scores on a test, or by presenting negative or positive feedback based on the score. You also can use it to create more compact flowline logic, as you'll see later in the chapter in "Using calculated paths."

TIP In each type of decision path branching, you can assign a time limit value for the decision icon so that Authorware automatically exits the decision icon when the time limit is reached.

In the next section, you'll begin looking at ways of integrating decision paths into your piece by looking at how to set up sequential paths.

Using Sequential Paths

Frequently when designing a piece, you'll need to set up branching that moves through several consecutive sequences of icons. These might be images or scenes that you're trying to display in a specific order, or a series of steps that the user must pass through in order to continue with the piece.

Rather than creating a long sequence of display icons, wait icons, and erase icons, as shown in **Figure 13.2**, you can simply use the decision icon to control presentation of the sequence of icons. Authorware then erases them automatically as it moves along the decision paths attached to the decision icon, as shown in **Figure 13.3**.

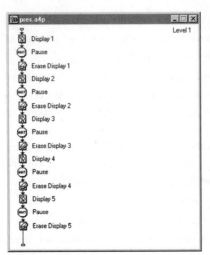

Figure 13.2

Creating a sequence of icons using the wait and erase icons can be problematic—especially if it is a large sequence.

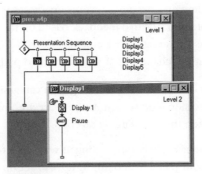

Figure 13.3

The decision icon is a much more efficient way to present sequential icons in the flowline.

Setting up the decision icon

When setting up sequential paths, Authorware presents each segment of an icon sequence in the order in which each path is attached to the decision icon from left to right. In the next set of steps, you get a feel for how sequential paths are created. You'll use some of these same techniques to create other types of decision paths later in the chapter.

To set up the decision icon:

1. Drag a decision icon to the flowline where you want the sequence to happen and give it a name.

2. Double-click the decision icon to open it.

The Decision Icon Properties dialog box appears, as shown in **Figure 13.4**. You will see several default options displayed for the Sequentially branching options.

Time Limit field ———
Repeat option ———
Branch option ———
Reset Paths option ———

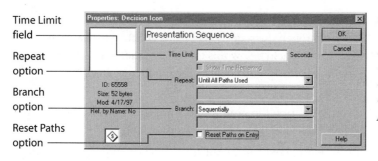

Figure 13.4
The Decision Icon Properties dialog box, showing the sequential path options.

Take a quick look at the default options already set for you inside the decision icon. You'll learn about the other options available in this dialog box in a moment.

In this example, you need to make an adjustment to the Repeat option so that all paths in the sequence display before Authorware exits the decision icon.

3. Select Until All Paths Used for the Repeat option.

NOTE If you leave this option set to Don't Repeat, you will only see the first path icon of the sequence displayed.

4. When you have finished, click OK to close the dialog box. Notice that the decision icon is displayed with an "S" in the flowline. This indicates that you've set up the decision icon to use sequential branching.

Before you continue setting up paths for the decision icon, you can get a feel for how different types of branching are set up by looking at the other options in the Decision Icon Properties dialog box. These options, labeled for you in **Figure 13.4**, are explained in more detail below:

■ The Time Limit field enables you to specify a time limit (in seconds) for the decision icon. When the time limit expires, Authorware automatically exits the currently selected path of the decision icon and continues down the flowline. The default setting for the Time Limit field is no time limit; if you enter a value in this field, you also can select the Show Time Remaining option, which displays a timer on screen (as you saw when working with time limit responses in Chapter 10, "Responding Automatically to Events").

- The Repeat option controls the number of times Authorware repeats through the sequence of paths attached to the decision icon. Use the field below this to type in either a number or a variable expression that defines the number of times the sequence should repeat.

  If you select Don't Repeat, Authorware goes through the sequence once and then exits the decision icon.

  If you select Fixed Number of Times, you can type a value in the Repeat field that controls the number of times the sequence repeats.

  If you select Until All Paths Used, Authorware continues to loop through the sequence until it selects all the paths. You use this option with Random branching only.

  If you select Until Click/Keypress, Authorware continues to loop through the sequence until the user clicks the mouse or presses a key. However, be careful when using this option—especially if you've placed an interaction inside the path map icon that requires a click or a keypress to match a response. When this happens, Authorware disregards the interaction and automatically exits the decision icon when the user clicks the mouse or presses a key.

  If you select Until True, the loop repeats indefinitely until a variable condition is met. You'll learn more about this option later when creating decision loops is discussed.

- The Branching option lets you select the type of branching you want to use for the decision icon. Notice that there are four options listed, including Sequentially (default), To Calculated Path (used with calculated decision paths), and Randomly to Any Path and Randomly to Unused Path (both of which apply to setting up random decision paths, as you'll learn later in the chapter).

- Below the Branching option is the Reset Paths On Entry option. This option is used to allow Authorware to go to the same paths each time the decision icon is entered. Having this option checked resets the list of used paths for the decision icon that Authorware maintains internally. You should check this option if you plan to access the decision icon repeatedly in a piece and if you want to reset the branching each time.

You will work with these options throughout this chapter as you learn how to set up the different types of decision paths that are used in Authorware. The next section continues explaining how to set up sequential branching by looking at how to add paths to the decision icon.

Setting up the decision icon paths

As explained earlier, the sequence or order of a decision icon that you have set to use sequential branching is defined by the order in which you attach the paths to the decision icon. For example, if you're simply using display icons as your path icons, the first display icon to the right of the decision icon always displays first, followed by the next display icon to the right, and so on, until all of the paths have been used.

NOTE Regardless of the decision path types you're creating, the process for adding a path icon to the decision icon is the same as explained below. However, the type of decision path you use determines which path or paths Authorware selects when entering the decision icon.

To set up the first path icon in the sequence:

1. Drag the type of icon you want to use to the right of the decision icon.

When you add the path icon, Authorware creates a decision response symbol above the path icon. You edit the options for this path before you continue so you can use the same path settings for each successive path icon you add to the decision icon.

2. Double-click the decision response symbol.

The Decision Response Properties dialog box appears, as shown in **Figure 13.5**.

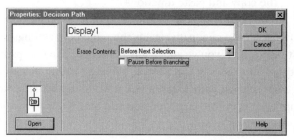

Figure 13.5
The Decision Response Properties dialog box controls automatic erasing of the decision path.

As shown in the figure, there are two options available in this dialog box:

■ The Erase Contents option controls how Authorware erases the contents of each path from the screen before continuing to the next path in the sequence (or exiting the decision icon). If you select Before Next Selection, Authorware erases the contents of each path icon before the next icon in the sequence displays. If you select Don't Erase, Authorware keeps the contents of each path icon in the sequence on screen, even after you exit the sequence. If you select Upon Exit, Authorware keeps the contents of each path icon in the sequence on screen, but erases the screen when you exit the sequence.

■ The Pause Before Branching option is similar to the Pause Before Exiting option used with the interaction icon. When you check this option, a wait button appears on screen before Authorware exits the current path. As soon as the user clicks the button, Authorware branches to the next path, or if it is the last path, exits the decision icon.

3. Choose an Erase Contents option. In sequential branching, it's best to use the Upon Exit setting if you are displaying a sequence of icons in the Presentation window. However, if you want to clear the screen between paths, select Before Next Selection.

NOTE If you select the third Erase Contents option, Don't Erase, all display objects in the path remain on screen when Authorware exits the decision icon.

4. Click OK to close the dialog box.

Now that you've set up the first decision path icon and selected the path options, you can add additional paths to the sequence by dragging new map icons to the right of the first decision path, or by using the copy and paste functions.

If you copy and paste the first response to create additional responses, each new path retains the same path settings used by the first response. If you've added any content to the first path map icon, Authorware pastes in that as well, allowing you to quickly duplicate the logic of each path. Later, if you want to modify icons in a path, you simply can open the map icon and add new icons or modify the existing ones.

As you continue adding additional paths to the decision icon, Authorware builds out the path sequence to the right. When you add a sixth path to the decision icon, Authorware creates a scroll bar that enables you to scroll through the paths attached to the decision icon, as shown in **Figure 13.6**. This is the same type of scroll bar that Authorware creates when adding responses to the right of an interaction icon.

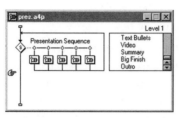

Figure 13.6

You can use the scroll bar to view additional paths attached to the decision icon.

After you've set up the paths for your sequence, run the piece to test it. You should see each path attached to the decision icon displayed before Authorware continues to the next path.

If you do not see the objects in your sequence, you may need to look at the Erase Contents settings you've used for each path and make sure that you've selected Until All Paths Used for the decision icon Repeat option. The next section shows you how to use this option to set up sequential branching that repeats a set number of times.

Looping through a sequence

As mentioned earlier, decision paths are useful when you need to repeat a series of steps, or you need to set up some kind of loop that repeats until a condition is met. While you could set this up using the options contained within an interaction, it is much easier to set up these types of loops using the decision icon.

In **Figure 13.7**, you can see an example of how you might use this functionality in a presentation piece to update the screen with a new image every 30 seconds (timed with a wait icon) and then cycle back through the images after the last image in the set displays.

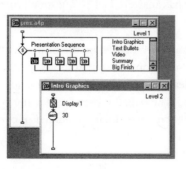

Figure 13.7

This decision icon is set to loop through a series of images that will update in the Presentation window.

Setting up the sequence you created earlier to loop is a matter of adjusting one option in the Decision Icon Properties dialog box:

1. Double-click the decision icon.

   The Decision Icon Properties dialog box appears.

2. Change the Repeat option from Until All Paths Used to Fixed Number of Times.

3. In the Repeat field, type in **2**.

4. Click OK to close the dialog box.

When you now run the piece, the sequence you created repeats two times before Authorware exits the decision icon. At times, you might want to use a variable expression in the Repeat field to set the number of times that Authorware repeats the sequence so that you can change this value by using a calculation script. As mentioned earlier, the decision icon is particularly handy when you need to repeat a sequence indefinitely until a variable condition is True.

To set up the decision icon to repeat until a variable condition is True:

1. Open the decision icon and change its Repeat option to Until True.

   The Until True field below the Repeat options drop-down list becomes active.

2. Type in the variable expression you want to use in the Repeat field.

3. Click OK to close the decision icon.

For example, you could use this type of sequential branching to cycle through a series of 10 questions until a user answers all of them correctly. After setting up a series of paths using judged interaction responses, you could include the following variable expression in the Until True field of the Decision Icon Properties dialog box to test whether or not the user has answered all 10 questions correctly:

`TotalCorrect=10`

The above expression works, based on the principle that you've set up all your interaction responses using Authorware's automatic judging option. (You'll learn more about using automatic judging of responses in Chapter 16, "Tracking the User.") Since the system variable `TotalCorrect` contains the total number of correct responses the user has made to all judged interactions in the file, and the total number of questions in this example is 10, Authorware continues repeating through the questions until each one is answered correctly (i.e., until `TotalCorrect`equals 10).

The examples above highlight several of the added benefits of using the decision icon—namely, it is much easier to set up and use the decision icon when you have complicated flowline logic that needs to be repeated in sequence. The decision icon also makes it much easier for you to modify the types of flowline loops you're using in a piece because you only need to modify the options inside its Icon Properties dialog box. You'll see other examples of how this can be used effectively later in this chapter.

TIP You can also use decision icon looping to repeat through a calculation icon script that you've included in one of the decision paths. However, looping through a script this way is slower than creating a loop inside the script by using the `Repeat With` or `Repeat While` system functions. For more information on using these functions to create script-based loops, see Chapter 15, "Controlling the Flowline through Scripting."

Using Random Paths

As mentioned earlier, there are two ways to set up random branching within a decision path structure. If you want to display a random path, and don't need to select a unique path each time you enter the decision icon, then you can select Randomly To Any Path when setting up the decision icon's Branching option.

You can use this type of branching if you want to randomly select from a group of images or sounds. If you use this type of branching, the decision icon displays with an "A" in the flowline, as shown in **Figure 13.8**.

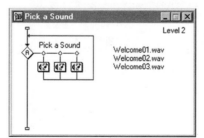

Figure 13.8
A decision path using Randomly To Any Path branching.

However, in some cases, you need to make sure that a unique decision path is used each time. For example, if you're setting up a group of questions for a test and want to randomize them, set up the decision icon to branch to a different path each time so that the questions do not repeat. To do this, select the Randomly To Unused Path setting when modifying the decision icon's Branching option. If you use this type of branching, Authorware displays a "U" in the decision icon on the flowline, as shown in **Figure 13.9**.

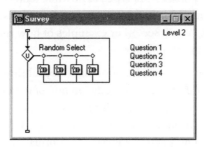

Figure 13.9
A decision path using Randomly To Unused Path branching.

By using this type of random branching, you can create a multiple choice test that has random questions. In **Figure 13.10**, you can see how you might set this up in the flowline, using a set of map icons that contain each question attached to the decision icon. In this example, Authorware selects randomly from the available questions, displaying each one before exiting the decision loop. When the decision loop is exited, the navigate icon below it takes the user to a separate page of a framework where final scores display.

Each question is a separate decision path. ———

The decision icon is set to Randomly To Unused Path branching. ———

The navigate icon jumps to a "Final Score" page. ———

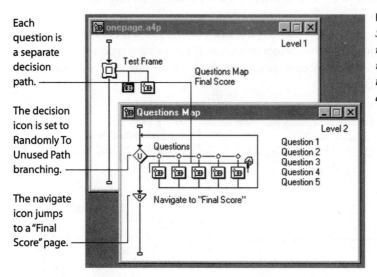

Figure 13.10
Setting up a randomized, multiple choice test, using the decision icon.

Figure 13.11 shows you how each separate question is set up inside the map icons attached to the decision icon. Notice that the interaction responses for all answers are set to exit the interaction. This allows Authorware to continue executing the decision loop and to select a new question after the user answers the previous question.

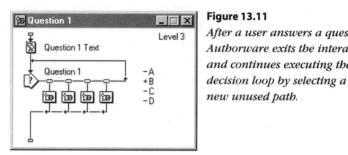

Figure 13.11

After a user answers a question, Authorware exits the interaction and continues executing the decision loop by selecting a new unused path.

When setting up the type of flowline structure shown in the example above, keep the following points in mind:

■ You need to leave the Reset Path On Entry option deselected for the decision icon so that Authorware remembers which decision paths it has already taken when selecting a new path. Otherwise, questions will display more than once.

■ You need to set the Erase Contents option for each decision path to Before Next Entry so that questions do not appear on top of each other in the Presentation window.

■ You need to make sure that the flowline logic for each question allows Authorware to continue executing the decision loop. In this case, each interaction response inside the question map icons is set to exit the interaction.

As you can see, both sequential and random paths are extremely useful in situations where you have a series of paths that you need Authorware to branch to in a specific order. However, calculated paths offer a different type of control over your flowline logic. Calculated paths allow you to select a decision path based on a variable condition in your piece—not unlike using a calculated navigate icon link to dynamically change page jumps.

Suppose, for example, that you're creating a training course for customer service representatives. Some of the people taking the course are current employees brushing up on department policies; some are new employees unfamiliar with the system; and some are seasonal workers who may have learned the system last year, but haven't used it since then. Because the backgrounds of the people taking the course are so varied, you decide to create a pretest to determine where each user should start the training course piece.

You can set this up easily by building the pretest at the beginning of the piece, and then using a calculated decision path in the flowline that branches to one of two destinations: a "Beginning Course" page and an "Advanced Course" page. The calculated path that Authorware takes in the piece depends entirely on how well the user scores on the pretest. You can see how this type of flowline structure might appear in **Figure 13.12**.

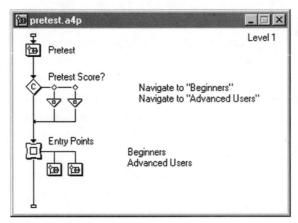

Figure 13.12
Using a calculated path, the user navigates to one of two framework pages based on the results of a pretest.

When setting up a calculated path inside a decision icon, Authorware selects a path to branch to based on the value of the variable expression you've specified. Calculated paths are determined dynamically by Authorware using the following rules:

■ Authorware numbers the icons attached to a decision icon from left to right, starting with 1. Each additional path to the right of the first path is given the next number. If you have 10 path icons attached to a decision icon, the last path icon has the assigned value of 10.

■ When you set up a calculated path, you insert a variable expression in the Branching field of the Decision Icon Properties dialog box. When Authorware enters the decision icon, it evaluates the expression and then branches to the path that equals this value.

■ If the value of the expression isn't a whole number, Authorware ignores the decimal part of a value; it considers 0.75 equal to 0 and 4.25 equal to 4. Authorware doesn't round the value to the nearest whole number—it simply drops the decimal part of the value.

■ If a value is less than 1 (0, for instance) or larger than the number of icons attached to the decision icon, Authorware bypasses all the attached icons and moves to the icon that follows the decision icon on the flowline, regardless of which Repeat option you've selected for the decision icon.

TIP If you want Authorware to automatically bypass the paths attached to a decision icon, use the value FALSE or 0 in the Branching field of the Decision Icon Properties dialog box. This is useful when debugging certain portions of the flowline and if you want to hide display elements, movies, or keep sounds from playing.

Since you've already had experience working with conditional expressions inside interactions, you should have little problem creating calculated decision paths. The next section describes one convenient way to use calculated paths in your piece when creating navigational structures.

Creating a calculated navigation path

When designing the navigation controls in your piece, you must determine what types of user controls are absolutely necessary to have on screen. Commonly, you simply don't have enough screen real-estate to include buttons for each type of navigation that occurs in the piece. However, you can help the interface designer by including calculated paths with your navigation controls.

Suppose that you have a topics menu that jumps the user to several nested paging sequences. When designing the navigation controls for this type of piece, you might decide that there are really three types of navigation controls needed:

■ A Next button to take the user to the next page in the paging sequence.

- A Back button to take the user to the previous page in the paging sequence.

- A Return To Topics button that takes the user back to the list of topics.

You may find yourself in trouble coming up with a creative way of managing three buttons on the screen at any given time, considering that you also have several other buttons to manage, including a Quit button, a Main Menu button, a Help button, a Find button, and so forth (you get the picture).

However, rather than squeezing in an extra button, you can take advantage of the decision icon's capability to pick a path based on a condition in the piece (in this case, the current page number) to integrate both the paging and return-to-menu functionality into the same onscreen button.

You can quickly set up your buttons by modifying the default paging controls created with the framework icon:

1. Open the framework icon where the paging controls are located.

2. Select the Next Page button, and then select Group from the Modify menu to make the button response a map icon with a single navigate icon inside it.

3. Do the same for the Previous Page button.

Once you've done this, you can quickly modify how each button handles its navigation by doing the following:

1. Double-click the map icon attached to the Next Page button.

   The map icon opens, displaying a single navigate icon on the flowline.

2. Drag a decision icon to the flowline, placing it above the navigate icon.

3. Drag a new navigate icon to the right of the decision icon, creating a single path response, as shown in **Figure 13.13**.

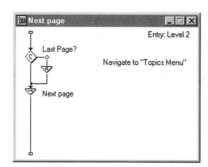

Figure 13.13

Adding a calculated navigation path to the Next Page button.

NOTE Because you're only using this path to navigate to a page, you don't need to worry about changing the path's Erase Contents option.

The original navigate icon for this button (the one below the decision path) already is set to navigate to the next page in the framework. However, you also need to set up the navigate icon you just created to jump to the topics screen. (Remember, you need to make this screen a page on another framework.)

To do this:

1. Double-click the navigate icon attached to the decision icon.

The Navigate Icon Properties dialog box appears.

2. Since you already have selected Anywhere for the Destination option, simply select the page where the topics screen is located, and then click OK to close the dialog box.

NOTE If you can't see the name of the topics page, select Entire File for the Page option to display all pages in the framework.

You've now created a flowline structure within the button response's map icon with two navigate icons that each point to a different destination page. You can now control which destination link is selected by setting up a calculated path inside the decision icon. This creates a button that automatically chooses between paging forward or returning the user to the topics screen.

To modify the decision icon path options:

1. Double-click the decision icon.

The Decision Icon Properties dialog box appears.

2. Leave the Repeat option set to Don't Repeat because you only want to branch to a single path each time the user clicks the button.

3. Select To Calculated Path for the Branching option. This displays the Calculate Path options, as shown in **Figure 13.14**.

Branching field for expression —

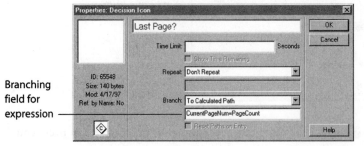

Figure 13.14
Creating a calculated path.

4. In the Branching field, type: **CurrentPageNum=PageCount**.

5. Click OK to close the dialog box.

Since you used the two system variables in the expression above when working with paging controls in Chapter 11, "Working with Pages," you already have a good idea of how the calculated navigation control works when the piece runs:

- If the value of `CurrentPageNum` equals the value of `PageCount` (i.e., if the user is on the last page of the section framework), then the variable expression evaluates to True (or 1). This means Authorware automatically branches to the path you've attached to the decision icon, sending the user to the topics screen.

- If the value of `CurrentPageNum` does not equal the value of `PageCount` (i.e., if the user is on any other page of the section framework), then the variable expression evaluates to False (or 0). In this case, Authorware ignores the calculated path, drops out of the decision icon, and uses the second navigate icon, sending the user to the next page of the section framework.

In order to complete your navigation controls, you can use the following set of steps to modify the Previous Page button:

1. Select the decision path structure you added to the Next Page button (this includes both the decision icon and the new navigate icon) and choose Copy from the Edit menu.

2. Close the Next Page map icon.

3. Select the navigate icon attached to the Previous Page button and choose Group from the Modify menu.

4. Double-click the map icon attached to the Previous Page button.

The map icon Display window appears.

5. Position the paste hand above the navigate icon you see and select Paste from the Edit menu.

This adds the decision path structure you copied from the Next Page button to the map icon Design window for the Previous Page button.

6. Double-click the navigate icon attached to the decision icon and change the expression in the Branching field to **CurrentPageNum=1**.

7. When you have finished, click OK to close the Decision Icon Properties dialog box.

After following these steps and running your piece, you can see that Authorware now navigates to the topics screen whenever you are on the first page of the framework and click the Previous Page button; otherwise, you will navigate to the previous page of the framework.

There are many similar situations where you might want to think about using the decision icon to help control the navigation in your piece. With both icons integrated into one interaction, you'll find that you can solve complex navigation issues and use fewer icons in the process.

TIP You'll especially want to keep this technique in mind when working on Shockwave pieces, since the most problematic aspect of doing Shockwave development is learning how to create compact flowline logic that takes up less file space and downloads quickly.

Decision paths are useful in many situations when you need quick and accurate control over presenting a sequence of icons in the flowline. They are also useful when you need to add a touch of randomness to a project (it is very easy to include random paths in the flowline). Calculated paths are equally easy to set up and offer the capability to work more efficiently in the flowline, as well as make decisions dynamically in your piece based on run-time conditions.

As you've learned more about using navigation and decision paths in this chapter, you may have recognized how powerful these two components are when designing a piece. However, regardless of how well you learn to use navigation and decision paths, you also need to develop a firm grasp of functions and variables if you intend to make your pieces more responsive to the user. The techniques you learned in this chapter—calculated branching and decision loops—help prepare you for Chapter 14, "Using Functions and Variables," which introduces you to working with Authorware's scripting language.

Using Scripting and Data Tracking

As your familiarity with Authorware grows, you start to look for shortcuts to get your work done efficiently. In previous chapters, you learned about the techniques you can use when working with the icons to gain productivity, while at the same time making your piece more fluid and dynamic. In many cases, however, productivity is enhanced when you integrate scripting into your work. When developing a piece, you need to ask yourself two questions: "How can I do this better?" and "How can I make this easier?" In many cases, you can find the answer to both of these questions by turning to Authorware's scripting tools.

Throughout this book, you've seen many examples of how you can integrate scripting components like variables and functions into the flowline to address specific issues. Scripting enables you to control many aspects of a piece, including icons on the flowline, objects displayed on screen, and data that is generated in the background. In Part IV, "Using Scripting and Data Tracking," you continue to learn more about the types of scripting and background data handling techniques that you can use in Authorware to solve complex issues more quickly and more efficiently.

Chapter 14

Using Functions and Variables

Of all the tools that you have at your disposal in Authorware, none of them are quite as powerful as Authorware's set of functions and variables. These are the built-in scripting tools that enable you to control many elements of your piece by using the calculation icon. They can be used in many ways to give you control over the icons, the interactivity, and the information contained in your piece.

This chapter discusses the basic techniques for harnessing the power of functions and variables. At times, it may seem like you're required to learn a completely new language—and in some ways, this is true. However, you don't have to be an expert in programming languages to use Authorware's scripting tools. You can easily integrate variables and functions into almost any context in a piece, whether you're controlling elements on screen, doing background data tracking, or reacting dynamically to a user's choice in an interaction.

One of the biggest challenges to authoring a piece is figuring out the best methods to control what is happening in the flowline at any given point. Because there may be many things happening simultaneously, you need to develop ways to efficiently monitor what is happening, and to react to it quickly and easily.

Scripting allows you to both monitor and react—and do it well. This is because you can integrate the three scripting components—variables, functions, and expressions—into almost any flowline structure by including a separate calculation icon in the flowline, attaching a calculation script to an icon, or inserting a variable or expression into a Properties dialog box field.

Before diving into your own scripts, you need to become familiar with how variables, functions, and expressions are used together in a piece. They are the three components that you will use to control what happens in your piece when you use scripting. The next several sections explore these components in more detail.

Using variables and functions

Every script that you create in Authorware utilizes variables or functions in some way. These two scripting components work hand-in-hand to give you multiple methods of manipulating the flowline and tracking the information that is generated when a piece runs.

Functions and variables are different in the following ways:

- A variable stores a value that you can access any time. For example, you've already worked with the system variable MouseDown, which continually keeps track of whether or not the user is pressing the mouse button. This is an example of a variable that you can use right away in a script without having to create it.

  You also have the option of creating your own custom variables if you need to store or keep track of specific information in a piece that Authorware is not tracking. You'll learn more about this later in the chapter in "Creating custom variables."

- A function performs a specific task for you. Authorware has different categories of functions that you can choose from to manipulate the content in your file, keep track of variables, or modify if needed. For example, you've already worked with the system function `TimeOutGoTo`, which tells Authorware which icon to jump to when there has been no keyboard or mouse activity for a specified number of seconds in your piece.

If there is a particular task that you want your program to do, but you can't seem to find a function in Authorware to do it, you can integrate custom functions into your piece with the help of Windows DLLs (Dynamic Link Libraries), Macintosh XCMDs (external commands), or Xtras that are available for either platform. You'll learn more about working with these types of files in Chapter 20, "Developing with External Code."

When variables and functions are used together in a piece, they enable you to manipulate, store, or retrieve information and to react to it in different ways. You've already seen several examples of this earlier in the book when you worked with such things as conditional interaction responses, calculated navigation links, and decision paths.

Variables are temporary containers that store a value and can change depending on the conditions in a piece. You can use variables in place of actual character or numerical values to create a piece that changes dynamically, as you might if you were setting up a variable motion path for an icon or creating a calculated link to a page of a framework.

NOTE You also can use variables to store sets of information in lists. Lists are a more complex type of data that allows you to store multiple values in the same variable and retrieve them using an index value or list property. See "Types of variables," later in this chapter.

After you've placed information into a variable, you can use Authorware's functions to perform different tasks with this information. For example, if you have a variable that stores a user's password, then you can use a function to encrypt the password or write it out to an external text file. If another person uses the piece, the contents of this password variable will change; however, the variable name remains the same throughout the piece.

Likewise, functions that you use in a piece never change because they don't contain a specific value in the same way that variables do. Functions are used to perform a specific task. Examples of this include getting the average value of a list of numbers using the `Average` system function; capitalizing all the letters in a word using the `UpperCase` system function; or resizing the Presentation window using the `ResizeWindow` system function.

Because most functions require that you state specific values when you use them (e.g., the width and height of the Presentation window when using the `ResizeWindow` system function), you have greater control over functions if you integrate variables into them.

The example script below shows how you can use variables with the `ResizeWindow` system function to resize the Presentation window:

```
WindowWidth := 520

WindowHeight := 400

ResizeWindow(WindowWidth, WindowHeight)
```

This script assigns a value of 520 to the custom variable `WindowWidth` and a value of 400 to the custom variable `WindowHeight`. The names of each variable are included as separate arguments in the `ResizeWindow` function. If you include this script in a calculation icon at the very top of the flowline, as shown in **Figure 14.1**, you will see the Presentation window resize to 520 x 400 pixels when you run the piece.

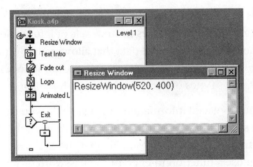

Figure 14.1
A script that resizes the Presentation window is placed at the top of the flowline.

Using variable names with functions enables you to adapt the function to fit a specific condition. In the example script above, for instance, you could easily adapt it to find the size (in pixels) of the user's current desktop monitor resolution, and then change the width and height values passed to the `ResizeWindow` function based on this information. You'll see an example of how to do this in Chapter 15, "Controlling the Flowline through Scripting."

Using expressions

In the example script you just looked at, there were three expressions created, one on each line of the script. Expressions are really the third component to using scripting in Authorware. You can use expressions to compare the values of two variables, to change the value of a variable, or to execute a specific function that may or may not use a variable.

For a moment, think of the way in which you were asked to solve problems in your high school geometry class. You might remember having to write out the equation $a2 + b2 = c2$ to find the hypotenuse of a right triangle. When doing this, you were actually building an expression. Authorware's scripting language enables you to build different types of expressions, including the one above. However, if you were to trying to solve the above equation using the calculation icon in Authorware, your expression might look something like this:

```
SIDE_C := SQRT((SIDE_A**2) + (SIDE_B**2))
```

In this example, both the custom variables `SIDE_A` and the custom variable `SIDE_B` are squared using the exponential operator (`**`), and then these values are added together. The `SQRT` system function then determines the square root of the final sum, and the result is assigned to the custom variable `SIDE_C`, solving the equation. All you need to do is supply initial numerical values for `SIDE_A` and `SIDE_B` in the script.

NOTE You'll take a closer look at working with different types of expressions and operators later in this chapter in "Building Expressions."

As you can see, Authorware's math functions and operators allow you to easily manipulate numerical values stored in variables. However, this is just one example of how you can build complex expressions that combine variables and functions to help you work with the data in your piece.

As you continue through this chapter and the next two chapters, you'll see other examples of how functions, variables, and expressions can all be integrated into a piece. In the next section, you will start by exploring how variables in particular are used when working with data.

TIP While this chapter and the next two chapters describe many commonly used functions and variables, you should continue to refer to either *Using Authorware* or Authorware Help for a comprehensive guide to the set of system functions and variables available to you in Authorware.

Exploring Variables

Variables are a powerful way to store data in your piece. Because you can interchange a variable with many different values (including a number, a character string, a logical True/False value, or a list), you can control many aspects of your piece by integrating variables and variable expressions into the flowline.

There are two types of variables in Authorware: system variables, which are integrated into Authorware already; and custom variables, which you create yourself in instances where Authorware does not have a system variable defined for the data value that you want to store.

Authorware's system variables keep track of a wide range of information in a piece including information about decision structures, files, frameworks, graphics, videos, icons, interactions, dates, and times. Authorware continuously updates these system variables so that you can access them any time to get the latest "report" on what's happening with your piece.

If you want to keep track of information that Authorware isn't storing in a system variable, you can create a custom variable. Custom variables reflect the values you give (or assign) them. The values change only when you explicitly change them using an expression.

For example, you might keep track of the currently playing sound icon by attaching the following expression to each sound icon in your piece:

```
CurrentSound := IconID
```

This allows you to restart or pause the current sound playing in a piece by using the custom variable CurrentSound to specify the current sound icon used by an Authorware system function like MediaPlay or MediaPause inside a calculation icon script. Chapter 15, "Controlling the Flowline through Scripting," takes a closer look at how to use the media system function.

Types of variables

All system and custom variables fall into a specific data type that corresponds to the type of data that the variable stores. Authorware automatically interprets the variable's type based on how you've used it. System variables automatically default to a specific type. However, when creating a custom variable, you define the type by entering in the correct initial value for it.

Variables in Authorware fall into one of several different data types, depending on how you use them:

- Numerical variables store numbers. Numerical variables can store positive or negative integers (e.g., 13 or -13), "real number" values (e.g., 0.006, 1.34), or numerical constants such as pi. The values stored in a numerical variable can range from $-1.7*10^{308}$ to $+1.7*10^{308}$. You might use a numerical variable to store a user's score, a topic number, or the result of a mathematical calculation.

- Character variables store groups of characters, or character "strings." A string is a sequence of one or more characters that consists of letters (e.g., "Mary Wagner"), numbers (e.g., "49931"), special characters (i.e., "*/"), or a combination of any of them (e.g., "Total is $5.00"). A character variable can contain up to 32,000 characters.

  Character strings are always enclosed in quotation marks (as you can see by selecting a variable that contains a character string, such as `FileName` in the Variables window, and then looking at its current value). You might use a character variable to store the text of a user's response, a list of spelling words, or today's date.

- Logical variables store a value of True or False. They're like a light switch that can only alternate between two states: on (True) or off (False). These types of values are often referred to as "Boolean" values; this is derived from Boolean logic, in which the number 0 equals false, and any nonzero number (usually 1) equals true.

  Logical variables are particularly useful for activating or deactivating options. As you've seen in earlier chapters, inserting a logical variable in an interaction response's Active If field is a good way to activate and deactivate the response.

■ Lists are a new data type supported by Authorware 4. Lists allow you to store a set of values that you can easily update, sort, and add to other lists. You can include numbers, character strings, logical values, and other lists within a list that you create.

Lists are created like other variables, but require that you use a special set of list system functions when working with them. Lists are particularly useful when tracking scores for multiple users or managing a large amount of data in a piece.

NOTE There are two types of lists in Authorware: linear lists, in which values are accessed by specifying an index number; and property lists, in which values are accessed by specifying a property of the list. You'll learn more about working with both types of lists in Chapter 16, "Tracking the User."

■ Rects and points are data types related to lists that you can use, respectively, to store rectangle coordinates or a specific X-Y points coordinate. When working with these data types, you can use a specific subset of the list system functions.

TIP You can use rect and point variables when working with Authorware's set of graphics functions. These allow you to create boxes and lines inside the Presentation window. For more information on using the graphics functions, see *Using Authorware* or Authorware Help.

■ Symbols are a data type that is complimentary to both the list and event data types. You can create a symbol if you need to add a property to a property list or to an event list. You also refer to symbols when working with Xtras such as the QuickDraw 3D Xtra. For more information on using symbols and Xtras, see Chapter 20, "Developing with External Code."

■ Events are a specialized version of the property list data type. Sprite or scripting Xtras that you use in a piece generate event data that you can access using the list system functions in the same way that you access property lists. For more information on working with Xtras, see Chapter 20, "Developing with External Code."

TIP When working with variables, you can determine the type of data stored in a variable by using the `TypeOf` system function. For more information on this function, see *Using Authorware* or Authorware Help.

Naming variables

Every variable (either system or custom) in Authorware must have a unique name that identifies it. When creating a custom variable, you should try to follow the naming scheme used for system variables. Every system variable begins with an uppercase letter and consists of one or more words with no spaces in-between (e.g., `Tries`, `UserName`, or `MediaPlaying`).

Some system variable names are followed by the "at" operator symbol (@) and the title of an icon. These are "referenced" variables; they make it possible to find out a variable's value at a specific icon within a file. Referenced variables are very powerful because you can incorporate them into expressions and functions to make dynamic data handling easier.

Before you start working with system variables, decide what you want to accomplish with the variable. Do you want to give Authorware information, or do you want to extract information from Authorware? For example, you can provide Authorware with information by setting the system variable `Movable` to True to allow the user to drag a display object. An example of extracting information is retrieving the value stored in the system variable `EntryText` after you enter your name into a text entry field.

After you decide what you want to accomplish using the variable, finding one and putting it to use is easy when you know how to use the Variables window.

Working with the Variables window

Authorware lists every system and custom variable available to you in the Variables window. You can open this window to paste a variable name into a calculation icon, the Presentation window, or a Properties dialog box field. You also can use the Variables window to create new custom variables, view the current value of a variable, or modify the initial value of a variable. You'll learn about these techniques later in this chapter.

To open the Variables window:

1. Choose Variables from the Window menu or click the Variables window button on the toolbar.

The Variables window appears as shown in **Figure 14.2**.

Shortcut: To open the Variables window, use Ctrl+Shift+V (Windows), or Command+Shift+V (Macintosh).

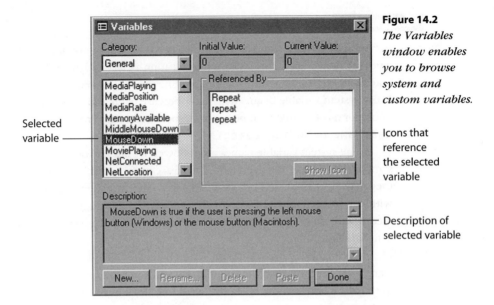

Figure 14.2
The Variables window enables you to browse system and custom variables.

Selected variable ——

Icons that reference the selected variable

Description of selected variable

2. After opening the Variables window, you can use it to browse through all system and custom variables to select the one you want by clicking on the Category drop-down list and selecting a category.

The variables for this category appear in the scrolling list. If you want to look at the description or values of a specific variable, simply select it by clicking on it (see **Figure 14.2** above).

When browsing variables inside the Variables window, there are nine individual categories of system variables (Decision, File, Framework, General, Graphics, Icons, Interaction, Time, and Video), all related to the type of information that the variables track in a piece. If you want to display all system variables in the list, select the All category. Authorware places any custom variables you've created in the file name category at the end of the Category list.

NOTE If you haven't named the file yet, the custom variables set appears as "[Untitled]" in the Category drop-down list.

If you've selected the name of a variable inside the Variables window, the following information displays (see **Figure 14.2** above):

■ The Description field describes how you can use the variable. It also gives information about the type of data that you have stored in the variable, as well as the other system variables you can use in tandem with it.

- The Initial Value field displays the initial value of the variable. The variable's initial value indicates its type (e.g., 0 for numerical and logical variables; an empty string ("") for character variables; or an empty list ([]) for list variables).

- The Current Value field displays the current value of the variable. By looking at this field while your piece runs, you can quickly see how Authorware updates your variables—a useful tool when troubleshooting problems you may come across while authoring.

- The Referenced By field displays the names of all icons in the piece in which you have referenced the currently selected variable. If you want to view a specific icon, select the icon, and then click the Show Icon button. The Design window opens to display the selected icon.

Pasting in a variable

The Paste button in the Variables window is useful whenever you want to add a variable to the calculation window, the Presentation window, or to a Properties dialog box field. While you can type in the name of the variable, make sure that you spell it correctly; otherwise, Authorware thinks you're creating a new custom variable. Pasting the name of the variable into place ensures that you will use the correct name each time.

NOTE Authorware's custom and system variables are not case-sensitive when typing in the name.

To paste a variable into the Calculation window:

1. Open the calculation icon where you want to paste the variable.

2. Position the cursor where you want to paste in the name of the variable, as shown in **Figure 14.3**.

Name of variable

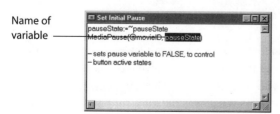

```
Set Initial Pause                          [_][□][X]
pauseState:=~pauseState
MediaPause(@movieID, pauseState)
 — sets pause variable to FALSE, to control
 — button active states
```

Figure 14.3
Adding a variable to the Calculation window.

3. Choose Variables from the Window menu.

The Variables window appears.

4. After choosing the appropriate category from the Category field, select the name of the variable you want to paste by clicking it in the scrolling list of variables for this category.

TIP You can type the first few letters of the variable's name to scroll to the variable in the list.

5. Click Paste and Authorware pastes the variable into the Calculation window.

The process for pasting a variable into an icon's Properties dialog box is similar:

1. Open up the Properties dialog box where you want to paste the variable. For example, if you add a variable name to the Active If field of an interaction response, double-click on the response to open its Properties dialog box.

2. Position the cursor in the field where you want to paste in the name of the variable.

3. Open the Variables window, select the name of the variable you want to paste, and click Paste.

Authorware pastes the variable into the field, as shown in **Figure 14.4**.

Name of variable pasted into field. ────

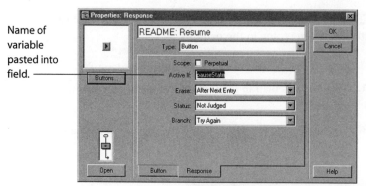

Figure 14.4
Pasting a variable into the Active If field of the Response Properties dialog box.

The Variable window is especially useful when working because you can have it open all the time. Simply move it out of the way when you don't need it. If you want to close it, click the Done button. Working with the Variables window is the same for both system and custom variables; however, to paste in a custom variable, you have to create it first.

TIP If you are viewing variable descriptions and are having trouble seeing the entire description in the Description field, you can resize the Variables window by dragging one of its corners.

Creating a custom variable

Authorware automatically creates custom variables any time you use a variable name not currently defined in the list of system or custom variables. The easiest way to create a custom variable is to type its name into a Calculation window or a Properties dialog box field.

TIP You also can create a custom variable by typing its name into a text field. However, when doing so, you need to enclose the name of the variable in braces ({}) so that Authorware recognizes it as a variable. For more information, see "Updating data on screen."

When doing this, Authorware automatically opens the New Variable dialog box (see **Figure 14.5**) so you can assign a default value for it. After defining the variable, it appears inside the Variable window in the list of custom variables for the piece.

Figure 14.5
The New Variable dialog box.

However, using the Variables window, you also can quickly create a custom variable by using the following steps:

1. Open the Variables window.

2. Click the New button.

The New Variable dialog box appears, as shown in **Figure 14.5** above.

3. Type the name you want to use for the variable in the Name field.

Keep in mind that a new custom variable name must be unique—
that is, other system or custom variables cannot use it. If you ever
want to change the name of the variable, you can simply click the
Rename button in the Variables window after selecting the
variable, and then rename it.

NOTE When renaming a custom variable, Authorware automatically
renames all references to that variable in your scripts as well, unless
you've enclosed the variable name inside the Eval system function.
For more information about using this function, see *Using
Authorware* or Authorware Help.

Variable names always begin with a letter, but can contain any
combination of letters, numbers, underscores, and spaces.
Capitalization doesn't matter, but spaces do; for instance, Score
and score are the same variable, but Score1 and Score 1
are not. You can use up to 40 characters when creating the name
of a custom variable.

After you've typed in the name, you need to define its
default value.

4. Type a value in the Initial Value field.

This is the value that Authorware initializes the variable to when
the piece first starts. It's recommended, but not required, that you
specify the default value based on the type of data you want to
store in the variable.

TIP At any time, you can change this initial value by selecting the
name of the custom variable in the Variables window, and then typing
a new value in the Initial Value field.

For instance, if you're creating a new numerical or logical variable,
you should specify 0 as the initial value; when creating a new
character variable, you should specify an empty string ("") as the
initial value. If you don't enter a value in the Initial Value field,
Authorware sets the initial value to 0 automatically.

NOTE When creating a new linear list, you should specify empty
brackets ([]) as the initial value. When creating a new property list,
place a colon between the brackets ([:]). For more information on
working with lists, see Chapter 16, "Tracking the User."

5. Type a description in the Description field.

It's important that you include a description with the variable so you can quickly refer to this field if you need to recall how you are using the variable in the piece.

Provide as much information as possible about the variable. As with the Initial Value field, you can change the description of a custom variable by modifying the text in the Description field after selecting the icon in the Variable window.

6. When you have finished setting up these fields, click OK to close the dialog box.

Authorware adds the custom variable you've created to the list of custom variables in the Variables window. After you have created the variable, you can continue adding new variables to the piece using the same technique.

Deleting a custom variable

At times, you may have custom variables that you want to delete. This is especially true if you remove portions of the flowline that reference variables. While unused variables take up a negligent amount of memory, periodically you should "clean house" by deleting variables that you are not using. This helps cut down on the amount of time spent looking for a custom variable inside the Variables window, and also prevents you from accidentally pasting the wrong variable into a script.

Before you can delete a custom variable, make sure that it isn't referenced elsewhere in the piece. If an icon references the variable, the icon's name is listed in the Referenced By field of the Variables window (see **Figure 14.2** above). If you want to delete the custom variable, you first must go into the icon that references it and delete it from the Calculation window, or from the Properties dialog box field in which it's used.

To delete a custom variable:

1. Open the Variables window.

2. Select the list of custom variables (listed under the name of the piece in the Category drop-down list).

The names of the custom variables in the file appear in the scrolling list.

3. Select the variable you want to delete.

4. Click the Delete button.

Authorware removes the variable from the file.

As you begin using variables more often in a piece, you will recognize similar techniques you can use to keep them better organized and easily accessed. It's important to have a firm grasp of the ways in which you work with variables so that you can apply these techniques to working with functions.

Exploring Functions

As explained earlier, a function performs a specific task. You can set up a function to do something simple, like capitalizing the first letter of a word. You also can use a function to do more complicated tasks, such as searching your file for instances of a word or phrase, or writing out the scores of a series of tests to an external text file.

There are two types of functions: system functions, which are built into Authorware; and custom functions, which are located externally. While the techniques for integrating both types of functions into your piece are the same, custom functions require that you load them from an external file. This chapter concentrates on using the Authorware system functions. Later, in Chapter 20, "Working with External Code," you'll learn the basic techniques of adding custom functions to your piece.

Using system functions

Authorware's system functions enable you to directly manipulate text, files, navigation structures, icons, graphics, and video. You can access much of the functionality that icons provide through system functions. They also allow you to control processes that happen behind the scenes (such as manipulating, storing, and retrieving data).

System functions in Authorware follow certain naming conventions. They always begin with an uppercase letter and consist of one or more words with no spaces (e.g., `Beep` or `DisplayIcon`). This is true of custom functions as well.

NOTE As with variables, you can add the name of the function to a calculation icon or Properties dialog box field by typing in its name, or by pasting it into place using the Functions window.

Each function has its own format (or syntax) that you need to follow to include it in a section of your piece. When including a function, you use the name of the function, followed by parentheses. For example, if you want to trigger a system beep when a button is clicked, you would include the following expression in a calculation icon attached to the button response:

```
Beep()
```

This is a simple function that doesn't require any arguments to work. However, many system (and custom) functions require that you specify one or more arguments when using a function. A function "argument" is simply a piece of information that you pass to the function that allows it to do its job. For example, the **SQRT** function takes one argument, the number that you want to find the square root of:

```
result := SQRT(4)
```

As shown in the above example, the number 4 is the only argument that requires the **SQRT** system function. You could just as easily use a numerical variable in place of the "literal" value of 4 (as you saw earlier in this chapter):

```
x := 4
result := SQRT(x)
```

Also notice that you can use the function as part of an expression to get the result of the function and store it in a custom variable. In the example expression above, the custom variable `result` contains the result of the function after it is used—in this case, `result` equals 2.

Viewing function descriptions

If you want to see what arguments you need for a specific function, open the Functions window and view the function's description. You can take a look at the information provided for the **SQRT** function to see how this works.

To view the **SQRT** function's description:

1. Select Functions from the Window menu.

Shortcut: To open the Functions window, press Ctrl+Shift+F (Windows), or Command+Shift+F (Macintosh).

The Functions window appears, as shown in **Figure 14.6**.

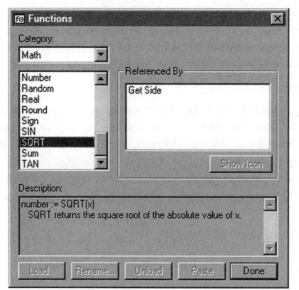

Figure 14.6
The Functions window enables you to browse system and custom functions.

2. Select the Math category from the Category drop-down list.

   The list of Math system functions appears in the window.

3. Scroll through the list of Math functions and click on SQRT to select it.

   The description of the SQRT function appears in the Description window, as shown in **Figure 14.6** above.

   This description tells you that you need to provide only one argument for the function, and that it returns a number. Because of the type of return value, you would want to provide a numerical value for the argument when using this function.

   NOTE Authorware has a set of data type conversion rules that it follows when an argument value does not fit the argument type included in the function description. See "How does Authorware convert data types?" later in this chapter for more information.

When using other types of functions, you need to include other types of arguments with them, as indicated by their function definitions. For instance, you can use the `UpperCase` function to change all letters in a character string to uppercase. When using this function, you can include a character string as its argument:

```
NameInCaps := UpperCase("tom")
```

After using this function, the custom variable `NameInCaps` contains the value "TOM." In other cases, you may need to include both character and numerical values, as you would when using the `SubStr` function to return a set number of characters of another character string:

```
resultString := SubStr("Mississippi", 1, 4)
```

The first argument tells Authorware which string to select the characters from; the second and third arguments tell Authorware the range of characters to select. In the above expression, the characters "Miss" are assigned to the custom variable `resultString`. Notice that commas separate each argument. This is the standard way of separating all arguments when using a function in Authorware.

NOTE Don't place quotation marks around variable names; otherwise, Authorware interprets your variable name as a string, rather than the value of the variable in its place.

Working with the Functions window

If you take a closer look at the Functions window, you will notice that Authorware's system functions are grouped into 15 categories: Character, File, Framework, General, Graphics, Icons, Jump, Language, List, Math, Network, OLE, Platform, Time, and Video.

These system functions are explained briefly in the following table:

Function category...	These functions are used for...
Character	Manipulating characters in character strings.
File	Working with external files and folders.
Framework	Setting up scripting control over paging and frameworks.
General	Setting up files and paths; controlling interactions and icon Xtras.
Graphics	Creating and modifying one-bit graphics.
Icons	Setting up scripting control over icons.
Jump	Controlling navigation from one Authorware file to another.
Language	Setting up scripting operators, If-Then statements, and Repeat loops.
List	Creating and manipulating lists.
Math	Performing standard math operations.
Network	Controlling Shockwave-specific functionality.
OLE	Controlling OLE applications through Authorware.
Platform	Checking for platform-specific properties.
Time	Setting and updating system date and time values.
Video	Setting up scripting control over external video sources.

In addition, there is a category called Xtras [All], as well as specific function categories for any specific scripting Xtras you've placed in the Authorware Xtras folder. You'll learn about working with Xtra functions in Chapter 20, "Developing with External Code."

TIP A good way to learn the Authorware system functions is to browse through each category of functions in the Functions window, and then look at the description of each function in the category. *Using Authorware* and Authorware Help also explain all of Authorware's system functions in detail and provide some examples of how to use them.

When you have the Functions window open, you can paste a function into a calculation icon or a Properties dialog box field using the same kind of process that you used when you worked with variables and the Variables window.

To paste a function into a calculation icon or Properties dialog box field:

1. Open the calculation icon or Properties dialog box.

2. Select the position where you want to paste the function (either in the Calculation window or the Properties dialog box field).

3. Open the Functions window.

4. Select the category that contains the function you want to use.

If you don't know which category the function is in, select All.

5. Select the function from the list, and then click Paste.

Authorware pastes the function at the place where you have positioned the cursor.

TIP When using a variable with a function in a calculation script, it is easier to paste in the function first so that you can tell where to place the variable name.

Integrating functions into Properties dialog box fields is a powerful way to control decision and interaction paths. For example, you can use the `GetLine` function to retrieve a user's previous logon name that you've stored in another character string variable, compare it to the user's current logon name, and then branch to a separate new user logon screen to get more information from the user if the two do not match.

To do this, you could include an expression in the Condition field of a conditional interaction response similar to the one below, which causes Authorware to branch to a separate screen:

`CurrentUser <> GetLine(2, UserData)`

The expression above compares the value of `CurrentUser` with the result returned by the `GetLine` function (in this case, the second line of the character variable `UserData`). If the two are not equal (i.e., if the names do not match), the conditional response matches and the correct feedback displays in the Presentation window. You might also attach a navigate icon to the response so that you could navigate to a separate framework page where you can handle new user registration, as shown in **Figure 14.7**.

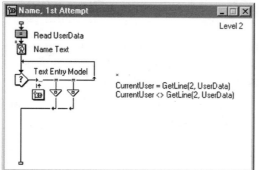

Figure 14.7

You can integrate functions into interaction responses to control navigation.

Before setting up this type of conditional response, you need to set up a custom variable called `CurrentUser`, which contains the user's current logon name, and another custom variable called `UserData`, which contains the user's session information (this might include information such as the user's first and last name, social security number, and date and time of the last logon). You might even want to store the `UserData` information in an external text file to keep the information available each time the user logs into the piece.

Using optional arguments with functions

If you take a closer look at the function descriptions, notice that some functions have optional second or third arguments that you can use if you need to provide additional information to the function you're using. A pair of brackets separates these optional arguments from the rest of the arguments, as shown in **Figure 14.8**.

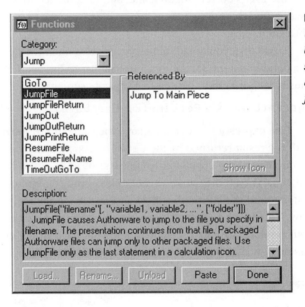

Figure 14.8
Use a pair of brackets to specify optional arguments for functions.

For instance, take a look at the `JumpFile` function, which is listed under the Jump category. If you look at its description, you will see the following syntax used with this function:

```
JumpFile("filename"[, "variable1, variable2,
...", ["folder"]])
```

The JumpFile function jumps to the Authorware file you specified in the first argument. Since you call this function when you want to jump out to another file, you need to include this argument each time you use the function. However, the second and third arguments (enclosed in brackets) are optional. Notice that the third argument is placed inside the second argument. This is known as "nesting" arguments.

If you use this function, you can include the second optional argument if you want to pass the values of current custom variables to the other file. You can use the third optional argument to specify a new folder name where the file you jump to stores its records. When writing out the statement in the Calculation window, you should omit the brackets as shown below:

```
JumpFile("Main.a4r", "UserName, UserID", ¬
"Records")
```

Notice that each argument is enclosed in separate quotation marks; the character spaces between the arguments are optional, but make the statement a little easier to read. This example illustrates how you may have to include additional arguments if you need the function to do a specific task. The best place to find out whether you need additional arguments is to view the function's description inside the Functions window.

The JumpFile function is another example of an Authorware system function that doesn't return a value—it simply does its job, allowing Authorware to continue to other statements that you've entered into the calculation icon. (In the case of the JumpFile function, Authorware jumps to the current file to another Authorware file you've specified. You'll learn more about using this function in Chapter 16, "Tracking the User.")

However, as you've seen earlier, your scripts and flowline logic can improve dramatically when you learn to integrate functions and variables into expressions to manage and manipulate data in your piece. In the next section, you'll learn some additional techniques for building expressions inside Authorware.

An expression is a statement that produces a result by performing a calculation, or it carries out an operation such as placing a value in a variable. You can use expressions in the Calculation window and Properties dialog box fields, or you can embed them in text. In addition to variables and functions, you can use numbers, character strings, and constants to build your expressions.

Each expression that you build requires that you define the "operators" for the expression. An operator is a symbol that you use to connect parts of the expression together to form a complete statement.

You can view the various operators in Authorware's scripting language by opening the Functions window and selecting the Language category. The various operator symbols are displayed at the top of the Language functions list, as shown in **Figure 14.9**.

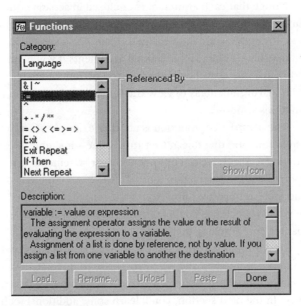

Figure 14.9
The operator symbols displayed in the Functions window.

The assignment operator

You already have seen how you can use the assignment operator (:=) in an expression. The assignment operator assigns the value or expression on its right to the variable on its left.

Here are some examples of how you can use the assignment operator:

Expression...	*What it does...*
`Path := 2`	Assigns a value of 2 to the custom variable `Path`.
`Counter := Counter + 1`	Adds 1 to the current value of the custom variable `Counter`, and then assigns the new value to `Counter`.
`City := "Cape Town"`	Assigns the character string `Cape Town` to the custom variable `City`.
`Result := GetLine(2, UserData)`	Assigns the result of the `GetLine` function to the custom variable `Result`.

You need to include an assignment operator in an expression when you want to assign a value or the result of a function to a variable. You can assign new values to any custom variable you've created, as well as many of the system variables in Authorware.

NOTE For a complete list of the system variables that you can reassign a value to in an expression, see *Using Authorware* or Authorware Help.

The assignment operator is one of five categories of operators available to you in Authorware. The other categories of operators allow you to perform arithmetic, character, relational, and logical operations inside your expressions. The sections below explain these types of operators in greater detail.

Arithmetic operators

Use the set of arithmetic operators to build numerical expressions that perform many of the mathematical functions common to other types of programming languages.

The arithmetic operators available to you in Authorware are listed below:

Operator...	*What it means...*
+	Add
-	Subtract
*	Multiply
/	Divide
**	Exponentiate

You can include arithmetic operators anywhere in the expression where you want to perform a mathematical operation. For instance, you can include a minus sign (-) in the expression to indicate a negative number, or place the minus sign between the names of two variables to subtract one value from the other.

Here are some other examples of how you might use arithmetic operators in an expression.

Expression...	What it does...
Score := Score + 1	Increases the value contained in custom variable Score by 1.
WrongPercent := 100*(Total/Missed)	Assigns a percent-missed value to the variable WrongPercent after dividing the value of Total (total number of questions) by the value of Missed (total missed questions), and then multiplies by 100.
TempC := (TempF-32)/1.8	Converts Fahrenheit degrees to Celsius degrees by subtracting 32 from the value of TempF; divides the result by 1.8, and then assigns the result to the variable TempC.

Although you can use the arithmetic operators to manipulate numerical data, there are certain rules you must follow when using them. As mentioned earlier, Authorware evaluates expressions from right to left—that is, the value of the expression on the right is assigned to the variable on the left of the assignment operator.

Parentheses help define the order of steps in which Authorware evaluates the expression. Any part of the expression inside parentheses is evaluated before Authorware continues to evaluate the rest of the expression, as shown in the examples above.

NOTE When creating numerical expressions, don't use commas or periods to separate numbers in the thousands or millions range. You can add separators later when displaying the numerical data on screen (see "Updating Data On Screen"). You shouldn't use any other special symbols, including currency and scientific notation symbols, in the expression.

Concatenation operator

The concatenation operator (^) is used to join character strings or a set of character variables together. For instance, you might have two variables: one that stores the value of the user's first name, and one that stores the value of the user's last name. If you want to combine these two variables, set up an expression as follows:

```
UserName := FirstName ^ " " ^ LastName
```

Here, the value of the custom variable `FirstName` is joined (or "concatenated") with the value of the custom variable `LastName` and assigned to the custom variable `UserName`. You also can write the expression in the following way using literal strings:

```
UserName := "John" ^ " " ^ "Smith"
```

Here, the value of `UserName` is John Smith. Notice that a character string containing a single space (" ") has also been inserted between the two names using the concatenation operator. This prevents the characters in the two variables from running into each other. If you omit the middle part of the expression, you end up with JohnSmith as your result (which probably is not the way you want to display the name on screen).

When working with character strings, you can use the concatenation operator to add a Return or Tab character constant to the end of a line of characters. This makes it possible to format the characters that you're writing to an external file with the help of the `WriteExtFile` function.

The syntax of the WriteExtFile function looks like this:

```
WriteExtFile("filename", "string")
```

When using this function, you can either type in the values for each argument or use a variable that contains a character string in each place. If you want to write out more than one variable to the text file, you can use a line continuation character (¬), which allows you to organize your statements into shorter lines without breaking up the syntax, as shown below:

```
WriteExtFile("Score.txt", UserName ^ FinalScore)
```

Shortcut: To add a continuation character to a line, press Alt+Return (Windows), or Option+Return (Macintosh) when typing in the Calculation window.

When using the `WriteExtFile` function to write multiple variables to a text file, you probably will want to include a Return character after each variable name so that each variable is stored in a different line. This makes it much easier for you to retrieve values later using Authorware's `GetLine` function.

TIP The `GetLine` function has an optional argument that allows you to specify a line delimiter other than a Return character. For more information on this function, see *Using Authorware* or Authorware Help.

When creating a user records file using variable names and Return characters, your final expression might look something like this:

```
WriteExtFile("Score.txt", UserName ^ Return ^ ¬
"Your final score is " ^ FinalScore ^ Return)
```

Here, the function writes the user records information to an external text file called Score.txt. If you don't specify a path to the file, Authorware creates the file in the same folder that contains the piece. Because the expression includes a Return character on each line, it creates two separate lines in the text file, as shown below:

```
John Smith
Your final score is 100
```

If you want to include a period at the end of the second line (as you might if you were having the user print out the results of the test), you need to enclose the period in quotation marks and concatenate it to the end of the second line before the Return character:

```
WriteExtFile("Score.txt", UserName ^ Return ^ ¬
"Your final score is " ^ FinalScore ^ "." ^
Return)
```

You also can use a literal string for the Return character by using a backslash (\) followed by an "r":

```
WriteExtFile("Score.txt", UserName ^ "\r" ^ ¬
"Your final score is " ^ FinalScore ^ ".\r")
```

Notice that in this example, the return string (\r) is inside the character string that contains the period in order to shorten the statement. (Otherwise, you need to include an extra concatenation character.)

TIP The Return character is an example of a "constant," meaning you can include it in an expression without specifying it as a character string. When working with character strings, you can use Tab in the same way to insert a tab character into a string.

Relational operators

Any time you need to compare information, you need to use a relational operator. Relational operators compare two values and return a logical (True or False) result. You can use relational operators to compare numbers, character strings, or numerical and character variables. The relational operators available in Authorware are listed below:

Operator...	What it means...
=	Equal to
<>	Not equal to
<	Less than
>	Greater than
<=	Less than or equal to
>=	Greater than or equal to

Relational operators are especially helpful when including expressions in calculated interaction paths or decision branching paths. They are the second most commonly used operators behind the assignment operator.

Here are some examples of how you might use relational operators in an expression:

Expression...	What it does...
Fuel > 15	Compares the value of custom variable Fuel to 15, returning a value of True or False.
TempQuiz <= Total	Returns a value of true if TempQuiz is less than or equal to Total; otherwise, returns a value of False.
Completed = False	Compares the value of Completed with False. If Completed is False, returns a value of True; if Completed is True, returns a value of False.
Lines = 15	Returns a value of True if the custom variable Lines equals 15; otherwise, returns a value of False.

Notice that, in the last two examples the equal sign (=) is used rather than the assignment operator (:=). Use the assignment operator to assign a value to a variable; use the equal sign to compare two values or variables. Otherwise, your scripts may not work properly.

Logical operators

Use logical operators to help build logical "not," "and," and "or" expressions. You can use them to assign a logical value to a variable or to test for multiple cases with the same expression. The logical operators for Authorware are listed below:

Operator...	What it means...
~	Not (changes a value or expression to its opposite state).
&	And (both values or expressions must be true for result to be true).
|	Or (if either value or expression is true, the result is true).

You may remember that you frequently use logical operators when creating expressions. However, you also can build expressions with them, as shown in the examples below:

Expression...	What it does...
`Switch := ~ Switch`	A "toggle" is created using the custom variable `Switch`. If `Switch` is True, it is set to False; if it is False, it is set to True
`ReadyState := MouseDown & Clicked`	`ReadyState` is True if `MouseDown` and `Clicked` are both true; `ReadyState` is False if either or both variables are False
`ReadyState := MouseDown | Clicked`	`ReadyState` is True if either `MouseDown`, `Clicked` or both are True; `ReadyState` is False if both variables are False

The last two expressions are examples of how to use "compound conditions" in an expression. You can include two or more different test cases when using compound conditions. When entering compound conditions in an expression, you can use a shorthand form for relational and logical operators.

For example, the following condition is True if `Choice` is between 1 and 5:

Long form   `Choice > 1 & Choice < 5`

Short form   `Choice > 1 & < 5`

You also can use shorthand forms when comparing character strings. For example, the following condition is True if the variable `Name` contains "Jim," "james," or "James."

Long form   `Name = "Jim" | Name = "james" |¬`
                  `Name = "James"`

Short form   `Name = "Jim" |= "james" |= "James"`

When working with logical expressions, you can use the constants True and False to assign a logical value to a variable. You also can substitute 1, On, or Yes for True; and you can substitute 0, Off, or No for False.

Keeping these rules in mind, you can see that the following expressions are all equivalent:

`SwitchStatus = True`

`SwitchStatus = 1`

`SwitchStatus = On`

`SwitchStatus = Yes`

NOTE When assigning a logical value, Authorware does not require you to be case-sensitive. The values "True" and "true" are both interpreted the same way.

Logical expressions can seem a bit perplexing when comparing variables that contain two different data types. You can prepare yourself by learning how Authorware converts different data types to logical values (see "How does Authorware convert data types?" below).

Order of operations

As mentioned earlier, Authorware has an order of operations that it follows for each type of operator, including the arithmetic operators. In numerical expressions, multiplication and division are performed before addition and subtraction, unless you use parentheses.

The order that Authorware follows when evaluating expressions using different types of operators is shown in the table below. Authorware starts with the row at the top and continues down.

If several different operators from the same row are in an expression, Authorware carries them out in the order they appear from left to right.

Name...	Order...	Operators (left to right)...
Parentheses	1	()
Referenced	2	@
Unary	3	~,+,-
Exponential	4	**
Multiply/Divide	5	*,/
Add/Subtract	6	+,-
Concatenate	7	^
Relational	8	=,<>,<,>,<=,>=
Logical	9	&,|
Assignment	10	:=

The order of operations is especially important when you nest functions and variables within other functions when building an expression. For instance, look at the following example:

```
SIDE_C := SQRT((SIDE_A**2) + (SIDE_B**2))
```

In this expression, the result of the SQRT function is not evaluated until after the two custom variables SIDE_A and SIDE_B are squared using the order of operations. If you wanted, you could take the right-hand side of this expression and use it within another function as the numerical argument. This technique can help you create more powerful scripts using fewer variables, as shown below:

```
MyInteger := INT( SQRT((SIDE_A**2) + (SIDE_B**2)) )
```

This expression uses the INT system function to convert the results of the SQRT function to an integer by stripping the numbers to the right of the decimal point. Since the original part of the expression is included inside the INT function as its argument, you are not required to create a third custom variable to store the result value of the SQRT function (unless you need to save it for use later). Authorware evaluates the entire expression using its rules of operation. The parentheses determine the order in which each part of the expression gets evaluated.

How does Authorware convert data types?

You don't always need to define a variable as a numerical, character, or logical variable when you set it up. Authorware automatically interprets each variable's type based on how you use it in an expression. This is important to keep in mind when using a variable in a function argument because it can affect how well your function does its job.

Since the `SQRT` function is a mathematical function, you might assume that you need to provide a number for the argument as well. This is partially correct. For instance, take the following script:

```
number := "four"
result := SQRT(number)
```

This second line in this script is a "nonsense" expression (at least for Authorware). Because Authorware is looking for a numerical argument for the `SQRT` function, it disregards any non-numerical characters passed to it. What you end up with for this expression is a return value of 0 because the custom variable number doesn't actually contain any numbers (even though it spells one). In other words, Authorware can't understand what you mean by "four"—instead it looks for the number 4 or a variable that contains a value of 4.

However, Authorware follows certain data type conversion rules in cases where you've provided a variable value for a function argument that it can convert properly and use with the function. Taking these rules into consideration, the following script would be valid:

```
number := "4"
result := SQRT(number)
```

In this expression, Authorware converts the string value of number ("4") to an integer value (4) before taking its square root and getting the result of 2. Authorware's data type conversion rules work in this case, producing the result that you expected.

You commonly run into issues like this when reading and writing external files because Authorware's character and file functions all return character string values. For example, if you've stored the number 4 in an external file using the `WriteExtFile` system function, Authorware converts it to "4" when you retrieve the value using the `ReadExtFile` function. However, you can still work with this value in both numerical and character expressions because Authorware converts its data type as needed.

In general, Authorware's type conversion rules for variables are summarized as follows:

- When you use a character string in place of a numerical value, Authorware goes through three different comparisons. If the string is True, T, Yes, or On, Authorware interprets it as 1 (capitalization isn't important). If the string is False, F, No, or Off, Authorware interprets it as 0. If it is any other value, Authorware looks for a number at the beginning of the string and ignores all other characters except for the plus (+), minus (-), and decimal point (.) characters. Null strings (those with no characters) are interpreted as 0.

- When you use a character string in place of a logical value, Authorware uses the same rules to convert the string to an integer. If the integer is any value other than 0, Authorware interprets it as 1.

- When you use a numerical value in place of a logical value, Authorware interprets any value other than 0 as 1.

- When you concatenate two variables together in a character string expression, Authorware converts both variables to strings before combining them into one string.

- Numerical values converted from strings and displayed in the Presentation window display up to 15 decimal places and the decimal separator inside the string. However, separators between thousands aren't added. Because of this, it's usually better to display the numerical value inside the Presentation window, as you can use the Number Format dialog box to add thousands separators. (For more information on using the Number Format dialog box, see "Updating Data On Screen.")

Keep these rules in mind as you continue to work with variables and functions inside a piece.

TIP You can use the system functions `Number`, `Real`, `String`, and `Symbol` to change the data types of variables in a piece to a specific type (indicated by the name of the variable).

As you've seen, you can use variables, functions, and expressions in calculation scripts to control what happens behind the scenes. However, you also can display data for the user on screen to give additional feedback.

Updating Data On Screen

Updating information on screen is a particularly useful way to provide the user with dynamic visual feedback that changes throughout a piece. For instance, you might want to have a score summary screen for a particular training piece. Using embedded variables, you can quickly create a display icon that updates the user's score after each lesson, and then displays the appropriate information.

This might include the total number of questions answered, the total number of questions answered correctly, the total percent correct, and any other information that you feel is relevant feedback about the user's progress through a section.

TIP Embedding an expression in a text object makes it possible to display the result of a calculation without adding a calculation icon to the flowline.

To display the value of a variable or an expression on screen, create a text field inside a display icon and add the variable or the expression to the field. You can add any other text (such as a label) that you want to appear on screen, along with the results of the expression to the same text field.

To create the text object where you want the value of the variable or expression to appear:

1. Drag a display icon to the flowline and double-click it to open it.

   The Presentation window and toolbox appear.

2. Select the text tool from the toolbox and click text cursor at the spot where you want the result of the expression to appear.

3. Use the Variables and Functions dialog boxes to paste the variables and functions you want to use into the text field.

   Each time you paste a variable or function into the text field, Authorware encloses it in braces, as shown in **Figure 14.10**.

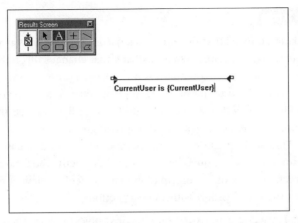

Figure 14.10
Pasting a variable into a display icon text field.

NOTE You also can place variable or function names into the text field by typing in the name, but you need to enclose it inside braces.

4. Add any additional text you want to the field.

TIP If you need to display a left brace character ({) in a text field, you should precede it with a backslash (\) character. Otherwise, Authorware assumes you have placed a variable expression into the text field.

5. When you have finished, deselect the text tool.

When you deselect the text tool, the text field becomes selected in the Presentation window. The braces around the variable expression disappear, and the current value for the expression displays inside the field, as shown in **Figure 14.11**.

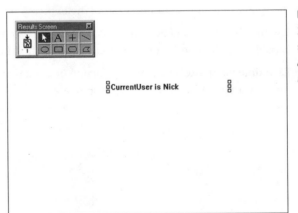

Figure 14.11
The embedded variable after deselecting the text tool.

However, if you restart the piece, the value of the embedded expression does not update correctly unless you select the Update Displayed Variables option in the Display Icon Properties dialog box.

To change the Display Icon Properties dialog box option for updating displayed variables:

1. Choose Icon > Properties from the Modify menu before closing the display icon.

The Icon Properties dialog box appears.

2. Select the Display tab at the bottom of the dialog box and check the Update Displayed Variables option.

3. Click OK to close the dialog box.

If you run the piece now, you'll see that the variable updates properly. You need to do this for each display or interaction icon in which you've embedded data. Otherwise, the user doesn't get the correct feedback displayed on screen.

The Number Format dialog box

When including numerical variable values inside a text field, you may want to adjust the way the numbers appear in the Presentation window. For instance, you might want to include commas or other types of numerical separators that help format the numbers when they display. You can do this quickly using the Number Format dialog box.

To set number formatting for a displayed text field:

1. Select the text field inside the Presentation window.

2. Choose Number Format from the Text menu.

The Number Format dialog box appears, as shown in **Figure 14.12**.

Figure 14.12

The Number Format dialog box.

The default options in the dialog box automatically display the numerical value with digits after the decimal point and with a Thousands/Millions comma separator.

You quickly can change the format of the numbers using the options in the Decimal area and the Before Decimal area to update the text field using the number format you select. For example, selecting the Leading Zeros option in the Before Decimal area displays the number with a 0 before the decimal point, if it is a fractional number, as shown in **Figure 14.13**.

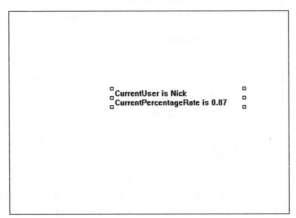

Figure 14.13
Number formatting affects how numbers display on screen.

3. Select the number formatting options you want to use and click OK to close the dialog box.

Displaying numerical values is useful when working with percentages and other mathematical data. The next section explains how to integrate all types of variable data that updates on screen into results screens that explain to the user in greater detail how their progress is tracked.

Combining embedded variables and text

It's very easy to provide different types of results feedback to the user based on system and custom variables. Suppose, for example, that you want to display the percentage of responses a student gets right on the first try. You probably would paste the `FirstTryCorrect` and the `JudgedInteractions` variables into the text field, since these system variables track this information for you.

The field should look like this:

```
{FirstTryCorrect} {JudgedInteractions}
```

If you use an expression in a text field, you need to include the correct operator symbol for the type of expression you're building. For instance, you can immediately get the percentage of responses a student gets right on the first try by inserting the division operator between the names of the two embedded variables, like this:

```
{FirstTryCorrect/JudgedInteractions}
```

Notice that there is only one set of braces. This makes it easier to edit the entire expression when you open the display or interaction icon.

When embedding data on screen, you also may want to add text before or after the expression to clarify what you are displaying. For example, you could tell students that the percentage on screen represents only the questions answered correctly on the first try by typing in something like this into the text field:

```
You got{FirstTryCorrect/JudgedInteractions}%
of the questions you answered right on the
first try.
```

When you run the piece, Authorware continues to update the field and replace the variable or expression inside the braces with its associated value, as shown in **Figure 14.14**.

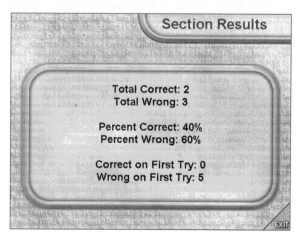

Figure 14.14
A results screen in the Presentation window.

This technique is used frequently to give the user other types of feedback. For instance, including the system variable `CurrentPageNum` in a display icon inside the entry pane of a framework allows you to display the current page number inside the Presentation window. You can use on screen feedback as well to track custom variables while you are authoring to isolate problems that occur in your scripts or in the flowline.

Looking Ahead...

This chapter introduced you to the basic ways of working with variables, functions, and expressions. Learning to integrate these three components into your pieces can help you exhibit more control over all aspects of your piece, including the flowline, the icons, and the data being generated in the background while the piece is running. If you need to provide the user with visual feedback, you can use embedded variables and expressions directly inside the Presentation window to create automatic feedback that is updated while a piece runs.

As you begin to work more closely with Authorware's scripting components, you'll find that they greatly enhance your productivity by giving you additional control over how your piece runs from start to finish. As you'll see in Chapter 15, "Controlling the Flowline through Scripting," scripting can be a great asset when creating larger pieces that require variable control over specific icons on the flowline.

Controlling the Flowline through Scripting

When authoring, keep in mind there isn't a single "right" answer for every problem you face. As you become more familiar with the tools available in Authorware, you can figure out the solutions that make sense for you. To solve a problem, you may need to modify your flowline or change the way you've integrated graphics, text, movies, or sounds into your piece. At other times, however, you may run into bottlenecks that you can't solve with these techniques alone.

In such cases, you may need to look at scripting techniques to address flowline-specific issues that you cannot resolve by working with the icons or content that you've added to your piece. Authorware's functions and variables give you far more flexibility in controlling what is happening in the flowline than the techniques discussed so far. The techniques in this chapter are by no means the only solutions to the types of icon-specific issues you may face; however, they are the ones most commonly used by Authorware developers to work around issues that they encounter frequently when designing a piece.

Frequently, you will need to find ways of working directly with specific icons on the flowline to improve the fluidity of your piece. In Authorware, the most common way to do this is to use its scripting tools to create referenced expressions, which point to a specific icon on the flowline.

When you add a new icon to the flowline, Authorware adds the icon to its own internal reference list. This list provides Authorware with a way of tracking what's happening on the flowline at any given moment. The list tells Authorware which icons are being presented, which icons need to be erased, and other types of icon-specific information that is required to keep the piece running.

Because this information is always available, you can use it to point or "refer" to specific icons on the flowline inside your scripts. By doing this, you can control such events as grabbing the text a user enters in a text entry field, displaying and erasing graphics, or even playing, pausing, and searching through a digital movie frame-by-frame directly through the calculation icon.

While Authorware handles these types of tasks through different system variables and functions, what they have in common (as you might suspect) is their reliance on you to specify the icon that you want to target when using this scripting technique. Before you begin working with referenced expressions, it is helpful to understand the ways in which you can refer to the icons on the flowline inside a script.

Referencing icons by title

Here's a pop quiz question for you: Why is it so important to give your icons unique titles? If you recall from Chapter 1, "Getting Started," the reason you want to do this (aside from keeping your flowline better organized) is that you may want to refer to an icon by using its title when you are working in the calculation icon. Hopefully, you can also recall that you must give the icon a unique title because you can't have any other icons in the flowline with the same name when referring to them inside a script.

Referencing icons by title is one of the most common ways to refer to icons inside a piece. You can refer to the icon's title by including the system variable IconTitle in an icon properties field, or as a variable embedded in a text field if you're working with display or interaction icons. Because each icon maintains its own `IconTitle` value, you can use this to your advantage when working with specific icons.

For example, you can use the value of `IconTitle` to make it easier to edit a wait icon's time limit directly from the flowline:

1. Add a new wait icon to the flowline; double-click it to open it.

   The Wait Icon Properties dialog box appears, as shown in **Figure 15.1**.

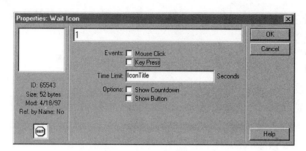

Figure 15.1
The Wait Icon Properties dialog box.

2. Type in 1 in the title field at the top of the dialog box.

   This number appears as the icon's title in the flowline.

3. In the Time Limit field, type in `IconTitle`.

4. Deselect the Key Press and Show Button checkbox options.

5. Click OK to close the dialog box, and then run the piece.

When Authorware encounters the wait icon, it pauses for one second, and then continues. Authorware uses the value of `IconTitle` (in this case, "1") to control the duration of the pause. By changing the wait icon's title in the flowline, you can automatically change the duration of the pause (as long as you use a number for the title). This can save you a lot of time if you need to tweak synchronization issues inside a large piece that uses wait icons to control the timing.

Using this same technique, you can embed the system variable `IconTitle` in a display or interaction icon text field to display the title of the icon inside the Presentation window, as shown in **Figure 15.2**. Because `IconTitle` contains only the title of the icon in which it is embedded, you can quickly create topic headings and title fields for your piece that you can update easily by changing the titles of the display icons in which you've embedded the icons.

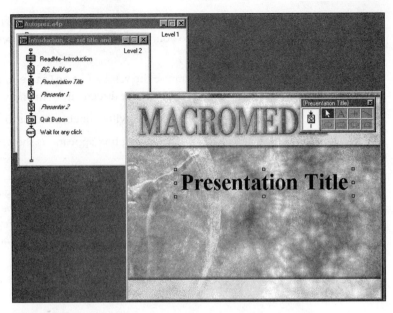

Figure 15.2
Embedding the icon title of a display icon in the Presentation window.

These are two common ways of working directly with the `IconTitle` system variable when creating your piece. However, many functions also require you to use the expression `IconID@"IconTitle"` when referring to a specific icon. This is an example of a referenced variable, discussed in more detail in the next section.

Using referenced variables

Because a variable's contents can change throughout a piece, its value may change at specific icon locations along the flowline. For example, the system variable `EntryText` may contain many different values throughout a piece, depending on the text the user enters in each text entry field interaction that you've included in your piece.

Many of Authorware's system variables enable you to find out their value at a specific location in the piece by including a reference to a specific icon in the flowline when using them within a script or a Properties dialog box field. You do this by typing the variable's name followed by the "at" (@) symbol and the title of the icon:

`ReferencedVariableName@"IconTitle"`

NOTE You cannot use all system variables in a referenced variable expression. You can look at a variable's definition inside the Variables window to see if you can use it in this way.

For example, you might have a text entry response in the flowline that the user can type into (one of many text entry fields that you've included in the piece). If you want to grab the specific text entry response information at another position in the flowline, you could either store the value of EntryText in a custom variable, or you could reference the interaction icon that contains the response in a script and quickly grab the value.

To do this, you would use the following expression:

```
UserEntry := EntryText@"Text Interaction"
```

Regardless of the number of text-entry fields in the piece, EntryText@"Text Interaction" always contains the value the user typed at the interaction named Text Interaction (the title of the interaction icon). By using a referenced variable, you can avoid creating new variables for every text-entry field where the user enters information you want to store.

NOTE Authorware automatically tracks changes to icon names used with referenced variables. If you change the title of an icon, Authorware automatically makes the same change wherever you have used it in a referenced variable expression.

Referenced variables are useful in expressions. For example, suppose that you want to add the values a user enters as responses to three interactions entitled Planes, Trains, and Automobiles. You can use the NumEntry system variable followed by the @ symbol in an assignment expression, like this:

```
VehicleCount := NumEntry@"Planes" + ¬
NumEntry@"Trains" + NumEntry@"Automobiles"
```

It's generally a good idea to use a custom variable in place of the icon title when working with a referenced variable expression. This also applies to functions that require a referenced variable expression. Many times you will create a script that refers to an icon by title, but later delete the icon or replace it with another icon. It's much easier to make changes to your piece later, if you refer to an icon using a variable rather than the exact title.

When specifying an icon title within a referenced variable expression, you must spell the icon's title exactly as it is spelled on the flowline, including capital letters. Otherwise, Authorware may mistake it for another icon on the flowline with a similar name.

Referencing icons by ID

If you look at the system functions that require you to specify an icon title as the first argument (e.g., functions like `DisplayIcon` or `MediaPlay`), you may notice that the first argument that you must provide is something that looks like this:

```
IconID@"IconTitle"
```

This argument is another example of using a referenced variable in a piece. It's the same type of referenced variable that you looked at in the last section. Referenced variables enable you to refer to a specific icon by title. However, you can shorten the syntax for this argument by simply including the `IconID` of the icon instead, as you'll see in a moment.

TIP A shorthand way of writing a referenced variable expression is simply `@"IconTitle"`. You don't need to include `IconID` in the expression every time you use it.

Each icon on the flowline has its own unique `IconID` value when you add it to the flowline. (Remember, Authorware maintains an internal list of every icon you add to the flowline.) The `IconID` value that Authorware assigns to each icon is actually a system variable that updates continually while the piece runs. As soon as a new icon in the flowline is executed, the value of `IconID` updates as well to reflect the current icon being presented.

Consequently, you can use an icon's `IconID` value in the same way that you use its icon title. (The system variable `IconTitle` functions in much the same way as the system function `IconID`.) You can use a simple scripting technique to grab the `IconID` value of a specific icon in the flowline, and then assign this value to a custom variable that you've created. This allows you to target specific icons in the flowline when using Authorware's system functions.

To do this, you simply attach a calculation script to the icon that contains the `IconID` value you want to store. Adding a script to an icon is sometimes referred to as creating a calculation "ornament" because a small calculation symbol appears on the flowline and is attached to the upper left-hand corner of the icon, as shown in **Figure 15.3**. You can attach calculation scripts to any icon, except calculation icons. Authorware executes the script attached to the icon before executing the icon.

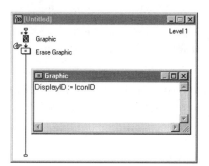

Figure 15.3
Attaching a script to an icon to grab its ID value.

To see how this works, try the following steps:

1. Drag a new display icon to the flowline, give it a name, and then select it.

2. Choose Icon > Calculation from the Modify menu.

Shortcut: To open the Calculation window when you have selected an icon, press Ctrl+= (Windows), or Command+= (Macintosh).

The Calculation window appears.

3. Type in the following two-line script:

TEMPID := IconID

Trace("TempID=" ^ TempID)

The second line of the script calls the `Trace` system function, which displays the value of the variable or expression you specified inside the parentheses inside the Trace field of the Control Panel window. You can use this function to quickly test whether or not a numerical `IconID` value is stored correctly in the custom variable `TempID`. You'll learn more about working with the Control Panel window in Chapter 18, "Debugging Your Piece."

4. After typing in the script, close the Calculation window.

The New Variable dialog box appears, asking you to define an initial value for the custom variable `TempID`.

5. Type in **0** for the initial value and click OK.

TIP It's a good idea to create several custom variables for different types of icons. For instance, you might store the `IconID` values of display icons in a custom variable named `DisplayID`; and, you could store movie `IconID` values in a variable named `MovieID`, and so on. This would help you keep track of your `IconID` information easier.

6. Before you run the piece, open the Control Panel window by choosing Control Panel from the Window menu.

The Control Panel window appears, as shown in **Figure 15.4**. The Control Panel window includes buttons for many of the same commands in the Control menu, including Restart, Pause, and Resume.

The Show Trace button ————

Figure 15.4
The Control Panel window.

You also can use the Control Panel window to display a Trace field to trace what is happening on the flowline.

7. For now, click the Show Trace button of the Control Panel window (see **Figure 15.4** above).

The Control Panel expands to show the scrolling Trace field, as shown in **Figure 15.5**.

Figure 15.5
The Control Panel window expanded to show a separate Trace field.

Now go ahead and run the piece, noting the message that pops up immediately in the Trace field. You should see something like the following:

— TempID=65543

Here, Authorware displays the character string you specified in the `Trace` function, concatenated with the five-digit value of the `IconID` assigned to the custom variable `TempID`. This is the same `IconID` value that Authorware assigned to the display icon in the flowline. Now that your script has assigned this value to a custom variable, you can quickly refer to this display icon later in the piece when using another system function or referenced variable expression. Simply replace the expression `IconID@"IconTitle"` with the name of your custom variable (in this case, `TempID`) when you want to include it in an expression.

The list below shows you some possible ways of using this new technique in a script:

Old expression	*New expression*
`EntryText@"Sign On"`	`EntryText@TextID`
`DisplayIcon(IconID@"Main Background")`	`DisplayIcon(DisplayID)`
`EraseIcon(IconID@"Balloon.mov")`	`EraseIcon(MovieID)`

Using an `IconID` value in an expression makes your scripts easier to write and a great deal more flexible because you now have the capability to reference any icon using an expression—as long as you've updated the custom variable you're specifying in the expression with the correct `IconID` value of the icon you want to reference.

How does this work in practice? The next two sections of this chapter take a look at some ways you can use this technique when working with icons on the flowline.

Displaying and Erasing Icons

Now that you've learned how to create referenced variables by storing `IconID` values, it is a good time to look at some ways you can use this technique to improve your handling of events on the flowline. One particularly good way to use referenced variables is to control what Authorware displays or erases from the screen by using the `DisplayIcon` and `EraseIcon` functions.

The `DisplayIcon` function

The `DisplayIcon` function is just one of several functions that enables you to work directly with display and interaction icons. You might use this function if you already have erased the display or interaction icon in another part of the flowline, but need to redisplay its contents in the Presentation window.

To get around this issue without using the `DisplayIcon` function, either copy the icon you want to redisplay and paste it into the other section of the flowline, or create another link to the icon on the flowline if you've placed it in a library. As you will see later, the `DisplayIcon` function is a simpler alternative to both of these—especially if you're setting up responses that need to take into consideration several possible combinations of icons to provide the correct user feedback.

To get a feel for how the `DisplayIcon` function works, you can create a simple example that redisplays the graphic after it erases:

1. Drag a display icon to the flowline and title it **My Graphic**.

2. Open the display icon and draw an object inside the Presentation window by using the toolbox. When you have finished, close the display icon to return to the flowline.

3. Place a wait icon below the display icon; set it to wait for a mouse click.

4. Place an erase icon below the wait icon; set it to erase the display icon.

5. Copy the wait icon and paste it below the erase icon to create another pause in the piece.

6. Add a calculation icon to the flowline below the second wait icon and double-click it to open it.

7. In the Calculation window, type in the following expression: **DisplayIcon(@"My Graphic")**.

When you have finished, close the calculation icon and run the piece. Your flowline should look similar to the one in **Figure 15.6**.

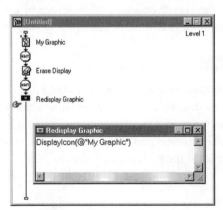

Figure 15.6
Displaying and erasing graphics using a calculation script.

If you run the piece, you'll see that the graphic erases on the first mouse click. However, when you click a second time, the graphic displays again inside the Presentation window in the same position where it initially appeared. It's as if the same display icon was copied and pasted into a different position on the flowline. The only difference is that you're using only one display icon and a system function.

TIP When you display an icon using the `DisplayIcon` function, it conforms to the automatic erasing options that you've set inside the piece. If you want to prevent Authorware from automatically erasing the icon, use the `DisplayIconNoErase` function in place of the `DisplayIcon` function.

Although this example doesn't show it, the `DisplayIcon` function is extremely useful when creating an interaction response where you want to dynamically display a different icon each time the user chooses the response. Rather than creating several decision paths for the response, with each one displaying a different icon, you can place one calculation icon in the response map that controls which icon should display.

Of course, another way to do this is to place the display icons in a library, and then create additional links to them in the flowline. However, this isn't a very flexible approach to the problem. Using the `DisplayIcon` function enables you to react to several situations at the same time. Because you can specify the `IconID` argument for this function using a custom variable, you could easily display a different icon each time, if you need to use the same function call. Later in this chapter, you will learn how to set something like this up, using If-Then statements inside your scripts.

The `EraseIcon` function

If you want to remove the display icon from the Presentation window in the last example you created, you can erase it by using another erase icon or use the `EraseIcon` function to do the same thing. You can use the `EraseIcon` function in place of the erase icon to remove graphics, text, or digital movies from the Presentation window.

Because the erase icon requires that you "target" specific icons you want removed from the screen, sometimes it is more difficult to use the erase icon when you have many icons that you need erased at a particular place in your piece. While you can set up the erase icon to erase specified icons from the screen, this quickly becomes a problem of its own as you find that some of the graphics you didn't want to erase in the first place are disappearing.

For example, you might have a help screen that displays when the user clicks a perpetual button. However, if the user clicks this button while a digital movie is playing, you will find that the movie still plays on top of the help screen.

You could add an erase icon to the help screen interaction, but if you use many movie icons in your piece, it quickly becomes a trying task to go through the entire piece and target every movie icon with the same erase icon.

It's good to know that there's a more elegant way around this problem. It involves using the `EraseIcon` function to target only the current movie that's playing. To set up this type of erasing in your piece, you need to do two things:

■ Attach a calculation script to each movie icon that assigns its `IconID` to a custom variable. For example you might use the expression `MovieID := IconID`.

NOTE The next several steps refer to the custom variable `MovieID` in the scripts that are used.

To take into account any movie that might be playing when the user presses the help button, you would add the same calculation script to each movie icon in your piece. This allows you to erase any movie appearing on screen (unless you are displaying two or more movies at the same time, which isn't recommended).

■ Add a calculation icon to the perpetual interaction that erases the currently playing movie.

After setting up your movie icons, add a calculation icon to the perpetual interaction using the following steps:

1. Drag a calculation icon into the map attached to the perpetual response that activates the help screen. **Figure 15.7** shows you how this type of flowline structure might appear in a piece.

Help button displays help screen. ——

Calculation script erases any movie playing. ——

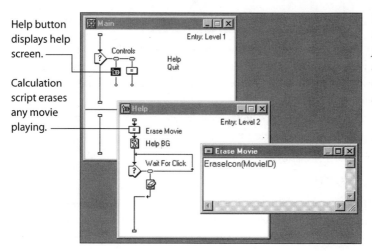

Figure 15.7
Setting up a perpetual help screen to erase any movies that are playing.

2. Open the calculation icon and type in the following expression: **EraseIcon(MovieID)**.

3. When you have finished, close the Calculation window and run the piece.

When you click on the perpetual response, you should see that any movie that is currently playing is erased from the screen.

NOTE If you do not see this, make sure that you've attached the same script to each movie icon, assigning its `IconID` value to a custom variable; also make sure that you have used the name of this custom variable in the argument for the `EraseIcon` function.

If you try this with your own piece, you may notice one additional issue that could be a problem. Because Authorware erases the movie when the user clicks on the perpetual interaction, it stops playing and does not continue playing again when the user returns to the previous screen. To get around this issue, you might rely on one of Authorware's media functions to restart the movie. In the next section, you'll learn how to work with this set of functions.

When you begin integrating more scripting into a piece, it's helpful to provide comments with your scripts so that you can refer to them later if needed. Comments are also useful when sharing code with other developers, since it helps them understand how your piece works.

To include comments in a script, you simply place two hyphens before the line you want to comment, as shown below:

```
--This line is commented.

statement := "This line is not."
```

You can include comments in calculation icons that are in the flowline or attached to another icon. You also can use comments directly in the flowline in the same way that you include comments in calculation icons. This can be particularly helpful in larger pieces where you need to keep track of what is happening in specific interactions.

As you may remember from Chapter 10, "Responding to Events and Conditions," you can edit a conditional response directly in the flowline by modifying its title. You can quickly include a comment after the expression you've entered for the conditional response in the same way that you would add comments to a calculation script. An example of what this might look like is shown in **Figure 15.8**.

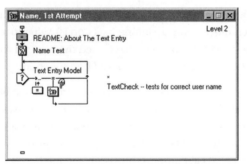

Figure 15.8
A conditional response with a comment added in the flowline.

To include a comment on the flowline with a conditional response:

1. Click on the title of the conditional response to which you want to add a comment. If there are more than five responses in the interaction, you may have to use the scroll bar to find the response title that you want to edit.

2. Type in a pair of hyphens at the end of the title, and then add your comment.

NOTE You also can add and change comments to a response by double-clicking on the response and editing the icon title or Condition field inside the Response Properties dialog box.

When executing the interaction, Authorware only looks at the part of the conditional expression to the left of the hyphens and ignores the rest of the line. You can add, change, or delete the comment at any time without affecting the conditional response's functionality.

TIP You can add comments to keypress and text entry responses by using the same technique.

Using the Media Functions

As your pieces become more complicated, you may frequently run into situations where you would like more control over the media elements appearing on screen. In the case of the last example, having the capability to restart a movie after it's erased can help you out of a difficult situation.

You can refine how you integrate sound and video into your piece by taking advantage of Authorware's set of media functions, which give you more control over the movie, sound, and video icons on the flowline. This section discusses how you can integrate them into your scripts.

Using `MediaPlay`

At times, you may want to play or replay a movie or sound—especially if it's already erased; or, in the case of a sound icon, if it's stopped by another sound that interrupts it on the flowline. Using the `MediaPlay` function, you can play any sound, movie, or video icon on the flow-line through the calculation icon. This function only needs one argument—the icon (either specified by icon title or `IconID`) that you want to play, as shown below:

```
MediaPlay(IconID@"IconTitle")
```

When you call the function, Authorware starts playing the clip contained in the digital movie, sound, or video icon you've specified. If the sound, movie, or video clip is already playing when you call the function, Authorware restarts the clip from the beginning.

To see how this works, you can create a simple button interaction that plays a movie or sound you've imported into Authorware from a calculation icon attached to the button:

1. Create a new file, then import a movie into the piece and title it **Sample Clip**.

2. Drag a new interaction icon to the flowline by placing it below the movie icon.

3. Add a button response to the interaction by dragging a calculation icon to the right of the interaction icon, and then title it **Play**.

4. Double-click the calculation icon to open it.

   The Calculation window appears.

5. Type in the following expression: **MediaPlay(@"Sample Clip")**.

6. When you have finished, close the Calculation window and run the piece to test it.

The movie should start to play while the button displays inside the Presentation window. When you press the Play button, the MediaPlay function is called, and the movie starts playing again from the beginning. You might have to reposition the movie the first time you run the piece so that it doesn't display on top of the button you've created.

In this example, the movie already is playing on screen when you press the button. However, the movie will still play, regardless of where it's positioned on the flowline. To see what is happening, try dragging the movie icon below the interaction, and then run the piece again. To see the movie play this time, you must press the Play button first.

Using MediaPause

The last example showed you how you might create your own custom movie controls on screen. Using a button interaction enables you to import custom graphics to control the movie. If you want, you can improve the design of the previous example by adding two additional buttons to the interaction: one that pauses the movie, and one that resumes playing.

To do this, you could use the MediaPause function. The syntax for this function looks like this:

```
MediaPause(IconID@"IconTitle", pause)
```

Like the MediaPlay function, you must specify the icon you want to pause or resume. This function also uses a second argument (the "pause" argument), which tells the function whether to pause or restart the movie. If you specify 1 for this argument, the movie or sound pauses; specifying 0 causes the movie to resume playing from the location where it paused.

NOTE You also can use other Boolean values like On, Yes, or True (in place of 1) and Off, No, or False (in place of 0) for this argument.

You can add the pause and resume buttons to your movie control interaction by doing the following:

1. Create two more button responses for the interaction, using the calculation icon as you did in the previous example. Title the buttons **Pause** and **Resume**, as shown in **Figure 15.9**.

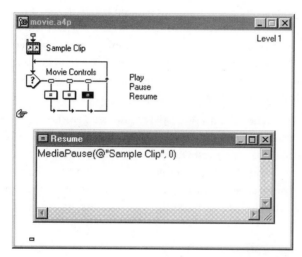

Figure 15.9
Adding Pause and Resume buttons to the movie control interaction.

2. Double-click the calculation icon attached to the Pause button response.

   The Calculation window appears.

3. Type in the expression **MediaPause(@"Sample Clip", 1)** and close the Calculation window.

4. Double-click the calculation icon attached to the Resume button response.

5. Type in the expression MediaPause(@"Sample Clip", 0) and close the Calculation window.

Now that you've set up your pause and resume buttons, go ahead and run the piece to see how it works. As you might expect, clicking the Pause button freezes the movie at the current frame. Clicking on the Resume button while the movie plays has no effect because the movie hasn't paused yet. If you pause the movie and then click the Resume button, the movie restarts from the current frame where it has paused.

 If you would like to see a more complete example of how to create a custom movie control interaction, you can look at the example included on the CD accompanying this book. It's in the Chapter 15 examples folder in the file MOVCNTRL.A4P.

Not every piece requires that you create interactions like this. Remember that if you're using QuickTime movies, you can easily add a QuickTime-style control bar to the movie simply by selecting the Under User Control option inside the Movie Icon Properties dialog box. However, if you're working with AVI, MPEG, PICS, or FLC movies, you might want to add this type of control to your piece.

NOTE In addition to `MediaPlay` and `MediaPause`, there are several other functions and variables that you can use to further refine the playback of sound and video in your piece. These include the `MediaSeek` function, and the `MediaPlaying` and `SoundPlaying` system variables. For more detailed descriptions of these functions and variables, see *Using Authorware* or Authorware Help.

Using the Language Functions

You might remember from earlier in the chapter that one of the advantages of using scripting to control the flowline is that you can quickly adapt your piece to one of several conditions. For instance, when using the `ResizeWindow` system function to resize the Presentation window (as discussed in Chapter 14, "Using Functions and Variables"), you might find it desirable to adjust the piece's window size based on the user's current display resolution.

Another example might be to combine the Pause and Resume buttons used in the movie controller example into a single button to control the pause and resume functions. Doing so makes your movie controls behave more like the kind of movie controls you find in other applications such as Movie Player (Macintosh) or Media Player (Windows).

At other times, you might find when working with data in the background of your piece that you need to update a large number of lines in a character variable with the same information. You simply can't hard-code it into a script, however, because it is information that is generated by the user while the piece runs.

Using the language functions, you can add all these types of functionality to a piece. The main language functions that you need to learn how to use are the If-Then function and the Repeat functions.

If-Then statements

The If-Then function allows you to test for a condition before executing a script. You use If-Then statements to instruct Authorware to perform actions, depending on different conditions. Whenever you create a statement like this in a calculation script, it always follows the same format, as shown below:

```
if (case 1 is true) then
(do something)
else
(do something else)
end if
```

For example, you could use an If-Then statement to resize the Presentation window to one of two dimensions, depending on whether or not the user's current display resolution is set to 640 x 480 (VGA) or something larger. If you were to write an If-Then statement like this in plain English, it might read something like this:

```
if (the user's display resolution is larger ¬
than 640x480) then
(change the Presentation window size to 640x480)
else
(change the Presentation window size to 400x300)
end if
```

To put this statement into a calculation script, you would need to rephrase it somewhat:

```
if ScreenWidth >= 640 then
    myWidth := 640
    myHeight := 480
    ResizeWindow(myWidth, myHeight)
    else
    myWidth := 400
    myHeight := 300
    ResizeWindow(myWidth, myHeight)
end if
```

In this example, you use the system variable ScreenWidth to set up the If-Then condition that Authorware tests. Because ScreenWidth contains the current pixel width of the user's display resolution, you can use the value of this variable to dynamically adjust the size of the Presentation window when the piece first launches.

The If-Then statement looks at the condition that is defined at the top of the statement, and if it is True (if ScreenWidth is greater than or equal to 640), then the Presentation window resizes to 640 x 480; if it is not True (if ScreenWidth is less than 640), the Presentation window resizes to 400 x 300.

Notice that both sets of "case" instructions within the If-Then statement are indented to make the statement easier to read. While Authorware doesn't automatically indent lines for you in an If-Then statement, try to format your scripts this way so they are easier to view and troubleshoot. It also helps to compact your statements into as few lines as possible.

To compact the example script above, you could also write the statement this way:

```
if ScreenWidth >= 640 then
    myWidth := 640
    myHeight := 480
    else
    myWidth := 400
    myHeight := 300
end if
ResizeWindow(myWidth, myHeight)
```

Because the `ResizeWindow` function takes the same arguments in both cases, you don't need to repeat it in the statement. You can simply include the lines of script that need to be executed differently inside the If-Then statement, and then add the function below it.

When creating other kinds of If-Then statements in which you're only including one line of instructions for each possible case, you can compact the statement by writing it as follows:

```
if (case is true) then (do something)

else (do something else)
```

When structuring your statement this way, you don't have to include the `end if` at the end of the statement as you did in the previous example. For example, if you want to set up a simple If-Then statement that updates a custom variable embedded in a display icon with a different message depending on what the user has typed into a text entry field, write the statement as follows:

```
if EntryText="boy" then PickUpLine := "I'm a girl!"

else PickUpLine := "I'm a boy!"
```

Another variation of the If-Then statement allows you to test for multiple conditions at the same time. For instance, if you want to display a different help graphic on screen depending on a preference setting the user makes, you could use an If-Then statement similar to the one below:

```
if HelpOption = 1 then

    DisplayIcon(@"Pict01")

    DisplayIcon(@"Help1 Caption")

    else if HelpOption = 2 then

    DisplayIcon(@"Pict01")

    DisplayIcon(@"Help2 Caption")

    else

    DisplayIcon(@"Pict01")

end if
```

If-Then statements are powerful tools when you need to set up decision-style branching in a script. However, when you need to repeat through a series of steps, consider using repeat loops.

The `Repeat With` function—and its system function siblings `Repeat While` and `Repeat With In`—enable you to repeat a set of instructions until a specific condition is met. While you can do this with a decision icon, repeat loops you create inside a calculation icon script are executed more quickly and are in some ways easier to set up.

NOTE You should still use a decision icon loop if you need to loop through entire sections of flowline logic, as you saw in Chapter 13, "Using Decision Paths."

Sometimes you may need to repeat a series of steps in a script many times. For instance, you might want to update a series of lines in a character variable with the same information. At other times, you may want to "populate" a list variable with the same data in each position. Rather than typing out line after line of script, you can simply use Authorware's set of `Repeat` functions to do the work for you.

There are three basic types of repeat loops you can use in a script:

■ Repeat With loops repeat a series of steps a given number of times.

■ Repeat While loops repeat a series of steps for as long as a condition is True.

■ Repeat With In loops repeat a series of steps for each position in a list variable.

When setting up a Repeat With loop, you use the following general format:

```
repeat with (index value) from (start) to (end)
          (do something)
end repeat
```

For example, you can set up a Repeat With loop that draws a box on screen, and then cycles through randomly selected colors. The statement would look something like this:

```
repeat with Counter := 1 to 256
          Red := Random(0,255,1)
          Green := Random(0,255,1)
          Blue := Random(0,255,1)
          SetFill(1,RGB(Red,Green,Blue))
          Box(1,100,100,200,200)
end repeat
```

In this example, you begin the loop by setting a custom variable (in this case, `Counter`) equal to 1. It goes through each of the statements in the loop. After it finishes the last one, it compares the value currently in `Counter` with 256 (the number of colors in the Authorware palette). If the value is less than 256, it adds 1 to the value and starts over again. Authorware repeats the process until `Counter` is equal to 256.

NOTE In this example, you don't necessarily need to begin with 1. You could set the initial value of `Counter` to 101, but then you would only get 156 repetitions instead of 256.

Repeat While loops are similar, except that instead of repeating the loop for a given number of times, you begin the statement by setting up the condition for which you are you're testing:

```
repeat while (condition is true)
          (do something)
end repeat
```

Since you can continue to execute the same steps repeatedly, Repeat While loops are especially useful for situations where you need to modify characters contained in a variable. For instance, you can set up a Repeat While loop that removes one character at a time from a custom variable until there are no more characters left:

```
repeat while Characters > 0
Characters := SubStr(MyString, 1,
CharCount(MyString))
end repeat
```

Here, you use the `SubStr` function to reduce the length of the custom variable `MyString` one character at a time, and then assign it to the custom variable `Characters`. After each repetition, Authorware compares the value of `Characters` to 0; if there are still characters left in MyString, then the action repeats until Authorware has stripped all characters.

These examples illustrate the types of control that the If-Then and Repeat functions provide when working with more complex types of scripts. You'll see other examples of using If-Then and Repeat functions in the chapters ahead.

Looking Ahead...

While scripting does not always offer you an instant solution to icon and flowline-related issues that you encounter, it is certainly one of the most valuable tools to use if you need additional control over what is happening in the flowline. Scripting not only allows you to control specific icons in a piece, but it also allows you to create logic that anticipates how a user might react to a specific interaction. The scripting language functions provide many shortcuts to you, including moving quickly through a series of repetitions while updating the information contained in custom variables that you are using.

You'll find these types of skills a tremendous asset when you begin creating pieces that track a user's progress and react to it accordingly. Chapter 16, "Tracking the User," teaches you the basic Authorware components for building this type of functionality into your piece.

Tracking the User

With the kind of information tracking you have at your disposal in Authorware, you don't need to confine its use to training or learning applications. In fact, just about any piece you create can benefit from the additional power that information tracking provides.

While it's extremely useful to record test scores and other performance-based data, you also can use information tracking to give you detailed information about your audience or to provide hands-on feedback from the user about a piece during the preliminary prototyping phase of development.

In this chapter, you'll learn about the basic techniques used to track, record, and store run-time information in your piece. While this is a fairly broad subject, this chapter focuses on the main aspects that you should know when fine-tuning your piece for information tracking. These include working with performance tracking system variables, creating user records, working with lists and external files, and creating logon routines.

What you'll learn...

Tracking performance

Creating a user record

Using lists to improve data handling

Working with external files

Using variable paths

Creating a logon routine

Authorware automatically tracks a wide range of user performance information, which it handles through the performance tracking system variables. You might remember that you can use automatic judging of responses when you create your interactions. Authorware tracks this information internally each time the piece runs. At any time, you can access this information through a calculation script, or you can display it on screen inside a text field.

However, the number of correct and incorrect responses the user selected in the interactions isn't the only type of information that Authorware maintains when using performance tracking in a piece. In addition to the number of automatically judged responses, you can find out the following details about a user's performance:

- How many tries the user takes to get the right answer in an interaction.

- How much time it takes the user to match a response in an interaction.

- How much time it takes the user to exit an interaction.

- How much time the user spends in the current session.

- How much time is left in a time limit interaction before the user moves on to another interaction.

The sections ahead describe a few of the most commonly used performance tracking system variables. Many of these are included in the Interactions and Time categories of variables inside the Variables window. For a complete description of these variables, take a look at the system variable descriptions included in *Using Authorware* or Authorware Help.

However, before you look at ways of working with the performance tracking variables, it's important to understand how to set up your piece to use automatic judging of responses to generate run-time performance data for the user.

Using automatic judging in interactions

When you set up an interaction response to be judged either correct or incorrect, Authorware automatically stores this information in a special set of system variables. This set, found under the Interaction category of the Variables window, includes system variables such as

`TotalCorrect`, `TotalWrong`, `PercentCorrect`, and `PercentWrong`.

NOTE The system variable `FirstTryCorrect` is also among this group. You may remember working with `FirstTryCorrect` in Chapter 14, "Using Functions and Variables," when you set up a display icon to display a results screen using embedded variables.

It's important to remember that in order to track a student's performance, you have to set up each response to use Authorware's automatic judging features. Otherwise, the information that you get back is not accurate.

You can use automatic judging with any type of response in Authorware. To set up an interaction response using automatic judging, simply create the response, and then use the Status option in the Response Properties dialog box to mark the response as either the Correct Response or the Wrong response, as shown in **Figure 16.1**.

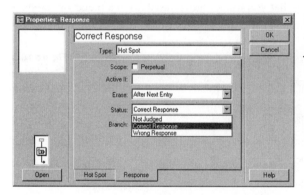

Figure 16.1
Automatic judging of responses is set up in the Response Properties dialog box.

When you assign a judging status to a response, it appears in the flowline next to the response title. Correct responses display with a plus sign (+) to the left of the title; incorrect responses display with a minus sign (-) next to the title. You can see how this appears in **Figure 16.2** for both types of judged responses.

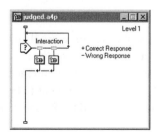

Figure 16.2
Judged responses appear with symbols to the left of the response title.

Note that in **Figure 16.2**, the response named Time Out (a time limit response) was not set up to be judged in the interaction. In general, you don't want to assign judging status to responses that have no bearing on the final score. (These might include time limit responses and tries limit responses, as well as perpetual navigation controls and other responses that you've set up to handle user interface issues.) You can do this by leaving the Status option for the response set to its default setting, Not Judged.

Shortcut: You can assign a judging status to a response by clicking to the left of the response's title while pressing the Ctrl key (Windows), or Command key (Macintosh).

After you set up judged responses in the interactions you need to track, you can begin using the set of performance tracking variables that are included in the Interaction category of the Variables window, as shown in **Figure 16.3**. You can work with these variables in the same way that you use all other variables in a piece—namely, in calculation scripts, Properties dialog box fields, or in the Presentation window.

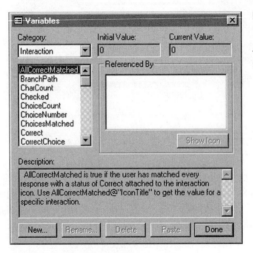

Figure 16.3
Viewing the set of Interaction system variables.

Using multiple correct responses

When using automatic judging, you can mark more than one response in an interaction correct if this applies to the way you want the interaction judged. For example, if you set up an interaction in which students drag the right animals into an environment to create a balanced ecosystem, there might be half a dozen correct answers.

Authorware is able to determine whether all the response type symbols you've labeled as correct have matched by checking the value of the variable `AllCorrectMatched`. If the value of `AllCorrectMatched` is True, it means that a user has matched all the responses in the interaction whose Status is set to Correct Response. The value of `AllCorrectMatched` remains False until this happens.

TIP Many of the performance tracking variables, including `AllCorrectMatched`, enable you to include them in a referenced variable expression to determine their values at a specific interaction.

Tracking more complex interactions

If you want an accurate picture of how the user is doing in a piece, it may not be enough to track whether or not the user has matched all correct responses in each interaction. You may need to look at other performance tracking variables that track a user's score. However, in order for this information to be accurate, you must use judged responses in any interactions that you want to track.

The most common variables used in performance tracking are listed below:

Variable Name...	*Description...*
`CorrectChoicesMatched`	Contains the total number of judged interactions that a student answered right in the piece.
`WrongChoicesMatched`	Contains the total number of judged interactions that a student answered wrong in the piece.
`FirstTryCorrect`	Contains the total number of judged interactions that a student answered right on the first try in the piece.
`FirstTryWrong`	Contains the total number of judged interactions that a student answered wrong on the first try in the piece.
`PercentCorrect`	Contains the percentage of all judged responses that a student answered wrong in the piece.
`PercentWrong`	Contains the percentage of all judged responses that a student answered wrong in the piece.
`TotalCorrect`	Contains the total number of correct responses the user made to all judged responses in the piece.
`TotalWrong`	Contains the total number of correct responses the user made to all judged responses in the piece.

It's important to realize when creating performance tracking in your piece that these variables record exactly what they are meant to record—meaning, if you don't think about how you set up your interactions, you may run into problems when you want an accurate view of a user's performance later.

For example, you might set up an exam with 10 questions. Each question has three wrong responses and one right response for a total of 40 judged responses. Later, if you want to get an accurate picture of how many questions a user missed in the exam, you might decide to use the TotalWrong system variable to track this and display it on screen at the end of the exam.

However, because TotalWrong records the total number of judged "responses" that are matched incorrectly in the piece, you should build your interactions so that each wrong response exits the interaction, as shown in **Figure 16.4**. This increases the value of TotalWrong by one after each interaction, giving you a total of 10, if you missed each question.

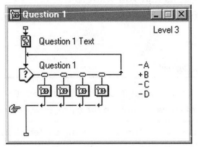

Figure 16.4
Setting up a judged interaction.

You get very different results if you set each wrong response to Try Again branching. This is because after each wrong response is matched by the user, the value of TotalWrong increases by one. You could possibly end up with a value of 30 for TotalWrong by the end of the exam (10 questions multiplied by 3 wrong responses each), throwing off your performance tracking.

In this case, it might be better to use the FirstTryWrong variable instead; this way you allow the user to make as many mistakes in an interaction as he needs to continue, but you still give an accurate picture of how many questions the user missed on the first try.

Providing feedback for the user when using performance tracking is an important part of creating an effective training or learning piece because it allows users to get a feel for their strengths and weaknesses.

If you don't want to provide this feedback in the Presentation window, you can record the information in an external text file for later use, or print it for the user. You'll learn how to do this later in the chapter, in "Working with External Files."

Tracking response time

Information about the time a user spends in an interaction can be crucial to performance tracking. If the user spends too little time in an interaction, it may mean that a question or problem is too easy; likewise, you also can use this information to determine whether a section of your piece is too difficult or too confusing for the user.

Authorware handles response time tracking with three system variables listed below:

Variable Name...	*Description...*
ResponseTime	Tracks the amount of time it takes a user to respond to an interaction.
TimeInInteraction	Tracks the amount of time it takes for a user to exit an interaction.
TimeRemaining	Tracks the amount of time left in an interaction, if you have attached a time limit response to it.

Each of these variables tracks time in seconds (and fractions of seconds) so that you can quickly compare values from one interaction to another. You can get information about the amount of time a user has spent in a specific interaction by using a variable with an icon title or an IconID value inside a referenced variable expression.

To understand how these variables differ from each other, you can create a simple interaction with a button response and time limit response, and then embed the resonse time tracking variables into the interaction icon to see how their values change.

To do this:

1. Drag an interaction icon to the flowline and name it **Time Out**.

2. Create a button response and a time limit response for the interaction. Make sure that you set the button response to Try Again branching, and the time limit response to Exit Interaction branching.

3. Open the time limit response and set the duration to 10
   seconds. Also select Restart after the Each Try option.

4. Open the interaction icon and select the text tool. Create
   a new text field.

5. Open the Variables window, select Interaction from the
   Category drop-down list, and then paste the variables
   named `TimeRemaining`, `ResponseTIme`, and
   `TimeInInteraction` into the text field.

   The variable names appear in the Presentation window inside
   separate braces.

6. Using the keyboard, separate the variables into three separate
   lines in the text field. After doing this, insert the name of each
   variable in front of the variable name in braces, as shown in
   Figure 16.5.

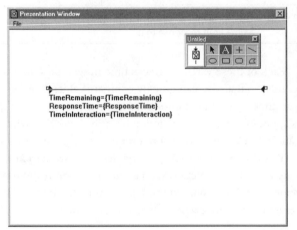

Figure 16.5
*Creating a
display field that
allows you to
track the response
time variables
in an interaction.*

By embedding the variables into the interaction icon, you can
easily view their values when running the piece. At times, you may
want to include this type of information on screen for the user.

TIP Another way to display the time remaining in an interaction is
to select the Show Time Remaining option for the time limit response.
For more information on working with time limit responses, see
Chapter 10, "Responding Automatically to Events."

In order to update this information properly, remember to turn on the Update Displayed Variables option for the interaction icon.

To do this:

1. Choose Icon > Properties from the Modify menu. (If you've closed the interaction icon already, select it first in the flowline before choosing this menu command.)

   The Interaction icon Properties dialog box appears.

2. Change the Erase option to Don't Erase so that the variable information remains displayed when you exit the interaction.

3. After doing this, click the Display tab and select the Update Displayed Variables option.

4. When you have finished, click OK to close the dialog box, and then run the piece.

When testing your example piece, you should see how each of the variables update differently on screen. If they do not change at all, go back and make sure that you've turned on the Update Displayed Variables option for the interaction icon.

As soon as you enter the interaction, the `TimeRemaining` value begins to count down from 10 seconds. At the same time, the `TimeInInteraction` value increases. Clicking the button response sets the `ResponseTime` variable to the number of seconds it took you to click the button and changes its value each successive time you respond to the interaction.

Notice also how `TimeRemaining` resets each time you click the button. This is because you've turned on this option in the time limit response. If you allow the time limit to expire, you exit the interaction, and you can see how long it took you by checking the value stored in `TimeInInteraction`. Although you only used one interaction in this example, you could use the same type of response tracking throughout your piece to get user performance information for each interaction.

TIP Embedding system variables in a display or interaction text field, as shown in the example above, is an excellent way to troubleshoot particular problems that you may come up against when developing. You'll learn more about this in Chapter 18, "Debugging Your Piece."

When developing a training piece, you also may want to track the amount of time a user spends in a session. A session is defined as the amount of time that expires between the time that the user first launches the piece and the time that the user quits it. Authorware's system variables enable you to time both the current session, as well as the complete amount of time it takes to complete an entire course that consists of multiple sessions.

Using the variables listed below, you can provide accurate and up-to-date session information to the user or an administrator:

Variable Name...	Description...
SessionTime	Contains the duration of the current user session in hours and minutes. Measures time from when the user starts the file.
FirstDate	Contains the first date the user used the current file. If the file is set to Restart, FirstDate always contains the date on which the current session started. The date format is set according to local standards based on system localization.
TotalTime	Contains the total amount of time the user spends in the file for all sessions, expressed in hours and minutes. If the file is set to restart when the user returns to it, TotalTime equals SessionTime.
SystemSeconds	Contains the total amount of time in seconds since you turned on the computer or restarted it.

These variables are included (along with many others) in the Time category inside the Variables window. As with the response tracking variables, you can include these in calculation script expressions, Properties dialog box fields, and text fields.

If you need a way to accurately time a section of your piece and the response tracking variables don't seem to work, you can use the system variable SystemSeconds. Because SystemSeconds contains the number of seconds that have elapsed since a student turned on or restarted the computer, you can use it as an internal clock to help time sections.

To use SystemSeconds as an internal clock to help time sections, use a custom variable to record the value of SystemSeconds at the beginning of the section you want to time, using an expression like the one below:

```
startTime := SystemSeconds
```

By placing another calculation icon at the end of the section, you can quickly see how much time has elapsed by subtracting your custom variable value from the current value of `SystemSeconds`, as shown below:

```
elapsedTime := SystemSeconds - startTime
```

Finding different ways of tracking the time spent in a piece is useful. However, when using performance tracking, you usually maintain this information in a separate location so that you can access it later for administrative purposes.

Managing User Records

User records allow you to maintain information about a user's performance in a piece. While you can use Authorware's system variables to track the progress of a user, you usually store these values in a separate custom variable or in an external file so you can manage your records more easily and retain information between sessions. This is especially true when a piece has multiple users working with it.

Managing user records falls into three basic steps:

1. Use Authorware's system variables to record a user's progress. This was explored above in "Tracking Performance."

2. Assign these values to a custom record-keeping variable, array, or list, so that you can store multiple pieces of information in one place. This also makes it easier to manipulate stored information, as you might need to do if you want to create a score report or compare the scores of several users.

3. Write this information to an external (ASCII) text file to save the information for later sessions or so an administrator can access it. (You'll learn more about this in the chapter, in "Working with External Files," below.)

For example, you might have a piece that collects information from the user through a series of text entry responses. Authorware automatically keeps track of the text the user enters in each response by using the `EntryText` system variable. However, to better manage this information, you should create a separate custom variable that you can use as a temporary storage variable for the information.

TIP If you have a lot of information that you need to track, you might want to consider using an array or a list. These types of data "objects" enable you to index the information stored in them so that you can more easily manage, store, and retrieve large amounts of data.

As the user enters information that you requested into each text entry interaction, you need to grab each value (using the `EntryText` system variable) and store it in a custom record variable that you've set up. This type of process usually happens in the background while the piece runs.

For example, perhaps you have several sections of content with a quiz at the end of each section. You might want to update the user record variable after each section in the event the user quits the piece before completing all quizzes; or you might include a script that updates the user's records inside a map icon attached to the quit button or the main menu button (if you are using one), as shown in **Figure 16.6**.

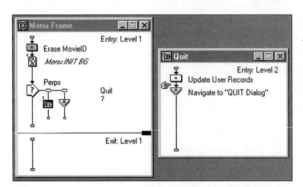

Figure 16.6
A calculation icon is included in the Quit button map to update the user record variable before the user exits the piece.

TIP Another flowline location that is useful for updating user record variables is in the exit pane of each section's framework, as you learned in Chapter 12, "Creating Links and Hyperlinks."

Setting up a record variable

You can create a simple user record by joining a series of variables together using the concatenation (^) character and line delimiters like a Return or Tab character. This technique allows you to store each piece of information in a single line within a custom variable. Because each item is stored in a different line, you can quickly retrieve or update this information using the character system functions GetLine and ReplaceLine.

To demonstrate how this is done, create three test variables that represent the types of information that you might want to track inside a piece, and then add them to another custom variable that is storing a user record.

Before following the steps below, create the custom variables first. In this example, you need to create a variable called `User` that stores the user name; a variable called `QuestionScore` that stores the total number of questions scored correctly; a variable called `PercentScore` that stores the percentage scored correct; and the variable `UserRecord` that stores the user record. After creating these variables, you are ready to begin.

NOTE If you were developing a real piece, you would probably want to replace the custom variables `QuestionScore` and `PercentScore` with the Authorware system variables `TotalCorrect` and `PercentCorrect` to take advantage of Authorware's automatic response tracking.

To place the values of your custom tracking variables into a user record variable:

1. Add a calculation icon to the flowline where you want to update your user record and double-click it to open it.

The Calculation window appears.

2. Type in the following lines:

```
User := "Susan Lee"

QuestionScore := 8

PercentScore := 80

UserRecord := User ^ Return ^ QuestionScore ^ Return ^ ¬
PercentScore ^ Return
```

This expression assigns each of the custom variables you want to store to a separate line in the record variable. To demonstrate how the user record variable is created, "dummy" values have been assigned to each of the custom tracking variables.

NOTE When setting up a record variable, it's important to specify the same line separator (or "delimiter") for each variable that you store. Otherwise, you may have problems later when working with these values using the character system functions.

Now that you've set up a script to update your record variable, you need a way to look at the values contained in it. The easiest way is to use the `Trace` function to display the value of the record variable in the Trace field of the Control Panel window:

1. Add the following line at the bottom of your script:
   Trace(UserRecord)

2. When you have finished, close the Calculation window and choose Control Panel from the Window menu.

   The Control Panel window appears.

3. Click the Show Trace button on the right-hand side of the window to display the scrolling Trace field.

4. As soon as you have everything set up, go ahead and run the piece.

When Authorware executes the calculation script, the value of UserRecord appears inside the Trace field, as shown below in **Figure 16.7**.

Figure 16.7
The record variable as it appears in the Trace field.

The value of UserRecord is a combination of the three variables you have assigned to it. Each variable is stored on a separate line. Alternatively, you can view the value of UserRecord by opening the Variables window and looking at its current value. You should see the following value displayed in the Current Value field when you select UserRecord in the Variables window:

"Susan Lee\r8\r80\r"

As you can see, Authorware replaces the Return constant that you specified when building the record variable with a Return character string (\r). However, this doesn't change the way you retrieve values from the record variable. Because each variable is now stored as a separate line in a single character variable, you can quickly retrieve and update specific values using Authorware's character functions.

Using the character line functions

Working with record variables is a quick and reliable way to reduce your authoring "overhead" by placing the system and custom variables you need to keep track of in a single location. Because you're really creating a long character string, you can refer to this string by name and manipulate it in many ways. The two most common ways to manipulate a variable are retrieving and replacing the values it stores.

For instance, you quickly can grab a stored value from one of the lines in the record variable you've created and assign it to another variable using an expression. To do this, you can use the `GetLine` function (listed in the Character functions category in the Functions window) to retrieve a value or a series of values.

The function's syntax looks like this:

```
resultString := GetLine("string", n [, m, delim])
```

For the first argument, you need to specify the character string from which you want to retrieve the value. You can use either a literal string (enclosed in quotes), or the name of a character variable that you've already created. In the second argument, you specify the number of the line where the value is stored.

Using the `GetLine` function, you could retrieve the `User` value from the `UserRecord` variable used in the last example, using the following expression in a calculation script:

```
User := GetLine(UserRecord, 1)
```

If you want to retrieve more than one line from the record variable, specify the last line to retrieve in the third (optional) argument. For instance, if you want to retrieve the first two lines from the `UserRecord` variable, you would write the following expression:

```
resultString := GetLine(UserRecord, 1, 2)
```

The `GetLine` function is especially useful because its fourth (optional) argument enables you to specify the type of line delimiter that you're using in a character variable. Because the Return character is the default delimiter, you don't need to specify a value for this argument if you're using the Return character to separate the lines of your record variable (as you did in the last example).

However, in some cases you may need to work with other delimiters like tabs or commas—especially if you're formatting your record variable in a specific way to import it into another application.

For instance, you could grab the third "line" separated by a tab delimiter using the following type of expression:

```
resultString := GetLine(UserRecord, 3, 3, Tab)
```

If you use a special character delimiter like a comma, place it inside quotes when using the GetLine function, as shown below:

```
resultString := GetLine(UserRecord, 3, 3, ",")
```

In this example, the GetLine function never actually changes the value of the custom variable UserRecord. It simply grabs a specific line that you have stored in this variable so that your original record variable stays intact. However, if you need to replace one of the values stored in a record variable, you can do so by updating a line using the ReplaceLine character function.

The ReplaceLine function is similar to the GetLine function. You define the string you want to work with, the line you want to replace, the new value that you want to replace this line with, and the line delimiter in the string to separate lines if you're not using the default Return character. The function's syntax is shown below:

```
resultString := ReplaceLine("string", n, ¬
"newString"[, delim])
```

Because you're modifying the original string by replacing a line value, you have to reassign the result of the ReplaceLine function to the same variable that you specified for the first argument. For instance, you would use the following expression to update the QuestionScore value in the record variable UserRecord from the last example:

```
UserRecord := ReplaceLine(UserRecord, 2, 18)
```

Assigning the result of the ReplaceLine function to the same record variable you're manipulating keeps your data intact. Rather than tracking multiple variables, you only need to keep track of one. It's much simpler in the long run when you work with character functions this way.

However, you can see that while record variables are an effective way of managing small amounts of data in your pieces, they also require you to keep careful track of the lines in which you're storing separate tracking variables. Once you begin working with multiple sets of data, you may want to think about using lists instead to manage data-handling in your piece.

Using Lists to Improve Data Handling

Lists are a much more powerful way to manage the information in your piece than custom record variables. This is because lists enable you to store multiple pieces of information in the same variable. As you saw in the last section, it gets pretty cumbersome stringing together separate variables to create a single record variable. Lists are a much more flexible alternative when you need to track a lot of information—especially if you need to create multiple sets of performance data.

For example, you might want to store user information (name, password, address, telephone number, and so forth) in one variable, and use another variable to store response tracking data generated when the piece runs. As you learned earlier, the character, numerical, and Boolean variables (like `EntryText`, `TotalCorrect`, or `MouseDown`) that you use in a piece can hold only one piece of information at a time. Even a record variable, like the one you worked with in the last section, contains a single multiple-line character string.

Using lists, you can store related sets of information in one place, and then refer to each specific piece of information using its position in the list. You can store any type of variable data that Authorware supports inside a list. This can include other lists that you've created.

Because Authorware can store any kind of variable data in a list, you have a more sophisticated way to work with the data that you're tracking, allowing you to organize it numerically, alphabetically, or by defined categories (or "properties"). This technique is shown in the example below, which stores information about an album recorded by the Beatles:

```
["Rubber Soul", 1965, [#Song:"Eleanor Rigby", ¬
#Track Number:2]]
```

Notice that in the example above, the song title is labeled `#Song` and the track number of this song is labeled `#Track Number`; this is an example of assigning specific properties to information that you store in a list. You'll work with these types of lists (property lists) below in "Creating a property list."

As you can see from the example above, a list is very similar to a small database table that you might create in a database program. You put each piece of information in a list into its own smaller container, which you can reference using the Authorware functions specific to lists. You can find these functions in the List category of functions when you open the Functions window, as shown in **Figure 16.8**.

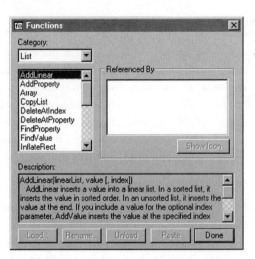

Figure 16.8
The List category of functions.

In addition to retrieving and updating the information stored in a list, the List functions also provide a way to sort your information, as well as the capability to combine sets of data or to perform calculations with a set of data (e.g., finding the highest value or the average value of a set of numbers).

As mentioned earlier, there are two types of lists that you can work with in Authorware: linear lists and property lists. Linear lists enable you to create a numerical index to the information you want to store. Property lists are different than linear lists because you can refer to a piece of information stored in a property list in the context of how you're using it in a piece.

NOTE For a complete description of the List functions new in Authorware 4, see Appendix A, "New Authorware 4 Functions and Variables."

Creating a linear list

Linear lists store a single piece of information in a separate numerical position of the list. For instance, you might have a list of city names that you want to store. Writing this list by hand, it might look something like this:

`Spokane, Seattle, Vancouver`

Using the list functions in Authorware, you can create a linear list that you use to store each name in a separate position. The linear list in Authorware has three values (index positions 1, 2, and 3). If you viewed the value of this list in the Variables window, it would look like this:

```
["Spokane", "Seattle", "Vancouver"]
```

As you can see, a linear list is a bit different than other variables. Brackets surround the items in the list, and commas separate each item. In order for Authorware to recognize a custom variable as a linear list, you have to specify it as a list when you first create the variable, or "initialize" it.

You can get a feel for how lists are used by going through the following steps:

1. Choose Variables from the Window menu or click the Variables window button on the toolbar.

   The Variables window appears.

2. Click New to create a new custom variable.

   The New Variable dialog box appears.

3. Type the name **MyList** into the Name field.

   As with any other variable, you can use any name when creating a new list variable. (The following examples, however, continue to refer to the list variable MyList when explaining how to work with lists.)

4. To define this new variable as a linear list, type a pair of empty brackets into Initial Value field, as shown: [].

   If you don't use brackets, Authorware won't recognize the variable as a list, causing problems when you want to add new values to the list in a calculation script.

5. When you have finished, click Done to close the Variables window.

Now that you've created your list variable, you can populate it with the values you want to store in it.

You can use the AddLinear function to add a value to a specific list position. For example, you can add this function to create the list of cities that you looked at earlier:

1. Drag a new calculation icon into the flowline and double-click it to open it.

   The Calculation window appears.

2. Open the Functions window and select the List category from the drop-down list of available functions.

The List functions appear in the scrolling window.

3. Click on the function named `AddLinear` in the scrolling window to select it, and then click Paste to paste this function into the calculation icon.

The `AddLinear` function appears in the Calculation window, as shown in **Figure 16.9**.

Figure 16.9

Pasting a list function into the Calculation window.

4. Click Done to close the Functions window.

As you can see from looking at the function arguments pasted into the Calculation window, the `AddLinear` function requires two separate arguments: the name of the list and the value that you want to add to the list.

In the next set of steps, you will use the `AddLinear` function to add the names of the three cities to your list variable. You can quickly type in the arguments for the first statement, and then copy and paste this statement two more times:

1. Change the line you've pasted into the Calculation window to read as follows: **AddLinear(MyList, "Spokane")**.

When first creating a new list, you don't need to worry about the third (optional) argument for this function. It simply allows you to specify an initial index position for the value if you want. Otherwise, Authorware adds the value to the first available index position in the list. Because there are no values currently assigned to this list, Authorware adds the word Spokane to list position 1.

NOTE Authorware inserts a 0 value for any list position that doesn't yet have an assigned value but falls between two positions that already have assigned values.

2. Use the cursor to highlight the line you just typed inside the Calculation window, and then copy and paste this line two times below the first line, creating three lines of the same statement.

3. In the second line, change Spokane to Seattle. In the third line, change Spokane to Vancouver. When you have finished, the Calculation window should appear as shown below:

AddLinear(MyList,"Spokane")

AddLinear(MyList,"Seattle")

AddLinear(MyList,"Vancouver")

4. Type in the following statement underneath the third line:

Trace(MyList).

When you have finished, close the Calculation window.

5. Before running the piece, open the Control Panel window (if it is not already open) and click the Show Trace button to display the Trace field.

Go ahead and run the piece. You can check the value of the list that you've created by looking at the Trace field. As you can see, your list now contains all three city names, separated by commas.

Notice that each city name is treated as a separate character string enclosed in quotation marks. However, the separate character strings are all contained inside one variable, allowing you to work with the information stored in the list in various ways.

Sorting a list

Because lists usually contain related sets of information, Authorware has the capability to average and sort the data stored in lists. For example, using the SortByValue function, you can quickly rearrange the names included in the list of cities you just created.

To do this:

1. Open the calculation icon and add the following lines to the bottom of the script:

SortByValue(myList, 0)

Trace(MyList).

The SortByValue function looks at the list specified in the first argument and sorts it by using the value order specified in the second argument. Using a 1 (or True) for the second argument sorts the list in ascending order (from lowest to highest); using a 0 (or False) for this argument sorts the list in descending order (from highest to lowest).

2. Close the calculation icon and run the piece again.

You now see the list of cities organized in reverse alphabetical order, as shown below:

```
["Vancouver", "Spokane", "Seattle"]
```

You also can use the SortByValue function to sort numerical values in a list the same way. If you've placed character strings and numerical values together in a list, Authorware evaluates each type of data separately.

For example, you might want to perform an ascending order sort on a list that contains the values:

```
[1, "Vancouver", 34, "San Francisco"]
```

Using the SortByValue function on this list produces the following result:

```
[1, 34, "San Francisco", "Vancouver"]
```

Performing operations with lists

You also can perform other types of operations with lists that enable you to change the information stored inside them. For instance, you can update a set of numbers stored in a list by adding another list to it:

```
List01 := [1, 2, 3]
List02 := [10, 10, 10]
List01 := List01 + List02
```

When adding lists, Authorware adds together the values that occupy the same position in each list. In the example above, each value stored in List02 is added to the corresponding value in List01. The end result is that each value in List01 has been increased by 10, as shown below:

```
[11, 12, 13]
```

Because the values in List02 are all the same, you can perform the same type of operation on List01 without creating an additional list by simply using the Repeat With In function (mentioned in Chapter 15, "Controlling the Flowline through Scripting"). This function enables you to repeat a set of instructions for each position in the list you specify. The syntax for this function is shown below:

```
repeat with (variable) in (list)

        statement(s)

end repeat
```

This type of repeat loop works a bit differently than the others you worked with in Chapter 15. The `Repeat With In` function takes the value stored in each list position of the list you specified, assigns it to the variable you specified, and then uses this value when executing the statements included inside the repeat loop.

To see how this works, take another look at how you added the value of 10 to each list position of `List01` in the previous example. Using the `Repeat With In` script shown below, you can get the same net result you saw earlier when adding two lists together:

```
repeat with number in List01
    number := number + 10
    repCount := repCount + 1
    SetAtIndex(List01, number, repCount)
end repeat
```

In the example above, Authorware assigns the first value stored in `List01` to the variable `number`. Once Authorware is in the repeat loop, it increments the value of `number` by 10. In the second line within the repeat loop, another variable named `repCount` is used to keep track of the current list position. The third line in the repeat loop uses the `SetAtIndex` function to replace the value stored in the current list position with the new value assigned to `number`. Authorware repeats this set of steps until all values in `List01` are used.

NOTE For more information on using the `SetAtIndex` function, look at the description of this function found inside the Functions window.

You also can perform other types of operations on multiple lists, including subtraction, division, multiplication, and concatenation. However, these types of list operations only work on lists of the same size (i.e., the same number of values stored in each list). Take this into consideration when sorting lists that contain other lists. All lists nested inside the parent list must be of the same size as the parent list— otherwise, Authorware disregards them when performing the sort.

Because you can store any type of variable information in a list, it's an ideal way to store different data types in the same place. For instance, you might want to store the number of a question (a numerical value), the correct answer (a character string value), and a True/False value, which indicates whether the question was answered correctly. You could assign this list to another results list, as shown in the example expression below:

```
Question_A_List := [4, "Vancouver", FALSE]
```

At any time, you can retrieve a single piece of information from the list by referring to the item's position in the list by using the list function ValueAtIndex. For example, if "Vancouver" is the correct answer for the question stored in the above list, you can retrieve this answer by including the following expression in a calculation script:

```
correctAnswer := ValueAtIndex(Question_A_List, 2)
```

Notice, however, that in order to get a value from a linear list, you need to refer to its numerical position in the list. In a way, you're back to the same problem you had when working with record variables. Keeping track of the numerical list position of an item may be difficult—especially if the list you've created has many different values stored in it. Because of this, you may want to look at using property lists to handle larger amounts of data in a piece.

A property list stores two "values" for each position in the list: the information that you want to store in the position, and a property value that you can use to refer to the information. Property lists are easier to work with in some ways than linear lists because you can refer to a piece of information using its property. Although you need to keep track of two values for each item in a list, it frequently is easier to refer to a property name rather than a number (as you do with a linear list) when retrieving the information you want.

For instance, you might create a property list to store user profiles in your piece. You could assign a specific property value to each type of value you want to store and use the property later to retrieve a value. The properties you might assign are listed below, along with the values that you might store with the properties:

Property Name...	Value...
Name	"Schultz, Peter"
LastDate	"8/10/97"
SessionTime	"4:38"

After creating the property list defined above and taking a look at it in the Variables window or the Trace field, you would see the information stored in a list, as shown below:

```
[#Name:"Schultz, Peter", #LastDate:"8/10/97", ¬
#SessionTime:"4:38"]
```

Each property that you specify is stored as a symbol in the list. This is indicated by the pound sign (#) which precedes each property name (e.g., #Name, #LastDate, #SessionTime). Properties are stored in the same list position as the values they refer to, and they are separated from the values by a colon (:).

Because you can refer to a value by name rather than number in a property list, you don't have to worry about the translation process when trying to grab a value. For example, in the list above, you simply ask Authorware for the value of "LastDate," rather than the value of "list position 2." While it may not be difficult to keep track of three values (as shown in the example above), it is quite a different story when you are trying to keep track of many different sets of values that are constantly being updated inside your piece.

Creating a property list

When you create a new property list, use the Variables window to create a new variable and then define the initial value of the variable in a special way that's different from a linear list. The value that you use is two brackets, with a colon placed between them, as shown below:

```
[:]
```

This specifies the new variable as an empty property list. After you've created the property list, you can work with it using techniques similar to the ones you learned earlier when working with linear lists.

For example, the AddProperty function allows you to add a new value to the property list as well as specify a property to store with the value. The syntax for this function is shown below:

```
AddProperty(list, #property, "value"[, index ¬
position])
```

You can see that the function requires three arguments: the list name, the value being added, and the property for this value. The optional fourth argument enables you to specify a position in the list when inserting the value. However, Authorware automatically creates a new position for the value if this argument is not used. You can see how to use this function in a calculation script by looking at the example below, which adds the user profile values you saw earlier to the list named UserProfile:

```
AddProperty(UserProfile, #Name, "Schultz, Peter")
AddProperty(UserProfile, #LastDate, Date)
AddProperty(UserProfile, #SessionTime, SessionTime)
```

The property names that you specify must be preceded by the pound sign (#) for Authorware to treat them as symbols. You also must enclose the first value added to the list in quotation marks because it is a literal character string.

TIP You can use the Symbol system function to convert any variable to a symbol and then assign the result to a custom variable. This allows you to use the name of the custom variable in place of a literal property name when using the property list functions. For more information on the Symbol function, see *Using Authorware* or Authorware Help.

However, notice in the last two lines of this script that the system variables Date and SessionTime are used as the values to insert into the list. This technique lets you to take advantage of Authorware's system variables when adding new values to a linear or property list. You might include a script like this at the beginning of a piece when updating a user record before jumping to a specific section of the piece.

Retrieving a property list value

As mentioned earlier, to grab a piece of information you've stored, you simply ask for it by name using the name of the property list, followed by the name of the property in brackets. For example, if you want to get the current value of the property #Name in the UserProfile list created earlier, you can include the following line in a calculation script:

```
User := UserProfile[#Name]
```

In the example expression above, Authorware would assign the custom variable User the value "Schultz, Peter." You can see that there aren't any numeric hassles to speak of when retrieving a value this way, just the satisfaction in knowing that your value is safely tucked away for you to retrieve later.

NOTE You don't need to worry about case-sensitivity when referring to a value by the name of the property.

The downside to using property lists is that you need to keep your property names unique when you create the list or add additional values to the list. If you accidentally use the same property name twice in a property list, Authorware doesn't warn you. However, you'll find out soon enough that you can retrieve only the first value added to the list with the name of the property that is shared by other values. This may throw off other scripts that you've included in your piece.

You can use property lists (like linear lists) in many ways to improve how you store, modify, and retrieve data. While you may need to spend some time working with lists to see the numerous ways you can use them, it is a step that you should take because lists offer significant advantages over other types of variables when managing information in a piece.

Working with External Files

While record variables and lists are essential to tracking data within a piece, you also need to know how to work with external files if you want to access this information later after a user quits a piece. There are three basic techniques for working with external files in Authorware: writing to a file, reading from a file, and printing a file.

TIP You can use the FileIO Xtra to perform additional functions with external files. Chapter 20, "Developing with External Code," looks at how to use this Xtra.

Writing to a file

You can set up a calculation script to save run-time data on the user's hard disk or on a file server using the WriteExtFile function. When Authorware saves information using this function, it creates an external file in plain text (ASCII) format. This enables you to open the file with a word processor or text editor and print it if needed.

The `WriteExtFile` function is one of several file-handling functions, which are listed in the File category of functions in the Functions window, as shown in **Figure 16.10**.

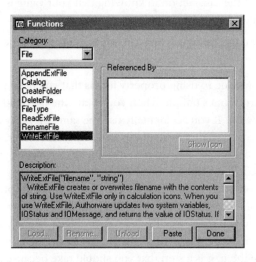

You can either paste the `WriteExtFile` function into a calculation icon script, or you can type it in directly. However, you should use this function only in a script; you can't use it in the field of a Properties dialog box, as you can other system functions. If you take a look at the `WriteExtFile` function inside the Functions window, you'll see the following syntax used:

```
WriteExtFile("filename", string)
```

There are two arguments that you need to specify with this function to create the text file. The filename argument specifies the location where you want to store the information. This usually includes the filename and the path to the file.

NOTE Specifying only a filename without a path stores the file in the folder where you have Authorware or the run-time application located. In general, you should try to specify a path to the file that you can write to, regardless of where it's delivered. This is especially true if you're delivering from CD-ROM because you are unable to write a file to a CD-ROM drive.

The string argument specifies the information that you want to write to the file. You can either include a literal string enclosed in quotation marks, the name of a variable, or the name of a list. You also can specify a series of variables and/or lists using the concatenation operator (^).

For example, if you wanted to store a variable or list called UserScores in a file called Records.txt, you would use the following syntax:

```
WriteExtFile("C:\\Records\\Records.txt", UserScores)
```

To write two variables to the same file (in this case, UserScores and UserPrefs), you could set up the function like this:

```
WriteExtFile("C:\\Records\\Records.txt", ¬
UserScores ^ UserPrefs)
```

If you set up the function as it is in the last example, you would first want to make sure that you've placed a Return character at the end of the last line of the variable UserScores. Otherwise, the last line of UserScores and the first line of UserPrefs write to the same line of the text file.

Each time you use the WriteExtFile function to write information to a file, it replaces the information that was previously written in the file. If the file doesn't exist, Authorware creates a file the first time you call the function.

TIP You also can use AppendExtFile if you want to add information to an existing file without erasing the information that's already there. For a description of this function, see *Using Authorware* or Authorware Help.

When you specify a location to write the file to, you should always think about the easiest and most reliable location to use. If you're unsure how you will deliver your piece or would like to have the location dependent on the delivery platform, you can set up a variable path to the file you're creating. (You'll learn more about this later in the chapter in "Using Variable Paths.")

Reading data from the file

Reading in information stored in an external file is the reverse process of writing out the information to a file. Authorware reads the entire file using the ReadExtFile function first and then stores it in a temporary custom variable that you've set up. This may be the same variable you specified when using the WriteExtFile function. Then you can use a character function like GetLine to grab a specific value and reassign it to the custom variable to which it applies.

NOTE There is a 32K (32,000-character) limit to the amount of data that you can store in a single custom variable in Authorware. If you find that the amount of information you need to store or retrieve from an external file exceeds this limit, one solution is to break your information down into smaller, more manageable chunks by using multiple text files.

It's a good idea to set up a standard procedure of reading in information from an external file at the beginning of your piece—especially if you want to reset custom variables to their previously saved states.

NOTE This is especially true if you're using a router file that jumps to another Authorware file. You can use the second argument of the `JumpFileReturn` function to pass variable data between pieces. "Creating a Logon Routine" discusses this in more detail later in the chapter.

For example, you might create a file called Records.txt, which contains four lines of information, separated by Return characters, as shown in the table below:

Line Item...	Description...
Mark Rivera	User name
22-1665	User ID number
34	Number of questions attempted
28	Number of questions correct

To read this information into the piece, simply paste or type the `ReadExtFile` function into a calculation script and assign its result to a custom variable you've created. For example, you might have a temporary variable called `UserRecords` that you can use to store the records file:

```
UserRecords := ReadExtFile(RecordsLocation ^ ¬
"Records.txt")
```

As you can see, the `ReadExtFile` function only requires one argument, the path and filename of the file. After Authorware reads in the file, it stores the file's contents in the custom variable you've specified. In the above example, notice that you have used the system variable `RecordsLocation` in the pathname to point to the location of the Records.txt file.

After Authorware reads the file and stores it in a custom variable, you can use the same technique to grab a value from a record variable to retrieve a specific line from the text file. For instance, to get the user's name from `UserRecords`, you could include the following expression in the calculation icon:

```
UserName := GetLine(UserRecords, 1)
```

In this example, Authorware assigns the user's name, Mark Rivera, to the `UserName` system variable because Authorware has stored it in the first line of the text file. It may seem a bit awkward at first to read in the complete text file at once, but this is the only way to retrieve specific values from the file you've saved.

Printing an external file

Using the `JumpPrintReturn` function, you can print the information you've stored in an external text file. You also can use this function to print other types of documents that use an application already installed on the user's system.

The syntax for printing a document is shown below:

```
JumpPrintReturn("program", "document"[, ¬
"creator type"])
```

The `JumpPrintReturn` function opens the application you specified in the program argument and prints the file you specified in the document argument. After the other application launches, its print options appear. After printing, Authorware continues presentation from the point in the flowline where the function was called.

As with the `WriteExtFile` and `ReadExtFile` functions, you need to specify the exact filenames and—on machines running Windows—any filename extensions. Unless the application and document that you want to jump to are stored in the same folder as the Authorware file, you also need to specify the path to the file.

If you're not sure where the program is located on the user's system, you can insert an empty string for the program argument. Authorware then selects an application that is capable of printing the file (in the case of text files, either Notepad or SimpleText). If it can't find such a program, Authorware displays a standard file dialog box that prompts the user to select a program to print the file.

If you plan to deliver on the Macintosh platform, you can use the optional third argument to specify the printing application's creator type (a 4-letter code). If a creator type is specified—but not a program,

Authorware uses the system information to locate a program suitable to print the document. The creator types for some common documents types are listed below:

Document Type...	Creator Type...
SimpleText	TTXT
Adobe Acrobat	CARO
Microsoft Word	MSWD

TIP You can find a document's creator type by opening the document using Apple's ResEdit resource editor and choosing Get Info from the File menu.

Using Variable Paths

As you saw in the last section, saving information in an external file requires that you first set up the file's path and filename. While you can probably keep the same filename each time, think about creating a variable path to the file so that you can change it automatically based on conditions that change during run time.

Creating a variable path

The path identifies where the file will be stored (i.e., whether it's on the user's hard disk, on a file server, or in another location). In the path, you also need to specify the folder(s) where you want to store the file. While you might know the exact name of the hard drive and folder on your own machine, it's almost guaranteed that this will change when you deliver the piece—especially if you're delivering for both the Windows and Macintosh platforms.

While there are some creative ways to get around this, the easiest method is to include one of Authorware's system variables in the path you specify. Using a system variable in the path lets you dynamically change the path based on run-time conditions. The primary system variables used when setting up variable paths in Authorware are `FileLocation` and `RecordsLocation`, which are described below.

Variable Name...	*Description...*
FileLocation	Contains the current path to the file location.
RecordsLocation	Contains the current path to the Authorware records file location.

You can include either of these variables in the path when calling the WriteExtFile function. The value of FileLocation varies depending on where the file is currently located. If you run your piece while authoring, the value of FileLocation contains the path to where you have Authorware installed on your hard drive. After packaging your piece, it contains the path where your packaged files are located.

NOTE If you have packaged your piece without run time, FileLocation contains the path where the RunA4W (Windows) or RunA4M (Macintosh) run-time player application is located. If you are distributing your piece using the Shockwave for Authorware Plug-In, FileLocation contains the path to the folder in which the Shockwave Plug-In is installed. For more information on packaging options in Authorware, see Chapter 17, "Distributing Your Piece." For more information on Shockwave paths, see "External paths and Shockwave" later in this chapter.

For example, if you deliver your piece from a separate folder on the Windows 95 platform, the value of FileLocation might contain:

```
"D:\\Example Files\\"
```

If you've placed the piece in a separate folder on the Macintosh, it might contain:

```
"My Drive:Authorware Files:"
```

The FileLocation variable always contains the path in the format of the platform on which you're running Authorware. Because it is a character variable, you can add it to the rest of the path where you want to store your external file. You add it the same way you create other character strings, which are shown in the example below:

```
WriteExtFile(FileLocation ^ "Records.txt", ¬
UserScores)
```

NOTE To use long file names when assigning paths to an external file on the Windows platform, select the Long File Names option in the File Properties dialog box. Otherwise, Authorware is unable to find the file during run time.

Sometimes it's not appropriate to use `FileLocation` when setting up a path to your external file. If you deliver on CD-ROM and your piece runs from the CD, you soon discover that you can't create new files directly on the CD. You can rely on the `RecordsLocation` system variable when setting up the path to the external file. The path location contained in this variable is different for each platform, as shown below:

Platform...	Records Location Path...
Windows	[Windows Location]\A4W_data\
Macintosh	[System Folder Location]:Preferences:RunA4M Data:

The `RecordsLocation` variable points to a directory on the user's hard drive that Authorware creates each time you run a piece. Authorware uses this directory to store file records to enable it to resume play from the same location, if you've set your file to Resume on Return in the File Properties dialog box. For more information about setting up a file to resume, see Chapter 2, "Beginning a Piece."

What do I need to know about external paths and using Shockwave?

If you plan to deliver your piece using Shockwave, you need to know that there are several minor differences in the way that Authorware handles variable paths when running a piece within a web browser using the Shockwave Plug-In. You need to address these issues before you deliver the piece to end-users because it may cause problems with the scripts you've included in your piece.

Although `FileLocation` and `RecordsLocation` are still available to you, there are slight differences in how you can use them in a Shockwave piece. The value of `FileLocation` points to the current folder where the Shockwave for Authorware Plug-In is installed on the user's system. This location depends on the platform, as shown below:

Platform...	Browser...	Plug-in Location...
Windows	Netscape Navigator, Microsoft Internet Explorer	[Folder where browser is installed]:\Plugins\Np32asw\
Macintosh	Netscape Navigator, Microsoft Internet Explorer	[Folder where browser is installed]:Plugins:Np32asm:

On the other hand, the value of RecordsLocation doesn't change; however, it is virtually off limits to you because the Plug-In only allows you to write to a location within the folder where the Shockwave for Authorware Plug-In is installed.

There is a third system variable used with Authorware to set up variable paths to external content when working with Shockwave pieces. The name of this variable is NetLocation. You can view its description by opening the Functions window and selecting the Network category of functions.

When a Shockwave piece runs, the NetLocation variable contains the URL path to where you have your Shockwave map file stored on the web server. However, the Shockwave Plug-In does not allow you to write a file to the web server—even if you've included NetLocation as part of the file path when calling the WriteExtFile function. You can, however, read in data from an external file stored on a web server by using the ReadExtFile function.

If your Shockwave piece depends on writing information to an external file location (i.e., from a location other than the folder where the Plug-In is installed), you need to look at using the custom functions found in FTP.UCD, an Authorware custom function library included on the Authorware 4 CD.

> **NOTE** This file is also available for download from the Authorware software updates area of the Macromedia web site: **(http://www.macromedia.com/support/authorware/upndown/updates/)**.

The set of custom functions included in the FTP.UCD allows you to store and retrieve data from a web server in the same way that you would when using an FTP program like WinFTP (Windows) or Fetch (Macintosh).

> **TIP** More information on how to use FTP functions is included in the ReadMe file accompanying FTP.UCD or in the Shockwave for Authorware tech notes area of the Macromedia web site: **(http://www.macromedia.com/support/authorware/how/shock/)**.

Creating a variable filename

When developing a piece that many users will run from the same machine, use a variable to name the folder or file where you have stored the information. You use a variable so that previously saved records aren't overwritten when a new user runs the piece.

One of the simplest approaches is to ask a user to enter his or her name at the beginning of a piece, store the name in the custom variable User, and then use User as part of the path you have specifed in the WriteExtFile function, as shown in the example below:

```
WriteExtFile(RecordsLocation ^ User ^ ".txt", ¬
UserRecords)
```

You also may want to create a unique folder for each user if
you are creating multiple records files for users. You can do this by
creating a script that uses the same custom variable for both the
folder name and the file name. However, because the Windows
and Macintosh platforms treat path names differently, you can create
a simple platform test using the If-Then function at the start of
the script:

```
if OSNumber=1 then
            FolderPath := User ^ ":"
else
            FolderPath := User ^ "\\"
end if
WriteExtFile(RecordsLocation ^ FolderPath ^ ¬
User ^ ".txt", UserRecords)
```

In the example script above, the OSNumber system function
returns a 1 if the user is running on a Macintosh, or a 3 if the user
is running on a Windows machine. When the user is running on a
Macintosh, the colon (:) is concatenated to the User custom variable,
creating the correct Macintosh path name to the folder; likewise, the
double-backslash is used on the Windows side (this is actually a
backslash character preceded by another backslash character so
that Authorware correctly recognizes it). The folder path is then
assigned to the custom variable FolderPath and used in the
WriteExtFile function as part of the file's path name.

TIP There are other ways of writing this script that don't require you
to create a separate custom variable to store the folder path. Play
around to come up with some variations of your own.

Specifying separate user records locations like this is much easier
to do if you use some type of logon procedure in which the user
provides a unique logon name and password at the start of a piece.
When you begin to develop larger training pieces, you also may need
to set up access to more than one piece at a time. In order to manage
this, you need to know how to create and use logon routines.

TIP You also can take a look at the Show Me example files included
on the Authorware 4 CD for a working Authorware example of using
routers in Authorware.

Creating a Logon Routine

Often a project is so big that you need to create several Authorware files to comprise the entire project. Separating content into smaller pieces is a good way to keep your content organized. For example, if you're creating a digital magazine, you might want to make each article a separate file. When you break a project into a number of files, you need to create an additional piece that connects all the other parts together. This file is usually referred to as a router.

Jumping to a file

A router can take many forms. Much of the time, it's built like a button menu with several buttons that can take you to other files. At other times, you might want the user to type in a logon user name and password, and then automatically jump to the appropriate file so the user can resume where he or she left the file. In either case, you can use one of two system functions, `JumpFile` or `JumpFileReturn`, to jump the user to the other piece.

The `JumpFileReturn` function enables the user to return to the router after quitting the second file. For this to work, you need to use the `Quit` function with a 0 specified for the `Quit` function's argument, as shown below:

```
Quit(0)
```

You can place this in a calculation icon anywhere in the piece. When the `Quit` function is called, Authorware exits the piece and returns to the router. This also happens if the user selects Quit from the default menu bar created for a piece.

TIP You can specify values other than 0 for the `Quit` function. To find out more about using the `Quit` function, see *Using Authorware* or Authorware Help.

The `JumpFile` function is similar to the `JumpFileReturn` function except that it doesn't automatically return you to the router. To return to the router, you must include another `JumpFile` function call in the piece you're navigating that points to the router.

When including either of these functions in a calculation icon script, the syntax is the same. You can see the syntax for the `JumpFileReturn` function below:

```
JumpFileReturn("filename"[, "variable1, vari-
able2, ...",["folder"]])
```

You can specify the file you want to jump to in the first argument of the function. You should try to include a full path to the file unless it's in the same folder as the router file. If you don't include a path to the file, Authorware uses the search path settings you've specified to locate the file.

You can use `JumpFileReturn` in a sequence of files to control nested jumping between segments. This simply means that Authorware remembers all previous jumps that were made. For example, if File1 uses `JumpFileReturn` to jump to File2, and File2 uses `JumpFileReturn` to jump to File3, quitting File3 causes File2 to resume, and quitting File2 causes File1 to resume.

TIP When specifying the filename, you don't need to include the extension of the file to which you're jumping because Authorware automatically searches for files with an .A4W or .A4M extension when it executes a jump. Similarly, RunA4W and RunA4M automatically search for files with an .EXE or .A4R extension when you run a packaged piece.

In the second (optional) argument for these functions, you can specify the variables that you want to pass to the file to which you're jumping. These values are passed back to the original file when you quit the second file. This provides a way to maintain performance tracking information and other system variable information between files. If you list several variables, be sure to separate them with commas and to enclose the entire list in quotation marks.

As a shortcut, you can use an asterisk (*) as a wildcard character when specifying the variables to pass to the other file. This is helpful when you have several variable names with a common prefix, such as `Temp1`, `Temp2`, `Temp3`, and so on. To pass all three variables without listing each one of them separately, you could include the following expression:

```
JumpFileReturn("MyFile", "Temp*")
```

TIP If you want to pass all variables in a file to the file to which you're jumping, simply use a single asterisk (*) character as the only character in the second argument of the `JumpFile` or `JumpFileReturn` function.

In the third (optional) argument for these functions, you can specify a new folder name and path for the `RecordsLocation` system variable. By defining different folders for user records, you can create a separate records folder for each user. This ensures that separate records files are maintained for each user. (For more information on RecordsLocation, see "Saving records when resuming," later in this chapter.)

As mentioned earlier, the easiest way to create a router is to have a series of buttons on a menu screen that jump out to different files when clicked. When the user quits the second file, Authorware returns to the same menu screen each time—as long as you've selected Try Again branching for the menu buttons. In **Figure 16.11**, you can see what a typical menu router flowline structure might look like.

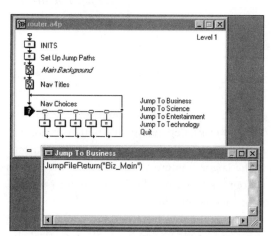

Figure 16.11
Setting up a router menu.

As you can see, it doesn't look all that different from the type of menu that you created when working with frameworks. However, notice that each of the buttons has a calculation icon attached to it in which you have placed the script that calls the JumpFile or JumpFileReturn function. Notice also that each button response is set to Try Again branching. This is important when using the JumpFileReturn function because Authorware returns to the point in the flowline from where it jumped when the file it jumps to is quit by the user.

Setting up a logon routine

A router is usually used for the purpose of maintaining peformance tracking information over a period of time for your users. If you are maintaining separate performance data for each user, you need to include a simple logon routine at the beginning of the router piece that goes through a series of interactions, helping you identify the user.

While there are many ways to handle this type of procedure, the common approach is to use a series of text entry responses that require the user to type in a unique user ID. This can be a last name, a Social Security Number, a pre-assigned numerical ID, or any combination of items that you require. **Figure 16.12** shows you what the flowline structure for a sample logon routine looks like inside the Design window.

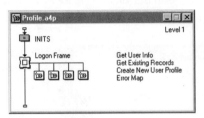

Figure 16.12
The flowline structure for a sample logon routine.

The example above is built around pages of a framework that perform different tasks, depending on whether or not the user's profile record already has been created. The Get User Info map icon attached to the Logon framework requires that the user enter a name and the last four digits of his or her Social Security Number. Using a series of map icons containing calculated decision paths, the logon routine verifies that the user has typed in a name (i.e., only alphabetical characters) and a valid ID number (only numerical characters). **Figure 16.13** shows you how this area of the flowline appears.

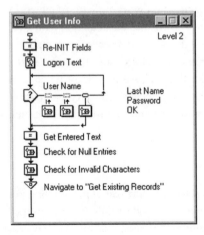

Figure 16.13
The section of the flowline that checks the user-entered information for valid characters.

Authorware uses the user name and ID number when jumping to the Get Existing Records map icon attached to the Logon framework to see if any previous records for the user have been saved.

Authorware attempts to read the file specified by the user name and ID number entered earlier; if it cannot be found, a calculated decision path jumps the user to a separate map icon attached to the Logon framework, named Create New User Profile. If a previous profile exists, the user's previous records are assigned to a custom variable and then Authorware jumps to the specified location of the main piece, passing the user's session information to the main piece using the JumpFile system function. **Figure 16.14** shows you how this area of the flowline appears.

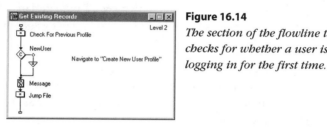

Figure 16.14

The section of the flowline that checks for whether a user is logging in for the first time.

This is the kind of approach that is used generally to set up a logon routine that enables you to create new user profiles if the user is logging in for the first time, and to retrieve previously saved information about the user on subsequent log-ins. While there are many ways of handling this type of procedure, you will certainly want to store separate records for each user and use a logon ID for the user so that you can update a user's performance information each time he or she uses the piece.

If you want to see an example of the logon routine discussed above, you can take a look at the example file named PROFILE.A4P. It's included in the Chapter 16 examples folder on the CD accompanying this book.

Saving records when resuming

Sometimes, it's convenient to use Authorware's Resume On Start option when using a router. This allows the user to resume the piece from the point in the flowline where the user quit the piece.

TIP Another way to resume a piece is to use the PageHistoryID function to store the IconID value of the last viewed page in a custom variable; then use a navigate icon set to a calculated link at the beginning of your piece to navigate to the correct location. For more information on using the PageHistoryID function, see Chapter 12, "Creating Links and Hyperlinks."

If you've selected Resume for the On Start option located inside the File Properties dialog box (see Chapter 2, "Beginning a Piece"), Authorware creates a records file inside the records location folder, which allows it to resume the file in its last saved flowline location. The records file that Authorware creates is used by Authorware to set any system variables used in the piece to the state in which they were saved before the file was quit. The filename that Authorware uses to store these records is the name of the file, followed by an .rec extension.

NOTE If the On Start option for a piece is set to Restart, all system variables automatically reinitialize to their default values the next time the piece runs.

Regardless of how you've set up the resume features of a piece, you will need to externally store any custom variables that you use because they initialize to their default values each time the piece runs. This is why it's very important to design a way to track variable information in your piece by using the types of techniques discussed in this chapter. In most cases, you will want to store your custom variables in an external file if you want to maintain this information between sessions.

NOTE You can use the `SaveRecords` function to write out the .rec file for your piece by including the function in a calculation script. For more information on this function, see *Using Authorware* or Authorware Help.

Looking Ahead...

Authorware excels at doing performance tracking. The techniques you learned in this chapter help prepare you for developing larger-scale pieces that track the user's progress and allow you to manage the information more easily. Using record variables and lists as well as external files, you can improve your data handling and, in the process, improve the type of feedback you provide your users.

By now, you should have a firm grasp of how an application is developed by using Authorware's content, navigation, and data-management tools. Everything that you've learned so far prepares you to now take your piece from the planning and design stages to the delivery stage. Chapter 17, "Distributing Your Piece" covers many of the issues that you will need to prepare for when taking a piece beyond your own desktop.

The Final Stages

The final stages of a project (when you are preparing your piece for delivery) are often the most critical stages of development. While it's important to have your delivery platforms and delivery medium decided upon well before testing, you no doubt will encounter specific platform and delivery issues that you hadn't anticipated while developing. The first two chapters of Part V, "The Final Stages," address these issues by showing you how to prepare your piece for delivery, as well as providing you with some common troubleshooting techniques that can help you isolate problems that you encounter while testing your piece.

Testing is a process that you should do throughout development, since it can cause you to reassess your original design plans for a piece. While introducing features to your piece half way through development is something that you should avoid if at all possible, you nonetheless may find that you sometimes overlook certain functional aspects that are critical to the type of application you are developing. If you can't create this functionality in Authorware, it's time to look at other alternatives. This book concludes by focusing on the main ways you can expand the functionality of your piece by using Director movies, external functions, and Xtras.

Distributing Your Piece

Chapter 17

What you'll learn...

Packaging a piece

Shocking a piece

Distributing external files

Preparing your piece for distribution

When entering the final stages of development, you need to prepare your piece for distribution to the user. In some ways, this is the most crucial step in developing an Authorware piece because your previous hard work may be unexpectedly derailed by problems that you experience when delivering it. These issues mainly relate to the ways in which you distribute the various elements needed to play the piece on another computer.

The issues discussed in this chapter—including packaging a piece, and delivering it as a stand-alone or a Shockwave application—are ones you need to consider carefully when moving into the final stages of development.

The point in creating Authorware pieces is to distribute them to your audience. However, most of your target users probably don't have Authorware installed on their systems. When you distribute an Authorware piece, you need to provide a packaged piece—a separate version that users can run but not edit.

When you package a piece, the authoring menus and commands are no longer available, and the user doesn't need Authorware to run it. After you package a piece (if all goes well), it plays back the same way you created it, with all of its content and functionality intact.

Creating a packaged run-time piece

When you package a piece, you have two basic options:

- Packaging the piece with the run-time player creates a self-executable file that the user can simply double-click to run. Use this option to create a stand-alone application that you can distribute on CD-ROM or run from a LAN (local area network) server.

- Packaging the piece without the run-time player creates an .A4R format file that the user can run but not edit. Use this option for files that you are jumping to from a router application (packaged with the run-time player), or for pieces that you are going to shock and deliver from a web server.

NOTE "Shocking a piece" describes the way you prepare your piece to run from an Internet or intranet web server. Before shocking a piece, however, you must follow the steps in this section to package your piece.

When packaging a piece, Authorware also prompts you to package any libraries attached to your piece. You must package and distribute libraries along with your executable files. For more information, see "Packaging libraries," later in this section.

To package a piece:

1. Save your piece using the Save and Compact command from the File menu.

2. Choose Package from the File menu.

The Package dialog box appears, as shown in **Figure 17.1**.

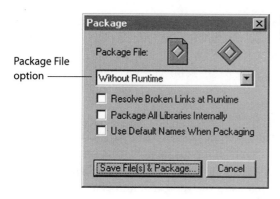

Package File
option

Figure 17.1
The Package dialog box.

There are several options in this dialog box, including the Package File option drop-down list that you can use to select the type of packaged piece you want to create. By default, you see Package Without Runtime already listed here, which packages the piece without the run-time player. If you package your piece as a self-executable file, you need to change the Package File option to the type of system on which you plan to deliver your piece.

NOTE The options in the Package dialog box are covered in more detail later in "Customizing your packaged piece."

3. Select the packaging option you want to use from the Package File drop-down list.

4. If you want to customize your packaged piece, select one or more of the checkbox options.

5. Click Save File(s) and Package.

   The Save File As dialog box appears.

6. Add a file name in the File field, and then click OK to save your packaged piece. Authorware displays the name of your piece in this field by default. You can modify it if you want.

   After doing so, a progress dialog box tells you that Authorware is saving the file and packaging it.

   Files packaged without the run-time player have an .A4R extension that you should not edit. Authorware looks for this extension when you use the `JumpFile` and `JumpFileReturn` functions or when you launch the piece with the run-time player.

   When you package a Windows piece with the run-time player, Authorware automatically appends an .EXE extension to your packaged file. On the Macintosh, Authorware automatically appends a

.PKG extension to the packaged file. Do not change the extension on the Windows side because it tells Windows that the file is an executable file. On the Macintosh side, you can modify the file name either when you package the piece or after you have saved it.

Opening a piece packaged without the run-time player

It's important to test your packaged file after you've packaged it to make sure that it is functioning properly. If you've packaged your piece with the run-time player, you can simply double-click to open it. If not, you need to open it using the version of RunA4W or RunA4M included on your machine in the Authorware folder.

To do this:

1. Open the folder where you have installed Authorware.

2. Double-click on RunA4W32.EXE (Windows), or RunA4M.fat (Macintosh).

   A dialog box appears that asks you to select the packaged file to open.

3. Select the name of your packaged piece (remember, it has an .A4R extension) and click OK.

   Authorware opens the packaged piece, allowing you to test it.

   While going through the procedure above, you may have noticed other versions of the run-time player installed in your Authorware folder. In the next section, you'll learn more about how you select the correct run-time player when deciding on which platform you will deliver your piece.

Using the Package File options

When you package a piece with the run-time player, Authorware creates an executable file that includes the RunA4W application (Windows), or the RunA4M application (Macintosh). The Authorware run-time player files are installed in the same folder as the Authorware application.

There are actually several run-time packaging options available, depending on the type of machine and platform on which you want to deliver your piece. Each option packages your piece with a different version of the Authorware run-time player.

These options, explained in more detail below, are listed in the Package dialog box when you package your piece (see **Figure 17.1** above):

Packaging option...	Platform...	Run-time file name...	Description...
Package for Windows 95, Windows NT	Windows	RUNA4W32.EXE	Creates a 32-bit executable file that you can deliver only on systems running Windows 95 or Windows NT.
Package for Windows 3.1	Windows	RUNA4W16.EXE	Creates a 16-bit executable file that you can deliver on systems running Windows 3.1, Windows 95, or Windows NT.
Package for Power Macintosh Native	Macintosh	RunA4M.ppc	Creates a Power Macintosh native executable file that you can deliver only on Power Macintosh systems.
Package for Standard Macintosh	Macintosh	RunA4M.68k	Creates a 68K executable file that is optimized for standard Macintoshes. You can also deliver this on Power Macintosh systems, but it will not be Power Macintosh native.
Package for All Macintosh Models	Macintosh	RunA4M.fat	Creates a Macintosh fat-binary executable file that you can deliver on any Macintosh computer. It includes both the 68K and Power Macintosh run-time player, and is optimized for both types of Macintosh systems.

You also can distribute these files with a piece that you have packaged without the run-time player in order to deliver it on another system. Keep in mind, each run-time player file adds an additional 2 MB to the total size of your packaged Authorware piece, except for the fat-binary Macintosh run-time file, which adds approximately 3 MB to the packaged piece. Depending on the amount of disk space you have available, think carefully about how you will package your piece because packaging increases the total file size (in MB) of your piece.

The following guidelines can help you determine which packaging options to use for each platform:

- When packaging a Windows piece, you can limit the amount of file space your piece uses by packaging only one run-time executable file using the 16-bit (Windows 3.1) option, since this will also run under Windows 95 or Windows NT. However, you will see better performance for your piece if you also include a version of the piece packaged with the 32-bit (Windows 95, NT) option.

- Likewise, if you want to distribute only one executable file with your Macintosh piece and are planning to run it on any Macintosh, package your piece using the fat-binary, run-time file (the All Macintosh Models packaging option).

- You can improve performance of your final piece by splitting it into separate files connected by a router application using the JumpFile or JumpFileReturn functions.

- When using a router, you only package the router with the run-time player—not the other pieces to which you're jumping. This is unnecessary and wastes additional file space because Authorware can run all of them using the run-time player file packaged with the router.

- If you're packaging a piece to deliver only as a Shockwave piece, package it without the run-time player. Otherwise, you cannot open it using Afterburner, the utility that creates your final Shockwave file segments.

NOTE The Authorware run-time player files are used by the Shockwave for Authorware Plug-In to run shocked Authorware pieces with the user's web browser. The run-time player files are installed with the Shockwave Plug-In on the user's system, so you don't need to include these files when distributing a Shockwave piece. For more information on installing the Shockwave for Authorware Plug-In, see the technical notes available on the Macromedia web site (**http://www.macromedia.com/support/authorware/how/shock/**).

Customizing your packaged piece

When packaging a piece, you will see several additional options in the Package dialog box (see **Figure 17.1** above). These options enable you to customize certain features of your packaged piece:

- Select Resolve Broken Links At Runtime to have Authorware relink broken links to libraries when the user runs the piece. Relinking icons may take several seconds when the piece first runs.

- Select Package All Libraries Internally to package libraries as part of the piece. Using this option is helpful so that you do not need to worry about distributing separate library files with your packaged piece.

  However, if you intend to deliver your piece on both the Windows and Macintosh platforms, and you are not using a separate router file to launch the piece, avoid using this option so that you can use the same library files for both the Windows and Macintosh versions without taking up additional file space when delivering your piece.

NOTE Try to avoid packaging large libraries with your piece because this creates a larger run-time executable file that takes more memory to launch.

- Select Include Fonts (Macintosh) if you want to add to the packaged file the resource files for the TrueType or screen (bitmap) fonts that you have used in your piece.

- Select Use Default Names When Packaging to skip the Save File As dialog box and to package your piece using its current name.

How do I add a custom icon to my executable file?

You can customize not only the way the packaged file runs, but also its appearance. One of the most common ways to do this is to change the default icon for the executable file that appears on the Windows or Macintosh desktop.

On the Macintosh platform, this is a fairly simple process:

1. Create an icon that is 32 x 32 pixels using a graphics editing tool such as xRes or Photoshop, and then copy it to the Clipboard using the Command+C keyboard shortcut.

2. Select the executable file you've created in Authorware and choose Get Info from the Macintosh File menu.

   This opens the Get Info dialog box, showing you the current icon for your run-time file at the upper left-hand corner.

3. Click on this icon, and then use the Command+V keyboard shortcut to paste your new icon into the icon field.

Your new icon now appears on the desktop. Authorware uses the new icon when you distribute your piece to other users.

On the Windows platform, the process for replacing the packaged executable file icon is a more difficult process. First, you need to create a custom icon and save it in the .ICO format. Then you need to actually replace the icon resources of the RUNA4W16.EXE or RUNA4W32.EXE file before you package your Authorware piece as an executable file.

If you're creating a 16-bit run-time executable file, modify RUNA4W16.EXE. If you're creating a 32-bit run-time executable file, modify RUNA4W32.EXE. Editing the icon resources for these files requires that you have an application resource editor available, such as those that ship with the 32-bit versions of Microsoft Visual C++ or Borland C++.

TIP If you don't have access to one of these tools, you can get a shareware program called MicroAngelo. This tool enables you to create and save icon resources, as well as edit icon resources for a run-time file on the Windows platform. It's available from the Shareware site at **http://www.shareware.com** (do a search for MicroAngelo).

Once you have the necessary tools, use the following technique to replace the default Authorware icon with your own icon:

1. Create a custom icon that is 32 x 32 pixels using an icon editing utility (see TIP above).

2. Create a backup copy of the RUNA4W16.EXE or RUNA4W32.EXE file, and place it in a safe location so that you can restore this file later.

3. Open the original RUNA4W16.EXE or RUNA4W32.EXE file stored in the Authorware folder using a resource editor.

NOTE You cannot simply open the packaged file in a resource editor and modify its icon resources. If you try to do this, it creates a damaged .A4R file that you cannot open using RUNA4W32.EXE or RUNA4W16.EXE.

4. Paste your custom icon into the ID space reserved for the RUNA4W desktop icon. This is the first icon space displayed for RUNA4W in the resource editor window.

NOTE When editing the run-time executable file, there may be several versions of the icon that you may need to replace, including an icon for black-and-white monitors and the smaller 16 x 16 icon that displays in the small icon view on the Windows desktop.

5. After replacing the icon, save the file. Make sure that you save it with the same file name, and that you save it in the same directory as the A4W.EXE application that you are using to package your Authorware files.

When you package a piece now with the run-time executable file, the custom icon appears on the Windows desktop. After performing these steps, copy the original version of RunA4W32.EXE or RUNA4W16.EXE back into the Authorware folder; otherwise, every new file you package will have the custom icon that you last added to the run-time files.

NOTE You can get around modifying the icon of the Authorware run-time player by using an installation program that links the .ICO file to your executable file when the user installs your piece. However, the user still sees the default Authorware icon in the Windows taskbar when switching between the packaged file and other open applications. For the web addresses of companies that make custom installer software, see Appendix C, "Authorware Resources on the Internet."

Packaging libraries

When packaging an Authorware piece that contains icons linked to a library file, you also must package each library (if you have not packaged your libraries internally) and distribute them to the user along with any other files needed to run the piece.

As mentioned earlier, if you plan to distribute a piece to both Windows and Macintosh users, you must package each library separately so that the Macintosh and Windows run-time executable files can share the libraries. This helps conserve disk space for your final piece.

NOTE RunA4W and RunA4M read libraries, but don't write to them. Therefore, libraries can be shared by more than one piece at a time when you distribute a piece over a LAN network. For more information on this, see "Delivering from a Network," later in this chapter.

How you package a library separately depends on whether or not your piece has a linked icon. If you're packaging a piece linked to a library, you can use the following procedure to package the library at the same time:

1. Package the piece, but don't check the Package All Libraries Internally checkbox.

   After packaging starts, the Package Library dialog box appears, as shown in **Figure 17.2**.

Figure 17.2
The Package Library dialog box on the Windows platform.

2. Select the In Separate Package option at the top of the dialog box.

   Several additional options are available in this dialog box:

   - Selecting Internal to Piece overrides the Package dialog box option and packages the current library as part of the piece.

   - Selecting Referenced Icons Only packages the library with only those icons that you've linked to your piece—other icons are not included. This can help cut down on file size.

   - Selecting Use Default Name packages the library using the current library name.

   - Selecting Package With Fonts (Macintosh option only) enables you to include TrueType or screen (bitmap) font resources in your library.

3. Select the options you would like to use, and then click Package.

   The Open dialog box appears, as shown in **Figure 17.3**.

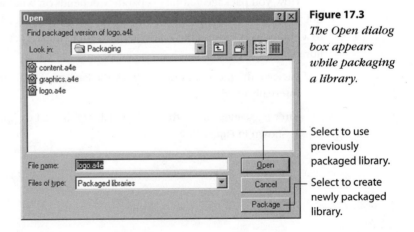

Figure 17.3
The Open dialog box appears while packaging a library.

Select to use previously packaged library.

Select to create newly packaged library.

If you are packaging your piece for the first time, use the following steps:

1. Use the file and folder browser to select the folder where you want to save the packaged library file.

2. Type in a name in the Name field for the packaged library you're creating.

3. After entering a name for your packaged library file, click Package.

   A status dialog box appears, which indicates that Authorware is packaging the library file. After Authorware packages the library file, a second status dialog box appears, which indicates that Authorware is packaging the piece.

NOTE Authorware automatically adds the .A4E extension to any library file that you package for both the Macintosh and Windows platforms. Don't change this because Authorware uses this extension to locate libraries attached to a packaged piece.

Using a previously packaged library

When packaging a piece, the Open dialog box enables you to attach a previously packaged version of the library to the piece you're packaging. Because you may be packaging the piece again (and you haven't actually made any changes to your libraries since the last time you packaged them), this dialog box enables you to get around repackaging your library files and saves you time in the process.

To use a previously saved version of your library when using the Open window:

1. Use the file and folder browser to find the name of the previously packaged library, and then select this packaged library file in the browser window.

   The name of the packaged library file appears in the File field at the bottom of the dialog box.

2. Click Open to continue packaging your piece without repackaging the library.

   If you have multiple linked libraries for a piece, the Package Library dialog box displays again, and you can repeat the above procedure for each additional library. Otherwise, a status dialog box appears, which indicates that Authorware is packaging the piece.

After packaging your piece this way, Authorware attempts to connect all linked icons in your piece to the library you've selected in the Open dialog box when you launched your packaged piece. Make sure that the packaged library files that you've linked to your piece are included in the same folder as your packaged application.

NOTE Pointing Authorware to the wrong packaged library or libraries when using the Open dialog box creates broken links in your piece. The piece still runs—however, some of the content is missing.

Packaging a library separately

Likewise, if you've made changes to a library file, but you haven't actually modified the piece to which the library file is attached, you can use the Package command to package the library file separately:

1. Make sure that you have selected the library you want to package in the Design window. (If the library is not already open, you'll need to open it using the Open > Library command from the File menu.)

2. Choose Package from the File menu.

   The Package Library dialog box appears.

3. Select any options for packaging the library.

4. Click Save File(s) and Package.

   The Package Library As dialog box appears.

5. Type in a name for your library and click Save.

   A status dialog box appears, which indicates that Authorware is packaging the library.

Distributing libraries

When you package libraries as separate files (as opposed to packaging a library internally), you need to distribute your packaged library files in the same folder as the piece. Putting packaged libraries in the same folder as the piece ensures that Authorware can find them when the piece runs.

If you've included your libraries in a separate folder, you may have trouble finding them when you distribute your piece, unless you've specified the folder name in the Content Search Path field in the File

Setup dialog box. If Authorware cannot find a library when you run a packaged piece, it displays a standard dialog box that asks you to locate the names of the library files linked to your piece.

NOTE When a link between an icon and a library breaks, the icon's contents don't appear. However, Authorware still presents the icons and evaluates all other information about the icon, such as option settings and attached calculations. Even though no content displays, the broken link can affect variables.

Shocking a Piece

Shockwave is Macromedia's technology for delivering media over intranets or the Internet. Shockwave technology consists of two elements: Afterburner, which prepares your application for delivery on the web, and the Shockwave for Authorware Plug-In, which runs your Shockwave piece inside a web browser.

NOTE Currently, Netscape Navigator and Microsoft's Internet Explorer are the only browsers that support the Shockwave for Authorware Plug-In. For the latest news on browser compatibility with Shockwave, see Macromedia's web site (**http://www.macromedia.com/ support/shockwave/**).

When you package a piece, Authorware automatically compresses the graphics that you have stored. This saves a great deal of file space when delivering your final piece. However, if you are creating a Shockwave piece, you also need to use the Afterburner utility (included with Authorware 4) to segment your packaged piece for delivery over the web.

The segments that Afterburner creates enables Authorware to "stream" the content in your piece. Streaming allows the Shockwave for Authorware Plug-In to play the piece from a web site without downloading the entire piece at one time. When you save a packaged piece using Afterburner, it splits the piece into small segments that you can upload to your web server. When the user runs the piece from within a web browser using the Shockwave Plug-In, these segments are downloaded by the Plug-In as they are needed to play back a particular segment of the piece.

Streaming is used only with content that you've stored internally in an Authorware piece—namely, graphics and sounds—and can include any libraries that you have packaged with the piece. Since external graphics, sounds, or movies that you link to your piece cannot be streamed by the Shockwave Plug-In, they are downloaded to the user's local hard drive when the Shockwave piece first launches. Consequently, this can make the initial start-up time of a Shockwave piece a bit longer, unless you've modified the default options for handling external Shockwave content by editing the Shockwave piece's map file.

TIP Shockwave audio (.SWA) files that you either have imported into your sound icons or linked to a sound icon are optimized for delivery by using Shockwave. For more information about using Shockwave audio, see Appendix B, "Using Shockwave Audio."

The process for creating a Shockwave piece using Afterburner is fairly straightforward. First, you package the piece without the run-time player using the techniques described earlier; then open Afterburner to save your piece in segments. This creates a separate map file that the Shockwave Plug-In uses to download the necessary components of your piece when the user runs it from within a web browser.

To prepare a packaged piece for Shockwave delivery:

1. Double-click on the Afterburner application installed in your Authorware folder to open it. The file's name on the Windows platform is AB32A.EXE; on the Macintosh, it's Afterburner-MacFat-AW.

   The Select Packaged Source File dialog box appears, as shown in **Figure 17.4**.

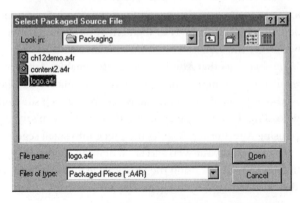

Figure 17.4
Select a packaged file in the Select Packaged Source File dialog box.

2. Select the name of your packaged file and click OK. (Remember, it will have an .A4R extension, since it has not been packaged with the run-time player file.)

After selecting the piece, the Select Destination Map File dialog box appears, prompting you to type in a map file name for your shocked piece.

3. Type in the name you want to use. In general, use the same name for the map file that you use for your piece.

NOTE This is especially important if you are jumping to the shocked file from another shocked Authorware file because Authorware looks for the file name you specified inside the piece when calling the `JumpFileReturn` or `JumpFile` system function.

The Afterburner Segment Settings dialog box appears, as shown in **Figure 17.5**.

Segment
Prefix field ———

Segment
Size field ———

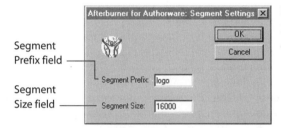

Figure 17.5
The Afterburner Segment Settings dialog box.

This is where you specify the size of the file segments for your piece, and the four-character prefix for each segment. These options default to a segment size of 16000 (16K) and the first four characters of your map file name. It's a good idea to keep the segments named the same as your map file; however, occasionally you may need to adjust the segment size.

4. If you want to change the default settings in this dialog box, type in new values in either of the fields, and then click OK to continue. If you choose to modify the segment prefix field, you have to use a prefix with four characters.

A progress dialog box appears as Authorware compresses the piece with Afterburner. If your piece has additional Authorware components (e.g., libraries, or other pieces that your file jumps to), you must repeat this process for each separate Authorware file. See "Handling libraries with Shockwave," for more information on this.

5. After all file segments have been created, the Map File window appears, showing you the map settings for your shocked piece. **Figure 17.6** shows you an example of what the Map File window looks like after using Afterburner. Each entry line in the map file contains a different piece of information about the Shockwave piece, as indicated below.

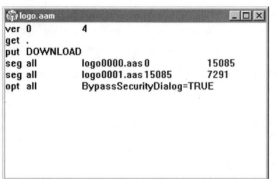

Figure 17.6
The Afterburner Map File window, which shows settings for a shocked piece.

6. Adjust the settings in the Map File window if needed, and then close Afterburner when you have finished to save the map file to your hard disk.

Afterburner creates a folder of segments (files with an .aas extension) that you need to upload to a location on your web server. If you've shocked a piece and then open the folder where you've saved your map file and segments, you will see that Afterburner automatically adds a numerical value to each segment in sequence, beginning with 0000. **Figure 17.7** shows you how your shocked piece appears inside a folder on the Windows desktop. You see the same result when you compress your file on the Macintosh.

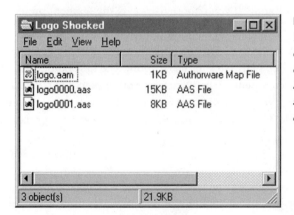

Figure 17.7
The folder that contains the compressed Shockwave segment files and map file.

Each segment is numbered so the Shockwave Plug-In knows which segment to download when the user runs the piece through a web browser. The map file is used to provide a reference for the Plug-In so that it knows which files it needs to download to present a particular section of the piece.

Because Authorware 4 is binary-compatible, you only need to shock your piece once (not on both platforms), and then upload your segments, map files, and external media to the same location on the web server. The Plug-In for both platforms comes with the platform-specific run-time player file so you do not need to create two run-time executable files for both platforms as you would when creating a stand-alone piece for delivery.

When creating a Shockwave piece, it is important when specifying the segment size that you take into consideration bandwidth constraints for your users. In general, 16000 (16K) is a good segment size to use for users who are running on connection speeds of 28.8 (28.8K/sec) or higher. However, if you are delivering your piece from an intranet server, it may be good to shock the piece using higher segment sizes because fewer downloads are needed in order to run the piece.

Handling libraries with Shockwave

When you shock a piece that you have linked to libraries, the libraries are also shocked at the same time. Authorware creates a separate map file for each library and saves the library in separate segments (unless you've packaged the piece with the libraries stored internally). It is extremely important when shocking your piece that you specify unique names for both the library map file and the library segment prefix; otherwise, you may overwrite the map file or the segments that you have already saved for the piece.

For example, if your packaged piece is named Startup.a4r and your library is named Startup.a4e, you should not use the name "Startup" for both the piece's map file and the library's map file. In this situation, save the piece's map file as Startup.aam and create a new name for the library map file.

When renaming the library map file, use a name that doesn't begin with the first four characters of the name of the piece because Authorware uses these characters when saving the library segments.

NOTE If you run into this problem, you can get around this by creating a new 4-character prefix for your library segments using the Afterburner Save Segments dialog box, as described earlier.

After you shock a piece linked to libraries, there is a line in its map file for each library that you have linked to the piece, as shown in **Figure 17.8**. The information contained in this line is labeled more clearly for you in **Figure 17.9**.

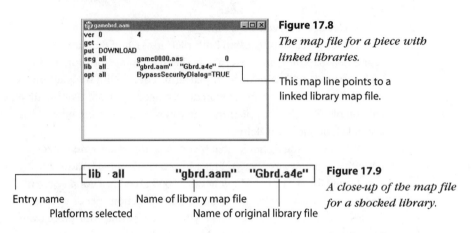

Figure 17.8
The map file for a piece with linked libraries.

This map line points to a linked library map file.

Figure 17.9
A close-up of the map file for a shocked library.

As mentioned earlier, Authorware saves a separate map file for each library in your piece that you have packaged externally. The library map file that Afterburner creates is much like the map file for the piece itself. As with the piece's map file, you can edit certain parameters specified in the library map file, but you need to be careful when doing so because it can create problems for you when you run the piece through a browser later.

The map file created by Afterburner stores information about the location of each segment of your piece, as well as any additional external files for your piece. You also can specify the name of the map file when creating the HTML page that the user loads to display the Shockwave piece. For more information on this, see "Embedding a Shockwave piece in an HTML page," below.

TIP Editing map files is covered more extensively in the Shockwave for Authorware Technote, "Editing a Map File with the Afterburner Editor." This Technote, along with many others, is available on Macromedia's web site in the Shockwave for Authorware Developer's Center (**http://www.macromedia.com/support/authorware/how/shock/**).

Testing your Shockwave piece

To see how your Shockwave piece runs, you need to test it using either the Netscape Navigator or the Microsoft Internet Explorer web browser installed on your system. Make sure that you've already installed the Shockwave for Authorware Plug-In for the type of web browser installed on your system.

NOTE The Shockwave for Authorware Plug-In can be installed only on systems with Netscape Navigator or Microsoft Internet Explorer already installed.

To open the Shockwave piece in Netscape Navigator:

1. Launch Navigator and select Open File from the File menu.

   The Open File dialog box appears.

2. Using the File Type drop-down list at the bottom of the dialog box, select Authorware (*.aam), and then select the name of the map file for the piece you want to test.

   A new browser window opens, and the piece loads.

To open the Shockwave piece in Microsoft Internet Explorer:

1. Launch Internet Explorer and select Open from the File menu.

   The Open Location dialog box appears.

2. Click Browse.

   The Browse dialog box appears.

3. Using the File Type drop-down list at the bottom of the dialog box, select Show All Files (*.*), and then select the name of the map file for the piece you want to test. Click OK.

   The Browse dialog box closes.

4. Click Open to open the file you've selected.

   A new browser window opens, and the piece loads.

Embedding a Shockwave piece in an HTML page

When you run a Shockwave piece by opening it in the browser, what you see is not how it actually will play after you have set it up for final delivery. You need a web page that users can load from their systems to see how it will actually appear in a web browser.

To create the embedded Shockwave page:

1. Use a text editor or an HTML editing tool to create a basic web page with the HTML, TITLE, HEAD, and BODY tags already entered.

2. Next, add the EMBED tag to the HTML file. This specifies the location of the map file you've created; it also specifies the way the piece displays when the browser loads it.

   After adding these lines to your HTML page, it should appear in the editor similar to what is shown below:

```
<HTML>
<HEAD>
<TITLE>Authorware Shockwave Demo</TITLE>
</HEAD>
<BODY>
<CENTER>
<EMBED SRC="demo.aam" WIDTH=400 HEIGHT=300
WINDOW="inPlace"></EMBED>
</CENTER>
</BODY>
</HTML>
```

Notice that there are several property settings specified in the EMBED tag. The WIDTH and HEIGHT property settings specify the width and height of the display area in pixels. Your browser crops the image to the size you specify; it's best, however, to use the size of your Presentation window for this setting.

TIP When creating Shockwave pieces for delivery on the Internet, you can improve the overall performance of your piece by using a smaller Presentation window size, which reduces the size of your graphics.

In the above example, the WINDOW property setting indicates how the Authorware piece will display in relation to the browser window. You have three settings from which you can choose:

■ The WINDOW="inPlace" setting displays the piece embedded in the HTML page in the browser window, as shown in **Figure 17.10**.

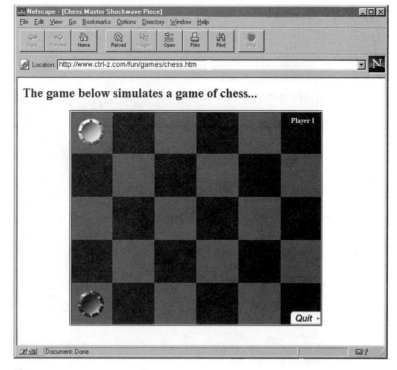

Figure 17.10

A Shockwave piece displayed in the browser window.

NOTE The WINDOW="inPlace" setting is ignored when the Shockwave piece runs on a Macintosh system.

- The WINDOW="onTop" setting displays the piece in a separate window on top of the browser window. This makes your piece look more like a separate application, as shown in **Figure 17.11**.

- The WINDOW="onTopMinimize" setting displays the piece in a separate window and minimizes (or hides) the browser. This setting makes your piece look the most like a separate, stand-alone application, appearing by itself on the desktop, as shown in **Figure 17.12**.

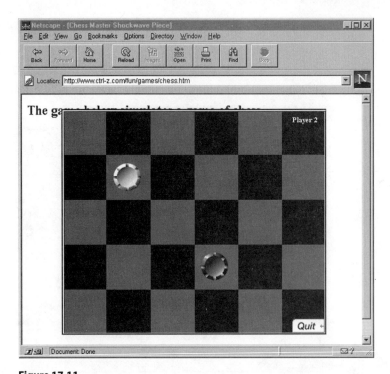

Figure 17.11
A Shockwave piece displayed on top of the browser.

Figure 17.12
A Shockwave piece displayed on top, with the browser minimized.

When working with Shockwave pieces and designing their appearance in the browser window, keep in mind these guidelines:

- Don't use a title bar on your Presentation window. (You can turn off the Title Bar checkbox option in the File Setup dialog box.) Embedding a Shockwave piece using the `WINDOW="inPlace"` setting reduces the height of your Presentation window by the height of the title bar.

- Take into account the user's monitor resolution when designing your piece. If your Presentation window size is 640 x 480 pixels, use onTop or onTopMinimize for your WINDOW property setting because users with monitor resolutions set to 640 x 480 must scroll vertically and horizontally to see the entire Presentation window.

- Avoid using the `ResizeWindow` and `MoveWindow` system functions, which can produce unpredictable results when inPlace is used for the WINDOW property setting. For more information on these functions, see *Using Authorware* or Authorware Help.

Working with the browser palette

A fourth (and optional) property setting for the EMBED tag is the PALETTE setting. This setting determines which color palette the browser uses on Windows computers. You have two options:

- If you specify the EMBED tag setting `PALETTE=Foreground`, the browser loads the color palette of the shocked Authorware piece. This can cause a noticeable color shift in other images that display in the browser on systems running in 256 colors. However, the color shift is corrected when the browser reloads its own color palette after the Authorware piece finishes.

NOTE If you don't specify the PALETTE setting, the browser defaults to loading the palette of the shocked Authorware piece.

- If you specify the EMBED tag setting `PALETTE=Background`, the shocked Authorware piece uses the browser's color palette. Using the Background setting avoids the color shift that happens when you use the Foreground setting. However, it has the disadvantage of changing the appearance of the

Authorware piece. (The colors you used when you created the Authorware piece are replaced with the colors in the browser's palette.)

To get around this issue, save your graphics using the default Netscape palette. This option is available when dithering your 24-bit or 16-bit graphics to 8-bit graphics inside Adobe Photoshop. You also can use Director to create a paint object using the Netscape palette, place it into the score, and then export it as a .BMP frame and load it into Authorware's Palette dialog box. For more information on creating custom palettes for your piece using Director, see Chapter 19, "Using Director Interactively."

Working with non-Shockwave browsers

If users don't have a Shockwave-compatible browser, you can set up the HTML page that contains your piece to display an optional JPEG or GIF image to these viewers. The image should include text that explains to users that they need a compatible browser and Shockwave to view the content. Use the NOEMBED tag to embed the image in the page.

This example shows how to display a GIF file named NoShock.gif in place of an Authorware piece named Demo:

```
<EMBED SRC="Demo.aam" WIDTH=400 HEIGHT=300
WINDOW="inPlace" Palette=Background>
</EMBED>
<NOEMBED><IMG SRC="Images/NoShock.gif">
</NOEMBED>
```

NOTE In browsers that are not compatible with Shockwave, users see a broken image icon (which indicates that a file could not be loaded into the browser window), in addition to the substitute image.

Distributing External Files

When you deliver a piece, not only are you required to deliver the packaged application and libraries, you also need to distribute any external files that you've used in a piece—regardless of whether you're delivering it as a stand-alone application or as a Shockwave piece.

While there are differences between the way you handle external file distribution for stand-alone pieces and Shockwave pieces, you can break down the types of files you need to distribute with your piece into five groups:

- The run-time files and libraries, discussed earlier in this chapter in "Packaging A Piece."

- External media (such as graphics, sounds, or movies) that you've linked to icons in your piece.

- External drivers used by Authorware to play back certain types of content, including QuickTime, Video for Windows, and Director movies, as well as external videodisc or video overlay content.

- Xtras that you've integrated into the piece, such as sprite and scripting Xtras, and those Xtras required by Authorware to display content and transition effects.

- External function libraries that you've used to integrate custom functions into your piece. Using these types of files is covered in more detail in Chapter 20, "Developing with External Code."

The files that a piece requires depends on the piece's components and the platform on which it runs. The following sections will outline the basic files that you need to include for different situations. This is an exhaustive list that you can refer to later as you move closer to distributing your final piece.

Distributing external media

In many cases, you may need to distribute the external movies, sounds, or graphics that you've linked to your piece. The most important issue to resolve when distributing external media is where to place them so that the final packaged piece can find them. (Actually, this is the most important issue for all types of external files that you distribute with your piece.)

You should place external graphics, movies, and sounds in the same relative location to your packaged piece as they were when you developed your piece in Authorware. This means that if your movies were placed in a folder called Movies, you need to include this entire folder when you distribute your final piece. Also make certain that you've included the name of the relative folder in your Content Search Path setting, which you can set in the File Properties dialog box, as described in Chapter 2, "Beginning a Piece."

Because the search path folder names entered in the File Properties dialog box are converted to a character string and then assigned to the `SearchPath` system variable, you can specify additional folders to add to the `SearchPath` system variable by using a calculation icon at the beginning of your piece. To do this, simply concatenate the additional folder name(s) to the current value of `SearchPath`, as shown in this example expression:

```
SearchPath := SearchPath ^ ¬
"Resources\;Movies\;Sounds\;"
```

A better way to avoid problems when delivering a piece is to specify the location of the file using a relative path. You can do this easily through the External Media Browser window, or directly in the Icon Properties dialog box of the graphic, sound, or movie that you have linked to your piece.

Whenever you specify an external path to your file, you can simply use the shorthand method of specifying the current run-time file location by placing a period (.) in front of the folder name and file name, and then separating the folder names with either a backslash (\), a colon (:), or a forward slash (/).

For instance, if you're storing your movies in a folder called Movies that you've placed in the same folder as your piece, you can point to the location of a movie named Tarzan.mov using the following shorthand expression inside the File slot of the movie icon:

```
.\Movies\Tarzan.mov
```

This technique also works for graphics and sounds that you have stored externally. Authorware uses this shorthand method by default when importing a new linked file into your piece.

Since Shockwave pieces locate all external files using the map file, you don't need to worry about setting up a different relative path for your movie, sound, or graphic if you have included a relative path as described above. However, keep the following issues in mind:

- Afterburner only adds the names of external files to the map file for your piece if you have pointed to them using either a literal path or a relative path as described above. If you are using an expression that points to an external file, you have to add the name of the file (and the file's location on the web server) to the map file manually so that the Shockwave Plug-In can locate the external file to download it.

NOTE For more information on how to specify external media locations in the map file, see the Shockwave for Authorware Technote, "Editing a Map File with the Afterburner Editor." This Technote, along with many others, is available on Macromedia's web site in the Shockwave for Authorware Developer's Center (**http://www.macromedia.com/support/authorware/how/shock/**).

- If you're working with external graphics or sounds, you also can use a URL to specify a graphic or sound stored on a web server. This eliminates some of the hassles of editing the map file as described above, but it makes it imperative that you know ahead of time where your content will be stored on the web server. For more information about linking to URLs, see Chapter 6, "Managing Your Content."

Handling external files for Shockwave pieces introduces other issues—since all external content must download before the piece can start. Because of this, consider creating two versions of your piece: one that uses external graphics and sounds, and another version where you've internalized most of your graphics and sounds for Shockwave delivery (for optimum network connection speeds and download times). Using the Shockwave Plug-In to run the piece enables Authorware to stream the data and to download it only when needed. While the size of your piece may increase, in the long run it proves more beneficial because the piece is easier to distribute.

TIP To minimize the size of your final packaged piece and improve performance when delivering it as a Shockwave piece, consider using the Shockwave Audio format for all sounds. This compresses sound by up to 75 percent without a noticeable difference in quality, and you can use the format for stand-alone applications as well. For more information about using Shockwave audio, see Appendix B, "Using Shockwave Audio."

Distributing external drivers

You must include the following external drivers in the same folder as your packaged piece when delivering it. The table below indicates the name of the driver file for each respective platform.

Type of content...	Files to include on Windows platform...	Files to include on Macintosh platform...
QuickTime movie	QuickTime for Windows installed. A4QT.XMO (16-bit) A4QT32.XMO (32-bit) You also must "flatten" the Quick-Time movie before you distribute it on the Windows platform.	QuickTime system extensions must be installed. No specific Authorware drivers are required.
Video for Windows movie	Video for Windows installed. A4VFW.XMO (16-bit) A4VFW32.XMO (32-bit)	Video for Windows is not supported on the Macintosh. Convert your AVI movies to QuickTime movies instead.
MPEG movie	MPEG hardware or software installed on playback system A4MPEG.XMO (16-bit) A4MPEG32.XMO (32-bit)	MPEG is only supported on systems running QuickTime 2.5 and the QuickTime MPEG 1.0 extensions. No specific Authorware drivers are required.
Director movie	See Chapter 19, "Using Director Interactively," for a list of the Director components required.	See Chapter 19, "Using Director Interactively," for a list of the Director components required.
Video Overlay devices	One of the following Author-ware drivers (depending on hardware): A4BRAVO.VDR A4MCI.VDR (16-bit) A4MCI32.VDR (32-bit) A4MMOTN.VDR A4VBLAST.VDR A4VLOGIC.VDR A4VSVW.VDR	One of the following Author-ware drivers (depending on hardware): QuickTime Overlay RasterOps 24STV RasterOps 24XLTV RasterOps ColorBoard RasterOps MediaTime TrueVision NuVista+ VideoLogic DVA-4000
Laser disc devices	One of the following Author-ware drivers (depending on hardware): A4PIOCLV.VDR (16-bit) A4PCLV32.VDR (32-bit) A4PIONER.VDR (16-bit) A4PION32.VDR (32-bit) A4SONY.VDR (16-bit) A4SONY32.VDR (32-bit)	One of the following Author-ware drivers (depending on hardware): Pioneer LDV Pioneer LDV CLV Pioneer LDV-6000 Sony LDP Series

For a complete list of the laser disc or video overlay hardware that each driver listed above supports, see *Using Authorware* or Authorware Help.

Distributing Xtras

You must ship certain Xtras that will display the content you've imported or linked to icons with your final piece. You should place them in a folder named Xtras that you have created inside the folder that contains your packaged files, or in the Authorware run-time player if you've packaged your piece without run time.

TIP If you're using Shockwave to distribute your piece, you don't need to include any of the Xtras listed in the tables below. They are installed with the Authorware 4 Shockwave Plug-In for both the Macintosh and Windows platforms.

NOTE All Windows Xtras are designated with either an .X16 extension (required for pieces packaged with the 16-bit run time), or an .X32 extension (required for pieces packaged with the 32-bit run time). All Macintosh Xtras (unless otherwise indicated) are fat-binary and you can distribute them on any Macintosh system.

Macromedia Content Viewers

Type of content...	Xtras to include on Windows platform...	Xtras to include on Macintosh platform...
MIX Viewer Xtras (required for all packaged pieces).	MIX16.X16 MIX32.X32 MIXVIEW.X16 MIXVIEW.X32 VIEWSVC.X16 VIEWSVC.X32	MIX Services MIX Viewer Viewer Services
Internet URL Xtras (required if you're using a URL to point to a linked file).	INETURL.X16 INETURL.X32	InetUrl Helper InetUrlFAT
A3 Sounds (required if piece was converted from Authorware 3.5 and includes sound).	A3SREAD.X16 A3SREAD.X32	A3Snd Reader

Graphics Formats

Type of content...	Xtras to include on Windows platform...	Xtras to include on Macintosh platform...
BMP (required if using imported or linked BMP files, and for pieces converted from Authorware 3).	BMPVIEW.X16 BMPVIEW.X32	BMP Import Export
EMF (required if using imported or linked EMF files).	EMFVIEW.X32 (only supported for Windows 95, Windows NT)	Not supported on the Macintosh platform.
GIF (required if using imported or linked GIF files).	GIFIMP.X16 GIFIMP.X32	GIF Import
JPEG (required if using imported or linked JPEG images).	JPEGIMP.X16 JPEGIMP.X32	JPEG Import Export
LRG (required if using imported or linked LRG images).	LRGIMP.X16 LRGIMP.X32	LRG Import Export
Photoshop 3 (required if using imported or linked Photoshop 3 images).	PS3IMP.X16 PS3IMP.X32	Photoshop 3.0 Import
PICT (required if using imported or linked PICT images).	PICTVIEW.X16 PICTVIEW.X32 (also requires QuickTime for Windows installed)	PICT Viewer
PNG (required if using imported or linked PNG images).	PNGIMP.X16 PNGIMP.X32	PNG Import Export
Targa (required if using imported or linked Targa images).	TARGAIMP.X16 TARGAIMP.X32	Targa Import Export
TIFF (required if using imported or linked TIFF images).	TIFFIMP.X16 TIFFIMP.X32	TIFF Import Export
WMF (required if using imported or linked WMF images).	WMFVIEW.X16 WMFVIEW.X32	Not supported on the Macintosh platform.

Sound Formats

Type of content...	Xtras to include on Windows platform...	Xtras to include on Macintosh platform...
AIFF (required if using imported or linked AIFF sounds).	AIFFREAD.X16 AIFFREAD.X32	AIFF Reader
PCM (required if using imported or linked PCM sounds).	PCMREAD.X16 PCMREAD.X32	PCM Reader
SWA (required if using imported or linked Shockwave Audio sounds).	SWADCMPR.X16 SWADCMPR.X32 SWAREAD.X16 SWAREAD.X32	Shockwave Audio Import SWA Decompression PPC Xtra (for Power Macintosh sytems) SWA Decompression 68K Xtra (for 68K systems)
WAV (required if using imported or linked WAV sounds).	WAVREAD.X16 WAVREAD.X32	WAV Reader

Transition Xtras

Cover In Transitions	COVERIN.X16 COVERIN.X32	CoverInTranzFAT
Cover Out Transitions	COVEROUT.X16 COVEROUT.X32	CoverOutTranzFAT
Corner Wipe In Transitions	CROSSIN.X16 CROSSIN.X32	WipeCornerInTranzFAT
Director Transitions	DIRTRANS.X16 DIRTRANS.X32	DirTransFat
SharkByte Transitions	THEBYTE.X32 (not available for 16-bit run time).	TheByeteFAT TheJawsFAT
XAOS Tools TransX	Not included with Authorware for Windows.	Trans-X LE 1 Trans-X LE 2 Trans-X LE 3 Trans-X LE 4 Trans-X LE 5

NOTE You also need to distribute any additional Xtras (including the ActiveX Xtra and the QuickDraw 3D Xtra) that you've integrated into your piece in the Xtras folder. This is described in more detail in Chapter 20, "Developing with External Code."

Depending on the platform you're using, you may have included DLL, UCD, or XCMD custom functions in your piece. You need to place these files in the same folder as your packaged piece, or in a folder that you've specified in your search path settings. For more information on working with custom function libraries, see Chapter 20, "Developing with External Code."

Preparing Files for Distribution

The last section of this chapter briefly covers the final stages of preparation before delivering your piece, which includes choosing a distribution medium, preparing your files for cross-platform delivery, and providing documentation for your users. These are the critical issues that you need to anticipate as they may affect your delivery schedule.

Choosing a distribution medium

You can distribute your stand-alone piece in several ways: on floppy disk, on CD-ROM, or from a LAN server. Authorware needs only to see an accessible disk; it makes no distinction between a local hard drive, a removable disk, or a LAN server.

- It is almost impossible to fit a piece on one disk because the run-time player alone takes up almost 1.2 MB. However, you can use a custom installation tool to create a multidisk installer, if needed. In order to do this, the installer will need to copy all components of the packaged Authorware file to the user's hard disk. For a list of companies that make installer software, see Appendix C, "Authorware Resources on the Internet."

TIP Another ideal way to distribute files is on 100 MB Zip cartridges, since this gives you more room to play with but does not require that you burn a CD-ROM.

- When you distribute several packaged files that can share the run-time application, package each piece without the run-time application and include only one copy of RunA4W or RunA4M. After you copy the pieces to a hard drive, an unlimited number of files can use the same copy of RunA4W or RunA4M.

■ You can use a hard drive, CD-ROM, or a LAN server when your piece does not fit on a manageable number of floppy disks. When distributing on a LAN server, more than one network user can run the file packaged with the run-time application, or the copy of RunA4W or RunA4M that you've placed in the same location as your packaged files.

NOTE Files distributed with Shockwave are handled differently because you first need to segment them with Afterburner, and then upload them to a web server that can be accessed using a URL address. You also must configure your server with the appropriate MIME types to handle delivering Shockwave content. For more information on using MIME types with Shockwave, see the Shockwave for Authorware Technotes area on the Macromedia web site (**http://www.macromedia.com/support/authorware/how/shock/**).

Preparing cross-platform files for delivery

If you plan to deliver a cross-platform application that you have packaged with the run-time player, you must create at least two executable files (one for the Windows platform and one for the Macintosh platform), and then distribute them along with any external files (including libraries) that you have used with your piece.

NOTE If you package a piece without the run-time player, you can use the same packaged .A4R piece on both platforms. Simply include the appropriate run-time player and Xtras for each platform, along with the packaged files.

Most hybrid applications (those designed to run under both Macintosh and Windows) are distributed from CD-ROM. This medium usually gives you a great deal of file space to work with when delivering your piece, and you can afford to package separate run-time executable files for each specific platform and system configuration on which the piece will be delivered. However, keep in mind the following issues:

■ You need to place both versions (Mac and Windows) of the run-time executables in the same disk location when delivering your final piece so that all resources (e.g., libraries, Xtras, external media) can be found when the piece runs. This is usually at the root level of the CD-ROM, or at the root folder that contains all other folders and external files for your piece (if you are placing your piece on a LAN server).

- In most cases, the best way to build a hybrid CD-ROM file structure is to prepare your piece on the Macintosh side so that libraries are already packaged, and then either copy these to the Windows side to package the Windows run-time executable file, or remember to use the same names for libraries when packaging your piece on the Windows side. This allows both platforms to share the same library files when your piece runs.

- If you have copied other external files such as QuickTime movies from a Windows machine that the Macintosh side also will need to access, make sure that you save these files again on the Mac side so they are mastered with their resource forks intact.

- If you're mastering a hybrid (Macintosh/Windows) CD, master it from a Macintosh hard drive to protect the resource fork information for your Macintosh files. Prepare your CD volume on a partitioned 640 MB hard drive that you have freshly formatted. Copy all Macintosh and Windows files to it using the same folder structure. Remember that files that the two platforms share (e.g., libraries, QuickTime movies) need to show up on both the Windows and Macintosh file partitions.

- When burning the CD, you will need CD formatting software that can create both an ISO-9660 (DOS format) and an HFS (Macintosh format) file partition on the same disc. Astarte's Toast and Sony's Hybrid Formatter software are both widely used CD formatting tools. Check with the manufacturer of your CD-ROM burner to see which software is recommended for your particular hardware.

Improving memory usage on Macintosh

Some pieces become quite large by the time you include all content and logic. At some point, the amount of available memory may not be enough for the piece to run efficiently. Increasing the amount of memory available for the piece can improve performance. (Of course, a piece that is so large that the computer doesn't have enough memory to hold it all at one time always has some performance problems.)

You can usually improve how large files run on the Macintosh by increasing the memory partition size for RunA4M or a file packaged with RunA4M.

To increase the partition size for the piece:

1. In the Finder, select RunA4M or a file packaged with RunA4M.

   For a piece packaged with RunA4M, select the file for the packaged piece itself. For a piece packaged without RunA4M, select RunA4M.

2. Choose Get Info from the File menu.

   The RunA4M Info dialog box appears.

3. Enter a number that provides an adequate amount of memory in the Preferred Size field.

   The optimum amount of memory is usually a trade-off between the amount that enables the piece to run smoothly and the amount of memory you expect to be available on computers on which the piece runs. When you allocate more memory than that available on the computer, the piece uses as much memory as is available at the time.

   NOTE The Windows task manager manages memory usage when running a Windows version of a piece, so you cannot modify this in the same way.

Decreasing file size

Considering the size of Authorware's run-time files, your piece won't fit on a single floppy disk. However, there are a few techniques that you can use to optimize how files fit onto the distribution medium you choose.

- Break the piece into several parts. It's a good idea to plan ways to modularize a file while authoring, rather than waiting until you're ready to package it.

- Use a compression utility such as WinZip (Windows) or StuffIt (Macintosh) to compress the file. These utilities enable you to break up and compress files into smaller parts that you can place on two or more disks and then reassemble during installation on a hard disk. (When you use WinZip or StuffIt, you can make the compressed files self-extracting, which means that the hard disk doesn't require its own copy of WinZip or StuffIt to decompress the files. If you don't make the files self-extracting, the computer must have WinZip or StuffIt available to decompress the files.)

Documentation is important when delivering your final piece because it informs the user of problem issues or functional issues that you may have been unable to solve before shipping the piece. You should include the following types of documentation with your final piece:

■ Write installation instructions and a Read Me file (if needed) and include them with the piece. Include information in the Read Me file about the minimum system requirements for your piece, as well as information about what files are installed and the known hardware or software issues that you've come across while testing it.

■ If you have created a logon procedure, you may want to tell users about the user records file location and warn them not to delete it.

TIP If you are including documentation for a Shockwave piece, consider creating it in an HTML format so that the user can view it when using a browser to link to your Internet or intranet web site location.

There are many issues that you need to be aware of when preparing your piece for distribution. While this chapter certainly does not cover all aspects of delivering a piece, the main issues that you should think about before you begin are delivery platform and delivery format.

As you begin to tackle more projects, you will find that CD-ROM offers the best way to deliver a large amount of content quickly, and with the least amount of overhead needed to prepare it for distribution. Delivering a piece using Shockwave is a more time-consuming process, but makes it easier to provide the user with future updates of your piece because your files are stored on a web server that can be quickly accessed.

You'll want to spend a great deal of time before you distribute your piece running through it and making sure that it functions properly. Keep in mind that no piece runs perfectly the first time. After many repetitions and testing, you can send it off feeling comfortable about the way it handles. In the next chapter, you'll learn the basic techniques for testing your piece and debugging the problems that you may encounter.

Chapter 18

Debugging Your Piece

Authorware does exactly what you tell it to do— but it doesn't always do what you expect it to do. You frequently will discover problems while authoring—especially if you consistently test the piece to make sure that you haven't introduced bugs into your code.

Although you may find some problems caused by hardware or software configuration issues on the delivery machine, most of the bugs you find in your piece occur as a result of the way you've constructed the flowline structures, the way you've set up specific properties for your icons, or the way in which you've integrated variables and functions into your calculation scripts and icon functionality. The debugging techniques in this chapter teach you how to isolate problems in your piece and fix them quickly.

As a new author, you may find that the way your piece runs inside Authorware isn't exactly how it runs as a packaged file on the end user's system. In some cases, this is a result of hardware or software installation problems on the playback system. Because this is something you can't always control, the best option is to abide by the golden rule of multimedia development, "Test early, test often, test on all target platforms." You'll see some examples of using troubleshooting techniques to narrow down a problem in "Putting Troubleshooting into Practice," later in this chapter.

NOTE It is especially important to periodically package, burn, and test your Shockwave piece. This doesn't mean you have to upload the file to the web server, but it does mean that you must run the piece from inside Netscape Navigator or Microsoft Internet Explorer. For more information on testing your Shockwave piece for delivery, see Chapter 17, "Distributing Your Piece."

When creating a piece, you can isolate most problems by looking at the set of icons where the problem occurs. Determining where the problem is in the flowline is really your best course of action when trying to debug your piece. You'll learn about the techniques for doing this in the sections ahead.

Isolating the problem

Unless your piece contains only a few icons, it can be difficult to analyze from beginning to end to determine where in the flowline the problem is occurring. Fortunately, when you discover a problem with the way your piece works, you rarely need to troubleshoot the entire piece. When debugging the flowline logic in a piece, you only need to consider the particular area where the problem is occurring. In many cases where an interaction is not working properly, you can narrow down the problem to a single set of icons quite easily.

When a section of the flowline doesn't perform as you want, it often helps to retrace the flowline's behavior in your head. At this point, you don't need to know why the problem is occurring; however, you do need to visualize where the problem is occurring in the flowline you've created for your piece. Many times, bugs occur when Authorware executes flowline logic in a manner different from what you expected after setting up your icons.

For example, interactions behave very differently when you change branching or erasing properties of the responses attached to the interaction icon—especially when modifying a response that uses continue branching, and then switching it to try branching again . You may find that this disrupts other conditional responses that you've created in the interaction.

Here are some common ways to isolate a problem in Authorware:

- If clicking a button produces the wrong result, look at the interaction that contains the button. Perhaps you have set up your branching incorrectly, or you are erasing feedback at the inappropriate time.

- If the contents of a display icon don't appear, check the position of the display icon in the flowline. It's probably positioned after a wait icon that prevents Authorware from displaying its contents; or it may be positioned before an erase icon that erases the image before you can see it.

- If you are using a navigate icon to jump to a specific section in a piece and Authorware does not navigate to the correct location, check the settings in the navigate icon to make sure that you haven't inadvertently selected a new destination page for the navigate icon. You also may have deleted the page that you previously selected as your destination page.

- If you are using a decision icon to loop through a series of actions in your piece and the loop doesn't execute properly, check the settings that you are using to control the repeat branching for the decision icon.

- If you are using a calculation script to assign a value to a custom variable and the custom variable does not update properly, check your script to make sure that you've named the custom variable correctly. If not, it's possible that another script in your piece is assigning a different value to the variable after the first script executes.

One of the easiest ways to isolate a problem is to run the piece from the beginning, and then pause the piece as soon as the problem occurs. You can then use the Jump to Current Icon command from the View menu to jump to the flowline.

Shortcut: To jump to the current icon while running a piece, use Ctrl+B (Windows), or Command+B (Macintosh).

Generally, after you've identified the area in your piece where the problem is occurring, test how the piece behaves when you run only that section of the flowline where the problem occurs. The simplest way to do this is to use the start and stop flags.

Debugging the flowline with flags

As you develop more complex pieces, you will find quicker ways to isolate the set of icons where the problem is occurring. If you first identify the section where the problem is occurring, you can use the start and stop flags to control the piece while you take a closer look at what is happening when the piece runs.

For example, you may have a map icon that contains several groups of icons. You have timed these icons to display and erase a sequence of images while a sound plays. The sound starts when the first graphic displays, and it is timed to stop when the last graphic erases. If you discover that the sound unexpectedly cuts out before the last graphic displays, it may be beneficial to first run the piece from inside the map icon to see if that changes how the sound behaves.

By placing the start flag at the beginning of the sequence and the stop flag at the end of the sequence, you quickly can see how only the sequence of icons runs when it is isolated. After doing so, you may find that the sound plays as normal. This may indicate that there are additional graphics, sounds, or movies from another section of the piece loaded into memory that cause the sound to stop playing when you hit the section of the flowline where the sound icon is located. You probably should take a look at how you've set up other erase icons in your piece to clear the screen while the current graphics display.

Checking icon settings

Continuing with the above example, suppose that the sound continues to stop playing each time you run that particular area of the flowline where you have positioned the sound icon. What then? Perhaps there is more going on than you first expected, requiring that you investigate further what is happening on the flowline.

Start by opening the sound icon and checking its settings. This is a quick test that tells you whether or not you've selected an option that causes the sound to stop playing. Perhaps you have used a custom variable that turns sounds on and off in your piece, and the variable resets when you enter the section of the flowline where it stops.

If you find that you have the icon set up correctly, you may want to look at how you've included the sound icon in the flowline. If the user is required to press a button before the sound and graphics display, you may be inadvertently stopping the sound if you have set the button response's Erase option to Before Next Entry. This prevents any sound icons attached to the response from playing.

This is a general example, but it shows the methods you need to use when isolating problems. You may have to modify the icon settings and run the piece again to see if that makes a difference. For example, what if you have a graphic that disappears from the Presentation window? A good way to troubleshoot this issue is to open the Properties dialog box for the display icon and change the layer setting to a higher value. Then restart the piece from the start flag and test whether or not you still see the display icon.

In some cases—especially where you've checked or modified icon settings and haven't seen a difference, you may want Authorware to bypass one or more of your icons while running the piece to see if the problem persists.

To have Authorware bypass selected icons:

1. Drag a new decision icon to the flowline where the problem is occurring.

2. Double-click the decision icon to open it.

   The Decision Icon Properties dialog box appears.

3. Change its Branching setting to Calculated Path, and in the field below the Branching drop-down list, type in **0** or **FALSE**.

   This forces Authorware to bypass the decision icon and any icons attached to it while running the piece.

4. Drag all icons you want Authorware to bypass and place them to the right of the decision icon.

5. Run the piece from the beginning, or from the start flag.

You can solve most of Authorware's simple problems by using one of the techniques described above. However, if you are working on a more complicated piece that uses many types of interactions and complex navigation, you may need some other methods to help debug the flowline.

The way icons connect in a piece is not always apparent when looking at a particular section of the flowline—unless you're working with pages of a framework or separate interaction responses. Even then, you may not see everything just by looking at the flowline.

This is particularly true if you're using frameworks and navigate icons to control your navigation. You may have a situation where several icons jump to the same page of a framework when they really should jump to different pages. You can open and inspect each navigate icon; however, this isn't an easy process. If you've discovered a problem with the way your piece jumps from one icon to another, you should consider using the Connections dialog box to debug your piece.

The Connections dialog box does more than just display connections between pages of frameworks. Many icons (including erase, motion, and display icons) in your piece may have connections to other icons on the flowline. For example, a motion icon is connected to the icon(s) that it moves, and an erase icon is connected to the object(s) that it erases. You also may have a display icon that is connected to a page of a framework, if you're navigating to the page by using a hot-text style.

Using the Connections dialog box, you can immediately find out how all the icons in your piece are connected. The Connections dialog box enables you to display connections between icons, and then go to one of the connected icons on the flowline.

To display the connections between icons:

1. Select the icon whose connections you want to find.

2. Choose Icon > Connections from the Modify menu.

The Connections dialog box appears, as shown in **Figure 18.1**. All the icons currently connected to the icon you've selected appear in the scrolling field in the middle of the dialog box.

View by connection types. ───

Displays connections. ───

Go to selected icon. ───

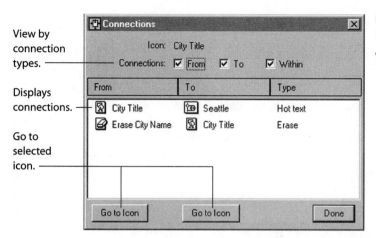

Figure 18.1
The Connections dialog box.

There are several options in this dialog box, which are explained in more detail below:

■ The Icon area shows the title of the icon you've selected.

■ The Connections area has three checkbox options: From, To, and Within. Selecting From shows you connections from the icon; selecting To shows you connections to the icon; and selecting Within shows you connections within a framework structure or a map icon.

■ The scrolling list in the middle of the Connections dialog box displays all connections for the option you've selected (From, To, or Within). When you first open this dialog box, all three options are selected—showing all connections to the current icon. You can select a connection to view by clicking on its name.

■ The Go To buttons at the bottom of the dialog box enable you to jump directly to the connection you've selected in the connections list. Click the Go To button under the From column of the connections list to jump to the From connection. Click the Go To button under the To category to jump to the To connection.

When using the Go To button to jump to a connection, the Connections dialog box remains open, and Authorware highlights the connection icon in the area of the flowline where you have placed it, as shown in **Figure 18.2**.

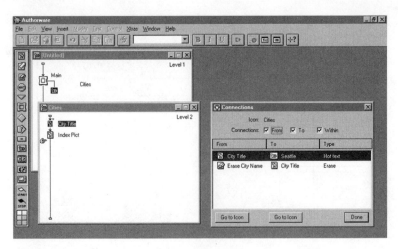

Figure 18.2
Viewing a connection using the Go To button.

Don't be afraid to change things in the piece to see if the change eliminates the problem or gives some result that points to the problem. However, don't trade one problem for another. Change things one at a time and then change them back if the change doesn't fix the problem. If you introduce too many changes before solving a problem, you may not determine the original problem—and, you may even introduce new ones.

If you haven't found the problem, try recreating the section from scratch in a new file. Don't copy and paste icons from the old flowline—you may just copy the problem.

Recreating the section enables you to reconstruct the logic at its most basic level and to verify that Authorware is working as expected. If the section that you recreate still doesn't work properly, chances are that there is something wrong in the logic for the section.

If the section that you re-create works properly, compare that section to the original piece to see where they differ. You also can place the new section into the original piece to see whether this corrects the problem by saving it as a model and then paste it into the original piece.

Tracing the flowline

In previous chapters, you worked with the Trace field of the Control Panel window when checking to see if variables in a piece were being assigned the correct values. However, you also can use the Trace field and the additional controls in the Control Panel window to simplify troubleshooting your piece in several ways:

- You can use the Control Panel controls to step over sections of the flowline to isolate a problem. For example, if you step over a map icon, Authorware executes the icons in the map but pauses when it hits the next icon in the flowline. When doing this, the Trace field generates a list of icons in the order in which they were executed. You'll see how this happens in more detail later in this section.

- You also can use the Control Panel to step into specific icons in the flowline. This is especially useful for studying interaction and decision icons. For example, if you step into an interaction, the piece enters the interaction and then waits for a response. When one occurs, the flow branches to the icon attached to the response type and pauses before the attached icon. Once again, the Trace field generates a list of icons that have been executed, allowing you to see clearly what is happening in the flowline.

- As mentioned earlier, the Trace field displays messages generated by the Trace system function. This is useful for tracking what happens to variables by reporting the values they contain as the piece runs.

You can access the Control Panel window by choosing Control Panel from the Window menu, or by clicking the Control Panel button on the toolbar. When the Control Panel window opens, several buttons will display that enable you to pause, proceed, or run the piece from the flag, as shown in **Figure 18.3**. These provide the same functionality as the Pause, Proceed, and Restart commands on the Control menu.

Figure 18.3
The Control Panel window buttons.

buttons from left to right:
Restart, Reset, Stop, Pause, Play, Show Trace

You already may have had a chance to look at the way the Control Panel window buttons work, if you've been exploring Authorware's features on your own. It's fairly simple to use. Because it displays on top of all other windows, it is useful for starting, pausing, and restarting your piece if you don't want to use the Control menu.

When the Control Panel window is open, you can display the Trace controls by clicking on the Show Trace button of the Control Panel window (see **Figure 18.3**). This displays the Trace control buttons and the Trace field, as shown in **Figure 18.4**.

Restart from Flag

Reset from Flag

Step Over

Step Into

Trace On / Trace Off

Show Invisible Items

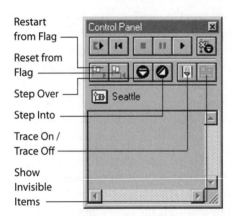

Figure 18.4
The Control Panel window with the Trace controls displayed.

Using the Trace field is particularly useful when you can't tell from looking at the flowline in what order Authorware is executing the icons. It is especially useful when you need to test whether or not Authorware is executing a perpetual interaction or a navigate icon.

To start a trace:

1. Place the start flag in the location where you want to start testing the piece, open the Control Panel window, and click the Show Trace button.

The Trace controls and Trace field appear.

2. Click the Restart from Flag button.

The Trace field updates to show you the icons that Authorware already has executed and the icon Authorware is about to execute, as shown in **Figure 18.5**.

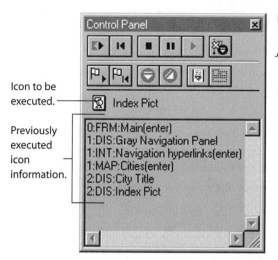

Figure 18.5

Tracing the flowline in the Trace field of the Control Panel window.

Icon to be executed.

Previously executed icon information.

For each icon in the window, Authorware displays the following information:

- The level of the icon's flowline

- The icon type

- The icon title

This information tells you exactly what's happening in the flowline at any given time. In addition, you can use the Trace controls to look at your flowline logic in greater detail. When using the Trace controls, you can step through the current segment of the flowline, see which icon Authorware is about to execute, and keep track of those icons that Authorware already has executed. These controls are explained in greater detail below:

- The Restart from Flag button starts the trace and runs the piece from the start flag's location. If you remove the start flag from the flowline, Authorware replaces this button with the Restart button.

- The Reset from Flag button resets the trace while the piece runs and starts a new trace from the start flag's location. When you remove the start flag from the flowline, Authorware replaces this button with the Reset button.

- The Show Trace button is turned on by default. Use this button to turn off the display of trace information.

- The Show Invisible Items displays all objects in the Presentation window that are currently hidden from view. These might include hot spots, target areas, or text entry fields. This button option is useful when you need to determine which interaction responses are currently active. When invisible items display, you can click this button to hide them again.

At any time, you can use the Step Over and Step Into buttons to walk through specific sections of the flowline that you have placed into a map icon, or that you have attached to a decision or interaction icon. If you are running a trace and Authorware encounters one of these types of branching structures, you have two options:

- Select the Step Over button if you want Authorware to enter the branching structure and execute sequentially all icons contained in it without pausing.

- Select the Step Into button if you want Authorware to enter the branching structure and execute each icon contained in it one by one.

NOTE If you have elected to pause at an interaction or a decision icon in which you've selected the Pause Before Branching option, you need to interact with the Presentation window to continue down the flowline.

Tracing return values of expressions

Problems in a piece often occur as a result of incorrect values assigned to a custom variable in one of your scripts. You can't always pinpoint the location of a problem, particularly in a piece that uses many calculation icons; however, you can use the Trace field to help you track down the cause of the problem. You've already worked with this feature a bit in previous chapters.

Because the Trace field displays messages generated by the `Trace` system function, you can use this function to track the value of a variable or variable expression you're using in a script. The `Trace` function automatically displays a message that shows you the current value of the expression you've specified in the argument for the `Trace` function. For instance, if you want to see what the value of `Tries` is in an interaction, you can attach the following script to the interaction icon:

```
Trace(Tries)
```

Each time you loop through the interaction, Authorware displays the current value of the system variable `Tries` in the Trace field, as shown in **Figure 18.6**.

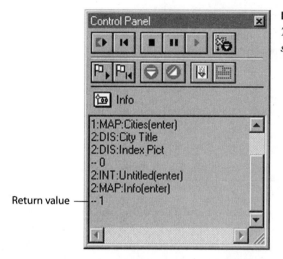

Figure 18.6
Tracing the value of a system function.

To make tracing variables easier, you can include literal character values in the argument for the `Trace` function in the same way that you can include them in any other function. For example, if you want to display the name of the variable you're tracing (in this instance, `Tries`), you could concatenate the name to the variable, as shown below:

```
Trace("Tries=" ^ Tries)
```

This is also a good technique for displaying comments about a particular area of the flowline, along with the relevant system variable that you may be tracking:

```
Trace("This should be the third page of this ¬
framework." ^   Return ^ CurrentPageNum)
```

The above commented line would appear in the Trace field, as shown in **Figure 18.7**.

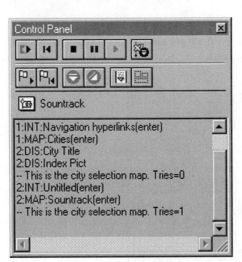

Figure 18.7
The commented line, as it appears in the Trace field.

TIP You don't always need to use the Trace function to check the values of the variable expressions you're using. A quick way to do this is to run the piece with the Variables window open, and then look at the current value for the variable you're using. This is particularly helpful when determining the value returned by a function. For more information about using the Variables window, see Chapter 14, "Using Functions and Variables."

Another useful way to track the values of variables and variable expressions is to create a debugging display icon and embed the name of the variable or the variable expression you want to view. Make sure, however, that you select the Update Displayed Variables option for the display icon. For more information about embedding variable expressions in display icons, see Chapter 14, "Using Functions and Variables."

Did someone say, "Help?"

If you've been working on a problem for some time and can't find a solution, it may be time to ask for some help. Help can come in many forms: another person you're working with on the project, the documentation and example files that ship with Authorware, a Macromedia technical support representative, or one of the many help resources available to you on the Internet.

TIP You'll find a complete list of where to go for help and information on using Authorware in Appendix C, "Authorware Resources on the Internet."

Remember that anyone you ask for help is probably less familiar with the piece than you are. You can help the person help you by having certain information available:

■ A brief description of the problem and the specific text of any error messages you received. Describe the problem accurately and create a concise problem statement that will help the other person zero-in on a solution faster.

■ A brief list of the steps you already have taken while trying to solve the problem. This might include steps you've taken while working in Authorware, or while checking the hardware or software configuration of the system on which you're testing the piece.

In addition, if you're troubleshooting an issue that you think may be hardware or software-related, try to have the following information gathered about the computer system on which you're testing the piece:

■ The platform (e.g., Windows or Macintosh) and type of system you are using.

■ The amount of memory and hard disk space installed on the system.

■ The type of video card installed.

■ The video resolution (i.e. 8-bit, 16-bit, 24-bit) at which you are testing the piece.

■ The operating system version number.

■ The type of networking software and web software installed on the machine—if you're troubleshooting an issue with a Shockwave piece.

Most importantly, if you recreate the problem section in a new file and it still doesn't work, keep the new file on your hard disk so that you can send it to the person helping you.

Putting Troubleshooting into Practice

Although it's impossible to predict every type of problem that may arise while creating a piece, you can benefit greatly from learning basic, reliable, troubleshooting techniques to detect and solve problems. While previous sections in this chapter have mentioned several techniques for isolating and fixing problems, you don't get a feel for how to use these techniques until you have your own problem and need to solve it.

This section looks at some examples of common issues that all Authorware developers face from time to time. It then gives you some advice on how you can solve these issues by using common troubleshooting techniques.

TIP Many additional technical notes on troubleshooting issues with Authorware are available at the Macromedia web site in the Authorware support area (**http://www.macromedia.com/support/authorware/**).

Troubleshooting Issue: Imported graphics appear discolored

The graphics that I've imported into Authorware don't look like they do in the application that created them. They appear blotchy or irregularly colored when I look at them in the Presentation window.

Problems with imported graphics are a common issue that you will come across soon—if you haven't already. One of three things may cause this problem:

- There could be a problem with the original file that you imported.
- There could be a palette conflict between Authorware and the graphic you imported.
- There could be a problem with the way you have configured your video display hardware or software.

To troubleshoot this issue, try the following steps:

1. Check the graphic.

Open the graphic in the program in which it was created; save a new copy of it; and make sure that you've selected the correct file format and file extension for the file—especially if you are working on the Windows platform.

To make sure that you've saved a graphic in the correct format, try opening BMP or DIB files in Paint (Windows) or PICT files in SimpleText (Macintosh). If you can't open the image in one of these applications, the graphic probably was saved in the wrong format.

NOTE You can use Netscape Navigator or Microsoft Internet Explorer to test any GIF or JPEG images that you want to import into Authorware. However, keep in mind that Authorware does not currently support the animated GIF, transparent GIF, or progressive JPEG file formats.

After saving a new copy of the graphic and testing it in another application to make sure that it opens correctly, reimport it into a new display icon in your Authorware piece. If it still looks wrong, continue following the steps listed below.

2. Check for a palette conflict.

When you create a new piece, it automatically uses the default system palette for the platform on which you're developing. As mentioned in Chapter 2, "Beginning a Piece," this palette consists of the set of 256 colors that the operating system uses to display bitmapped graphics on screen.

TIP If you do a lot of cross-platform development, you may want to stick with the Macintosh system palette for all your images because it tends to produce more accurate color dithering for 8-bit images across platforms.

However, in order for your image to look the same in Authorware as it looks in your graphics editing tool, make sure that you dither it to either the Windows or the Macintosh system palette before saving it. This is a built-in option for most graphics editing tools (including xRes, Photoshop, and Debabelizer).

If your 8-bit image looks different in Authorware, chances are you've saved it by using a custom palette. For it to appear correctly, you can either resave it after dithering the image to the system palette, or you can use the custom palette in your piece. See Chapter 19, "Using Director Interactively," for more information about working with custom palettes inside Authorware.

NOTE Many times, an image appears discolored or pixelated in Authorware because you've imported it as a 24-bit image—when your machine is running in 256 colors. In this case, either dither the image to the appropriate color depth, or change the color depth of your video display by using the Display control panel (Windows), or the Monitors control panel (Macintosh).

3. Check your system's hardware and software configuration.

Occasionally, you may have a problem with the way you have set up your video hardware or software on your system. On Windows computers, the display driver may not work properly with Authorware. On the Macintosh computer, there may be a conflict with an extension from another application.

The following are some ways to test whether you have a hardware or software conflict:

Platform...	Try these tests...
Windows	Quit all applications. Open the Display control panel and change your current display adapter setting to the standard Microsoft SVGA setting. (If you're unsure how to do this, use the Microsoft Help Wizard to walk you through the process.) After restarting your computer, open Authorware again and look at the image. If the image appears correctly in standard SVGAmode, you most likely have a conflict with the installed custom display driver. Contact the display card manufacturer for an updated version of the driver.
Macintosh	Quit all applications. Disable extensions by restarting and holding down the Shift key as extensions load. Open Authorware again and look at the image. If the image appears correctly, one of your extensions may conflict with Authorware. Use the Extensions Manager control panel to load your extensions one at a time to see which one is causing the problem, and then discontinue using the extension until you can get an updated version of it to use.

Troubleshooting Issue: A movie doesn't play when you click a button

I've created an interaction wherein I want the user to click on a button to play a QuickTime movie. When I test the piece and click the button, a dialog box appears that asks me to locate the movie.

1. Start by looking at how you have set up the movie's path and file name.

   When Authorware cannot locate an external movie, the Movie Icon Properties dialog box appears, asking you to locate it. So you can assume that the movie is at another location on your hard disk, or the path you are using to point to the location of your movie is incorrect. More likely it's the path to the movie—especially if you are using a variable expression to point to the location of the movie file.

   You can quickly check your hard disk to determine whether you've mistakenly moved the external movie to a different folder. If you find that it's in the same place where you last copied it, do some additional testing to find out why Authorware cannot locate it. If it has been moved, you can use the Import button in the

Movie Icon Properties dialog box to quickly relink the movie file to the movie icon, or you can open the External Media Browser and update the movie link using the Browse button.

2. If your movie is in the correct location, see what type of path you're using to point to the movie. As mentioned in Chapter 17, "Distributing Your Piece," it's usually best to use a relative path for the movie. If you open the Movie Icon Properties dialog box and see a literal path entered in the File slot, you can type in a new relative path to relink the movie.

NOTE If Authorware cannot find the movie using the relative path you've typed into the File slot, a separate dialog box appears that tells you it cannot locate the movie you've specified.

3. If you are using a variable path that has been assigned in the External Media Browser window, run the piece from the beginning to set the movie's path, and then open the External Media Browser window to view the current value of the expression. Most likely, your variable expression points to the wrong folder or file name. If this is the case, check the script in which you are assigning a value to the path expression. You might also need to reposition the script on the flowline so that the path is correctly updated before Authorware executes the movie icon.

This type of problem typically happens when running a packaged piece on another computer's hard disk or CD-ROM drive. Make sure that you've included the correct external movie drivers in the same location as the executable file (if you've packaged the piece with the run-time player), or in the same location as RunA4W or RunA4M (if you've packaged the piece without the run-time player). For more information on which drivers to include with external movies, see Chapter 17, "Distributing Your Piece."

■ If you only notice this problem after packaging your piece, make sure that you've included the correct movie folder name with your packaged files. Authorware must be able to find it by using either the relative path you've assigned the movie, or by using the search path settings you've specified. For more information on setting up the search path for your piece, see Chapter 2, "Beginning a Piece."

■ If you want to play an external movie file in a Shockwave piece, make sure that you have included the name of the movie in the Shockwave piece's map file. This is so that Authorware can locate it on the web server and download it when needed. You also need to make sure that you've copied the movie file to the web server where you have your shocked piece stored. This information is covered in more detail in Chapter 17, "Distributing Your Piece."

Troubleshooting Issue: The calculated decision path does not match correctly

I've created a calculated decision path that is supposed to branch to one of two icons when the piece hits it. However, each time I run the piece, Authorware goes to the second branch path.

Because you're using a calculated decision path, your first inclination may be to look at the way you've set up the variable expression inside the decision icon. In cases where you are using a variable expression to control branching, this is a smart decision. The smallest change in the way you've set up your variable expression can cause the problem described above.

1. Open the decision icon and look at the variable expression you're using. If you've placed the name of a variable in the Branching field, you can use the Variables window to check the value of the variable while the piece runs.

Restart the piece with the Variables window open. When you get to the point in the flowline where Authorware hits the calculated decision path, take a look at the current value of the variable you are using.

If you're using a custom variable to select the decision path, and it's assigned the incorrect value, check the calculation script where you have assigned the decision path.

If you're using a system variable to select the decision path, you may not be able to assign it a new value. In this case, your best option is to change the variable expression you are using in the decision icon.

2. However, you may be using a more complex variable expression to assign the calculated decision path. For example, you may be using the `Test` system function within a calculated decision path to branch to one of the two navigate icons—depending on the value of the custom variable `LessonsComplete`. The correct form for this type of expression is shown below:

```
Test(LessonsComplete=2, 1, 2)
```

In the example above, a calculated path of 1 is assigned to the decision path if `LessonsComplete` equals 2. If `LessonsComplete` does not equal 2, then a calculated path of 2 is assigned to the decision path. When using the `Test` function, a common mistake is to use the assignment (:=) operator in place of the equal sign in this type of expression:

```
Test(LessonsComplete:=2, 1, 2)
```

What you end up with is a calculated decision path that always branches to the second icon attached to the calculated path. Change the variable expression, and then restart the piece to test it again.

NOTE For more information about using the `Test` system function, see *Using Authorware* or Authorware Help.

Looking Ahead...

Trying to create a "bug-free" multimedia piece can be a lesson in futility. However, you should always try to make your piece as "bug-proof" as possible by using a common-sense approach to testing before you send the piece out the door. In this chapter, you learned some common techniques for isolating problems that you may encounter in your piece. You also saw some ways you can use troubleshooting techniques to narrow down the cause of a problem when testing your piece.

Learning to troubleshoot problems ahead of time is an invaluable step toward creating sophisticated applications that perform the way you've envisioned them. You need to be good at this when you start adding additional external functionality to your piece to handle more complex types of interactivity. One of the ways you can do this is to incorporate interactive Director movies into your piece. In Chapter 19, "Using Director Interactively," you will learn how to add Director functionality to your piece to expand the types of multimedia content that you can deliver.

Using Director Interactively

With Authorware, you can integrate Macromedia Director movies into a piece, allowing you to combine the capabilities of both tools to create more sophisticated approaches to delivering multimedia content. Because Authorware enables you to interact with Director movies in the same way you would if they were delivered as a stand-alone "projector" or a Shockwave movie, you can use Director to create more complex interactivity in your piece. At other times, you may find that a piece of animation is too difficult to create in Authorware, so you can take advantage of Director's strengths in this area.

Working with Director movies can be a mixed blessing because it requires that you not only learn how to work efficiently with Director, but also learn how to manage the additional performance and delivery overhead that a Director movie requires. While this chapter does not specifically discuss how to create Director movies, you do learn the basic techniques for integrating Director movies. This chapter also discusses issues you may confront before distributing Director movies with your final packaged piece.

When designing your piece, consider the advantages and disadvantages that Director movies bring to the table. Traditionally, Director is used for creating multimedia that relies heavily on animation synchronized with sound. It is also an extremely powerful tool for creating complex interactivity when you need to simulate real-world behavior of objects. Scripts you write in Lingo (Director's scripting language) handle the movie's interactivity.

NOTE This chapter focuses on using Director with Authorware. However, you are encouraged to spend some time with Director and create some simple Director movies before you begin working with the techniques discussed here. If you have questions on any of the Director terms mentioned in this chapter, refer to *Using Director,* part of the documentation included with Director.

Unlike Authorware, Director does not rely on icons to control the functionality and presentation of a Director movie. With Director, its scripting language controls functionality and presentation, so you need to know a bit about Lingo before you begin creating even simple interactivity. Authorware allows you to create simple interactivity rather quickly—without knowing a scripting language. (However, as you've seen in the examples in this book, you will get much farther down the road if you know how to utilize calculation icon scripts in your piece.)

Despite these differences, Director and Authorware can achieve many of the same results when creating multimedia content. However, you can get the most from both applications by having each one do the jobs that each one does best. Overall, it's best to use Authorware to implement features that either application performs. Rely on Director to do the things Authorware can't do or doesn't do well.

For example, Authorware excels at tracking user responses; one of Director's strengths is synchronizing sound with animation. Say that you are creating a piece that lets users choose from a set of animals; then it shows how the animal moves (e.g., crawling, walking, or twisting). In such a situation, you may want to create the interaction in Authorware, but use Director to simulate the animal in motion.

TIP You also could use Director to create the animation, and then export it from Director as a QuickTime or Video for Windows (AVI) movie. This would help improve playback performance of your piece when delivering on CD-ROM or the Internet.

The following are some of Director's core strengths:

- Animation—Director is noted for its capability to create animation efficiently and precisely, using its set of "tweening" and auto-animate features.

- Sound—Director can play two simultaneous sounds on Windows computers and up to eight simultaneous sounds on Macintosh computers. Director also gives you built-in sound volume control.

- Synchronizing sound and graphics—Director's timeline-based Score window provides more precision when synchronizing sound and graphics in a piece.

- Control through Lingo—Lingo gives you control of objects such as sprites, sound, and other movie components. For example, with Lingo, sprite size and location can change in response to some user action, or you can create a series of additional objects with real-world behaviors (e.g., objects that flock together, or bounce from side to side) through the use of parent scripts.

The following are some of Authorware's core strengths:

- Setting up interactivity—Authorware's interaction response types enable you to set up a variety of interactions quickly, using a set of built-in properties.

- Navigation and hyperlinking—Authorware's built-in framework, navigation, and hot text features make creating large hypertextual pieces much easier.

- Tracking user responses and scoring—Authorware's set of system functions, system variables, and response judging options enable you to track the user throughout an entire piece.

- External data storage and retrieval—Authorware's set of file system functions enable you to easily store and retrieve data external to your piece. Authorware also ships with a set of ODBC custom functions, which allows you to communicate with database software running in the background of a piece. For more information on using the ODBC custom functions, see Chapter 20, "Developing with External Code."

Use Director movies in your piece when it makes sense—that is, take advantage of Director's set of features if you can't accomplish the same thing in Authorware.

In Authorware, there are two ways to play a Director movie: by placing a movie icon at the appropriate place on the flowline, or by using the MediaPlay system function to play the movie from another position in the flowline.

TIP You can find information about working with the movie icon in Chapter 5, "Adding Sound and Video." Chapter 15, "Controlling the Flowline through Scripting," covers the media system functions in more detail.

The movie icon controls much of a Director movie's behavior when Authorware plays the movie. For example, the movie icon controls where the movie appears on screen, whether the Director movie repeats, and which frames of the movie play. The movie icon also controls whether you use the interactivity included in the Director movie. To allow interactivity to work for the Director movie, you need to turn on this option in Authorware:

1. Open the movie icon that you have linked to your Director movie.

The Movie Icon Properties dialog box appears.

2. Select On for the Interactivity option, as shown in **Figure 19.1**.

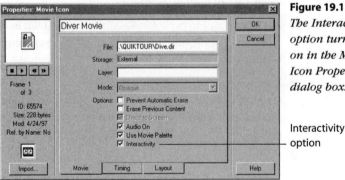

Figure 19.1
The Interactivity option turned on in the Movie Icon Properties dialog box.

Interactivity option

This turns on interactivity for the current Director movie.

NOTE This option is initially turned on when importing the Director movie into the movie icon.

When you have turned on the interactivity for a Director movie, most of the Director movie's Lingo elements work (except those listed in "Lingo not supported by Authorware" below) when the movie plays inside the Presentation window. Besides making the movie interactive for the user, this setting enables you to take advantage of Lingo's capability to precisely control movie components such as sprites, sound, palettes, and transitions.

For example, a Lingo script that you've included in the Director movie (which jumps the movie to frame 50 when the user click a button) continues to function in the same manner as it would when created in Director. However, unless you turn on the interactivity for the movie inside the movie icon, the same script won't work when the movie plays inside Authorware.

NOTE When working with the movie icon, you cannot set the Director movie to play in reverse—that is, from the end frame to the start frame.

When developing your piece, you frequently should ask yourself whether or not you can provide the same type of functionality for the user inside Authorware. In the above example, for instance, you can control the current frame of the Director movie through Authorware without actually turning on the interactivity option for the movie by using a variable expression to control the current frame that the movie icon is playing. Chapter 5, "Adding Sound and Video," covers this technique in more detail.

NOTE Lingo scripts in the Director movie work only when Authorware runs the piece. The Director movie's interactivity is turned off when Authorware pauses, when you preview the movie, or when the Movie Icon Properties dialog box is open.

Handling mouse and keyboard interactivity

When an interactive Director movie runs inside Authorware, the Authorware piece and the Director piece both can respond to mouse and keyboard interactivity. Authorware passes any mouse or keyboard events happening in the area of the Director movie to the Director movie itself.

For instance, if the user clicks a button created in Authorware, Authorware responds by displaying the feedback you've added to the button response. If the user clicks a button inside the Director movie, it lets Director handle the response.

Director movies always appear in front of everything else in the Presentation window. Any Authorware objects behind the movie appear to flash through the movie, unless the objects are assigned to a layer number of 0. Avoid problems by making sure that no Authorware objects are behind the movie, or by assigning these objects the lowest layer number in the object's Effects dialog box.

NOTE Be careful not to place any responses in the same area as the Director movie because the Director movie displays on top of everything else in the Presentation window, and the user cannot interact with your response.

Likewise, Authorware and Director both support text entry; however, only one of them can have text entry objects active at a time. A text insertion bar in the text entry object indicates which object is active. If you've placed a text entry field in the Presentation window at the same time that an interactive Director movie that contains a text entry field displays, the user must click between the two. In general, you should try to avoid this situation because it may confuse the user.

If you're using keypress responses or optional keys for a response in your Authorware piece, these features continue to function while the Director movie runs. Authorware takes priority for all keypress events in the piece. Because custom menus that you've included in a Director movie are not active when Authorware plays the movie, the user only can use custom menus that you have set up inside the Authorware piece.

NOTE When the mouse is over the Director movie, Director controls the cursor. As soon as the mouse moves out of the Director movie, Authorware regains control.

Quitting a Director movie

In some cases, you may use a Director movie to play only a sequence of animation, and then erase it from the screen. This is easy to set up. You simply set the movie icon's Play option to Wait Until Done, and then include an erase icon on the flowline that erases the movie.

However, when playing the Director movie inside the Authorware piece concurrently with other types of Authorware interactions, you need to include some type of functionality in your piece that erases the Director movie from the screen at the appropriate time. Usually, this is accomplished by including some type of interaction response inside the Authorware piece that the user selects to close the Director movie. For example, if you have a button that plays the movie, you can include a button that erases the Director movie as well.

NOTE When Authorware plays a Director movie, it ignores the Lingo commands `quit`, `restart`, and `shutDown`. Even if you've included these commands in your Director movie, you still need to erase the movie from the screen inside Authorware to close it.

In special instances where you are running a full-screen Director movie inside Authorware, interaction responses created in Authorware do not work because Director controls the entire Presentation window. Aside from the performance problems, this is another reason why you should avoid using full-screen Director movies.

However, if needed, you can include a decision icon loop in your Authorware piece to get feedback from the Director movie to determine whether or not the movie should erase. For an example of how to set up this type of functionality in your piece, see the Authorware Technote "Quitting Director Movies in Authorware," which is available in the Authorware support area of the Macromedia web site (**http://www.macromedia.com/support/authorware/ts/documents/**).

Adjusting Director Movies to Work in Authorware

Because many developers create content using Director, it makes sense to use this type of content in its original format without repurposing it. However, you may need to redo portions of a Director movie so it can play in Authorware successfully.

A couple of the problems that you may encounter when using a Director movie in Authorware are memory demands and the loading times for the portions of your piece that use Director movies. This is because you are running two separate executable files at the same time: the Authorware application and the application that controls playback of Director movies.

Consequently, performance issues tend to be the greatest deterrent to using large Director movies inside Authorware. You can overcome performance issues if you learn to work around limitations by making your Director movies smaller and easier to manage inside Authorware.

TIP Not every Director movie can run inside Authorware. If you want to deliver full-screen Director movies with lots of sound and video inside Authorware, you may find that this simply isn't possible on most machine configurations. In this case, you can go with either Director or Authorware—if you have the time to recreate the movie inside your Authorware piece.

The next few sections explore some of the problem areas that all developers face when utilizing Director-created content in Authorware. Keep this in mind as you begin to explore ways of integrating Director into your Authorware piece.

Controlling cross-platform playback issues

There are several differences in how a Director movie plays back in Authorware on the Windows platform as opposed to the Macintosh platform. These differences are explained in more detail below:

- In Windows, the Director movie's background appears the same as it does in Director. (This background is called the "stage" in Director.) The movie forms an opaque rectangle that covers everything underneath it—much like a QuickTime or AVI movie.

- On Macintosh systems, the Director movie's background becomes invisible when you bring the movie into Authorware, allowing the objects underneath the movie to show through. If you want the movie to appear the same as it does on the Windows platform, you must create a rectangular sprite in your Director movie that covers the entire size of the stage, and then insert it into each frame of your movie. (For more information on working with Director sprites, see *Using Director.*)

In addition to the background color issue, the two platforms handle sound playback differently:

- In Windows, only one application at a time can play sound. When no sound is playing, the sound channel is available for either Authorware or Director to start playing sound. When one application is playing sound, it has control over the sound channel until the sound finishes playing.

- On Macintosh systems, both Authorware and Director can play sound simultaneously.

If you plan to distribute the same Director movie and Authorware piece on both platforms, design your piece with these limitations in mind. The sound issue can cause problems when testing your piece on different hardware configurations. In general, try to avoid playing sound icons in the background of your piece, if you want the Director movie to play sound. This includes sounds that you've used for button clicks, as well as sounds that accompany the animation in your Director movie.

NOTE Authorware and Director maintain completely independent font mapping schemes. The mapping that you set up in the Authorware piece and the Director movie have no effect on each other.

Breaking a movie into smaller pieces

To improve performance in Authorware, it is recommended that Director movies not exceed 1MB. If you have a large Director movie that you want to play, break it into a set of smaller movies and distribute the group of movies with your piece.

If you need to play your movies in sequence at the same time, you can link them together using the play movie and play done Lingo commands in Director. For more information on these Lingo commands, see *Lingo Dictionary* or Director Help (which are included with Director). If you don't need the movies to play in sequence at the same time, you can simply play each smaller movie using a separate movie icon.

Controlling movie tempos and pauses

When importing a Director movie into Authorware, Authorware automatically defaults to playing the Director movie at the same tempo setting that you've saved when creating the movie. (In Authorware and Director, the movie rate is specified in frames-per-second.) However, if you've included tempo changes in the score of your movie, Authorware attempts to match these as closely as possible.

NOTE If you're playing back the Director movie on a system with a slower processor, you may not get accurate synching of sound and animation at a tempo setting much higher than 15 frames-per-second.

For example, if you have saved the Director movie with a tempo setting of 15 frames-per-second, then Authorware uses this value initially to play the movie at 15 frames-per-second. If the Director movie encounters a 1 frame-per-second setting in its tempo channel, the movie's tempo changes to 1 frame-per-second. Likewise, subsequent tempo settings become the movie's settings when they are encountered.

NOTE Tempo changes performed by the Lingo command puppetTempo work as long as you've turned on interactivity for the movie inside the Authorware movie icon. For more information on using this Lingo command, see *Lingo Dictionary* or Director Help.

The Wait For options in Director's tempo channel (which include Wait for Mouse Click or Key, Wait for Sound to Finish, and Wait for Digital Video Movie to Finish) have no effect when the movie plays within Authorware. If you're using these options to control timing of events in your Director movie, you may want to redo portions of the score using Lingo instead.

For example, you can set up the following `exitFrame` handler in a frame of your movie to pause the movie on the current frame until a sound in Sound Channel 1 finishes playing:

```
on exitFrame
  if soundBusy(1) then go to the frame
end
```

NOTE For more information on using Lingo to control presentation in your movie, see *Using Director*.

You also need to give special consideration to the ways you exit or pause your Director movie. When you use the `pause` Lingo command in the same frame that you have set in the End Frame field of the Movie Icon Properties dialog box, Authorware assumes that the Director movie is finished and stops it. Because of this issue, you should try to use the `go to the frame` Lingo command to pause a movie in the current frame.

Getting around palette issues

Many Director developers—who want the best possible look for their movies—tend to use multiple custom palettes in their movies. However, you soon find out that this can cause many problems when you bring the movie into Authorware.

If you deliver the piece on a system running in 256 colors, the screen goes through many contortions as it tries to adjust to each new palette that appears in the Director movie. This problem, known as "palette shifting," can give the person sitting on the other side of the screen a supreme headache. For this reason, you should limit your Director movie to one common palette. You must incorporate this same custom palette into your Authorware piece if you plan to deliver to end users who run systems in 256 colors.

NOTE There are always two sides to every issue. You don't see palette shifting issues on machines running in 16-bit color or higher. If you insist on using multiple custom palettes with a Director movie (or an Authorware piece), you should seriously consider changing your minimum system requirements to reflect the higher color depth.

In cases where you need very accurate color reproduction for graphics in your piece, you can use a graphics editing tool to save all your graphics using a single custom palette; then import this palette into Authorware before you import your Director movie. (Director automatically gives you the option to add a graphic's custom palette to your movie.) Save any graphics you're using in Authorware in the same custom palette. This is the only way to prevent the palette shifting problem.

You can use a tool like Debabelizer when working with graphics and palettes. This utility enables you to create a "super palette" for your images by taking a sample of the colors in each separate image and then averaging them into a single "super palette," which produces the best color dithering.

Before you can play a Director movie with a custom palette in an Authorware piece, you need to load the custom palette into the Authorware piece. To do this, you simply select one of the graphics you've saved previously using this custom palette.

NOTE In order for this procedure to work, you must save your graphic in a .BMP or a .PCT format.

To load a custom palette into your piece:

1. Choose File > Palette from the Modify menu.

The Palette dialog box appears, as shown in **Figure 19.2**. This dialog box shows you Authorware's default system palette (if you have not loaded a custom palette into your piece).

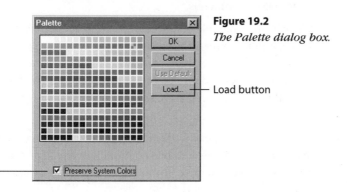

Figure 19.2
The Palette dialog box.

Load button

Preserve System Colors option

2. Deselect the Preserve System Colors option, if you want to use all the colors available in the custom palette. Leave this option checked if you want Authorware to continue to display system buttons, toolbars, and menus using the default system colors.

NOTE Deselecting this option can cause problems with the way your Authorware menus and controls display while in Authoring mode, if you are working in 256 colors.

3. Click the Load button, and then open the graphic file that contains the custom palette you want to import.

This replaces your current default palette with the custom palette.

NOTE All of your custom buttons and graphics remap to this custom palette when you import them into Authorware. Because of this, it's important that you save all your graphics using this custom palette before you import them into Authorware.

TIP In special instances where you need to use multiple custom palettes inside an Authorware piece, you can rely on the `SetPalette` system function included with Authorware 4. This function enables you to dynamically change the current palette while the piece runs. For more information on using this function, see *Using Authorware* or Authorware Help.

Unsupported Director features

As mentioned earlier, there are several features of Director that Authorware does not support when running your movie:

- Custom menus in a Director movie don't appear and have no effect when the movie plays within Authorware. Consider using a pull-down menu interaction in Authorware to recreate custom Director menus.

- When Authorware plays a Director movie that uses the `open window` and `close window` Lingo commands to play a Director movie in a window, the main movie plays, but the movie in a window does not. (For more information about using these Lingo commands, see *Using Director* or Director Help.)

  You often can work around this by extracting the movie that is in the window and then controlling it directly from Authorware. For example, if you've created a larger Director movie that lets users run and explore several smaller Director movies that run in a window, you should recreate the interface for the larger movie inside Authorware, and then play the smaller movies using the movie icon.

Can I play shocked Director movies in Authorware?

Director movies have become a standardized way to deliver multimedia content—especially on the World Wide Web. Many web developers are using Director to create tiny (20–30K) movies that add animation to their web pages.

When you compress a Director movie for playback with the Shockwave for Director Plug-In, it is saved with a .DCR file extension. Since Authorware only looks for Director movies with a .DIR (unprotected) or .DXR (protected) file extension, your shocked Director movie does not appear in the list of files when you try to import it through the movie icon.

However, using the following quick workaround, you can integrate a shocked Director movie into your piece:

1. Shock your Director movie using the Afterburner Xtra that ships with Director.

This creates a compressed Director movie with a .DCR file extension.

2. Make a copy of this file, and then change its .DCR extension to .DXR.

NOTE This is the extension that Director uses to save protected movies (ones that you cannot open and edit). Make sure that you don't rename the movie with a .DIR extension because this replaces the original Director movie, and you cannot make changes to it.

3. Open the movie icon in your piece and import the movie with the .DXR extension.

When Afterburner creates a .DCR file, it simply saves the Director movie after compressing its graphics and sounds. The movie still functions the same way as the original Director movie, except that it is much smaller. Using shocked Director movies enables you to save space when distributing your final Authorware piece as either a stand-alone piece or a Shockwave piece. Afterburner typically compresses a Director movie to 40 percent of its original size.

However, you still need to save the original .DCR file if you plan to embed it in an HTML document. For more information about working with Shockwave for Director, see the technical notes available on Macromedia's web site in the Shockwave support area (**http://www.macromedia.com/support/director/how/shock/**).

TIP You also can integrate shocked Director movies into your 32-bit Windows piece using the ActiveX Xtra and the ActiveX control for Director for Shockwave. See Chapter 20, "Developing with External Code," for more information on using the ActiveX Xtra.

While it may seem like there are a great number of issues to take into consideration when using Director in a piece, you should consider using some aspects of Director to enhance the presentation of your ideas.

Communicating with Director Movies

When using Director interactive movies with Authorware, you can control how the movie plays inside your piece by using Authorware's Lingo functions. Using the Lingo functions included with Authorware, you can send Lingo instructions to the movie and get feedback from the movie. In order to do this, you need to load the Lingo functions into your piece.

NOTE This is the same process that you would perform when loading any other custom function into your piece. Chapter 20, "Developing with External Code," covers loading custom functions.

The Lingo functions are included in the driver files named A4DIR32.XMO (32-bit Windows) and Director (Macintosh). The Windows driver is located in the same folder where you installed Authorware; the Macintosh driver is included in the folder called Director Folder, which was created inside the Authorware folder when you installed Authorware.

NOTE If you plan to distribute an Authorware piece to users running Windows 3.1, you must distribute the A4DIR.XMO file along with your piece if you use any of the Lingo functions described in the next several sections. The A4DIR.XMO file is included in the list of Director movie driver files in "Distributing Director Movies with Your Piece."

The following sections describe the four Lingo functions included with Authorware.

Using `LingoTell`

The custom function LingoTell sends a Lingo string to a Director movie that is playing within Authorware. After the movie executes the Lingo string, the function returns an error code indicating what has happened. The syntax for the LingoTell function looks like this:

```
errorCode := LingoTell(IconID@IconTitle, "Lingo")
```

The variable `errorCode` represents the error code returned by the movie. When its value is 0, no error occurred. Values other than 0 indicate an error. (The `LingoError` function, which is described in the next section, can help determine the meaning of the error code.) The function has two arguments:

Argument...	What you should include...
IconID@IconTitle	The ID of the digital movie icon that plays the Director movie.
Lingo	The Lingo statement sent to the movie. The Director movie defines either a complete statement or the name of a handler.

TIP When the Lingo statement includes quotation marks ("), place a backslash (\) before each quotation mark so that Authorware distinguishes it from the quotation marks used by the `LingoTell` function.

For example, the following calculation icon expression sends the Lingo statement `soundplayFile 1, "Elvis"` to the movie in the digital movie icon named JukeBox:

```
errorCode := LingoTell(@"JukeBox", "sound ¬
playFile 1, \"Elvis\"")
```

This type of `LingoTell` expression would result in the Director movie playing the sound you've specified in Lingo statement. If Authorware cannot pass this Lingo statement to the Director movie, a value other than 0 is assigned to the custom variable `errorCode`. The section on using the `LingoResult` function explains how to translate this error code into a character string that explains the problem to you in more detail.

NOTE Lingo statements that you send using `LingoTell` need to specify any arguments that you should include when calling the handler. For more information on using handlers in Director, see *Using Director* or Director Help.

Using `LingoResult`

`LingoResult` retrieves the result of the last Lingo statement that was sent to a Director movie by the LingoTell function. The syntax of `LingoResult` looks like this:

```
result := LingoResult(IconID@IconTitle)
```

The argument `IconID@IconTitle` represents the title of the digital movie icon for the Director movie that received the Lingo string sent by `LingoTell`. The expression assigns a value to the name of the variable that replaces `result`. You can use the `return` Lingo command in your Lingo script handler to return a specific value to Authorware when you call one of the movie's handlers using `LingoTell`.

For example, you might set up the following Lingo handler in a Director movie to set the sound level of the movie while it runs and then plays a sound:

```
on PlaySound level
    set the soundLevel to level
    puppetSound "Trumpet Blast"
    updateStage
    return level
end
```

This Lingo handler sets the sound level of the movie to the value contained in the argument `level`, plays the sound named Trumpet Blast, and then returns the value of `level` so that you can quickly see the sound level for the movie.

If you were to play this Director movie through a movie icon named Jazz Movie, you could use the `LingoTell` function to quickly mute the sound the Director movie is playing; then use the `LingoResult` function to determine if Director executed the handler.

To do this, you could include the following expression in a calculation icon:

```
errorCode := LingoTell(@"Jazz Movie", "PlaySound 0")
result := LingoResult(@"Jazz Movie")
```

Notice that you've included a value for the `level` argument for the `SoundLevel` handler inside the Lingo statement you're sending to the movie. In some cases, you may need to include multiple arguments for your `LingoTell` statement. To do this, just include comments between each argument, as shown below:

```
errorCode := LingoTell(IconID@IconTitle, ¬
"Statement arg1, arg2, arg3,...")
```

This is actually a technique that can give you more control over the Director movie through Authorware. Take the last example, for instance. Not only can you assign a sound level to the movie, you can tell the movie which sound to play. To do this, you need to modify both the Lingo handler inside the Director movie and the `LingoTell` expression inside Authorware.

For example, you could make the following change to your Lingo handler:

```
on PlaySound level, whichSound
   set the soundLevel to level
   puppetSound whichSound
   updateStage
   return level
end
```

You could then tell the Director movie to play the sound named Trumpet Blast, at a level of 4, using the following calculation expression:

```
errorCode := LingoTell(@"Jazz Movie", ¬
"PlaySound 4,\"Trumpet Blast\"")

result := LingoResult(@"Jazz Movie")
```

This gives you a great deal more control over how your Director movie runs. It also enables you to have the Director movie respond directly to what is happening in the Authorware piece.

Using `LingoError`

In the example above, you may find that there really isn't a sound in the movie named Trumpet Blast. If you run into a problem when passing a Lingo statement to a Director movie, you can use the `LingoError` function to convert the value of your `errorCode` variable into an error message. The syntax for the `LingoError` function looks like this:

```
string := LingoError(errorCode)
```

The variable `string` represents the descriptive string that is returned; the argument `errorCode` contains the error code that comes from the `LingoTell` function.

For example, error code number 38 indicates that there is a problem with a palette. The following function assigns the variable string a description of error code 38:

```
string := LingoError(38)
```

The value assigned to string is the phrase "Palette not defined." Since each type of error code is defined differently, you need to assign the result of the LingoError function each time to a character string variable to determine the type of error that is reported.

Using LingoShowErrors

LingoShowErrors controls whether Lingo error message dialog boxes display. If you don't set a value for LingoShowErrors, the error messages are off by default. This is a global switch that applies to all the Director movies currently playing. The syntax of LingoShowErrors looks like this:

```
LingoShowErrors(showErrors)
```

The argument showErrors controls whether Lingo error messages display. Replace showErrors with 1 to display Lingo error messages, or with 0 to turn off the error messages.

The setting for the LingoShowErrors function applies only while movies continue to play. When no movies play, the LingoShowErrors function reverts to off (0), which is its default setting.

Distributing Director Movies with Your Piece

The final hurdle to working with Director movies in Authorware is distributing the necessary drivers required to play the Director movie on another machine.

Including the Director run-time files

Authorware requires some additional files to run a Director movie. The required files are different for Windows and Macintosh computers. If these files aren't available on the user's computer, you must provide them. For information about including additional files when distributing a piece, see Chapter 17, "Distributing Your Piece."

The easiest way to make sure that you are including all necessary files for the Director movie is to simply copy the entire Director folder (located inside the folder where you have Authorware installed) to the hard drive or folder location where you have copied your packaged run-time files. The files that you need to include are listed in the tables below.

32-bit run-time files for Director movies

In order to run a Director movie in a piece that you have packaged for Windows 95 or Windows NT, Authorware requires that you include the following files in a folder named Director, placed in the same location as either the packaged executable file or the folder that contains RUNA34W32.EXE:

File name...	Description...	When it's required...
A4DIR32.XMO	The 32-bit version of the Authorware movie driver for Director external movies.	Always
A4DIR.U32	The 32-bit version of the DLL that contains the Lingo functions for Authorware.	Only when using Lingo functions in your Authorware piece.
ASIFONT.MAP	A resource file used by the Director for Windows projector file.	Always
ASIPORT.RSR	A resource file used by the Director for Windows projector file.	Always
DIRDIB.DRV	A resource file used by the Director for Windows projector file.	Always
FILEIO.DLL	The earlier Xobject version of the FILEIO Xtra.	Only when using FILEIO.DLL in your Director movie.
FONTMAP.TXT	The Director for Windows font and character mapping table.	Always
LINGO.INI	The Lingo initialization file for the Director for Windows projector file.	Always
M5DRVR32.EXE	The 32-bit version of the Director for Windows projector file.	Always
M5DRVR32.RSR	A resource file for M5DRVR32.EXE.	Always
M5IF32.DLL	A DLL that A4DIR32.XMO uses to interface with M5DRVR32.EXE.	Always
MACROMIX.DLL	A DLL that controls sound channel mixing for the Director for Windows projector file.	Always
XOBGLU32.DLL	A DLL that M5DRVR32.EXE uses to interface with Windows Xobjects.	Only when using Xobjects in your Director movie.

In order to run a Director movie in a piece that you have packaged for Windows 3.1, Authorware requires that you include the following files in a folder named Director, placed in the same location as either the packaged executable file or the folder that contains RUNA34W16.EXE:

File name...	Description...	When it's required...
A4DIR16.XMO	The 16-bit version of the Authorware external movie driver for Director movies.	Always
A4DIR.UCD	The 16-bit version of the DLL that contains the Lingo functions for Authorware.	Only when using the Lingo functions in your Authorware piece.
ASIFONT.MAP	A resource file used by Director for Windows projector file.	Always
ASIPORT.RSR	A resource file used by Director for Windows projector file.	Always
DIRDIB.DRV	A resource file used by Director for Windows projector file.	Always
FILEIO.DLL	The earlier Xobject version of the FILEIO Xtra.	Only when using FILEIO.DLL in your Director movie.
FONTMAP.TXT	The Director for Windows font and character mapping table.	Always
LINGO.INI	The Lingo initialization file for the Director for Windows projector file.	Always
M5DRVR16.EXE	The 16-bit version of the Director for Windows projector file.	Always
M5DRVR16.RSR	A resource file for M5DRVR16.EXE.	Always
M5IF16.DLL	A DLL that A4DIR16.XMO uses to interface with M5DRVR16.EXE.	Always
MACROMIX.DLL	A DLL that controls sound channel mixing for the Director for Windows projector file.	Always
XOBGLU16.DLL	A DLL that M5DRVR16.EXE uses to interface with Windows Xobjects.	Only when using Xobjects in your Director movie.

Macintosh run-time files for Director movies

In order to run a Director movie inside a packaged Macintosh piece, Authorware requires that you include the following files in a folder named Director, placed in the same location as either the packaged executable file or the folder that contains RunAPM:

File name...	Description...	When it's required...
Director	The resource file that contains the Lingo functions and the Director movie driver for Authorware.	Always
Fontmap.txt	The font and character mapping table for the Director movie player.	Always
MIX Services	Xtra for viewing content.	Always

NOTE If you include a Director movie in a Shockwave piece, you must distribute the Director drivers mentioned above for each platform. You must copy these files to the web server location where your Shockwave piece is stored. Each file name must also be added to your piece's map file so that the Plug-In can download them. For more information about adding external file names to a Shockwave piece's map file, see the Shockwave for Authorware area of the Macromedia web site (**http://www.macromedia.com/support/authorware/how/shock/**).

Distributing Xtras with Director movies

Authorware installs several Director Xtras in the same folder where the Director drivers are installed. These folder locations are different for each platform, as shown below:

Platform...	Folder Location...
Windows	[Authorware folder]\Director\Xtras
Macintosh	[Authorware folder]:Director:Xtras

These Xtras are used to play back sound inside the Director movie while it runs in Authorware. You need to include these files with your final piece when you distribute it. You should place them in the same relative folder as the Director drivers that you are distributing, as shown below:

Platform...	Folder Location...
Windows	[Packaged run-time folder]\Director\Xtras
Macintosh	[Packaged run-time folder]:Director:Xtras

NOTE Other Xtras that you have used with your Director movie can also be included in this same folder when distributing your final piece.

Different platforms require different sets of Xtras, depending on how you have packaged your final piece. If you've packaged your piece for Windows 95 or Windows NT, include the following Xtras:

File name...	Description...	When it's required...
MIX32.X32	Xtra for viewing content.	Always
SND_IMPO.X32	Xtra for normal sound file playback.	Always
SWADCMPR.X32	Xtra for playing Shockwave Audio files.	Only when using Shockwave Audio files in your Director movie.

If you've packaged your piece for Windows 3.1, include the following Xtras:

File name...	Description...	When it's required...
MIX16.X16	Xtra for viewing content.	Always
MIXSND.X16	Xtra for normal sound file playback.	Always
SWADCMPR.X16	Xtra for playing Shockwave Audio files.	Only when using Shockwave Audio files in your Director movie.

If you've packaged your piece for the Macintosh, include the following Xtras:

File name...	Description...	When it's required...
SWA Decompression 68K Xtra	Xtra for playing Shockwave Audio files.	Only when using Shockwave Audio files in your Director movie and delivering on a standard Macintosh.
SWA Decompression PPC XtraShockwave	Xtra for playing Shockwave Audio files.	Only when using Audio files in your Director movie and delivering on a Power Macintosh.
Snd Import Export	Xtra for normal sound file playback.	Always

Because many developers are using Director to create content, Director movies provide a convenient way to expand the scope of your Authorware piece. Including Director movies in a piece can help you expand the types of animation and interactivity that you can deliver to the user with Authorware. However, as you have seen, Director movies require special handling when integrating them into your Authorware pieces, so you should take some time to explore other options that may be available.

One of the best ways to integrate new functionality into your piece—without requiring the additional overhead of using Director movies—is to use Xtras and external functions. These types of external code enable you to fine-tune your piece and create customized features for your piece that you can't otherwise accomplish using Authorware alone. You'll look at some ways of working with Xtras and external functions in Chapter 20, "Developing with External Code."

Developing with External Code

Authorware multimedia features can take your creativity in new and unexpected directions. However, when investigating the ways you might design a piece, you may find that the icons and the system functions and variables fall short of the end result you want for your piece. For example, you might want to include interactive 3D models, integrate specific Windows or Macintosh functionality, or connect to a database to improve the way your piece handles user data.

You can include all of these types of functionality in an Authorware piece by using custom functions and Xtras created for Authorware. These types of tools expand your set of options when moving past the more difficult barriers you are sure to encounter when developing larger projects. The final chapter of this book explores briefly how you can begin integrating custom functions and Xtras into the pieces that you create.

Custom functions enable you to handle specific types of functionality that Authorware's set of system functions cannot handle. One example of this is the way you can use custom functions to send and receive Lingo messages to and from a Director movie (see example in Chapter 19, "Using Director Interactively"). All custom functions used with Authorware work similarly to the Lingo functions you have looked at already. Custom functions are stored in external function libraries that you can link to a piece, using the options in the Functions window.

There are three basic types of custom function libraries that you can use with Authorware, UCDs, DLLs, and XCMDs:

- On Windows computers, custom functions are stored in Dynamic Link Libraries (DLLs). DLL files remain separate from the piece.

- DLL files created specifically for Authorware are called UCDs (User Code) because they include function descriptions and defined arguments—much like the system functions you've already worked with in previous chapters.

- On the Macintosh, custom functions are stored in external command files (XCMDs) or external function files (XFCNs). Both are commonly referred to as XCMDs.

NOTE If you want more information about developing Windows UCDs and DLLs for Authorware, see the USERCODE.WRI file and example source code included on the Authorware 4 CD in the UCD.DEV folder. For information about writing your own XCMDs, see the Claris/Apple Computer publication *HyperCard: Script Language Guide*.

There are many custom function libraries already included on the Authorware 4 CD in the UCD folder (Windows) or XCMDs folder (Macintosh). Each UCD or XCMD includes documentation and an example file that show you how to use the functions included in the library. You will get a better feel for how custom functions are used later in this chapter in "Connecting to a Database," when you look at the set of custom functions included with Authorware that enable you to communicate with a database.

TIP In addition to the UCDs and XCMDs included on the Authorware 4 CD, many additional custom function libraries already exist and are available from online services or from other Authorware developers. The list of web sites in Appendix C, "Authorware Resources on the Internet," provides many locations where you can find existing custom function libraries to download and try.

There are two different versions of most UCDs included on the Authorware 4 CD. The UCDs that you can use with pieces running in Windows 95 and Windows NT are labeled with a .u32 extension (32-bit); those that you can use with pieces running in Windows 3.1 are simply labeled with a .ucd extension.

You need to distribute both versions of the UCD file with your piece if you are delivering for both platforms. However, when you load functions from the UCD into Authorware while developing your piece, you will need to link to the 32-bit version of the UCD. Authorware automatically links your piece to the correct version of the UCD during run time if you place both versions in the same folder location (usually the folder where you have placed the packaged piece).

On the Macintosh platform, you can use the same XCMDs for pieces packaged for either the Power Macintosh or the standard Macintosh platforms; however, you still must include them with your piece when you distribute it. As with UCDs, you need to place XCMDs in a location where Authorware can find them.

NOTE If you place UCDs and XCMDs in another folder location (other than the folder that contains the packaged file or the Authorware run-time file, if you've packaged without run time), you will need to specify this folder in your search path settings. For more information on setting up the search path settings for your piece, see Chapter 2, "Beginning a Piece."

Loading a custom function

When using a custom function, Authorware requires certain information about the function in order to load and use it. Many existing custom functions contain this information in a form that Authorware already can use. All of the UCDs and XCMDs included on the Authorware 4 CD contain function and argument descriptions that enable you to load them into a piece and use them in the same way you use Authorware's system functions.

NOTE When you move a piece from Authorware for Windows to Authorware for Macintosh, you cannot use DLLs with the Macintosh version of the piece. You need to write custom functions as XCMDs if you want them to work on a Macintosh; the same applies to pieces moved from a Macintosh to a Windows machine. You must recompile XCMD functions into a DLL or UCD format that Authorware for Windows can use.

Before Authorware can use a custom function, you need to link it to Authorware because the custom function resides in an external file location. After a custom function loads, Authorware can exchange information with the function and tell it when to execute. Loading a function links Authorware with the function and enables the two to communicate.

You can start the process of loading a custom function two ways:

- Clicking the New button in the Functions window.

- Typing in the name of a custom function you want to use in a calculation icon script before you load it into Authorware using the Functions window.

The steps below show you how to load a function using the Functions dialog box:

1. Choose Functions from the Window menu.

The Functions window appears, as shown in **Figure 20.1**.

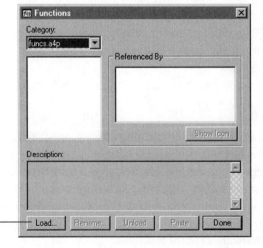

Click to load a custom function.

Figure 20.1
The Functions window enables you to load, delete, or rename custom functions.

2. Scroll down to the bottom of the Category list and select the name of the file on which you are currently working.

The names of the custom functions you've already loaded appear.

3. Click the Load… button (see **Figure 20.1** above).

The Load Function dialog box appears, as shown in **Figure 20.2**.

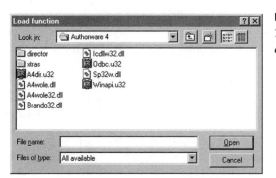

Figure 20.2
The Load Function dialog box.

This same dialog box appears when you have included the function's name in a calculation script, but haven't yet loaded the function into Authorware.

To select the function you want to load into your piece:

1. Find the file that contains the function you want to use and click Open.

If you are on a Windows machine, find the appropriate UCD file. (Remember, you want to use the 32-bit version of the UCD when you are authoring because your piece may run on either Windows 95 or Windows NT.) If you are on a Macintosh, select the name of an XCMD.

The Custom Functions dialog box appears, as shown in **Figure 20.3**.

Name of custom function selected.

Description of custom function selected.

Figure 20.3
The Custom Functions dialog box.

This dialog box lists all the custom functions contained in the file you've selected.

2. Select the function you want and click Load.

Shortcut: To load several functions at the same time, click on each function separately while pressing the Ctrl key (Windows), or Command key (Macintosh). If they are listed next to each other, select all of them at the same time by pressing the Shift key when clicking.

After you load the function you want, its name appears in the [Filename] category of functions for your piece, as shown in **Figure 20.4**. Any other custom functions that you load into the piece will appear in this same category.

List of currently loaded custom functions. —

Unload button —

Rename button —

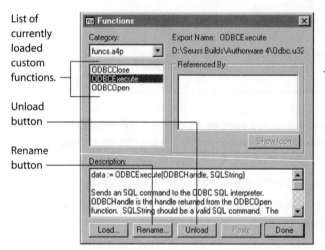

Figure 20.4
The Functions window, after loading a custom function.

NOTE If you select a function library that doesn't include Authorware function descriptions, another dialog box appears which tells you that the DLL you've selected doesn't have function definitions included. You'll learn more about this in "Loading DLLs that don't follow Authorware conventions," later in the chapter.

Several options are available in the Functions window when you select a custom function from the Category list:

■ Clicking on the function name shows you a list of icons that currently use the function you've selected.

■ You can rename a custom function by clicking the Rename button and typing a new name into the Rename dialog box. This changes the name of the function inside all the scripts that you've used in the piece; however, it doesn't actually change the name of the function inside the function library from where you've loaded it. Authorware still uses the original function name when sending commands to the function library.

■ If you want to remove the custom function, click the Remove button. You must remove the function's name from any scripts you're using, otherwise the Remove button is dimmed.

Loading DLLs that don't follow Authorware conventions

Many Windows DLLs are created for programmers, and are not as easy to integrate into a piece as UCDs and XCMDs. Standard DLL format and calling conventions often require that you refer to programming documentation and cope with API calls to the Windows operating system. To get around this, Authorware supports a transparent extension to the conventional DLL, known as a UCD (user code document).

When you load a UCD using the Functions window, Authorware lists the functions contained in the UCD. You can select the functions and paste them into a calculation window just as you would a system function, which makes it possible to load and call DLLs without coping with low-level programming conventions.

A C programmer who creates a DLL for use with Authorware can use the UCD to preload the information Authorware needs to recognize and link to functions within the DLL (including function names, arguments, return types, syntax templates, and online descriptions). You can store the additional resources with the DLL or separately, and they remain transparent to other programs that have access to the DLL.

However, Authorware also supports conventional DLLs by presenting a dialog box in which you can enter the specific calling parameters. Such conventional support makes it possible to link to DLLs that are not used by Authorware exclusively.

DLLs that don't follow Authorware's calling conventions require that you to enter the following information for each function that you load:

■ The function's name.

■ A list of arguments.

■ The type of value that the function returns.

■ A description of the function, if you want to include one.

After you load the function, Authorware prompts you to enter the information.

NOTE Because these DLLs do not include Authorware function descriptions with them, check the documentation that comes with the function to see what type of data each argument requires. If you are working with Windows API functions in particular, you can check the Microsoft API Reference included with the Visual C++ Development Kit, or any other API reference manual available in a technical bookstore.

To load an undefined DLL function into Authorware:

1. Load the function as described in "Loading a custom function," above.

For a function that doesn't follow Authorware's calling conventions, a separate dialog box appears that asks you for the function's name, arguments, return type, and description, as shown in **Figure 20.5**.

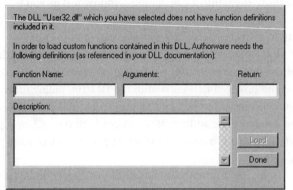

Figure 20.5
Loading an undefined DLL function into Authorware.

2. Enter the following information about the function:

- The function's name in the Function Name field.

- The function's arguments in the Arguments field. Separate the arguments with commas.

- The function's return type in the Return field.

- An optional description in the Description field (check the DLL's documentation to find out what information should go here).

3. Click Load.

After the function loads, it is listed in the custom functions category of the Functions window.

Using a custom function

After you've loaded a custom function, you can use it with your scripts in the same way you would use other system functions. As you saw in Chapter 19, "Using Director Interactively," when working with the Lingo functions, most custom functions require that you provide information for the function using specific arguments for the custom function to work.

You follow the same types of conventions that you used with system functions when passing arguments to custom functions. You can usually find out what a function's arguments are by looking at the description of the function, which is included with it. Before you use a custom function, make sure that you know its syntax and arguments, so that it will work correctly in the script you are creating.

Custom functions are useful for many specialized tasks; however, your choices are not limited to these alone when trying to do something complicated in a piece. In Authorware 4, you can now integrate additional types of functionality into your piece using sprite and scripting Xtras. In the next section, you'll see some examples of how these types of external code resources can help you develop more sophisticated types of applications.

Using Sprite Xtras

Authorware 4 includes several Xtras that enable you to introduce sophisticated new elements into your pieces. Because you can use many Xtras developed for Director 6 in Authorware 4, you have a wide selection of Xtras to choose from when looking at how to incorporate new types of functionality into your piece.

There are actually three types of Xtras supported by Authorware 4: transition Xtras, sprite Xtras, and scripting Xtras. The three types of Xtras are different in the following ways:

- Transition Xtras simply provide different types of on-screen transitions that you can use.

- Scripting Xtras include many types of scripting enhancements that enable you to control elements of your piece through the calculation icon. You'll learn about these later in "Using Scripting Xtras."

■ As you saw in Chapter 10, "Responding Automatically to Events," sprite Xtras enable you to display objects directly in the Presentation window with which the user running the piece can interact.

To get a better feel for the ways you can work with sprite Xtras, take a look below at how you can use the QuickDraw 3D Xtra to add fully interactive, textured 3D models to your piece. Later, you will see how you can use the ActiveX Xtra to include different types of components in pieces designed specifically for the 32-bit Windows platform.

Using the QuickDraw 3D Xtra

With the QuickDraw 3D Xtra, you can import files saved in the 3DM (3D Metafile) format. The Authorware 4 CD includes several models that you can integrate into your piece to get a feel for how they work. If you are unsure where these are located, refer to the documentation included on the Authorware 4 CD.

NOTE To use the QuickDraw 3D Xtra, you need to have QuickDraw 3D 1.5 or higher installed on your system. Keep in mind QuickDraw 3D also must be installed on the end user's system when you distribute your piece. You probably will want to install QuickDraw 3D at the same time other components of your piece are installed to make it easier for the user to run your piece.

To use the QuickDraw 3D Xtra, first insert a QuickDraw 3D sprite Xtra icon into the flowline using the following steps:

1. Choose ThreeD > QuickDraw 3D Model… from the Insert menu.

The Open file dialog box appears.

2. Select a model to import into the piece.

NOTE The next set of steps refers to working with the model named Globe.3dm. This is one of the models included on the Authorware 4 CD.

After importing the model, Authorware adds a new QuickDraw 3D sprite icon to the flowline, as shown in **Figure 20.6**.

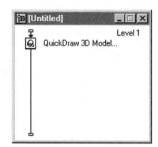

Figure 20.6
*Adding a QuickDraw 3D sprite
to the flowline.*

After you've added the QuickDraw 3D sprite to the flowline, you can assign different options to it.

3. Name the sprite icon **Globe**, and then double-click to open it.

The Icon Xtra Properties dialog box appears, as shown in **Figure 20.7**. This dialog box displays information about the location and version of the sprite Xtra you're using. It also contains separate options that allow you to customize the appearance and behavior of the sprite Xtra icon that you've added to the flowline.

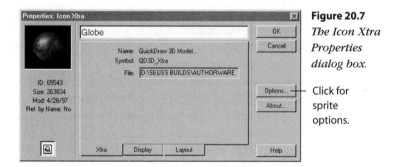

Figure 20.7
*The Icon Xtra
Properties
dialog box.*

Click for
sprite
options.

4. Click Options.

The QuickDraw 3D Xtra dialog box appears, as shown in **Figure 20.8**.

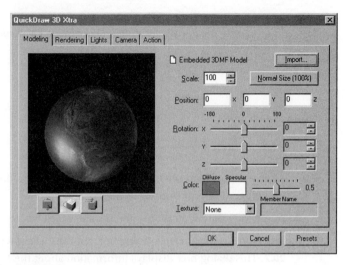

Figure 20.8
The QuickDraw 3D Xtra dialog box with the
Modeling options displayed.

Inside the QuickDraw 3D Xtra dialog box, you will find the options for customizing the way the model appears in the Presentation window. You also can adjust such parameters as its lighting, how it renders on screen, and what type of texture it uses. The available options are grouped into the following tab categories at the top of the dialog box: Modeling, Rendering, Lights, Camera, and Action. At any time, you can click on the preview of the model to play around and get a feel for how you can use it inside the Presentation window.

After you add a model to your piece, you can modify its properties dynamically through a calculation script to adjust how it appears in the Presentation window. You use the `SetIconProperty` function to do this. For example, you can change a model that displays as a textured model to display as a wireframe model by using the following script in a calculation icon:

```
SetIconProperty(@"Globe", #fillStyle, #q3Edges)
```

As you can see from the example above, QuickDraw 3D sprite icons store properties as symbols. In this case, the `#fillStyle` property is assigned the value of `#q3Edges`, a predefined value that is available for all QuickDraw 3D models. **Figure 20.9** shows you how the model appears in the Presentation window when you have set this property.

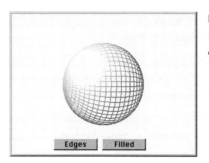

Figure 20.9
The globe model set to display as a wireframe model.

If you want to reset the model to its original textured look, simply change the property value you assign to the #fillStyle property from #q3Edges to #q3Filled, as shown in the example below:

```
SetIconProperty(@"Globe", #fillStyle, #q3Filled)
```

TIP You can set many QuickDraw 3D sprite properties in a calculation icon using the SetIconProperty function. For a complete list of these properties, see the QuickDraw 3D documentation included with the QuickDraw 3D Xtra.

Using the ActiveX Xtra

The ActiveX Xtra is a powerful new addition to the Authorware development environment. It takes advantage of Microsoft's ActiveX technology to allow you to embed customized Windows application controls into a piece in much the same way as OLE-style controls were used previously.

Because ActiveX is becoming a quickly adopted standard for both Windows and web-based applications, many developers are rushing in to design new types of ActiveX controls for every type of functionality that you may need to include in a piece.

TIP See the list of third-party developer sites included in Appendix C, "Authorware Resources on the Internet," for more information on where to go for additional ActiveX controls that you can download and use with Authorware.

You can use ActiveX controls with Authorware in a variety of ways:

- Insert a Calendar control that allows the user to flip through months and find a specific day of the week. (You'll see an example of this later in this section.)

- Include a Microsoft Word document that you can edit directly inside the Presentation window.

- Display an Adobe Acrobat document directly inside the Presentation window without opening the Acrobat Reader application from inside Authorware.

- Display an HTML document directly inside the Presentation window without opening a separate web browser application from inside Authorware.

- Play a Macromedia Flash animation directly inside the Presentation window. (Flash is Macromedia's latest Shockwave animation technology.)

In order to develop with ActiveX controls, you currently must author and deliver your piece on a Windows system running Windows 95 or Windows NT 4.0. There is no planned Windows 3.1 support for ActiveX.

NOTE At the time this book went to press, Microsoft had just released a Macintosh ActiveX Development Kit; however, it is still in its early stages, and isn't yet supported by Authorware or any additional third-party developers.

You can get a feel for how you can use ActiveX controls in a piece by working with the Microsoft Calendar control. The next example shows you how to integrate the Microsoft Calendar control into your piece, and introduces you to the ways you can manipulate the ActiveX sprite icons using a calculation script.

NOTE This example requires that you already have installed the ActiveX Xtra and ActiveX components that come with Authorware 4 for Windows. See the documentation included on the Authorware 4 CD if you need additional help in installing these to your system.

To insert the Calendar control into your piece:

1. Choose Control > ActiveX… from the Insert menu.

The Choose ActiveX Control dialog box appears, as shown in **Figure 20.10**. This lists all ActiveX controls that you have installed on your system.

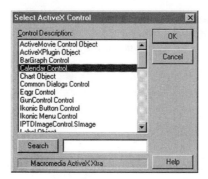

Figure 20.10

The Choose ActiveX Control dialog box lists all ActiveX controls installed on the system.

2. Select the control named Calendar Control and click OK.

   The ActiveX Control Properties dialog box appears, as shown in **Figure 20.11**.

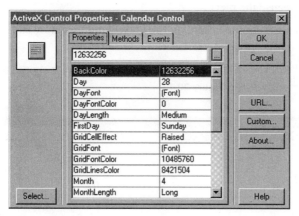

Figure 20.11

The ActiveX Control Properties dialog box.

You can use this dialog box to browse the properties, methods, and events available for this control by clicking the tab options at the top of the dialog box. These features enable you to control how the user interacts with the control when it displays in the Presentation window. They are explained in more detail later in this section.

3. When you have finished browsing, click OK to close the dialog box.

   Notice that a new ActiveX control sprite appears in the flowline, as shown in **Figure 20.12**.

Figure 20.12
The ActiveX sprite icon appears on the flowline.

4. Name the sprite icon **Calendar**, and then run the piece.

After running the piece, notice that it occupies only a small rectangle of the Presentation window, hiding most of its buttons from view. You can quickly resize the control using the following steps:

1. Pause the piece.

2. Click on the control in the Presentation window and drag one of its corners to resize it.

After resizing the control, restart the piece. It should now appear as shown in **Figure 20.13**.

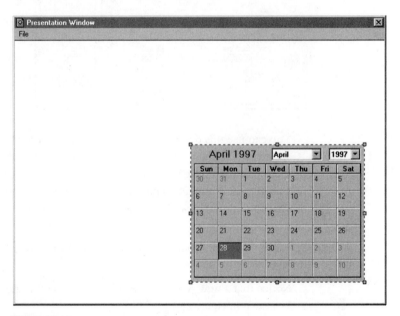

Figure 20.13
The calendar control, as it appears in the Presentation window.

If you click around on the calendar, you can select any day, or use the month and year drop-down lists to change the month or year. You could use a control like this in a training piece that allows users to select specific tasks according to a date or month. You also could use it to jump to preselected dates to show the user specific events that occur month-to-month. To do this, you need to know how to work with control methods.

Calling methods of the control sprite

When using ActiveX controls, you can use the `CallSprite` system function to control the sprite directly from a calculation script. When using this function, you must specify the method of the control that you are calling. If you remember from the last section, methods are defined in the ActiveX Control Properties dialog box. Each type of ActiveX control has different methods that enable you control the sprite icon.

NOTE When calling a method of a control sprite, the sprite Xtra generates an event. You can use event responses in an interaction to track events as well. For more information about setting up event responses, see Chapter 10, "Responding Automatically to Events."

Methods are useful if you need to set up automatic control over the sprite from within interactions in the flowline. The next example looks briefly at how to set up this type of control, creating buttons that automatically display the next and previous calendar months for the user.

> **TIP** This is just one example of the many methods you can use with ActiveX controls. Each control has its own set of methods that are listed in the ActiveX Control Properties dialog box.

To set up the interaction:

1. Drag a new interaction icon to the flowline, and name it **Change Date**.

2. Add two button responses to the interaction by dragging calculation icons to the right of the interaction icon. Name the button responses **Previous Month** and **Next Month**.

3. Double-click the calculation icon attached to the Previous Month response.

The Calculation window appears.

4. Type in the following line:
CallSprite(@"Calendar", #PreviousMonth).

As you can see, you specify methods in much the same way that you specify properties when working with property lists. Some methods require specific arguments; in this example, however, you simply include the name of the method only.

Note that you are calling a specific sprite icon by specifying its icon title; you also can use a variable to set the sprite's IconID value, as you can with any other type of referenced variable expression.

5. When you have finished, close the Calculation window.

6. Double-click the calculation icon attached to the Previous Month response.

The Calculation window appears.

7. Type in the following line:
CallSprite(@"Calendar", #NextMonth).

8. When you have finished, close the Calculation window, and then run the piece.

NOTE If you cannot see your buttons, they are underneath the ActiveX control sprite. You can pause the piece, move the sprite, and reposition the buttons by dragging them to a new location; or, you can use the Response Properties dialog box to reposition each button one at a time.

You now can change the calendar month that displays by clicking the buttons. This is a simple example of how you can use methods to interact with ActiveX control sprites inside the Presentation window.

As you can see, ActiveX controls are very useful because they allow you to set up ways for the user to interact directly with the control through other types of interaction responses. You also can use the CallSprite function to control the sprite icon in the background of a piece in response to a user action.

TIP For complete documentation of how to work with the ActiveX Xtra, see the Windows Help file named ActiveX.hlp, located in the Xtras folder where you have Authorware 4 installed.

How do I distribute a piece that uses ActiveX controls?

Distributing a piece that uses ActiveX controls requires that you distribute both the ActiveX Xtra included with Authorware, and the control itself.

There are actually two ActiveX Xtras installed with Authorware 4: ActiveX.X32, the run-time component and ActXPriv.X32, the user interface component. These are located in the Xtras folder of your Authorware 4 application. When you go to distribute a piece that includes ActiveX controls, you only distribute the run-time component, ActiveX.X32, with your piece. You should place this Xtra in the Xtras folder for your packaged piece (see Chapter 17, "Distributing Your Piece," for more information).

The following files are also provided with the ActiveX Xtra on the Authorware 4 CD: APRXDIST.EXE, AXDIST.EXE and WINDIST.EXE. These are self-installing executable files provided by Microsoft that upgrade a Windows 95 or Windows NT 4.0 system to run ActiveX components.

It is extremely important that all three of these files are installed for each system on which you plan to distribute the piece; otherwise, the ActiveX Xtra and the controls that you are using do not work. These enable the system to run any ActiveX components that you include with your piece. You probably should install these components at the same time as you install the additional components of your piece, using an installation program that can launch the separate executable files listed above.

In addition, you must install the ActiveX controls that you have included in a piece and register each control with the user's system. In certain cases, the user may already have certain ActiveX components installed. For instance, if you are working with the Microsoft Web Browser control, it is already installed if the user has Microsoft Internet Explore 3.02 or higher installed.

However, in most cases you should include the files that install the control in the same location as your packaged run-time piece so that Authorware can find the latest version of the control to install (if it is not installed already on the user's system). You can handle this by either providing Authorware with a URL where the control can be downloaded, or by specifying a path to the file that contains the ActiveX control that you want to install. You add this information to your piece by using the options inside the ActiveX Control Properties dialog box.

You can distribute most ActiveX controls in a Cabinet (.CAB) file format, which allows the control to auto-install and register through the Microsoft ActiveX DLLs installed on the user's system. The CAB format is simply a compressed file format, much like the ZIP format created by WinZip or PKZip.

You can include the CAB file containing your control in the same folder as your packaged piece, and then simply include the name of the CAB file in the URL field of the ActiveX Control Properties dialog box. When Authorware goes to use the ActiveX control and finds it is not installed already on the user's system, the control is automatically extracted from the CAB file and installed on the user's system.

TIP You can find more information about the CAB file format and auto-installing and registering ActiveX controls in the following HTML document available on Microsoft's web site: **http://www.microsoft.com/visualc/reference/cab.htm**.

In addition, the ActiveX Xtra includes several functions that enable you to find out if the user has the control installed; and if not, install the new control and register it with the system. These functions are explained in more detail with the documentation that ships with the ActiveX Xtra (see ActiveX.hlp in the Xtras folder where you have Authorware 4 installed).

Using Scripting Xtras

Scripting Xtras enable you to add additional custom functionality to a piece. Unlike sprite Xtras, however, you can only use them within calculation icon scripts. To see how scripting Xtras compare to the sprite Xtras discussed in the last section, take a look at the FileIO Xtra included with Authorware 4. The FileIO Xtra enables you to store and retrieve data from an external text file in many different ways, and you can use it in place of the `ReadExtFile` and `WriteExtFile` functions to add text-handling capabilities to your piece.

Like sprite icons, all scripting Xtras (including the FileIO Xtra) contain their own custom methods that you call by using a calculation script. However, the way you call scripting Xtra methods is a bit different than calling ActiveX sprite controls. To work with a scripting Xtra, you first must create an instance of the scripting Xtra by using the techniques described below.

Creating a scripting Xtra instance

To use a scripting Xtra, you must create an instance of the Xtra in memory. The instance of the Xtra is represented by a numerical ID value called a "handle." You use this handle to refer to the specific instance of the Xtra that has been created whenever you call a method of the scripting Xtra.

NOTE The instance handle created by a scripting Xtra is similar to the ODBC handle created by the ODBC custom functions. "Connecting to a Database" later in this chapter, looks more closely at these functions.

The methods included with the FileIO Xtra are listed in the Functions dialog box. You can quickly view the methods included with the FileIO Xtra by doing the following:

1. Open the Functions window.

2. Select Xtra FileIO from the Category drop-down list.

The list of FileIO Xtra methods appears, as shown in **Figure 20.14**.

Figure 20.14
Displaying the FileIO Xtra methods.

Each method that you see in the list performs a specific task. For example, the `ReadLine` method allows you to read an external text file line-by-line. Since you can't read an external file line-by-line using Authorware's system functions, you instead would have to use the `ReadExtFile` function to read in the entire file, assign it to a custom variable, and then use the `GetLine` function to read each line. The FileIO Xtra greatly simplifies this task by providing methods that do the work for you.

However, before you can use them, you must create an instance of the FileIO Xtra because the FileIO methods require that you specify the instance handle when using them. To create an instance of the Xtra, you use the `DeleteObject` and `NewObject` functions in a script, as shown in the example below:

```
DeleteObject(fileInstance)

fileInstance := NewObject("fileio")
```

In the example above, the custom variable `FileInstance` is assigned the value of the instance handle created by the `NewObject` function. The `DeleteObject` function is called before the

`NewObject` function to kill any previously created instances of the scripting Xtra, to make sure that you're referring to the correct FileIO instance in your scripts each time you call a method.

Calling a scripting Xtra method

After you've created the instance of the FileIO Xtra, you can call different methods using the same `fileInstance` handle. For example, you can call the `displayOpen` method to display a standard Open dialog box that enables the user to select the text file that the FileIO Xtra uses to read in data, as shown in **Figure 20.15**.

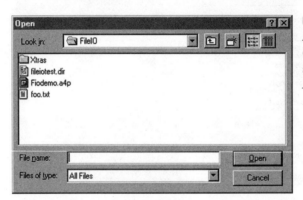

Figure 20.15
Displaying the Open dialog box, using the FileIO Xtra.

To call a method of the FileIO Xtra, you use the `CallObject` system function. This is similar to the `CallSprite` function that you used earlier with the ActiveX sprite control. However, the syntax is a bit different, depending on the type of scripting Xtra with which you're working.

When you paste a FileIO method into a calculation icon script, Authorware automatically inserts the `CallObject` function, along with the name of the method you've pasted in and any additional arguments that are required for the method. For example, if you paste the `displayOpen` method into the calculation window, it appears as shown below:

`CallObject(object, "displayOpen")`

The method name is called in the second argument of the `CallObject` function. The first argument is automatically reserved for the instance handle that you have created (named `object` by default). When using methods in a script, you can simply replace the `object` argument with your own instance handle variable that you have created, as shown below:

```
fileName := CallObject(fileInstance, "displayOpen")
```

Because the `displayOpen` method returns the path and name of the file the user has selected in the Open dialog box, the result of the `CallObject` function is assigned to another custom variable in the example above. Once you have located the file the user wants to read, you can use the `openFile` method to open the file, and then begin manipulating the text using other methods, as shown below:

```
CallObject(fileInstance, "openFile", fileName, 0)
CallObject(fileInstance, "writeString", NotesFromMe)
CallObject(fileInstance, "closeFile")
```

In the example above, the `openFile` method opens the file in read-and-write mode (specified by the 0 in the fourth argument of the first line of the script). The `writeString` method is used to write a character string variable called `NotesFromMe` to the end of the file, and then the `closeFile` method is called to close the file after you have updated all text in the file.

TIP Because each instance of the FileIO Xtra has a separate instance handle, you can create multiple instances of the Xtra in memory. However, this makes it essential to use the correct variable name of the instance whenever you call a new method in a calculation script.

Although the FileIO Xtra is more difficult to work with than Authorware's set of file functions discussed in Chapter 16, "Tracking the User," it does offer some additional functionality that you may find useful if you are storing much of your data in external text files. However, when you begin creating pieces that generate a great deal of run-time information, look at using Authorware's database connectivity features.

Combining Authorware's interactivity with the power and flexibility of a database gives you a powerful tool for retrieving and managing data quickly and easily. While you can use record variables, lists, and external text files to track the user, you can take advantage of Authorware's database connectivity features to improve the way that you handle data in your piece.

For example, combining Authorware's internal data-handling features with database connectivity enables you to do many things:

- A company that requires employees to complete regular training courses could use Authorware to constantly update its records when an employee completes an online course, and then provide an accurate list of who has completed which courses.

- A retail outlet or a group of restaurant owners could use Authorware to create an electronic product kiosk that is updated daily with current information about price and product availability.

- A referral agency for carpenters and plumbers could use Authorware to create a simple interface to its list of members, their specialties, and their current availability.

Of course, there are many possibilities for what Authorware and databases can do together. You probably will think of many more as you work with them. The next several sections describe the basic ways you can incorporate database connectivity into your piece.

Making the connection

Authorware makes connecting to databases relatively simple by relying on two industry database standards:

- Open Database Connectivity (ODBC), a common standard for connecting to a database was developed by Microsoft. This standard is used on both Macintosh and Windows platforms.

- Standard query language (SQL), a standard command language for sending information to and receiving information from a database.

Because it's a common standard, ODBC enables Authorware to communicate with a variety of commonly used databases such as Access, dBase, FoxPro, and Paradox. Macromedia simplifies work with databases by providing the external functions that you need to pass information from Authorware to a database file. These are contained in the following files, located in the folder where you have Authorware installed:

Platform...	*File name...*
Windows	ODBC.U32 (for authoring and delivery on Windows 95, NT)
	ODBC.UCD (for delivery on Windows 3.1)
Macintosh	ODBC XCMD

NOTE The same rules about delivering custom function libraries apply to the ODBC function libraries. For more information, see "Using Custom Functions" earlier in this chapter.

These custom function libraries include three different ODBC functions that enable you to open a database session, send the database SQL messages and retrieve the results, and then close the database session when you have finished. You can use the functions with any database that supports the ODBC standard.

NOTE The appropriate ODBC drivers must be installed on the end user's system in order to connect your piece to a database. You must license ODBC drivers for each platform from the appropriate third-party manufacturers. Windows ODBC drivers are included on the Authorware 4 CD. You can license Windows drivers directly from Microsoft for inclusion with your own projects.

Although Authorware's ODBC functions make it fairly easy to connect Authorware to a database, this doesn't eliminate the need for you to understand how to configure ODBC and how to use SQL syntax and logic. These are probably the most difficult aspects of working with a database and Authorware. While this section covers the main information you need to know, here are some places you can go for additional help:

- For information on installing ODBC drivers, see the manufacturer of the drivers that you are including with your piece. "Installing drivers" below covers installation of Microsoft's set of ODBC drivers for Windows.

- For information on setting up an ODBC data source for your piece, see the manufacturer of the drivers you are including with your piece. "Setting up a data source" below covers how to configure an ODBC data source for the Windows platform, if you are using Microsoft's set of ODBC drivers.

- If you have little or no SQL background, refer to the SQL documentation available from Microsoft, documentation from the database manufacturer, or a commercially available explanation of SQL.

After the ODBC-related functions are loaded in your piece, and the appropriate ODBC drivers are installed, Authorware can receive and send information to and from a database.

Installing drivers

Each database that Authorware connects with must have the appropriate ODBC driver in the Windows System directory. If the driver isn't in the directory, you must install it. Many database drivers are available from the database manufacturer or from other vendors such as Microsoft.

The Authorware package includes a set of ODBC database drivers from Microsoft. The set includes drivers for the following databases:

Database name...	Manufacturer...
Access	Microsoft
dBase	Borland
Excel	Microsoft
FoxPro	Microsoft
Paradox	Borland
SQL Server	Microsoft

The set includes Microsoft ODBC Setup, which enables you to select individual drivers and installs them in the Windows System directory. You can use the Microsoft ODBC Setup program included on the Authorware 4 CD. If you are installing database drivers from other suppliers, follow the instructions that come with those drivers.

For Authorware to connect to a database, the database must be available and you must define the path to the database. The combination of the database and its path is known as a data source. You must set up a data source for each ODBC database whose data you want to import, export, or attach to from Authorware.

NOTE You cannot specify a web location (URL) for a database. Databases that you connect to must be stored on the user's hard disk, the CD-ROM on which you are distributing your piece, or on a LAN server that the user can access.

If you've installed the set of Microsoft ODBC drivers included on the Authorware 4 CD, use the Data Sources dialog box to set up data sources. You can open the Data Sources dialog box in two ways:

- By running Microsoft ODBC Setup, if you haven't installed any ODBC database drivers yet. The Data Sources dialog box appears when Microsoft ODBC Setup has installed the drivers.

- By double-clicking the ODBC item in the Windows Control Panel. (Microsoft ODBC Setup installs this item when it first runs.)

The way you define the path to a database depends on the structure of the individual database:

- Databases (such as Access) that allow multiple tables within a file, require the database's filename in the path.

- Databases (such as dBase) that consist of one table, don't require the filename of the database in the path. Specify the path only to the directory that contains the database.

NOTE For more information about how to configure data sources for the type of database you are using, see the documentation included with your database software.

To set up a data source in Windows using the Microsoft ODBC Control Panel:

1. Open the Windows Control Panel.

- If you are running Windows 95 or Windows NT 4, Choose Settings > Control Panel from the Start menu.

- If you are setting up a data source on a Windows 3.1 or Windows NT 3.5.1 system, double-click on the Control Panels icon in the Main program group.

The Control Panel window appears.

2. Double-click the ODBC icon (Windows 3.1, NT 3.5.1) or the 32-bit ODBC icon (Windows 95, NT 4).

The Data Sources dialog box appears, as shown in **Figure 20.16**.

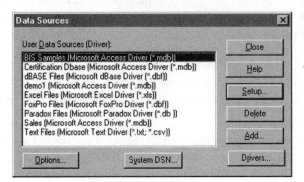

Figure 20.16
Configuring a Windows ODBC data source.

3. Click Add.

The Add Data Source dialog box appears, as shown in **Figure 20.17**.

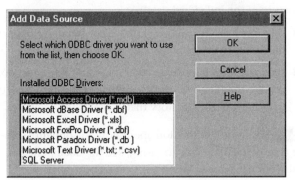

Figure 20.17
The Add Data Source dialog box provides a list of all currently installed ODBC drivers.

4. Select a driver from the Installed ODBC Drivers list.

NOTE If the driver for the type of database you're using doesn't appear in the list, check with Microsoft to see if it is supported by Microsoft's ODBC drivers. If it isn't included with the drivers you have installed, you may need to purchase drivers for your database separately.

5. Click OK in the Add Data Source dialog box.

The Microsoft ODBC Setup dialog box appears, allowing you to set up a data source that uses the driver you selected. **Figure 20.18** shows you how this dialog box appears when setting up a data source that uses Access drivers.

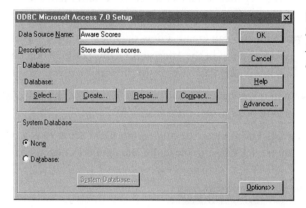

Figure 20.18
Setting up a Microsoft Access data source.

To set up the data source name:

1. Enter the name of the data source in the Data Source Name field.

The data source name can be any name that you want. For example, you can use a name that describes the database content, such as "User Scores."

NOTE The data source name that you specify in this step also needs to be used in Authorware when calling the ODBC functions.

2. Click Select Database in the ODBC setup dialog box.

The Select Database dialog box appears, as shown in **Figure 20.19**.

Figure 20.19
Setting the path to the data source.

3. Specify the path to the database file with which you are working.

For databases such as dBase that consist of one table in the file, select the directory that contains the database. For databases such as Access that can contain multiple tables in a file, select the directory that contains the database, and then select the database's filename.

TIP You also can create a new database file by using the Create option button in the Microsoft ODBC Setup dialog box. This creates a new database file of the type that you've selected.

4. When you have finished, click OK to close the Select Database dialog box.

5. Click OK to close the Microsoft ODBC Setup dialog box, and then click Close to close the Data Sources dialog box.

Working with the ODBC functions

After you've installed the necessary drivers and configured the data source that you are using, you can begin to add connectivity to the database using the functions included in the ODBC UCD (Windows) or ODBC XCMD (Macintosh).

The ODBC function libraries contain three custom functions (ODBCOpen, ODBCExecute, and ODBCClose) that enable Authorware to communicate with a database that supports the ODBC format. These functions are used within calculation scripts in a piece to execute specific ODBC commands using the name of the data source you've specified when setting up your ODBC drivers.

Each time you use the ODBC functions inside your piece (usually placed consecutively inside the calculation script), you must follow three basic steps:

1. Open the current ODBC session.

2. Execute update or retrieve commands.

3. Close the session.

The ODBCOpen function opens a session with an ODBC database and returns a handle that is used for subsequent access to the database during the session. The function's syntax looks like this:

```
ODBCHandle := ODBCOpen(WindowHandle, ¬
"errorVariable", datasource, "user", "password")
```

The custom variable `ODBCHandle` contains the "handle" that is returned by the function. This is a numeric ID value that you need to use when calling the other two ODBC functions so Authorware and the ODBC driver can keep track of which database transactions are being processed.

TIP You can open more than one database session by using different custom variables when calling ODBCOpen.

The ODBCOpen function has four arguments:

Argument...	What it's used for...
errorVariable	Contains the name of a variable that receives error messages from the function.
datasource	Contains the name of the data source for the database.
User	Contains the required user name for opening the database. This can be an empty string (""), if no user name is required.
Password	Contains the password for opening the database. This can be an empty string (""), if no password is required.

For example, the following function opens a session with the data source named Access Orders:

```
ODBCHandle := ODBCOpen(WindowHandle,"ODBC Error", ¬
"Access Orders", "Guttenberg", "")
```

In this example, the custom variable ODBCHandle receives the handle to the database. The other argument values used in this example are described below:

- `WindowHandle` is a system variable that contains the Presentation window's handle.

- `ODBC Error` is a string that receives an error message from the function.

- Guttenberg is the user's name.

- The password argument is left empty, since the database does not require the user to have a password.

After opening the ODBC session, you use the `ODBCExecute` function to send an SQL command to the data source. SQL commands are specified using a literal character string, or a character string variable to which you've assigned a value.

The function's syntax looks like this:

```
result := ODBCExecute(ODBCHandle, "SQLString")
```

The variable `result` contains the data that Authorware obtains from the database. The function has two arguments:

Argument...	What it's used for...
ODBCHandle	Contains the handle returned by the ODBCOpen function.
SQLString	Contains the SQL command.

For example, the following function sends an SQL statement to the database that has the handler returned by the **ODBCOpen** function. The SQL statement selects all addresses in a data source named Address:

```
data := ODBCExecute(ODBCHandle,"SELECT*FROM ¬
Address")
```

The custom variable data contains the data returned from the database. The arguments have the following purpose:

- **ODBCHandle** contains the handle to the database.
- **"SELECT*FROM Address"** is an SQL command.

NOTE Authorware can't handle a result from a database query result that exceeds 30K characters. When a query returns a record larger that 30K characters, Authorware lets you choose whether to disregard the query, or to continue—but to truncate any data that exceeds 30K. You can avoid the 30K-character limit by setting up queries to return smaller results by specifying fewer fields to be returned, or returning one record at a time.

After executing your SQL commands, you use the **ODBCClose** function to close the current ODBC session. The function's syntax looks like this:

```
ODBCClose(ODBCHandle)
```

The **ODBCClose** function only requires one argument: the handle returned by the **ODBCOpen** function call. You can call this function any time after the **ODBCExecute** commands have successfully executed.

Placing this function inside the same script that opens the ODBC session and executes the SQL commands is usually the best choice, unless you need to continuously update the database throughout your piece. In general, you should try to execute database transactions quickly because having a database connection constantly open slows down the performance of your piece.

TIP Make sure that you close all database connections before exiting Authorware. Otherwise, you get an error message and other applications may quit unexpectedly.

There are many SQL functions available for working with databases. The following table lists some frequently used SQL functions, along with a description:

SQL function syntax...	SQL function description...
SELECT*FROM TableName	Retrieves all records and all fields from the table specified.
SELECT* FROM TableName ¬ WHERE FieldName = 'value'	Retrieves records from all fields that contain a specific value in the table specified.
SELECT FieldName1, FieldName2, ¬ FROM TableName	Retrieves specific fields from the table specified.
INSERT INTO TableName VALUES ¬ ('value1','value2','value3')	Inserts a record into the table specified, using the values specified.
DELETE FROM TableName ¬ WHERE FieldName = 'criterion'	Deletes a record from the table specified.

These are just a few examples that illustrate SQL; it isn't a complete list of the functions you would typically use when working with a database. Most databases support different types of SQL commands that are unique to the database software you are using. Check the reference manuals that come with your database software for information on the types of SQL commands that are supported for the type of database you are using. In addition, you may want to look at the many third-party books available that are written about using SQL.

When building SQL statements in Authorware, you can include variables as part of the SQL statement to dynamically request information from a database or to write information to a database. Because the SQL statement is a character string that you pass to the ODBC data source using the `ODBCExecute` function, you can concatenate variable names to the SQL commands that you are using.

For example, the following expression updates the Total field of a database record stored in the Access data source named User Scores:

```
SQLString := "UPDATE User Scores SET Total = " ¬

^ TotalScore ^  " WHERE User = '" ¬

^ CurrentUser ^ "'"

ODBCExecute(ODBCHandle, SQLString)
```

In the example expression above, the value that is used to update the Total field is the value contained in the custom variable `TotalScore`, since this information is generated during run-time. To improve the readability of the script, the SQL string is formatted first, and then assigned to the custom variable `SQLString`, which is used as the string argument for the `ODBCExecute` function at the bottom of the script.

It's important to understand how the script performs the database record update. The script is set up to perform a single field update for a single record by including the keyword WHERE in the SQL string. The WHERE keyword allows you to specify the record to update based on the value of the record field that you specify. In this case, the SQL statement updates the record stored for the user specified in the custom variable `CurrentUser` so that no other user records are updated at the same time.

NOTE Many database drivers require a specific character format when executing SQL statements with the `ODBCExecute` function. For example, when working with an Access database, you need to enclose all field names inside single quotation marks if you reference them (see the example expression above) in the SQL statement. It's important to spend some time looking at the documentation that ships with your database software to determine how to format the SQL statements your piece uses.

Distributing a piece that uses ODBC

You must include more than the external files when distributing a piece that connects to a database:

- The ODBC.U32, ODBC.UCD, or ODBC XCMD file, which contains the ODBC-related functions.

- Drivers for any databases that the piece use. Obtain drivers from Microsoft or the database vendor. (Make sure that you observe the requirements of the licensing agreement when you distribute these files.)

The data sources that you set up when you author must also be set up on the computer that runs the piece. In order to avoid problems that you may encounter during delivery, it's a good idea to include installing the necessary drivers and configuring the correct data source as part of the installation process for your piece.

TIP Many developers install and configure the ODBC drivers at the same time they are installing their piece, using a third-party installation utility. Several different installation software companies are listed for you in Appendix C, "Authorware Resources on the Internet."

Looking Ahead...

As your projects become more difficult, you will at times need to integrate other external components into your pieces to provide additional functionality that Authorware cannot handle directly. This chapter explored some of the common ways of extending the Authorware environment using both external functions and Xtras— the newest set of tools made available for Authorware.

Now that you've seen how these types of tools can be used with Authorware, you will want to consider using them when you begin developing applications that need a bit of an extra push in the right direction. Your role as a developer is made a bit easier by knowing that these types of tools are being developed for you, allowing you to be able to deliver customized Authorware pieces that go beyond the scope of what other multimedia applications can do.

New Authorware 4 Functions and Variables Quick Reference

This appendix covers new Authorware functions and variables introduced in Authorware 4. The functions and variables are grouped according to how the developer would use them in a piece, and include a brief description and the proper syntax for each.

For more information on how to use these functions and variables (including examples), see *Using Authorware* or the online functions and variables reference included in Authorware Help.

NOTE An asterisk (*) indicates an existing function or variable that has changed since Authorware 3.5.

Character Functions

Syntax:	Description:
MapChars string := MapChars(*string, fromPlatform* [, *toPlatform*])	Performs character mapping from the *fromPlatform* to the *toPlatform* for each character in the string specified.
String string := String(*value*)	Converts the given value to a string.
Symbol string := Symbol(*value*)	Converts the given value to a symbol. Helpful in creating property lists.

General Functions

Syntax:	Description:
CallObject result := CallObject(*object, method* [, *argument*…])	Calls a scripting Xtra handler method of the object.
CallParentObject result := CallParentObject(*Xtra, method* [, *argument*…])	Calls a scripting Xtra handler parent method for the Xtra.
Call Sprite result := CallSprite(*sprite, method* [, *argument*…])	Calls a method of the sprite.
CallIcon result := CallIcon(*IconID, method* [, *argument*…])	Calls a method of the icon asset associated with a sprite Xtra.
DeleteObject DeleteObject(*object*)	Deletes an instance of a scripting Xtra object created by the NewObject function.
FlushEventQueue FlushEventQueue( )	Clears all pending events from the EventQueue system variable.
GetIconProperty result := GetIconProperty(*IconID, property*)	Returns the value of the property for the sprite icon.

General Functions (continued)

Syntax:	Description:
GetSpriteProperty result := GetSpriteProperty(*sprite, property*)	Returns the value of the property for the sprite.
NewObject object := NewObject(*Xtra* [, *argument*…])	Creates a new instance of the scripting Xtra and calls this new method of the instance with the optional arguments.
SendEventReply SendEventReply(*event, reply*)	Sends a reply to an event sent by an Xtra. The system variable EventLastMatched contains the value for *event*. The *reply* value can be any type.
SetIconProperty SetIconProperty(*IconID, property, value*)	Set the value of the property for the sprite icon.
SetKeyboardFocus SetKeyboardFocus(*IconID*)	Sets the current focus to the icon specified.
SetSpriteProperty SetSpriteProperty(*sprite, property, value*)	Sets the value of the property for the sprite.
TypeOf type := TypeOf(*value*)	Returns the data type of *value*, as one of the following: #integer ; #real ; #string ; #list ; #propList ; #rect ; #point ; #symbol

Language Functions

Syntax:	Description:
Repeat with x in list repeat with *variable* in *list* statement(s) end repeat	Repeats the statements with each element in *list*. Authorware keeps a reference to the original list for the duration of the loop. This means that the list will persist at least for the duration of the loop.

List Functions

Syntax:	Description:
AddLinear	
AddLinear(*linearList, value* [*, index*])	Inserts a value into a linear list.
AddProperty	
AddProperty(*propertyList, property, value* [*, index*])	Inserts the property and value into a property list.
Array	
myArray := Array(*value, dim1* [*, dim2, dim3, … dim10*])	Creates an array using the dimensions you specify. The *value* argument is assigned to each element of the array created.
CopyList	
newList := CopyList(*anyList*)	Returns a complete copy of a list, including all sub-lists.
DeleteAtIndex	
DeleteAtIndex(*anyList, index*)	Deletes the element from a list at the index specified.
DeleteAtProperty	
DeleteAtProperty(*propertyList, property*)	Deletes the element with the specified property from the list.
FindProperty	
index := FindProperty(*propertyList, property* [*, index*])	Returns the index of the first element in the list with the specified property.
FindValue	
index := FindValue(*anyList, value* [*, index*])	Returns the index of the first element of the list that matches the specified value.
InflateRect	
InflateRect(*rectangle, widthChange, heightChange*)	Changes the dimensions of the rectangle specified. The change is relative to the center of the rectangle. Negative values reduce the rectangle's size.
Intersect	
newRectangle := Intersect(*rectangle1, rectangle2*)	Creates a new rectangle for the intersection of *rectangle1* and *rectangle2*.
ListCount	
number := ListCount(*anyList*)	Returns the number of elements in the list.
OffsetRect	
OffsetRect(*rectangle, x, y*)	Creates a new rectangle offset from the rectangle specified. *X* is the horizontal offset specified in pixels; *Y* is the vertical offset.

List Functions

Syntax:	Description:
Point	
myPoint := Point(*x, y*)	Creates a point at the pixel location *x, y*.
PointInRect	
result := PointInRect(*rectangle, point*)	Returns true if the point specified is within the rectangle specified, or false if it is not.
PropertyAtIndex	
property := PropertyAtIndex(property*List, index*)	Returns the property of the element at the index. It returns a null value if the specified index is out of range or the first argument is not a property list.
Rect	
myRect := Rect(*x1, y1, x2, y2*) myRect := Rect(*point1, point2*)	Creates a rectangle at the specified *x* and *y* values, or points.
SetAtIndex	
SetAtIndex(*anyList, value, index*)	Replaces the value in a list at the specified index. This function differs from AddLinear and AddProperty because it replaces a value at the given index rather than inserting it.
SortByProperty	
SortByProperty(*propertyList1* [, *propList2, ... , propList10*]	Sorts the list(s) by property and marks [, *order*]) the list(s) as sorted. Specifying an *order* parameter of 1 sorts the list in ascending order (default); an *order* parameter of 0 sorts the list in descending order.
SortByValue	
SortByValue(*anyList1* [, *anyList2, ..., anyList10*] [, *order*])	Sorts the list(s) by property and marks the list(s) as sorted. Specifying an *order* parameter of 1 sorts the list in ascending order (default); an *order* parameter of 0 sorts the list in descending order.
UnionRect	
UnionRect(*rectangle1, rectangle2*)	Returns the smallest rectangle that encloses the two rectangles specified.
ValueAtIndex	
ValueAtIndex(*anyList, index*)	Returns the value at the given index.

Math Functions

Syntax:	Description:
Average value := Average(*anyList*) value := Average(*value1* [, *value2*, ..., *value10*])	Returns the average value of the top level elements of the specified list, or the average of up to ten values.
Fraction result := Fraction(*value*)	Returns the fraction of the specified value.
Max value := Max(*anyList*) value := Max(*value1* [, *value2*, ..., *value10*])	Returns the largest value in the specified list, or the largest value of up to ten specified values.
Min value := Min(*anyList*) value := Min(*value1* [, *value2*, ..., *value10*])	Returns the smallest value in the specified list, or the smallest value of up to ten specified values.
Number number := Number(*value*)	Converts the specified value into a number.
Real realNum := Real(*value*)	Converts the specified value into a real number.
Sum value := Sum(*anyList*) value := Sum(*value1* [, *value2*, ..., *value10*])	Returns the sum of the values of the elements of the specified list, or the sum of up to ten values.

Platform Functions

Syntax:	Description:
TestPlatform result := TestPlatform(*Mac, Win32, Win16*)	Tests the platform that a piece is running on and returns the appropriate argument. Used for setting up variable paths to files.

General Variables

	Description:
EventLastMatched Character	Use in an @"IconTitle" expression to return the last event matched by the given response.
EventQueue Character	A list of all pending unprocessed external events in order of arrival.
EventsSuspended Logical	When EventsSuspended is greater than zero, Authorware prevents all event responses from interrupting the current flow and saves all events in the EventQueue. When EventsSuspended is zero, Authorware processes the pending events.
GlobalTempo Numerical	Controls the rate at which sprite Xtras receive step events from Authorware, in steps per second.
KeyboardFocus Character	The title of the icon that currently has the focus.
MediaRate Numerical	Use in an @"IconTitle" expression to find the frame rate, in frames per second, for a given movie.
MediaLength* Numerical	MediaLength now dynamically reads the length of a movie, rather than the length when imported.
TimeOutRemaining Numerical	The amount of time, in seconds, left for Authorware to wait for any mouse or keyboard activity.

Variable @ References*

Authorware 4 now allows variables to be used in place of the icon title in an @"IconTitle" expression. The value of the variable can either be an IconID or an IconTitle.

Graphics Variables

	Description:
DirectToScreen	
Logical	Sets the icon property to draw direct to the screen.

Using Shockwave Audio

It takes a lot of data throughput to reproduce digital audio accurately. This is why sound files tend to take up a great deal of space—sometimes as much space as your compressed QuickTime and Video for Windows movies. The Shockwave Audio (SWA) format uses sophisticated MPEG audio compression techniques to create sound files that are much smaller in size but can be played back at an acceptable level of sound quality.

When you integrate Shockwave Audio files into a piece, you will find that you are able to include much more audio content than is normally possible with using uncompressed WAV, AIFF, or PCM files. You will also find that performance of your piece improves significantly, especially if you are creating Shockwave content for the Internet. This is because much less information needs to be downloaded first before the sound starts playing.

As with the other sound file formats that Authorware supports, SWA files can either be imported directly into the sound icon, or linked to a sound icon and stored externally. When a piece is running, these sound files are uncompressed and converted to a digital audio stream that can be played back on any system with a sound card installed. The next sections explain how to convert uncompressed sound files into the SWA format for use in Authorware.

NOTE If you use Shockwave Audio files in your piece, you will need to distribute the appropriate SWA Xtras included with Authorware 4. For more information, see Chapter 17, "Distributing a Piece."

Converting sounds to the SWA format in Authorware (Windows)

If you are working with the Windows version of Authorware 4, you can use the Convert WAV to SWA Xtra included with Authorware to convert any WAV format file to the Shockwave Audio (SWA) format.

To convert a WAV file to a SWA file inside Authorware:

1. Choose Other > Convert WAV to SWA... from the Xtras menu.

The Convert WAV to SWA dialog box appears.

2. Click the Add button.

The Select Files dialog box appears.

3. Use the folder browser window to select the file you wish to convert. You can select multiple files by Shift-clicking on the names of the files. When you are finished, click Open.

The name of the file you selected appears in the Files To Convert list inside the dialog box.

4. Select the compression and conversion settings you want to use. The options inside the Convert WAV to SWA dialog box allow you to select the appropriate data compression and conversion settings to use:

- Select the data compression rate for your file by choosing a bit rate (in kilobits per second) from the Bit Rate drop-down list (see "Adjusting data compression rates for SWA files," later in this chapter).

- You can adjust the level of the audio conversion filter used by selecting either Normal Quality or High Quality.

- Check the Convert Stereo to Mono check box if you want to convert a stereo file to mono. The Convert WAV to SWA Xtra automatically converts a file to mono if you choose a bit rate of 32kbps or less.

- Clicking the Destination Folder button allows you to select a new destination folder where your SWA file will be saved.

- Select the Prompt Before Overwriting option to have Authorware prompt you before overwriting files with the same file name that are saved in the destination folder.

5. When you have finished selecting these options, click Convert.

The files you have selected to convert are saved with the same file name and a .SWA extension, using the settings you have specified. Once conversion is complete, import each sound file into Authorware using the techniques discussed in Chapter 5, "Adding Sound and Video."

Converting sounds to the SWA format in SoundEdit 16 (Macintosh)

If you are working on the Macintosh platform, and want to convert your sound files to a SWA format, you will need to use the SWA Settings (SE16) Xtra and SWA Export Xtra that are available for SoundEdit 16 version 2. If you do not already have these Xtras, you can download the SoundEdit Streaming Audio Toolkit from the Macromedia web site (**http://www.macromedia.com/support/soundedit/how/shock/**).

NOTE The SWA Export Xtra and the SWA Settings (SE16) Xtra can only be used with a Power Macintosh system.

To use the SWA Export Xtra:

1. In SoundEdit 16 version 2, open the audio file you want to export.

2. Choose Shockwave for Audio Settings from the Xtras menu to configure the compression options.

3. Select the bit rate (kbps) you want from the Bit Rate drop-down menu.

4. Check the Convert Stereo to Mono check box if you want to convert a stereo file to mono. The SWA Export Xtra automatically converts a file to mono if you choose a bit rate of 32kbps or less.

5. Choose OK to close the Shockwave for Audio Settings dialog box.

6. Choose Export from the File menu to open the Export dialog box.

7. Choose SWA File from the Export Type pop-up menu.

8. Name the file, then choose Save.

The file is exported using the settings you specified in the Shockwave for Audio Settings dialog box. Once this is complete, import the sound file into Authorware using the techniques discussed in Chapter 5, "Adding Sound and Video."

TIP You can create the SWA files on the Windows platform using Authorware, import them into your piece, and then move the piece over to the Macintosh platform if you do not have SoundEdit 16 version 2 installed.

Adjusting data compression rates for SWA files

Shockwave Audio is scaleable, which means that you can adjust the compression rate for your sound files depending on the way in which you plan to deliver your piece. In pieces designed for CD-ROM or a fast Internet connection, you can afford to use lower compression settings (i.e., a higher data rate) since you have more bandwidth to work with. However, you will want to use higher compression settings (i.e., a lower data rate) when you are delivering Shockwave content to users with a slower modem connection speed (28.8 or less).

NOTE When delivering Shockwave Audio inside a Shockwave for Authorware piece, the entire SWA file is downloaded first before it is played by the piece.

It is useful to know the output sample rates that correspond to the various SWA settings used when converting your sound files to SWA files, since this will help you optimize your sound quality when using Shockwave Audio. It is not necessary to work at 44.1kHz, for example, if you are creating SWA files saved with a bit rate of 8kbps. The following table shows the correspondence between the SWA Bit Rate settings that are available, and the sample rates at which the files are output when played through Authorware.

Bit Rate (in kbps)	Output Sample Rate (in kHz)
8	8
16	16
24	16
32	22.050 (22.050, 44.100 input)
48 stereo	22.050 (22.050, 44.100 input)
48 mono	Same as input sample rate
56 stereo	22.050 (22.050, 44.100 input)
56 mono	Same as input sample rate
64 stereo	22.050 (22.050, 44.100 input)
64 mono	Same as input sample rate
96	Same as input sample rate
128	Same as input sample rate

As you can see from the table above, the SWA bit rate does not always match the output sample rate. For example, a SWA file compressed at a rate of 32kbps will still play at a sample rate of 22.050kHz. In general, however, higher bit rate settings produce higher audio quality in the final compressed SWA file.

The following table shows the suggested guidelines for compressing SWA files (depending on the delivery bandwidth), but you will need to experiment on your own in order to determine the data compression settings that work best for the delivery requirements and content of your Authorware piece.

Choose this bit rate...	For a target audience using...
64kbps - 128kbps	T1 delivery, CD-ROM, Ethernet LAN
32kbps - 56kbps	ISDN lines
16kbps	28.8 modem connections
8kbps	14.4 modem connections

When choosing a bit rate, keep the system resources of your users in mind. Low bit rates are generally appropriate for the Internet, while higher bit rates are appropriate for intranet and CD-ROM distribution. If you estimate that your users will have slower modem connections, choose a low bit rate. If you know your users are connecting to the

Internet using fast T1 lines, or you are delivering content over an Ethernet LAN connection, you can afford to choose a higher bit rate and get better overall sound quality in the process.

Preparing your sound files for conversion to the SWA format

When compressing a sound file using the SWA Xtras, you can improve the final quality of your compressed SWA files by using the following guidelines:

- Work with 16-bit 22.050 or 44.100kHz files (22.050kHz recommended).

- When using pre-existing 8-bit or 11kHz files, upsample them to 16-bit 22.050kHz and leave them at this resolution when exporting them to the SWA format.

If you are compressing your Shockwave Audio files at modem speeds (8kbps and 16kbps), you can improve the overall sound quality of them by pre-processing the original source files using equalization and filtering, before converting them to the SWA format. This can be done using a sound editing tool like SoundEdit 16 (Macintosh) or SoundForge (Windows). In addition, SoundEdit 16 supports the AudioTrack Xtra from Waves, Inc. (**http://www.waves.com**). This Xtra (Power Macintosh only) allows you to specifically pre-process audio files for Shockwave Audio output.

TIP More information on pre-processing your audio files before converting them to SWA files has been included in the SoundEdit Streaming Audio Toolkit documentation that can be downloaded from Macromedia's web site (**http://www.macromedia.com/support/ soundedit/how/shock/**).

Authorware Resources on the Internet

There are so many resources available on the Internet that you may feel a bit overwhelmed when you start browsing for information related to the types of Authorware projects you are creating. The list below is by no means comprehensive. It does, however, include the best selection of sites devoted to Authorware and those that deal with all aspects of multimedia development. Listed as well are some of the essential third-party software sites that offer valuable information and trial versions of tools that are essential for every multimedia developer.

For an HTML version of this list, including links to the web sites mentioned, open the file Weblinks.htm using any web browser. You can find this file in the Weblinks folder on the CD accompanying this book.

Macromedia Sites

The resources below provide additional information about using Authorware, and are maintained by Macromedia.

 Authorware Developer's Center
The one-stop Authorware area on Macromedia's web site where you can link to downloadable product updates and Xtras, product information, show-me examples, tips and tricks, and frequently asked questions about using Authorware and Shockwave for Authorware.
http://www.macromedia.com/support/authorware/

Macromedia Events Page
Includes the latest information on Macromedia events around the country. Highlights include the Macromedia International User Conference, an annual conference on developing multimedia, digital arts, and Internet content with Macromedia products. Online registration is available.
http://www.macromedia.com/macromedia/events/

Shockwave for Authorware "How-To" Page
Provides in-depth documentation of every aspect of working with Shockwave for Authorware, including shocking a piece, editing a map file, working with the browser, and configuring web servers to work with Shockwave for Authorware. Check out the cool Shockwave for Authorware Portfolio examples.
http://www.macromedia.com/support/authorware/how/shock/

Shockwave Developer's Center
Download the latest Shockwave Plug-Ins for all of Macromedia's products. Includes links to Shockwave frequently asked questions, as well as the Shockzone, an area devoted to showcasing the latest Shockwave content on the Internet.
http://www.macromedia.com/shockwave/

Authorware Sites

The resources below provide additional information about using Authorware, and are maintained by third-party Authorware developers.

down load **The Authorware FAQ (Frequently Asked Questions)**
A repository of frequently asked questions about developing with Authorware, including many links to other Authorware information on the Internet. This site is maintained by Jeff McGuire and Wade Wells, developers with the Media Shoppe. Also includes links to sample code and Authorware for Windows UCDs.
http://www.wadezworld.com/tmspages/aware_faq.html

The Authorware Intelligence Report
Includes tips and techniques on developing with Authorware, written by Joe Ganci (author of "Authorware 3 Internal System Functions Professional Reference").
http://www.mrmultimedia.com/

down load **The Aware Page**
This European host site, maintained by Danny Engelman and Peter Arien, provides the largest variety of resources and links for Authorware users. Includes links to "Danny's DLL Dungeon," a comprehensive collection of UCDs and DLLs for Authorware for Windows developers (see below), and a searchable archives of AWARE mailing list postings. Engelman is the list-owner of the AWARE mailing list (see below).
http://www.econ.hvu.nl/aware/

Multimedia Sites

The resources below provide additional information about multimedia development.

Authoring Web
Everything you always wanted to know about authoring on all platforms—and a little bit more. Hosted by Maricopa Center for Learning and Instruction, this site contains information on all types of authoring tools, techniques, commercial aspects of multimedia development, and links to some of the leading schools that provide multimedia education.
http://www.mcli.dist.maricopa.edu/authoring/

Director Web

A subset of the Authoring Web, this site contains a world of information for beginning and advanced users of Macromedia Director. Good reference tool if you're interested in integrating more Director content into your Authorware applications. Includes links to other Director sites on the Internet.

http://www.mcli.dist.maricopa.edu/director/

Index to Multimedia Information Sources

An exhaustive collection of links and information about all aspects of multimedia development.

http://viswiz.gmd.de/MultimediaInfo/

Macromedia Meta Index

An unofficial guide to all Macromedia-related sites on the Internet. Sponsored by PC Expanders, a Macromedia reseller.

http://www.pce.net/sales/petert/macromedia.html

Multimedia Authoring Systems FAQ

A general-purpose FAQ covering all aspects of multimedia development, maintained by Jamie Siglar. Includes conceptual overviews of authoring tools and hypermedia design.

http://www.tiac.net/users/jasiglar/MMASFAQ.HTML

NOTE You can find more multimedia links by using a search engine such as Yahoo!, Alta Vista, or Lycos.

Xtras

The resources below provide additional information about developing with Xtras, and include many sample Xtras that can be downloaded.

 g/Matter, Inc. Site

The leading developer of Xtras for Macromedia products, including Authorware and Director. Includes links for information on developing Xtras, as well as trial versions of g/Matter Xtras.

http://www.gmatter.com/

 Trial versions of several g/Matter Xtras for Authorware 4 are included in the 3RDPARTY folder on the CD accompanying this book.

Macromedia Xtras Developer Center

Find out everything you need to know about developing your own Xtras, with online reference material. Includes links for downloading versions of the Xtras Developer's Kit for Authorware, Director, FreeHand, and SoundEdit 16.

http://www.macromedia.com/support/xtras/

You can develop new Authorware 4 Xtras using the Authorware 4/ Director 6 XDK, included in the XDK folder on the CD accompanying this book.

Macromedia Xtras Studio

Links to the many Xtra developers for Macromedia's products. Many of the companies listed offer demo versions of their Xtras that you can download and try.

http://www.macromedia.com/software/xtras/

DLLs, UCDs, and XCMDs

The resources below provide additional information about developing with external functions, and include many sample UCDs, DLLs, and XCMDs that can be downloaded.

Danny's DLL Dungeons

One of the best collections of Authorware UCDs and DLLs. Maintained by Danny Engelman, owner of the AWARE Mailing List (see below).

http://www.econ.hvu.nl/aware/ddd/index.htm

Gary Smith's Download Page

A great collection of shareware UCDs for Authorware for Windows, including mFont, which enables you to embed TrueType fonts into your Authorware applications.

http://www.gil.com.au/~gsmith/download/index.html

Barry Wood's Authorware Page

Some great information on writing DLLs for Authorware for Windows, as well as tips and techniques for controlling sound and video through MCI (Media Control Interface) in Authorware for Windows.

http://www.ccc.nottingham.ac.uk/cal/pubc.htm

XCMD Hideout

The largest site for downloading custom XCMDs to expand the range of functionality in your Authorware for Macintosh application. Maintained by Director students at the University of California, Long Beach.

http://www.nmc.csulb.edu/projects/xcmdhideout/

Director Xobjects Page

Although the XCMDs that you can download from this site are Director-specific, you can find many that you can use with Authorware for Macintosh. Includes searchable index of XCMDs for both Macintosh and Windows. Maintained by the folks at Director Web (see above).

http://www.mcli.dist.maricopa.edu/director/xobj.html

Magazines & Newsletters

The resources below provide links to subscription publications which focus on multimedia and developing with Macromedia's products.

Hyperstand

Site sponsored by *New Media* magazine, a monthly subscription publication that focuses on emerging trends in multimedia. Includes many product reviews and tips on multimedia development.

http://www.hyperstand.com

Lingo User's Journal (LUJ)

Site sponsored by the *Lingo User's Journal*, a publication devoted to Lingo and XCMD/Xtra programming. A good all-around technical reference for those looking to integrate Lingo-controlled Director movies and Xtras into Authorware applications.

http://www.penworks.com/LUJ/lujinfo.htm

Macromedia User Journal (MUJ)

Site sponsored by the *Macromedia User Journal*, a monthly subscription publication that focuses on developing with Authorware and Director. Some areas of this web site are password-restricted for subscribers. There are some free goodies available for those checking out the site, including the Hot Links page, which contains excellent general multimedia information links.

http://www.muj.com

User Groups

The resources below are maintained by various Macromedia user groups.

Bay Area Authorware User's Forum
Information about Authorware events in the San Francisco Bay area, including information on the user group and some links to Shockwave applications created in Authorware.
http://www.thomson.com/wadsworth/auf/auf.html

Macromedia User Group Listings
Find out how to get in contact with a Macromedia User Group located near you. Includes international listings for those outside of the United States.
http://www.macromedia.com/support/authorware/resource/usrgrps/

New York Metropolitan Authorware Users Group
News, discussion groups, and links to cool Shockwave content created in Authorware. Sponsored by Blue Streak Digital, a New York-based Authorware developer.
http://www.nymaug.org/

FTP Sites

The resources below can be accessed from any web browser or FTP application. You can use an anonymous FTP login to connect to them.

down load **University of Kuleuven FTP Site**
FTP site maintained by Danny Engelman, creator of the AWARE Page. Includes example code, models, and DLLs.
ftp://pa.cc.kuleuven.ac.be/pub/authorware/

down load **University of Nottingham FTP Site**
A virtual gold-mine of Authorware DLLs and UCDs. Includes reference sources in text format, and example source code for creating UCDs for Authorware for Windows.
ftp://ftp.ccc.nottingham.ac.uk/pub/dlls/

The resources below provide information on Authorware through standard email and Internet newsgroups.

AWARE Mailing List
To subscribe, type in the body of the message: **subscribe aware (Your Name)**
listserv@cc1.kuleuven.ac.be

alt.authorware
General newsgroup for questions about using Authorware.

bit.listserv.authorware
Newsgroup version of the AWARE Mailing List.

Third-Party Developer Sites

The following resources are maintained by third-party developers.

Aladdin Systems Site
Creators of StuffIt Installer Maker, the leading utility for creating Macintosh installation programs for your multimedia applications. Includes trial versions of many of their installer packages, including StuffIt and StuffIt Expander, two of the most widely-used utilities for compressing and decompressing Macintosh files.
http://www.aladdinsys.com

Apple Computer Site
A necessary resource for multimedia developers creating software for the Macintosh platform. Includes links for software updates and technical information on all Apple products.
http://www.apple.com

Apple QuickTime Site
The official site for information about Apple's QuickTime technology, including links to the QuickTime VR (Virtual Reality) site and the latest versions of QuickTime for both the Macintosh and Windows platforms.
http://quicktime.apple.com

down load **CNET X-Lab Site**
A new specialty site hosted by the CNET computer site, featuring ActiveX controls that you can download, as well as information on all aspects of developing ActiveX controls.
http://www.activex.com

down load **CNET Shareware Site**
A new specialty site hosted by the CNET computer site, featuring an incredible amount of shareware tools for all aspects of multimedia software development.
http://www.shareware.com

down load **InstallShield Site**
The leading provider of software for creating custom installation programs for Windows 3.1, Windows 95, and Windows NT. Includes trial versions of many InstallShield installer packages.
http://www.installshield.com

down load **Microsoft Site**
A necessary resource for multimedia developers creating software for the Windows platform. Includes the latest Microsoft product updates and technical information about working with all Microsoft products, including ActiveX and Internet Explorer. Includes links for downloading the latest version of Microsoft Internet Explorer.
http://www.microsoft.com

down load **Microsoft ActiveX Developer's Site**
A departure point for exploring Microsoft's new web-ready technologies for multimedia development. Includes links to information on ActiveX, a component technology that you can use with Authorware for Windows and DirectX, the latest multimedia extensions for applications developed for Windows 95 and Windows NT. The ActiveX area includes custom ActiveX controls that you can download and install through Microsoft Internet Explorer 3.0 or higher.
http://www.microsoft.com/activeplatform/default.asp

down load **Netscape Site**

A must site for all developers creating Shockwave for Authorware content. Includes information on working with Netscape Navigator, creating HTML content, and using other Netscape component technologies, including Netscape Navigator Plug-Ins like Shockwave. Includes links for downloading the latest version of Netscape Navigator.

http://www.netscape.com

down load **WinZip Site**

Makers of WINZIP and WINZIP Self-Extractor, useful for creating compressed versions of your applications. You can download trial versions of WinZip software.

Using the CD

Bundled at the back of this book, you will find a
CD-ROM that can be run on both the Macintosh and
Windows platforms. Here is a brief listing of what's
included on the CD:

- All of the Authorware example files mentioned
  in the chapters of this book.
- Demo versions of the Macromedia products
  included with the Authorware Interactive Studio,
  as well as the Macromedia products included with
  the FreeHand Graphics Studio.
- Demo versions of third-party software mentioned
  in this book.
- An HTML document with links to web sites
  mentioned in this book.
- The Macromedia Xtra Developer Kit for Authorware
  4 and Director 6 is included for those interested in
  learning about how to create your own Xtras.

This appendix contains notes on viewing the
Authorware example files and how to install the
software demos included on this CD.

NOTE Additional copyright information is contained in the ReadMe
files that accompany each product demo.

You can browse the contents of the CD in Windows 95 or Windows NT 4 by using the following steps:

1. Place the CD in your CD-ROM drive.

2. Choose Programs > Microsoft Explorer from the Start menu.

The Microsoft Explorer window appears.

3. Open the disk named Guide_CD and then browse the contents of each folder.

You can browse the contents of the CD in Windows 3.1 or Windows NT 3.5.1 by using the following steps:

1. Place the CD in your CD-ROM drive.

2. Open File Manager, located in the Main program group.

The File Manager window appears.

3. Click on the disk named Guide_CD and then browse the contents of each folder.

Each folder on the CD contains the various sample files mentioned above. A description of the contents of each folder is listed below.

Guide_CD\Examples folder

Separate chapter folders are located inside the Guide CD:Examples folder that contains all Authorware example files mentioned in the chapters of this book. To view the example files, open each one separately using Authorware 4 or the Authorware 4 Working Model. You can open them directly from the CD, or copy them to your local hard disk and then open them. ReadMe information for each example file discusses how the example was created.

NOTE To run the example files, you need either Authorware 4 or the Authorware 4 Working Model installed on your system. For your convenience, a copy of the Authorware 4 Working Model for Windows is included on this CD in the Guide_CD\Macromed\Aware folder.

Guide_CD\Macromed folder

Located inside the Guide_CD\Macromed folder are several folders that contain demo versions of Macromedia products. Each folder listed below contains separate ReadMe information and files that you can install to your hard disk.

Aware This folder contains the Authorware 4 Working Model. Double-click on the file named **Setup.exe** to install it to your hard disk. This version allows you to create and save your own working files in Authorware 4. You can use the Authorware Working Model to view the Authorware example files included with this CD, if you do not already have Authorware 4 installed.

NOTE You only can install the Authorware 4 Working Model on systems running Windows 95 or Windows NT.

Bkstage This folder contains the demo version of Backstage Internet Studio 2. Double-click on the file named **Setup.exe** to install it to your hard disk. Director is used to create animation and interactive multimedia content that can be integrated into your Authorware pieces, delivered as a stand-alone piece, or delivered on the Internet using Shockwave.

NOTE You only can install the demo version of Backstage Internet Studio 2 on systems running Windows 95 or Windows NT.

Director This folder contains the demo version of Director 5. Double-click on the file named **Setup.exe** to install it to your hard disk. Director is used to create animation and interactive multimedia content that you can integrate into your Authorware pieces, deliver as a stand-alone piece, or deliver on the Internet using Shockwave.

NOTE The save-disabled version of Director 6 was not available at the time this book went to press. However, you can obtain it through Macromedia directly by ordering a free copy of the latest version of the Macromedia Showcase CD. You can order this from the Macromedia web site (**http://www.macromedia.com**).

E3D This folder contains the demo version of Extreme 3D 2. Double-click on the file named **Setup.exe** to install it to your hard disk. Extreme 3D is used for 3D modeling, animation, and rendering in a variety of formats that you can integrate into your Authorware pieces.

Fontog This folder contains the demo version of Fontographer 4.1. Double-click on the file named **Setup.exe** to install it to your hard disk. Fontographer is used to create and edit custom fonts.

Freehand This folder contains the demo version of FreeHand 7. Double-click on the file named **Setup.exe** to install it to your hard disk. Freehand is used for both print and multimedia design and illustration.

Shockwav This folder contains the Windows versions of the latest Shockwave for Authorware Plug-In. If you are running Windows 3.1, double-click on the file named **Shock16.exe** to install the latest Shockwave for Authorware Plug-In to your hard disk. If you are running Windows 95, Windows NT 3.5.1, or Windows NT 4, double-click on the file named **Shock32.exe** to install the latest Shockwave for Authorware Plug-In to your hard disk.

NOTE To install Shockwave for Authorware, you must either have Netscape Navigator or Microsoft Internet Explorer already installed on your hard disk.

Xres This folder contains the demo version of xRes 3. Double-click on the file named **Setup.exe** to install it to your hard disk. XRes is used to create and edit images for use in print, multimedia, and on the Internet.

Guide_CD\3rdparty folder

Located inside the Guide CD:3rdparty folder are several folders that contain demo versions of third-party tools that you can use with Authorware. Each folder listed below contains separate ReadMe information and files that you can install on your hard disk.

Dxm The Earshot SFX Sampler is a royalty-free collection of audio clips that you can integrate into any multimedia piece created in Authorware or Director. The demo allows you to preview the sounds included in the complete Earshot SFX library, a two-volume CD-ROM collection of over 2,000 sound effects.

Additional sales and ordering information is included in the ReadMe file inside the DXM folder. The Earshot SFX Demo was produced by DXM, a San Francisco-based multimedia studio that specializes in multimedia title and Shockwave development (**http://www.dxm.com**).

To run the demo, double-click on the file named **Demo.exe**. No installation is required.

Equilib The Equilib folder contains a demo version of DeBabelizer Pro for Windows. Double-click on the file named **Setupex.exe** to install it to your hard disk. DeBabelizer is the leading Windows tool for converting and dithering images from one format to another, and for creating custom palettes from 8-bit images that you have saved. For more information on this version of DeBabelizer, view the ReadMe file included with the installer, or check the Equilibrium web site (**http://www.equilibrium.com**).

Gmatter You can integrate the demo Xtras included in this folder into any multimedia piece that you have created in Authorware 4 or Director (versions 5 and 6). Additional sales and ordering information is included in the ReadMe file inside the Gmatter folder. The gMatter Xtras were produced by gMatter, Inc., a San Francisco-based software company that specializes in the development of Xtras for Macromedia products (**http://www.gmatter.com**).

To try the Xtras included in this folder, drag and drop them into the Xtras folder located inside the folder where you have installed Authorware 4.

Sfoundry The Sfoundry folder contains a demo version of SoundForge XP 3. Double-click on the file named **Setup.exe** to install it to your hard disk. SoundForge XP, created by Sonic Foundry, is the leading tool for recording and editing sound files for multimedia and professional audio on the Windows platform. It is included as part of the Windows version of the Authorware Interactive Studio. For more information on this version of SoundForge, view the ReadMe file included with the installer, or check the Sonic Foundry web site (**http://www.sonicfoundry.com**).

Guide_CD\Weblinks folder The Weblinks folder contains an HTML document named **Weblinks.htm** that any web browser can load. You can use this HTML document to connect directly to the web sites listed in Appendix C, "Authorware Resources on the Internet."

NOTE You may want to install the Shockwave for Authorware Plug-In before viewing many of these sites.

Guide_CD\XDK folder The XDK folder contains the complete Macromedia Xtra Developer Kit for Authorware 4 and Director 6 for Windows. If you are interested in creating Xtras and have access to a Windows C programming tool, you may want to look at the files and documentation included in this folder. Complete documentation, as well as sample source code files for creating transition, sprite, and scripting Xtras are included.

If You Have a Macintosh System...

You can browse the contents of the CD on a Macintosh system by using the following steps:

1. Place the CD in your CD-ROM drive.

2. Double-click on the disk icon named Guide CD, which appears on your desktop.

Each folder on the CD contains the various sample files mentioned above. A description of the contents of each folder is listed for you below.

Guide CD:Examples folder Separate chapter folders are located inside the Guide CD:Examples folder that contains all Authorware example files mentioned in the chapters of this book. To view the example files, open each one separately using Authorware 4 or the Authorware 4 Working Model. You can open them directly from the CD, or copy them to your local hard disk and then open them. ReadMe information for each example file discusses how the example was created.

NOTE To run the example files, you need either Authorware 4 or the Authorware 4 Working Model installed on your system. For your convenience, a copy of the Authorware 4 Working Model for Macintosh is included on this CD in the Guide CD:Macromedia:Authorware folder.

Guide CD:Macromedia folder Inside the Guide CD:Macromedia folder you will find several folders that demo versions of Macromedia products. Each folder listed below contains separate ReadMe information and files that you can install to your hard disk.

Authorware This folder contains the Authorware 4 Working Model. Double-click on the file named **Authorware Working Model Setup** to install it to your hard disk. This version allows you to create and save your own working files in Authorware 4. You can use the Authorware Working Model to view the Authorware example files included with this CD, if you do not already have Authorware 4 installed.

Deck II This folder contains the demo version of Deck II 2.5. Double-click on the file named **Deck II 2.5 Demo Installer** to install it to your hard disk. You can use Deck II to record and edit multi-track professional audio for everything from multimedia to music to the Internet.

Director This folder contains the demo version of Director 5. Double-click on the file named **Director 5 Demo Installer** to install it to your hard disk. Director is used to create animation and interactive multimedia content that you can integrate into your Authorware pieces, delivered as a stand-alone piece or delivered on the Internet using Shockwave.

NOTE The save-disabled version of Director 6 was not available at the time this book went to press. However, you can obtain it through Macromedia directly by ordering a free copy of the latest version of the Macromedia Showcase CD. You can order this from Macromedia's web site (**http://www.macromedia.com**).

Extreme 3D This folder contains the demo version of Extreme 3D 2. Double-click on the file named **E3D Demo Installer** to install it to your hard disk. Extreme 3D is used for 3D modeling, animation, and rendering in a variety of formats that you can integrate into your Authorware pieces.

Fontographer This folder contains the demo version of Fontographer 4.1. Double-click on the file named **Fontographer 4.1 Demo Installer** to install it to your hard disk. Fontographer is used to create and edit custom fonts.

Freehand This folder contains the demo version of FreeHand 7. Double-click on the file named **FreeHand 7 Demo Installer** to install it to your hard disk. FreeHand is used for both print and multimedia design and illustration.

Shockwave This folder contains the PPC and 68K versions of the latest Shockwave for Authorware Plug-In. If you are running on a Power Macintosh, double-click on the file named **Shockwave PPC Installer** to install the latest Shockwave for Authorware Plug-In to your hard disk. If you are running on a standard Macintosh, double-click on the file named **Shockwave 68k Installer** to install the latest Shockwave for Authorware Plug-In to your hard disk.

NOTE In order to install Shockwave for Authorware, you must have Netscape Navigator or Microsoft Internet Explorer already installed on your hard disk.

SoundEdit 16 This folder contains the demo version of SoundEdit 16 2. Double-click on the file named **SoundEdit 16 2 Demo Installer** to install it to your hard disk. SoundEdit 16 is used to record and edit professional audio for everything from multimedia to music to the Internet.

XRes This folder contains the demo version of xRes 3. Double-click on the file named **xRes 3 Demo Installer** to install it to your hard disk. XRes is used to create and edit images for use in print, multimedia, and on the Internet.

Guide CD:3rdparty folder Located inside the Guide CD:3rdparty folder are several folders that contain demo versions of third-party tools that you can use with Authorware. Each folder listed below contains separate ReadMe information and files that you can install on your hard disk.

Dxm The Earshot SFX Demo is produced by DXM, a San Francisco-based multimedia studio that specializes in multimedia title and Shockwave development (**http://www.dxm.com**). The Earshot SFX Sampler is a royalty-free collection of audio clips that you can integrate directly into any multimedia or Shockwave piece that you have created in Authorware or Director. The demo allows you to preview the sounds included in the complete Earshot SFX library, a two-volume CD-ROM collection of over 2,000 sound effects. Additional sales and ordering information is included in the ReadMe file inside the DXM folder.

To run the demo, double-click on the file named **Earshot SFX Demo**. No installation is required.

Equilibrium The Equilibrium folder contains a demo version of DeBabelizer 1.6.5. Double-click on the file named **DeBabelizer 1.6.5 DEMO** to install it to your hard disk. DeBabelizer is the leading Macintosh tool for converting and dithering images from one format to another, and for creating custom palettes from 8-bit images that you have saved. For more information on this version of DeBabelizer, view the ReadMe file included with the installer, or check the Equilibrium web site (**http://www.equilibrium.com**).

Gmatter You can integrate the demo Xtras included in this folder can be integrated into any multimedia piece that you have created in Authorware 4 or Director (versions 5 and 6). Additional sales and ordering information is included in the ReadMe file inside the Gmatter folder. The gMatter Xtras were produced by gMatter, Inc., a San Francisco-based software company that specializes in developing Xtras for Macromedia products (**http://www.gmatter.com**).

To try the Xtras included in this folder, drag and drop them into the Xtras folder located inside the folder where you have installed Authorware 4.

Guide CD:Weblinks folder The Weblinks folder contains an HTML document named **Weblinks.htm** that any web browser can load. You can use this HTML document to connect directly to the web sites listed in Appendix C, "Authorware Resources on the Internet."

NOTE You may want to install the Shockwave for Authorware Plug-In before viewing many of these sites.

Guide CD:XDK folder The XDK folder contains the complete Macromedia Xtra Developer Kit for Authorware 4 and Director 6 for the Macintosh. If you are interested in creating Xtras, and have access to a Macintosh C programming tool, you may want to look at the files and documentation included in this folder. Complete documentation, as well as sample source code files for creating transition, sprite, and scripting Xtras are included.

Index